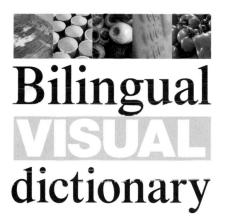

Bilingual VISUAL dictionary

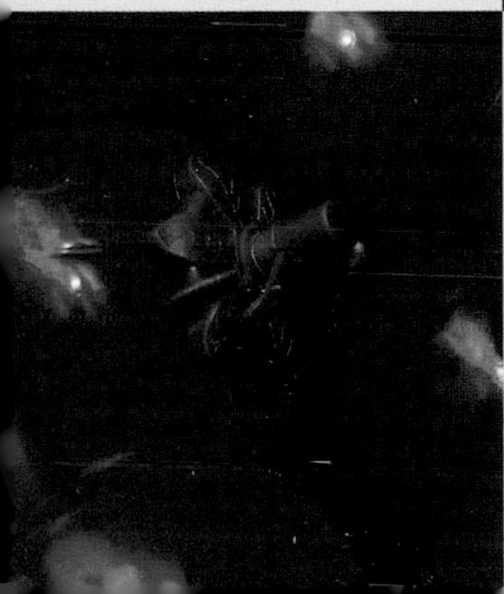

Bilingual VISUAL dictionary

DK

Penguin Random House

Senior Editor Angela Wilkes
Managing Art Editor Christine Keilty
Production Editor Lucy Baker
Production Controller Rita Sinha

Designed for Dorling Kindersley by WaltonCreative.com

Hindi Edition
Senior Editor Rohan Sinha
Editor Saloni Talwar
Design Manager Arunesh Talapatra
Senior DTP Designer Harish Aggarwal
DTP Designers Dheeraj Arora, Jagtar Singh
Production Manager Pankaj Sharma
Art Director Shefali Upadhyay
Head of Publishing Aparna Sharma

Hindi Translation by Yatra Books

First American Edition, 2008
This edition published in the United States in 2016
by DK Publishing, 345 Hudson Street, New York,
New York 10014

16 17 18 19 20 10 9 8 7 6 5 4 3 2 1
002 – HD160 – May/16

Published in Great Britain by Dorling Kindersley Limited.

A catalog record for this book is available from the Library of Congress.
ISBN: 978-1-4654-5164-4

Printed and bound in China

A WORLD OF IDEAS:
SEE ALL THERE IS TO KNOW

www.dk.com

contents
viṣaya sūchī
विषय सूची

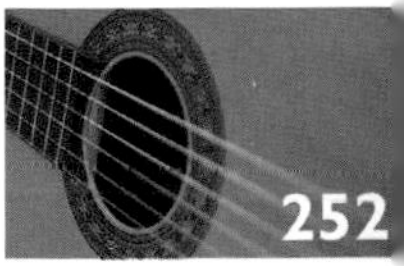

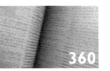

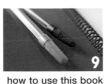

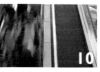

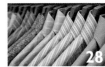

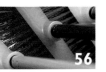

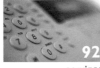

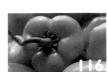

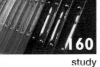

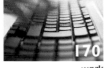

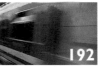

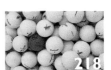

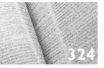

about the dictionary

The use of pictures is proven to aid understanding and the retention of information. Working on this principle, this highly-illustrated English-Hindi bilingual dictionary presents a large range of useful current vocabulary in the two languages.

The dictionary is divided thematically and covers most aspects of the everyday world in detail, from the restaurant to the gym, the home to the workplace, outer space to the animal kingdom. You will also find additional words and phrases for conversational use and for extending your vocabulary.

This is an essential reference tool for anyone interested in languages – practical, stimulating, and easy-to-use.

A few things to note

The Hindi in the dictionary is in the Devnagari script and this is accompanied by a romanization, showing you how to pronounce each word. The entries in the dictionary are always presented in the same order – English, the romanization, then Hindi. Where no suitable Hindi words exist, or are not commonly used, we have retained the English words, but the romanization has been adapted to show how native Hindi speakers pronounce them. You can find out more about this in the Hindi pronunciation guide on page 324-327.

Verbs are indicated by a (v) after the English, for example: **attend (v)**

There is an English index at the back of the book where you can look up a word and find out on which page it appears.

शब्दकोश के बारे में

तस्वीरों के ज़रिए किसी जानकारी को समझना और उसे ग्रहण करना हमेशा सहायक सिद्ध होता है। इसी सिद्धांत के आधार पर तैयार किया गया यह चित्रात्मक द्विभाषी शब्दकोश अंग्रेज़ी और हिन्दी भाषा में बड़ी संख्या में लाभकारी शब्दों को प्रस्तुत करता है।

यह शब्दकोश विषयों के आधार पर विभाजित है और इसमें रोज़मर्रा के जीवन से जुड़े अनेक पक्ष समेटे गए हैं, जिनमें रेस्तरां से जिम, घर से दफ़्तर और अंतरिक्ष से लेकर प्राणी जगत तक के क्षेत्र शामिल हैं। शाब्दिक क्षमता और बातचीत के कौशल को निखारने के लिए इसमें अतिरिक्त शब्द और वाक्यांश भी दिए गए हैं।

भाषाओं में दिलचस्पी रखने वाले व्यक्तियों के लिए व्यावहारिक, उत्साहवर्धक और प्रयोग में आसान यह संदर्भ पुस्तक एक अत्यावश्यक उपकरण सिद्ध होगी।

ध्यान देने योग्य बातें

इस शब्दकोश में हिन्दी मूल देवनागरी लिपि में लिखी गई है। शब्दों के उच्चारण को स्पष्ट करने के लिए उनका रोमन लिप्यंतरण दिया गया है। इस शब्दकोश में शब्दों को इस क्रम में प्रस्तुत किया गया है– अंग्रेज़ी, फिर हिन्दी रूप का रोमन में लिप्यंतरण और फिर देवनागरी में हिन्दी रूप। ऐसी स्थितियों में जहां अंग्रेज़ी शब्दों के समुचित हिन्दी पर्याय नहीं हैं या उनका आम चलन में प्रयोग नहीं होता, वहां हमने मूल अंग्रेज़ी के शब्दों को ही रखा है। हां, उनके रोमन लिप्यंतरण को उनके हिन्दी उच्चारण के अनुसार लिखा गया है। हिन्दी शब्दों के उच्चारण संबंधी विस्तृत जानकारी के लिए पुस्तक के अंत में (पृष्ठ संख्या 324–327) दी गई लिप्यंतरण गाइड देखें।

क्रियाओं को अंग्रेज़ी शब्द के बाद (v) के द्वारा बताया गया है, जैसे: **attend (v)**

इस शब्दकोश के अंत में अंग्रेज़ी तालिका दी गई है जिसमें किसी भी शब्द को देखकर आप उसकी पृष्ठ संख्या जान सकते हैं।

how to use this book

Whether you are learning a new language for business, pleasure, or in preparation for an overseas vacation, or are hoping to extend your vocabulary in an already familiar language, this dictionary is a valuable learning tool which you can use in a number of different ways.

When learning a new language, look out for cognates (words that are alike in different languages) and false friends (words that look alike but carry significantly different meanings). You can also see where the languages have influenced each other. For example, English has imported many terms for food from other languages but, in turn, exported terms used in technology and popular culture.

Practical learning activities

• As you move about your home, workplace, or school, try looking at the pages which cover that setting. You could then close the book, look around you, and see how many of the objects and features you can name.
• Challenge yourself to write a story, letter, or dialogue using as many of the terms on a particular page as possible. This will help you retain the vocabulary and remember the spelling. If you want to build up to writing a longer text, start with sentences incorporating 2–3 words.
• If you have a very visual memory, try drawing or tracing items from the book onto a piece of paper, then closing the book and filling in the words below the picture.

कोश का प्रयोग कैसे करें

आप भले ही व्यापार के लिए, शौक़ के लिए या विदेश में छुट्टी मनाने जाने के लिए कोई नई भाषा सीख रहे हों या पहले से सीखी हुई किसी भाषा का अपना शब्द ज्ञान बढ़ाना चाहते हों, आपके लिए यह शब्दकोश काफ़ी सहायक होगा और आप कई तरह से इसका प्रयोग कर सकते हैं।

कोई नई भाषा सीखते समय इस भाषा में प्रयोग होने वाले समानार्थी शब्दों (वे शब्द जो दूसरी भाषाओं में भी एक जैसे हों) और भिन्नार्थी शब्दों (वे शब्द जो एक जैसे दिखते हैं, परंतु उनके अर्थ अलग होते है) पर ध्यान ज़रूर दें। आप यह भी देख सकते हैं कि भाषाएं किस तरह एक–दूसरे को प्रभावित करती हैं। उदाहरण के लिए अंग्रेज़ी भाषा में खाने संबंधी अनेक शब्द यूरोपीय भाषाओं से लिए गए हैं जबकि इसने संस्कृति व तकनीक के क्षेत्र में बहुत से शब्द उन्हें प्रदान किए हैं।

सीखने के लिए व्यावहारिक अभ्यास

• आप अपने घर, दफ़्तर या कॉलेज में घूमते हुए, उन पन्नों को देखने का प्रयास करें, जो इन क्षेत्रों से संबंधित हैं। फिर इस पुस्तक को बंद करके अपने आसपास नज़र दौड़ाएं और यह देखें कि आपको कितनी चीजों के नाम याद हैं।
• किसी एक विशेष पन्ने पर दिए गए शब्दों का प्रयोग करके छोटी कहानी, पत्र या संवाद लिखने का प्रयास करें। इससे आपको शब्द और वर्तनी याद रखने में मदद मिलेगी। अगर आप कोई बड़ा आलेख लिखना चाहते हैं, तो दो–तीन शब्दों को मिलाकर छोटे–छोटे वाक्य बनाकर शुरुआत करें।
• यदि चित्रों की सहायता से आपको अधिक याद रहता है तो इस कोश में दिए गए चित्रों को अलग काग़ज़ पर बनाएं और बिना देखे उनसे संबंधित शब्दों को लिखें।

people
log
लोग

body • śarīr • शरीर

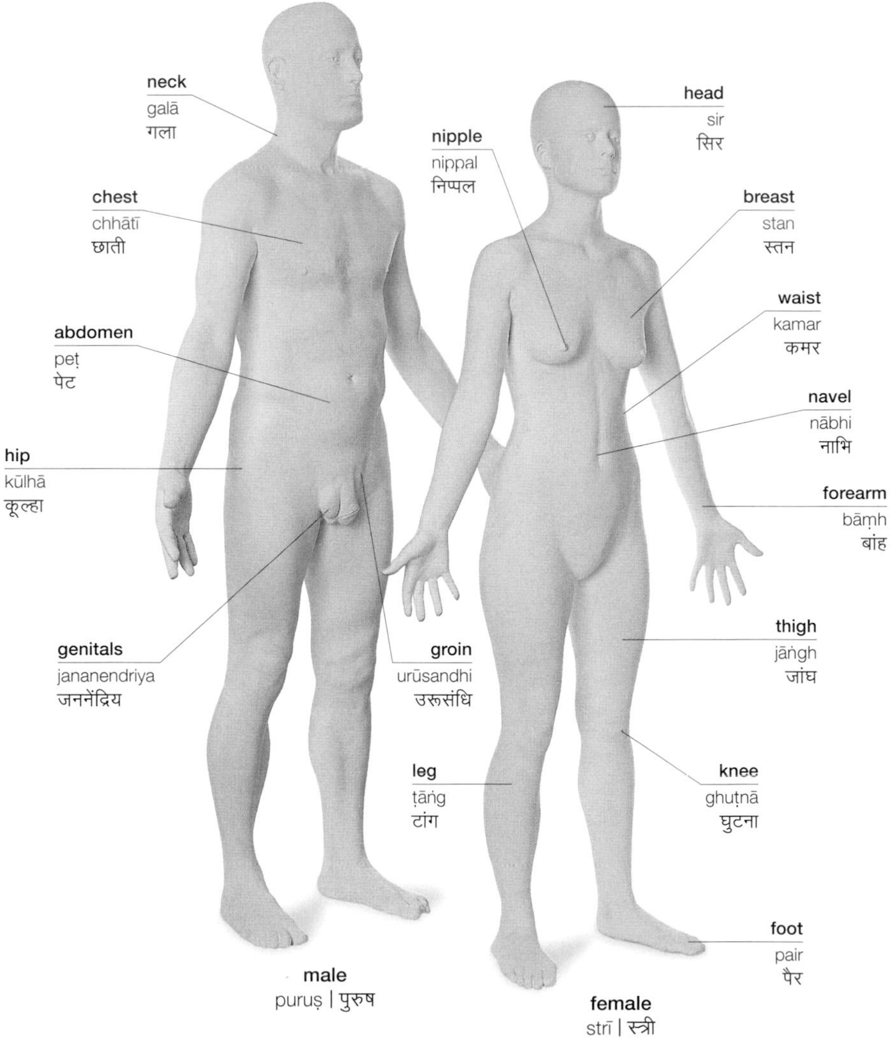
neck
galā
गला
chest
chhātī
छाती
abdomen
peṭ
पेट
hip
kūlhā
कूल्हा
genitals
jananendriya
जननेंद्रिय
groin
urūsandhi
उरूसंधि
nipple
nippal
निप्पल
head
sir
सिर
breast
stan
स्तन
waist
kamar
कमर
navel
nābhi
नाभि
forearm
bāṃh
बांह
thigh
jāṅgh
जांघ
leg
ṭāṅg
टांग
knee
ghuṭnā
घुटना
foot
pair
पैर
male
puruṣ | पुरुष
female
strī | स्त्री

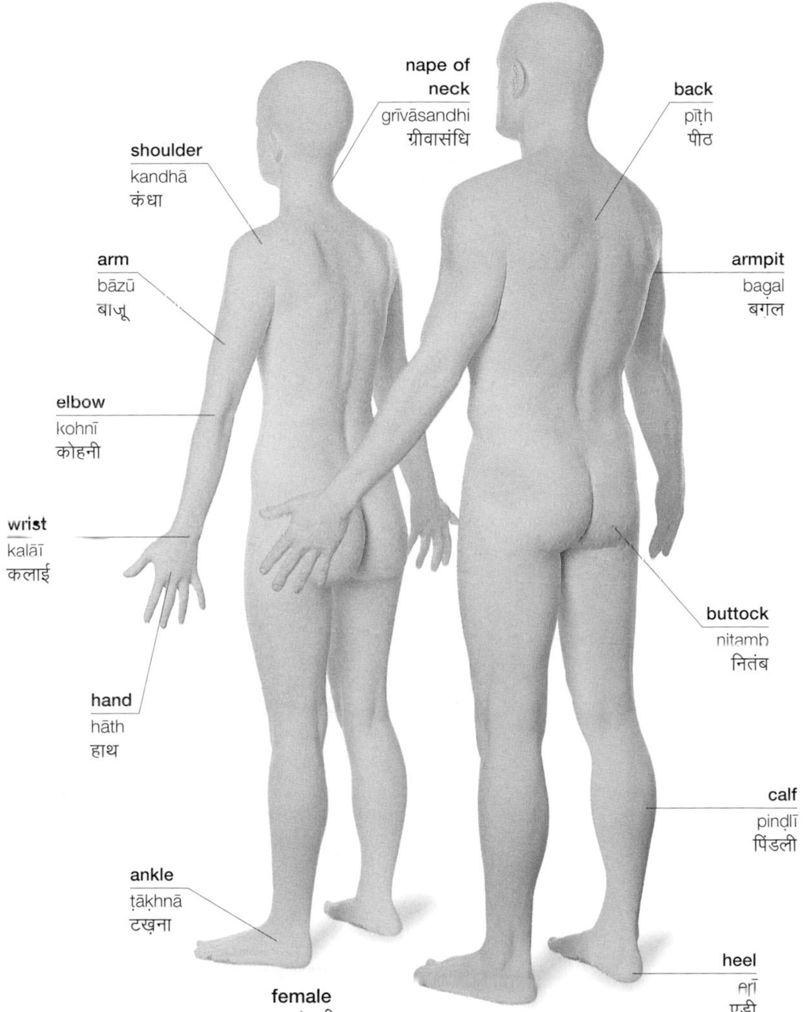
nape of neck
grīvāsandhi
ग्रीवासंधि
back
pīṭh
पीठ
shoulder
kandhā
कंधा
arm
bāzū
बाज़ू
armpit
bagal
बग़ल
elbow
kohnī
कोहनी
wrist
kalāī
कलाई
buttock
nitamb
नितंब
hand
hāth
हाथ
calf
pinḍlī
पिंडली
ankle
ṭākhnā
टख़ना
heel
eṛī
एड़ी
female
strī | स्त्री
male
puruṣ | पुरुष

face • chehrā • चेहरा

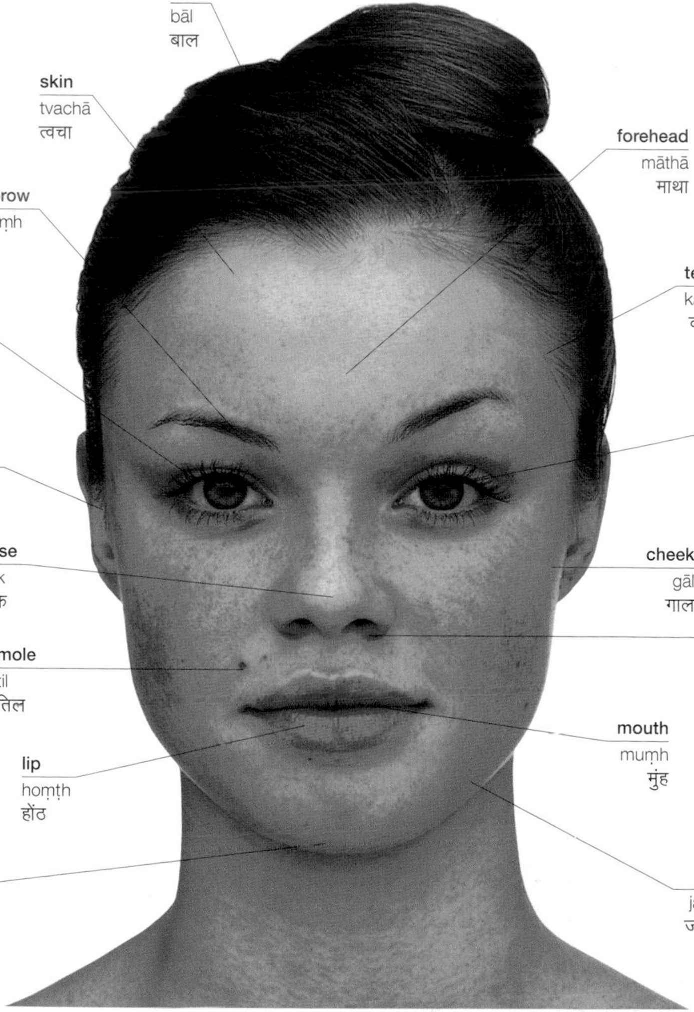
hair
bāl
बाल
skin
tvachā
त्वचा
forehead
māthā
माथा
eyebrow
bhaumh
भौंह
temple
kanpaṭī
कनपटी
eyelash
palak
पलक
eye
āṃkh
आंख
ear
kān
कान
nose
nāk
नाक
cheek
gāl
गाल
nostril
nathunā
नथुना
mole
til
तिल
mouth
muṃh
मुंह
lip
hoṃṭh
होंठ
chin
ṭhoṛī
ठोड़ी
jaw
jabṛā
जबड़ा

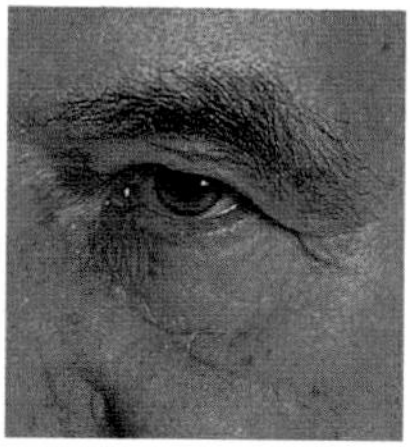

wrinkle
jhurriyāṃ | झुर्रियां

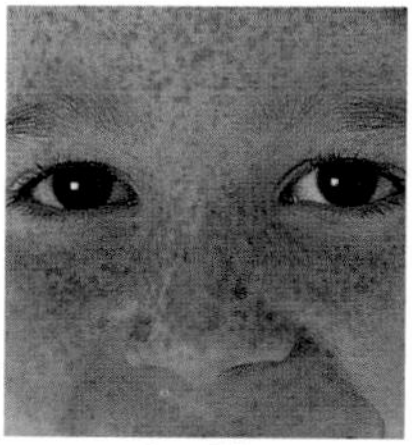

freckle
jhāīṃ | झाईं

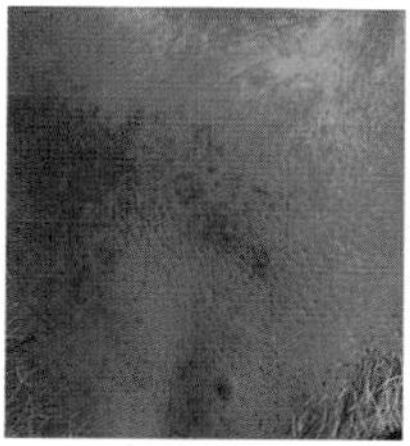

pore
rom chhidr | रोमछिद्र

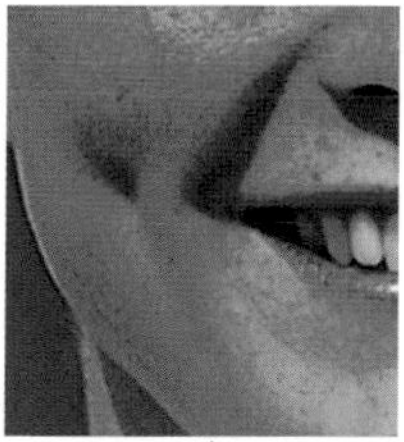

dimple | gāl kā gaḍḍhā | गाल का गड्ढा

hand • hāth • हाथ

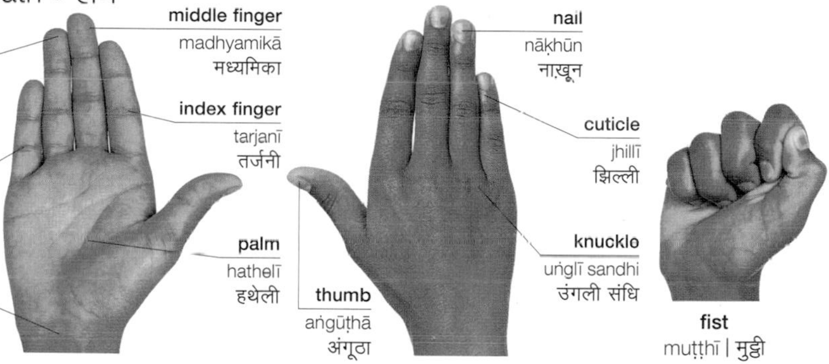
ring finger
anāmikā
अनामिका
little finger
kaniṣṭhikā
कनिष्ठिका
wrist
kalāī
कलाई
middle finger
madhyamikā
मध्यमिका
index finger
tarjanī
तर्जनी
palm
hathelī
हथेली
thumb
aṅgūṭhā
अंगूठा
nail
nāḳhūn
नाख़ून
cuticle
jhillī
झिल्ली
knuckle
uṅglī sandhi
उंगली संधि

fist
muṭṭhī | मुट्ठी

foot • pair • पैर

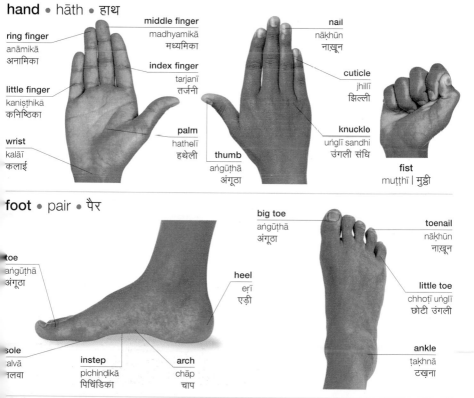

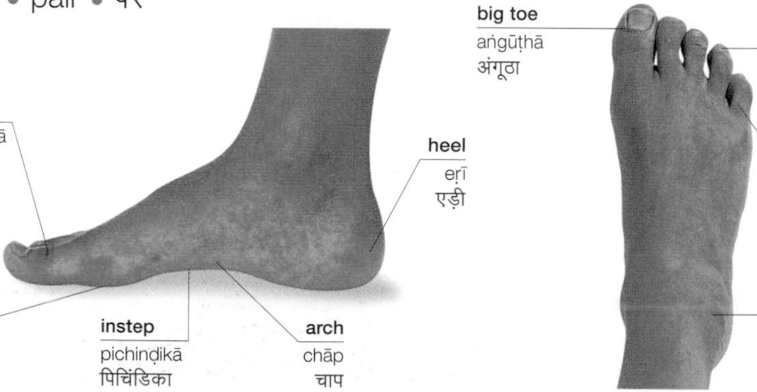
toe
aṅgūṭhā
अंगूठा
sole
alvā
लवा
instep
pichinḍikā
पिचिंडिका
arch
chāp
चाप
heel
eṛī
एड़ी
big toe
aṅgūṭhā
अंगूठा
toenail
nāḳhūn
नाख़ून
little toe
chhoṭī uṅglī
छोटी उंगली
ankle
ṭaḳhnā
टख़ना

muscles • māṃspeśiyāṃ • मांसपेशियां

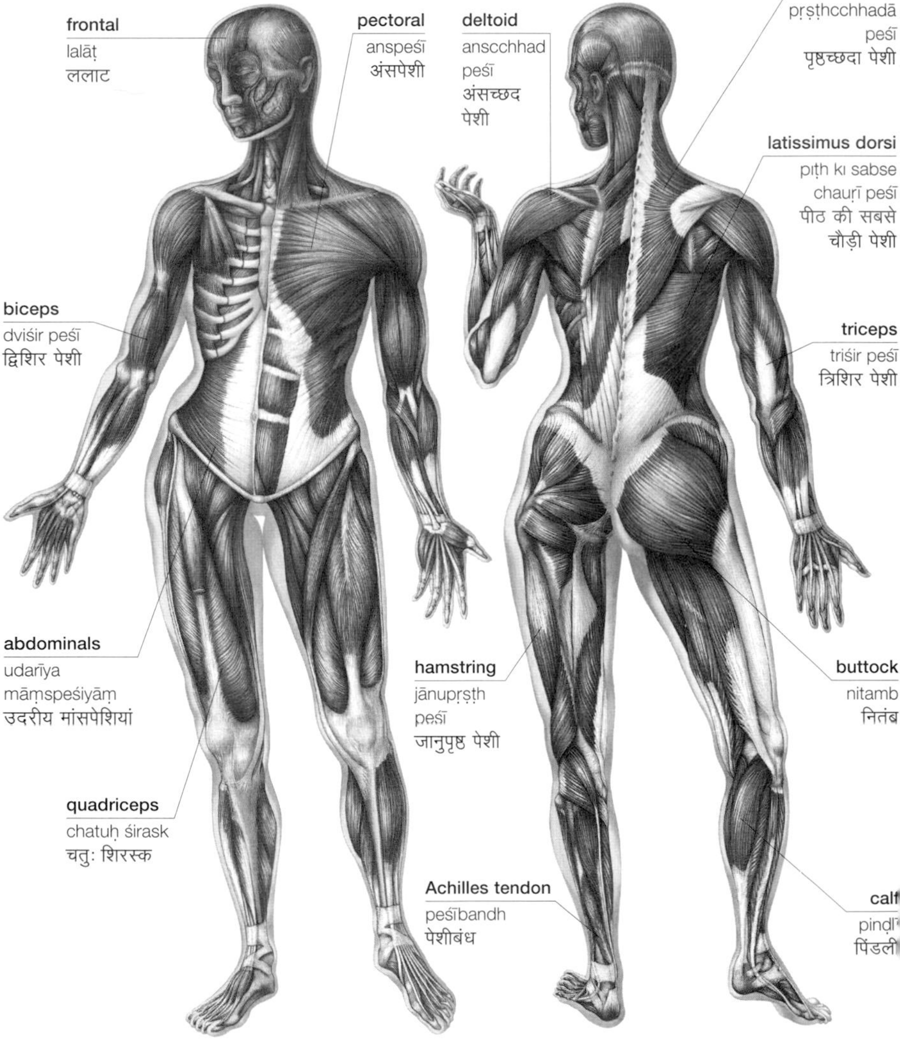
frontal
lalāṭ
ललाट
pectoral
anspeśī
अंसपेशी
deltoid
anscchhad
peśī
अंसच्छद
पेशी
trapezius
pṛṣṭhcchhadā
peśī
पृष्ठच्छदा पेशी
latissimus dorsi
pīṭh kī sabse
chauṛī peśī
पीठ की सबसे
चौड़ी पेशी
biceps
dviśir peśī
द्विशिर पेशी
triceps
triśir peśī
त्रिशिर पेशी
abdominals
udarīya
māṃspeśiyāṃ
उदरीय मांसपेशियां
hamstring
jānupṛṣṭh
peśī
जानुपृष्ठ पेशी
buttock
nitamb
नितंब
quadriceps
chatuḥ śirask
चतुः शिरस्क
Achilles tendon
peśībandh
पेशीबंध
calf
piṇḍlī
पिंडली

skeleton • asthipanjar • अस्थिपंजर

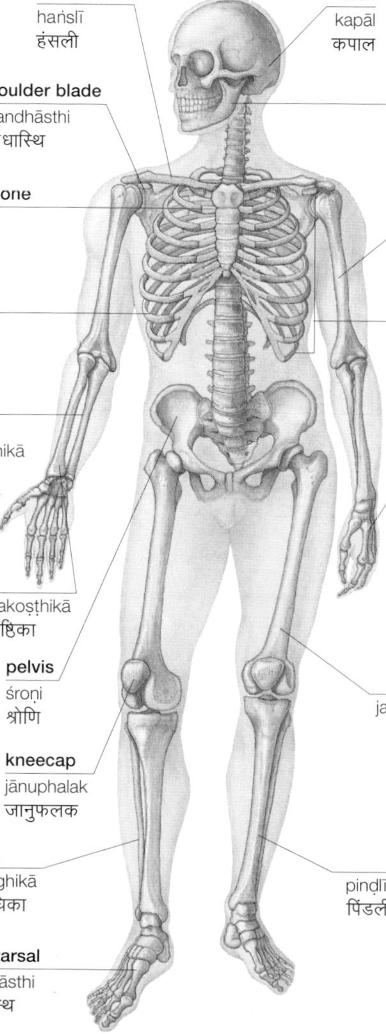
collarbone
haṅslī
हंसली
skull
kapāl
कपाल
shoulder blade
skandhāsthi
स्कंधास्थि
jaw
jabṛā
जबड़ा
breastbone
urosthi
उरोस्थि
humerus
pagaṇḍikā
पगंडिका
rib
paslī
पसली
rib cage
paslī panjar
पसली पंजर
ulna
antaḥ
prakoṣṭhikā
अंत:
प्रकोष्ठिका
metacarpal
panje kī asthi
पंजे की अस्थि
radius
bahiḥ prakoṣṭhikā
बहि: प्रकोष्ठिका
pelvis
śroṇi
श्रोणि
femur
jaṅghāsthi
जंघास्थि
kneecap
jānuphalak
जानुफलक
fibula
upjaṅghikā
उपजंघिका
tibia
piṇḍlī kī haḍḍī
पिंडली की हड्डी
metatarsal
prapdāsthi
प्रपदास्थि

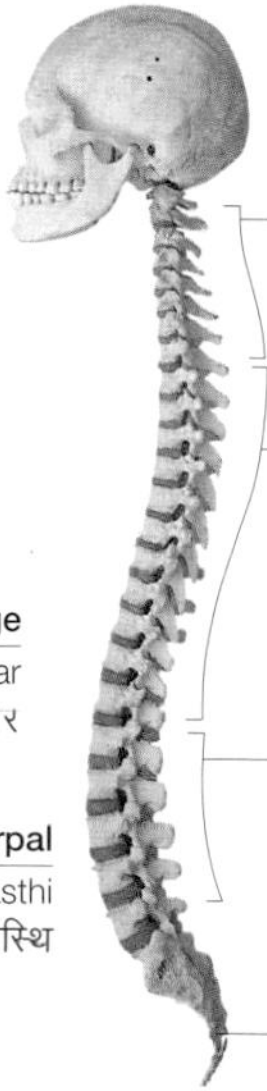
cervical vertebrae
grīvā kaśerukāeṃ
ग्रीवा कशेरुकाएं
thoracic vertebrae
vakṣīya kaśerukāeṃ
वक्षीय कशेरुकाएं
lumbar vertebrae
kaṭiparak kaśerukaeṃ
कटिपरक कशेरुकाएं
tailbone
puchhāsthi
पुच्छास्थि
spine
merudaṇḍ | मेरुदंड

joint • joṛ • जोड़

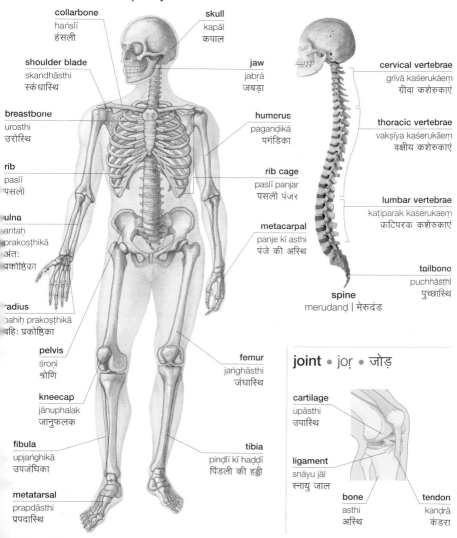

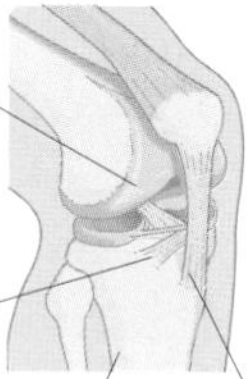
cartilage
upāsthi
उपास्थि
ligament
snāyu jāl
स्नायु जाल
bone
asthi
अस्थि
tendon
kaṇḍrā
कंडरा

internal organs • āntarik aṅg • आंतरिक अंग

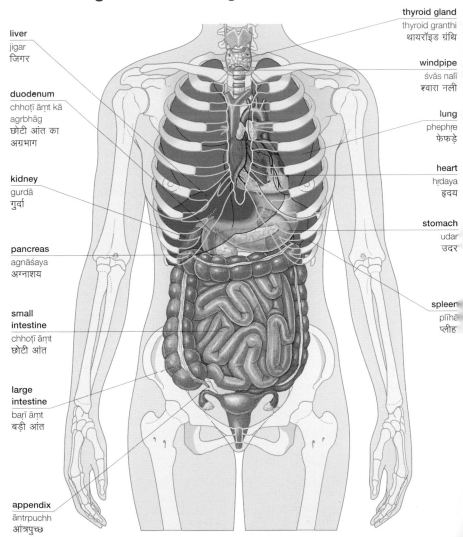

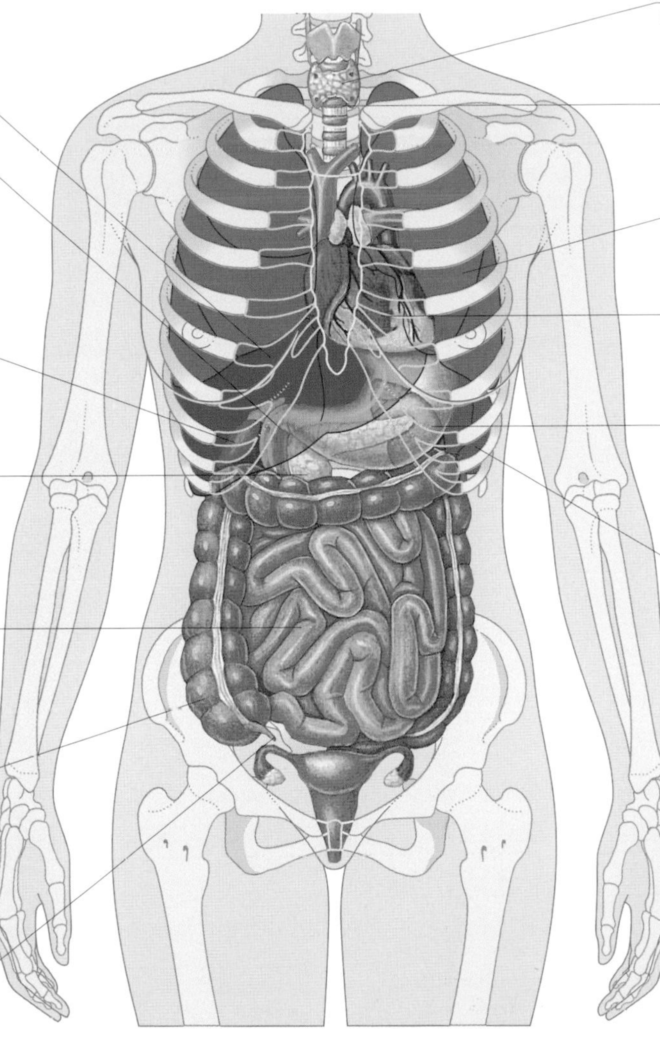
liver
jigar
जिगर
duodenum
chhoṭī āṃt kā agrbhāg
छोटी आंत का अग्रभाग
kidney
gurdā
गुर्दा
pancreas
agnāśaya
अग्नाशय
small intestine
chhoṭī āṃt
छोटी आंत
large intestine
baṛī āṃt
बड़ी आंत
appendix
āntrpuchh
आंत्रपुच्छ
thyroid gland
thyroid granthi
थायरॉइड ग्रंथि
windpipe
śvās nalī
श्वास नली
lung
phephṛe
फेफड़े
heart
hṛdaya
हृदय
stomach
udar
उदर
spleen
plīhā
प्लीहा

head • sir • सिर

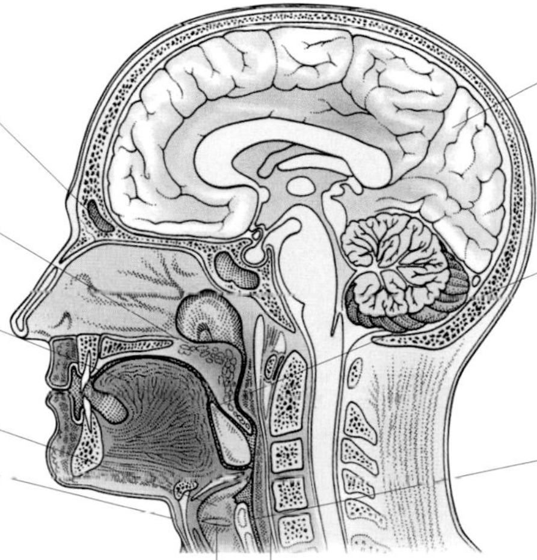

sinus
nālīvraṇ
नालीव्रण

palate
tālū
तालू

tongue
jībh
जीभ

larynx
kaṇṭh
कंठ

Adam's apple
kaṇṭhmaṇi
कंठमणि

vocal cords
svar tantr | स्वर तंत्र

brain
mastiṣk
मस्तिष्क

pharynx
śvās nalī
श्वास नली

oesophagus
āhār nalī
आहार नली

throat
galā | गला

body systems • śarīr tantr • शरीर तंत्र

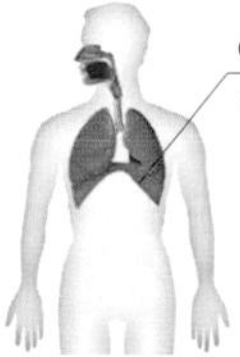

diaphragm
madhyapaṭ
मध्यपट

respiratory
śvasan | श्वसन

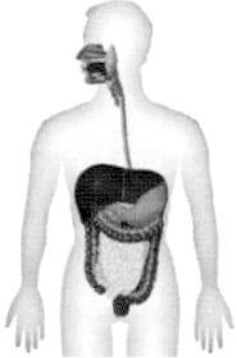

digestive
pāchak | पाचक

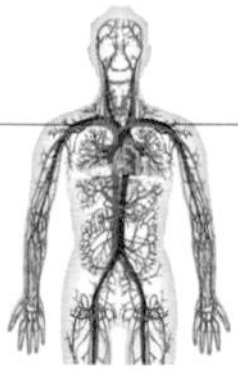

vein
nas
नस

artery
dhamnī
धमनी

cardiovascular
hṛdaya evam raktvāhinī
हृदय एवं रक्तवाहिनी

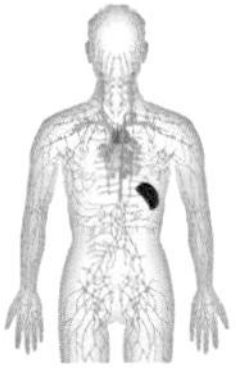

lymphatic
lasikā
लसिका

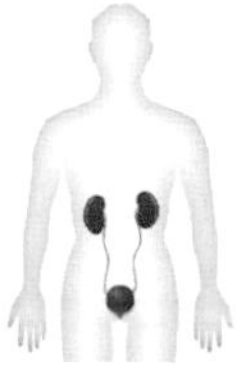

urinary
mūtr | मूत्र

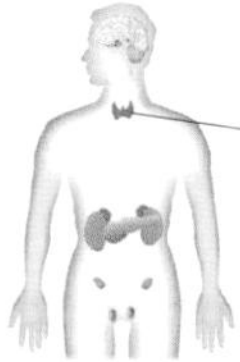

gland
granthi
ग्रंथि

endocrine
antaḥ srāvī | अंतः स्त्रावी

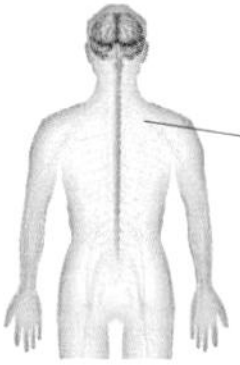

nerve
tantrikā
तंत्रिका

nervous
snāyu | स्नायु

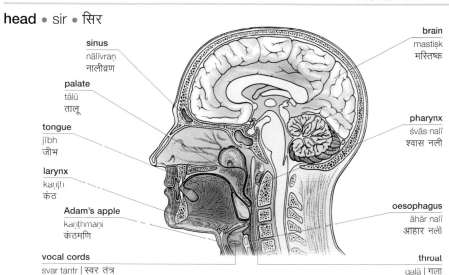

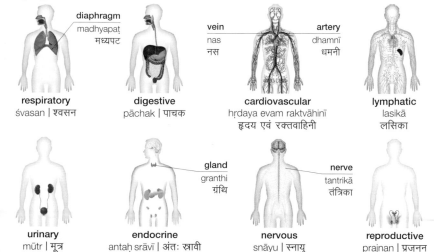

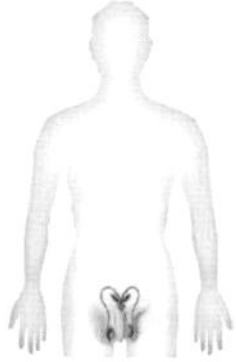

reproductive
prajnan | प्रजनन

reproductive organs • prajnanīya aṅg • प्रजननीय अंग

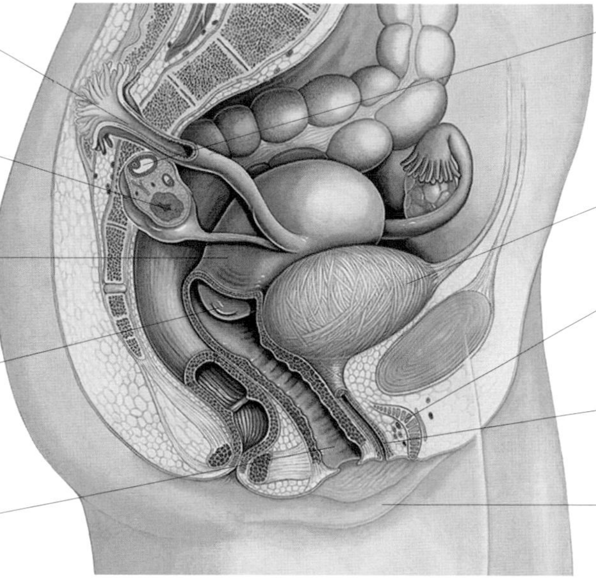
fallopian tube
ḍimb vāhinī
डिंब वाहिनी
ovary
aṇḍāśaya
अंडाशय
uterus
garbhāśaya
गर्भाशय
cervix
garbhdvār
गर्भद्वार
vagina
yoni
योनि
follicle
puṭak (jhillīdār chhoṭī thailī)
पुटक (झिल्लीदार छोटी थैली)
bladder
mutrāśaya
मूत्राशय
clitoris
bagśiśinikā
भगशिश्निका
urethra
mūtrnalī
मूत्रनली
labia
bhagoṣth
भगोष्ठ

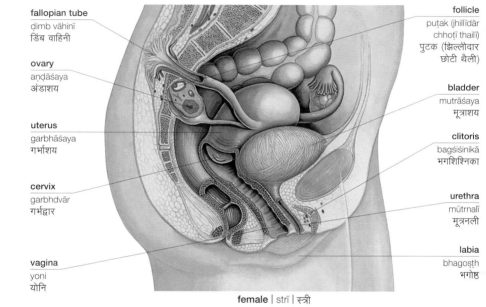

female | strī | स्त्री

reproduction • prajnan • प्रजनन

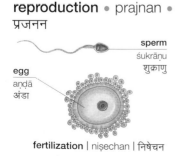

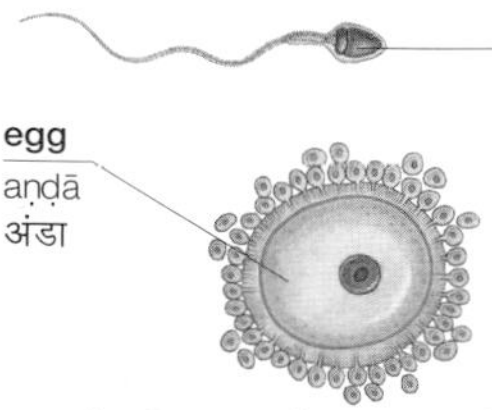
sperm
śukrāṇu
शुक्राणु
egg
aṇḍā
अंडा

fertilization | niṣechan | निषेचन

vocabulary • śabdavalī • शब्दावली

hormone hārmon हारमोन	**impotent** napunsak नपुंसक	**intercourse** sambhog संभोग
ovulation bīj janan बीज जनन	**menstruation** māhvārī माहवारी	**sexually transmitted disease** yaun rog यौन रोग
conceive garbhdhāraṇ karnā गर्भधारण करना	**fertile** urvar उर्वर	

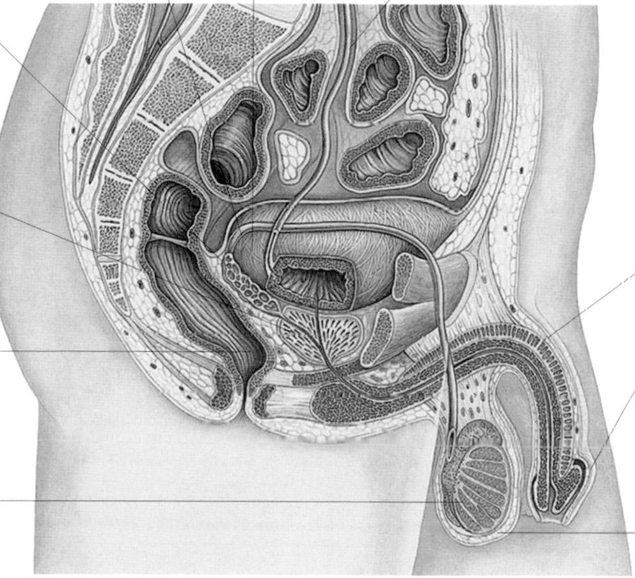

ejaculatory duct
skhalnīya nalī
स्खलनीय नली

vas deferens
śukravāhinī
शुक्रवाहिनी

ureter
mūtrnalī
मूत्रनली

seminal vesicle
śukrāśaya
शुक्राशय

prostate
purahsth granthi
पुर:स्थ ग्रंथि

penis
śiśn
शिश्न

rectum
gudā
गुदा

foreskin
śiśncchhad
शिश्नच्छद

testicle
aṇḍgranthi
अंडग्रंथि

scrotum
aṇḍkoś
अंडकोश

male | puruṣ | पुरुष

contraception • garbhnirodh • गर्भनिरोध

cervical cap
kaip | कैप

diaphragm
ḍāyafrām
डायफ़्राम

condom
kanḍom
कंडोम

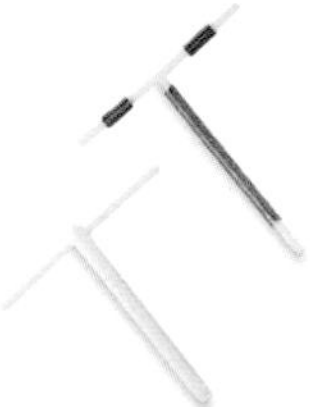

IUD
copper-ṭī
कॉपर–टी

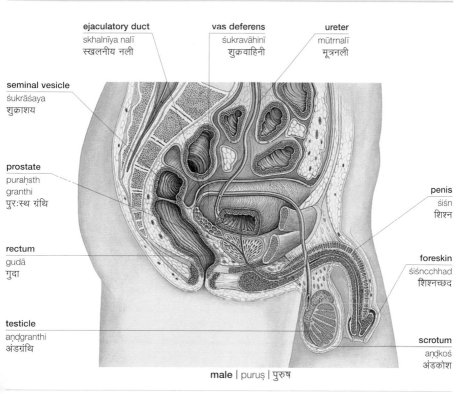

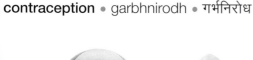

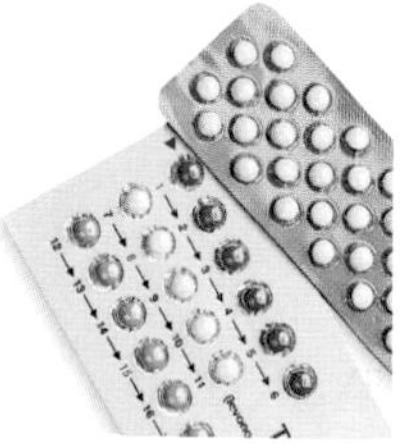

pill
garbh nirodhak goliyāṃ
गर्भ निरोधक गोलियां

family • parivār • परिवार

grandmother
dādī | दादी
grandfather
dādā | दादा
uncle
phūphā | फूफा
aunt
buā | बुआ
father
pitā | पिता
mother
mātā | माता
cousin
phūpherā bhāī
फूफेरा भाई
brother
bhāī | भाई
sister
bahan | बहन
wife
patnī | पत्नी
daughter-in-law
bahū | बहू
son
beṭā | बेटा
daughter
beṭī | बेटी
son-in-law
dāmād | दामाद
grandson
potā | पोता
granddaughter
potī | पोती
husband
pati | पति

vocabulary • śabdāvalī • शब्दावली

relatives riśtedār रिश्तेदार	**parents** mātā-pitā माता–पिता	**grandparents** dādā-dādī/nānā-nānī दादा–दादी/नाना–नानी	**stepfather** sautele pitā सौतेले पिता	**stepson** sautelā beṭā सौतेला बेटा	**generation** pīṛhī पीढ़ी
partner sāthī साथी	**children** bacche बच्चे	**grandchildren** nātī-nātin/potā-potī नाती–नातिन/पोता–पोती	**stepmother** sautelī mātā सौतेली माता	**stepdaughter** sautelī beṭī सौतेली बेटी	**twins** juṛvāṃ जुड़वां

mother-in-law
sās | सास

father-in-law
sasur | ससुर

brother-in-law
sāṛhū | साढ़ू

sister-in-law
sālī | साली

niece
bhānjī | भानजी

nephew
bhānjā | भानजा

titles • sambodhan • संबोधन

Mr.
śrī
श्री

Miss
kumārī
कुमारी

Mrs.
śrīmatī | श्रीमती

stages • avasthāeṃ • अवस्थाएं

baby
śiśu | शिशु

child
bacchā | बच्चा

boy
laṛkā | लड़का

girl
laṛkī | लड़की

teenager
kiśorī | किशोरी

adult
vayask | वयस्क

man
ādmī | आदमी

woman
aurat | औरत

relationships • sambandh • संबंध

manager
prabandhak
प्रबंधक

assistant
sahāyak
सहायक

business partner
kārōbārī
sājhedār
कारोबारी
साझेदार

employer
mālik
मालिक

employee
karmchārī
कर्मचारी

colleague
sahyogī
सहयोगी

office
kāryālaya | कार्यालय

neighbor
parosī | पड़ोसी

friend
dost | दोस्त

acquaintance
parichit | परिचित

pen pal
patr mitr | पत्र मित्र

boyfriend
puruṣ mitr
पुरुष मित्र

girlfriend
mahilā mitr
महिला मित्र

couple | yugal | युगल

fiancé
maṅgetar
मंगेतर

fiancée
maṅgetar
मंगेतर

engaged couple | bhāvī var-vadhū | भावी वर–वधू

emotions • bhāvnāeṃ • भावनाएं

smile
muskān
मुस्कान

happy
ḳhuś | ख़ुश

sad
dukhī | दुखी

excited
utsāhit | उत्साहित

bored
ūb | ऊब

surprised
āścharyachakit
आश्चर्यचकित

scared
bhayabhīt | भयभीत

frown
tyoriyāṃ
chaṛhnā
त्योरियां
चढ़ना

angry
ġussā | ग़ुस्सा

confused
bhramit | भ्रमित

worried
chintit | चिंतित

nervous
ghabrāyā | घबराया

proud
garvit | गर्वित

confident
ātmaviśvāsī | आत्मविश्वासी

embarrassed
lajjit | लज्जित

shy
śarmānā | शर्माना

vocabulary • śabdāvalī • शब्दावली

sigh (v) āh bharnā आह भरना	**shout (v)** chillānā चिल्लाना	**laugh (v)** haṃsnā हंसना	**cry (v)** ronā रोना
shocked sadmā lagnā सदमा लगना	**yawn (v)** ubāsī lenā उबासी लेना	**upset** pareśān परेशान	

life events • jīvan kī ḳhās ghaṭnāeṃ • जीवन की ख़ास घटनाएं

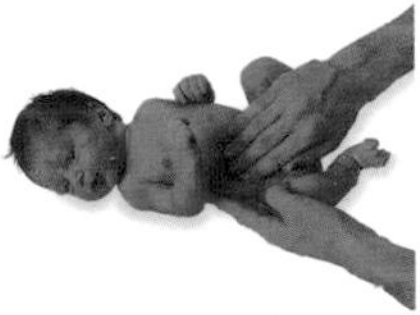

be born (v)
paidā honā | पैदा होना

start school (v) | skūl ārambh karnā | स्कूल आरंभ करना

make friends (v) | dost banānā | दोस्त बनाना

graduate (v) | snātak honā | स्नातक होना

get a job (v)
naukrī pānā | नौकरी पाना

fall in love (v)
prem honā | प्रेम होना

get married (v)
śādī karnā | शादी करना

have a baby (v)
santān honā | संतान होना

wedding | vivāh | विवाह

divorce
talāḳ | तलाक़

funeral
antyeṣṭi | अंत्येष्टि

vocabulary • śabdāvalī • शब्दावली

christening
nāmkaraṇ
नामकरण

bar mitzvah
yahūdī upnayan
यहूदी उपनयन

anniversary
sālgirah
सालगिरह

emigrate (v)
utpravās karnā
उत्प्रवास करना

retire (v)
sevānivṛtt honā
सवेानिवृत्त होना

die (v)
marnā
मरना

make a will (v)
vasīyat banānā
वसीयत बनाना

birth certificate
janm pramāṇpatr
जन्म प्रमाणपत्र

wedding reception
vivāh bhoj
विवाह भोज

honeymoon
hanīmūn
हनीमून

celebrations • utsav • उत्सव

birthday party
janmdin kī parṭī
जन्मदिन की पार्टी

card
kārḍ
कार्ड

birthday
janmdin | जन्मदिन

present
tohfā
तोहफ़ा

Christmas
krismas | क्रिसमस

New Year
nav varṣ | नव वर्ष

carnival
kārnival | कार्निवल

procession
śobhāyātrā
शोभायात्रा

ribbon
riban
रिबन

Thanksgiving
thaiṅks giviṅg | थैंक्स गिविंग

Easter
īsṭar | ईस्टर

Halloween
hailovīn | हैलोवीन

festivals • tyohār • त्योहार

Passover | yahūdī
parv | यहूदी पर्व

Ramadan
ramzān | रमज़ान

Diwali
dīvālī | दीवाली

appearance
veśbhūṣā
वेशभूषा

children's clothing • bāl paridhān • बाल परिधान

baby • śiśu • शिशु

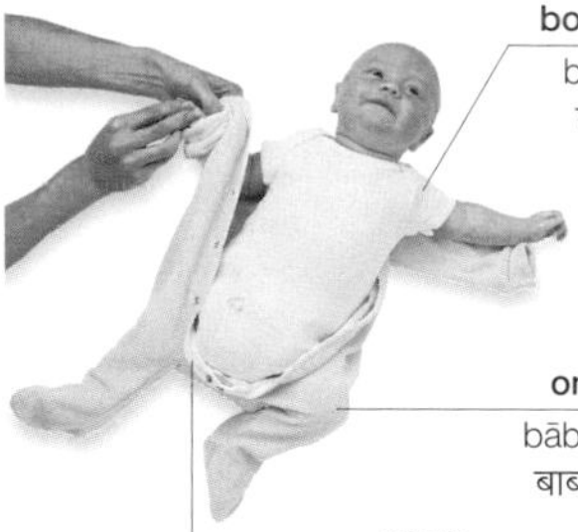

bodysuit
baniyān
बनियान

onesie
bābā sūṭ
बाबा सूट

snap
ṭich baṭan kā sūṭ
टिच बटन का सूट

sleeper | slīp sūṭ
स्लीप सूट

snowsuit
garm sūṭ | गर्म सूट

romper
rompar sūṭ | रोम्पर सूट

bib
bib | बिब

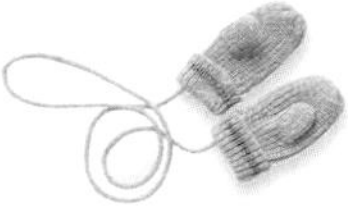

mittens
dastāne
दस्ताने

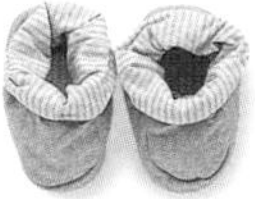

booties
bebī jūte
बेबी जूते

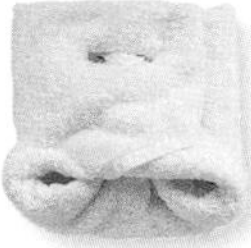

cloth diaper
ṭairī naipī
टैरी नैपी

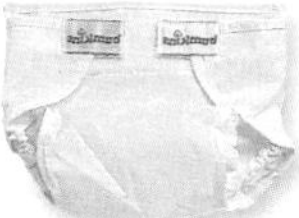

disposable diaper
dispozebal naipī
डिस्पोज़ेबल नैपी

plastic pants
plāsṭik kī laṇgoṭī
प्लास्टिक की लंगोटी

toddler • chhoṭā bacchā • छोटा बच्चा

sun hat
ṭopī | टोपी

apron
epran | एप्रन

shorts
nikar
निकर

overalls
ḍaṇgarī
डंगरी

t-shirt
ṭī śarṭ
टी शर्ट

skirt
skarṭ
स्कर्ट

child • bacchā • बच्चा

dress
ḍres
ड्रेस
sandals
saiṇḍil
सैंडिल

summer
garmī | गर्मी

hood
ṭopī
टोपी

raincoat
barsātī | बरसाती

jeans
jīns
जीन्स
backpack
piṭṭhū baig
पिट्ठू बैग

fall | śarad ṛtu
शरद ऋतु

toggle
lambā
baṭan
लंबा बटन

duffel coat
garm koṭ
गर्म कोट

scarf
skārf
स्कार्फ़
parka
barsātī
koṭ
बरसाती कोट
rain
boots
veliṅgṭan
būṭ
वेलिंगटन बूट

winter
sardī
सर्दी

bathrobe
ḍresiṅg gāun
ड्रेसिंग गाउन
nightgown
nāiṭī
नाइटी
slippers
chappal
चप्पल

nightwear
rātri pośāk | रात्रि पोशाक

logo
logo
लोगो
athletic shoes
ṭrenars
ट्रेनर्स

soccer uniform
fuṭball sṭrip
फुटबॉल स्ट्रिप

jogging suit
ṭraik sūṭ
ट्रैक सूट

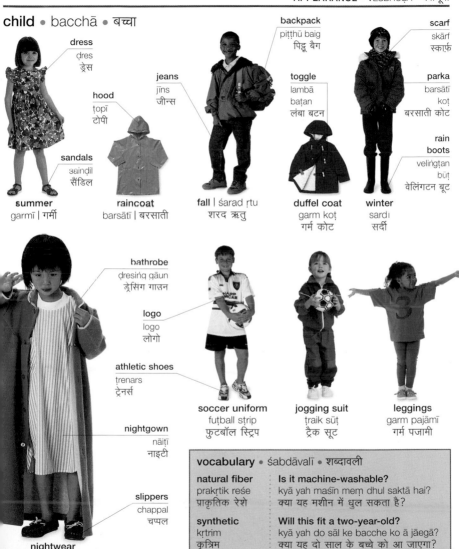

leggings
garm pajāmī
गर्म पजामी

vocabulary • śabdāvalī • शब्दावली

natural fiber prakṛtik reśe प्राकृतिक रेशे	**Is it machine-washable?** kyā yah maśīn meṃ dhul saktā hai? क्या यह मशीन में धुल सकता है?
synthetic kṛtrim कृत्रिम	**Will this fit a two-year-old?** kyā yah do sāl ke bacche ko ā jāegā? क्या यह दो साल के बच्चे को आ जाएगा?

men's clothing • puruṣ paridhān • पुरुष परिधान

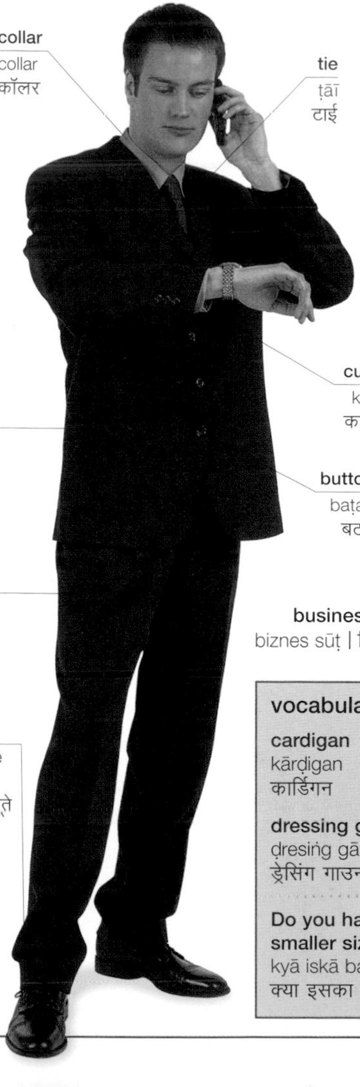

collar
collar
कॉलर

tie
ṭāī
टाई

cuff
kaf
कफ़

jacket
jaikeṭ
जैकेट

button
baṭan
बटन

pants
paiṇṭ
पैंट

leather shoes
chamṛe ke jūte
चमड़े के जूते

business suit
biznes sūṭ | बिज़नेस सूट

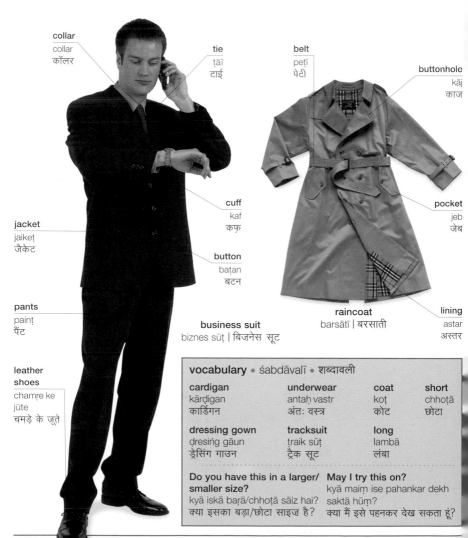

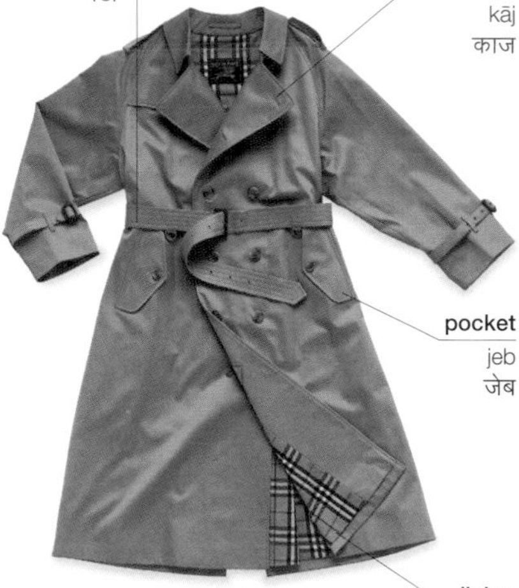

belt
peṭī
पेटी

buttonhole
kāj
काज

pocket
jeb
जेब

lining
astar
अस्तर

raincoat
barsātī | बरसाती

vocabulary • śabdāvalī • शब्दावली

cardigan
kārḍigan
कार्डिगन

underwear
antaḥ vastr
अंतः वस्त्र

coat
koṭ
कोट

short
chhoṭā
छोटा

dressing gown
ḍresiṅg gāun
ड्रेसिंग गाउन

tracksuit
ṭraik sūṭ
ट्रैक सूट

long
lambā
लंबा

Do you have this in a larger/ smaller size?
kyā iskā baṛā/chhoṭā sāiz hai?
क्या इसका बड़ा/छोटा साइज़ है?

May I try this on?
kyā maiṃ ise pahankar dekh saktā hūṃ?
क्या मैं इसे पहनकर देख सकता हूं?

blazer
blezar | ब्लेज़र

sport coat | sporṭs jaikeṭ | स्पोर्ट्स जैकेट

vest
vāskaṭ | वास्कट

V-neck
vī galā
वी गला
crew neck
gol galā
गोल गला
t-shirt
ṭī śarṭ
टी शर्ट
jeans
jīns
जीन्स

casual wear
rozmarrā ke vastr
रोज़मर्रा के वस्त्र

parka
barsātī koṭ | बरसाती कोट

sweatshirt
sveṭ śarṭ | स्वेट शर्ट

shirt
ḳamīz | क़मीज़

sweater
sveṭar | स्वेटर

pajamas
pajāmā sūṭ | पजामा सूट

undershirt
baniyān | बनियान

shorts
nikar | निकर

briefs
chaḍḍī | चड्डी

boxer shorts | boxer shorts | बॉक्सर शॉर्ट्स

socks
moze | मोज़े

women's clothing • mahilā paridhān • महिला परिधान

jacket
jaikeṭ
जैकेट

sleeve
āstīn
आस्तीन

hem
kinārī
किनारी

shoes
jūte
जूते

seam
sīvan
सीवन

skirt
skarṭ
स्कर्ट

knee-length
ghuṭne tak lambī
घुटने तक लंबी

formal
aupchārik vastr
औपचारिक वस्त्र

ankle length
lambī pośāk
लंबी पोशाक

evening dress
gāun
गाउन

strapless
sṭraip rahit pośāk
स्ट्रैप रहित पोशाक

sleeveless
āstīn rahit pośāk
आस्तीन रहित पोशाक

dress
paridhān | परिधान

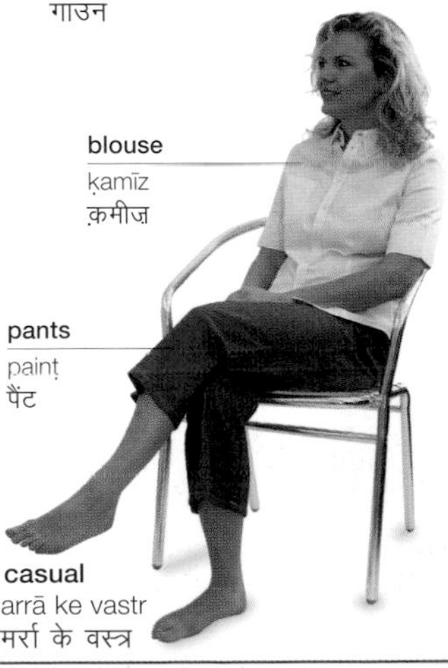

blouse
ḳamīz
क़मीज़

pants
painṭ
पैंट

casual
rozmarrā ke vastr
रोज़मर्रा के वस्त्र

lingerie • adhovastr • अधोवस्त्र

robe
ḍresiṅg gāun
ड्रेसिंग गाउन

slip
slip | स्लिप

strap
straip
स्ट्रैप

camisole
śamīz | शमीज़

bustier
aṅgiyā
अंगिया

stockings
lambe moze
लंबे मोज़े

pantyhose
taṅg pajāmī
तंग पजामी

bra
brā | ब्रा

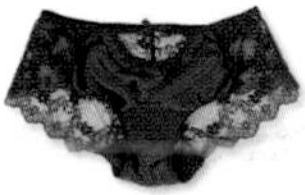

panties
nikar | निकर

nightgown
nāiṭī | नाइटी

wedding • vivāh • विवाह

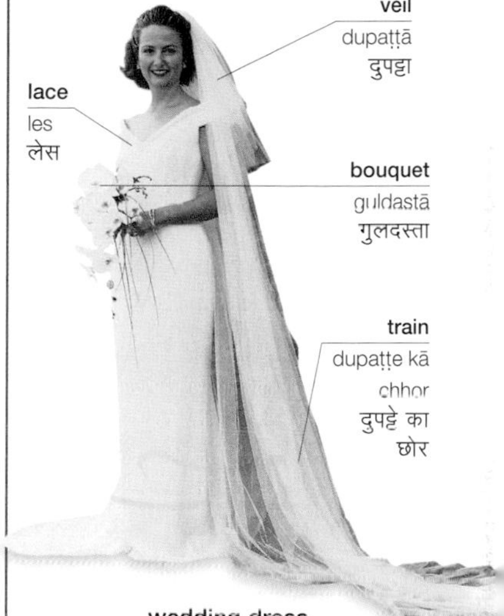
veil
dupaṭṭā
दुपट्टा
lace
les
लेस
bouquet
guldastā
गुलदस्ता
train
dupaṭṭe kā chhor
दुपट्टे का छोर

wedding dress
vivāh kī pośāk | विवाह की पोशाक

vocabulary • śabdāvalī • शब्दावली

corset
cholī
चोली

garter
geṭis
गेटिस

shoulder pad
śolḍar paiḍ
शोल्डर पैड

waistband
kamarband
कमरबंद

tailored
sile vastr
सिले वस्त्र

halter neck
ḍorī vālā galā
डोरी वाला गला

underwired
aṅḍarvāyarḍ
अंडरवायर्ड

sports bra
sporṭs brā
स्पोर्ट्स ब्रा

accessories • sahāyak vastueṃ • सहायक वस्तुएं

cap
ṭopī | टोपी

hat
ṭop | टोप

scarf
gulūband | गुलूबंद

buckle
baksuā
बकसुआ

belt
peṭī | पेटी

handle
hatthā
हत्था

tip
nok
नोक

umbrella
chhātā | छाता

handkerchief
rūmāl | रूमाल

bow tie
bo-ṭāī | बो–टाई

tie-pin
ṭāī pin | टाई पिन

gloves
dastāne | दस्ताने

jewelry • zevar • ज़ेवर

pendant
locket | लॉकेट

brooch
jaṛāū pin | जड़ाऊ पिन

cufflink
kafliṅk | कफ़लिंक

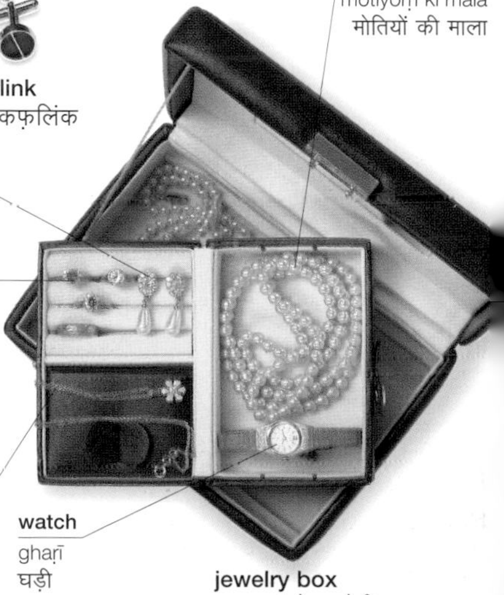

string of pearls
motiyoṃ kī mālā
मोतियों की माला

earring
bunde
बुंदे

ring
aṅgūṭhī
अंगूठी

necklace
hār
हार

watch
ghaṛī
घड़ी

jewelry box
zevar peṭī | ज़ेवर पेटी

link
kaṛī
कड़ी

bracelet
bresleṭ | ब्रेसलेट

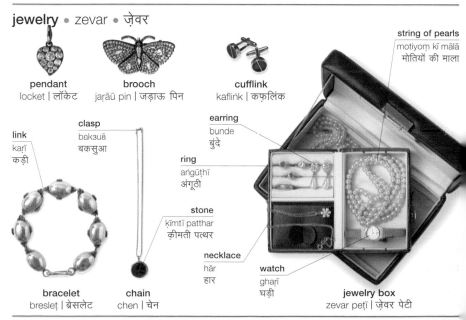

clasp
baksuā
बकसुआ

stone
ḳīmtī patthar
क़ीमती पत्थर

chain
chen | चेन

bags • baig • बैग

wallet
wallet | वॉलेट

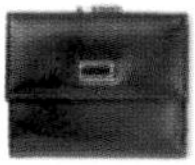
purse
baṭuā | बटुआ

fastening
kasanī
कसनी

shoulder bag
śolḍar baig | शोल्डर बैग

shoulder strap
baig kī tanī
बैग की तनी

handles
taniyāṃ
तनियां

duffel bag
bistar band | बिस्तर बंद

briefcase
brīfkes | ब्रीफ़केस

handbag
hainḍ baig | हैंड बैग

backpack
piṭṭhū baig | पिट्ठू बैग

shoes • jūte-chappal • जूते–चप्पल

lace
tasme/fīte
तस्मे/फ़ीते

tongue
jībh
जीभ

eyelet
chhed
छेद

heel
eṛī
एड़ी

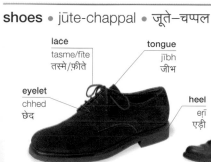

sole
talā
तला

lace-up
fīte vāle jūte | फ़ीते वाले जूते

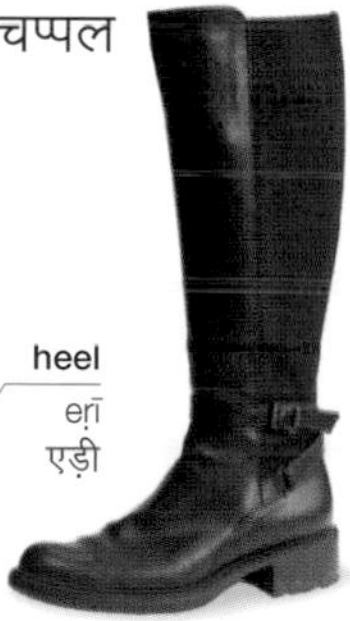
boot (women's)
būṭ (mahilā)
बूट (महिला)

hiking boot
būṭ | बूट

athletic shoe
ṭrenars
ट्रेनर्स

flip-flop
chappal
चप्पल

leather shoe
chamṛe ke jūte
चमड़े के जूते

high-heeled shoe
ūṃchī eṛī ke jūte
ऊंची एड़ी के जूते

wedge
chauṛī eṛī ke chappal
चौड़ी एड़ी के जूते

sandal
sainḍil
सैंडिल

slip-on
jūtiyāṃ
जूतियां

pump
pamp śūz
पंप शूज़

hair • bāl • बाल

comb
kaṇghā
कंघा

comb (v)
kaṇghī karnā | कंघी करना

brush
braś
ब्रश

brush (v)
braś karnā | ब्रश करना

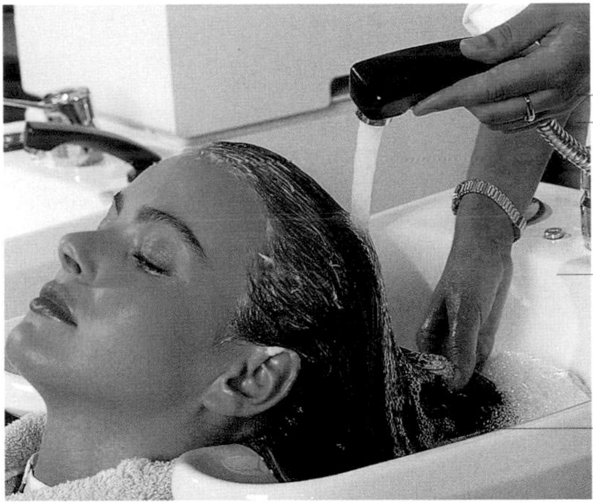

hair stylist
heyar ḍraisar
हेयर ड्रैसर

sink
besin
बेसिन

client
grāhak
ग्राहक

wash (v)
bāl dhonā | बाल धोना

rinse (v)
bāl dhonā | बाल धोना

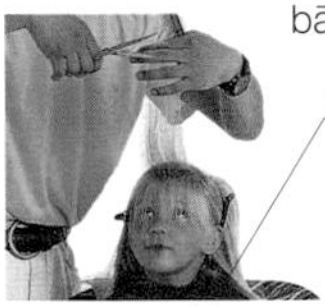

cape
vastr
वस्त्र

cut (v)
bāl kāṭnā | बाल काटना

blow-dry (v)
bāl sukhānā | बाल सुखाना

set (v) | bāl seṭ karnā | बाल सेट करना

accessories • saundarya prasādhan • सौंदर्य प्रसाधन

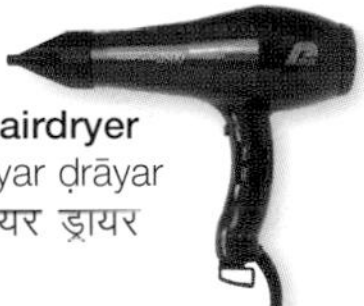

hairdryer
heyar ḍrāyar
हेयर ड्रायर

shampoo
śaimpū | शैम्पू

conditioner
kanḍiśnar | कंडीशनर

gel
jail | जैल

hairspray
heyar spre | हेयर–स्प्रे

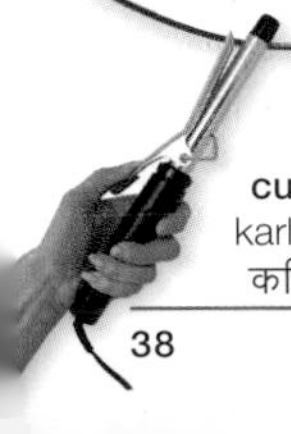

curling iron
karliṅg chimṭā
कर्लिंग चिमटा

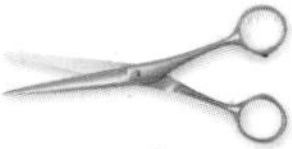

scissors
kaiṃchī
कैंची

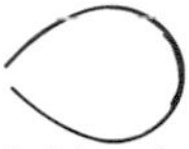

hairband
heyar baiṇḍ
हेयर बैंड

hair straighteners
bāl sidhā karne kā upkaraṇ
बाल सीधा करने का उपकरण

bobby pin
heyar pin
हेयर पिन

styles • keś sajjā • केश सज्जा

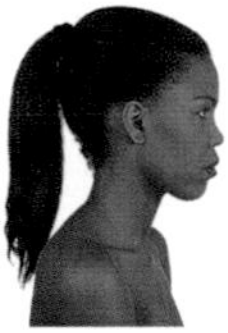

ponytail
ponī ṭel | पोनी टेल

braid
choṭī | चोटी

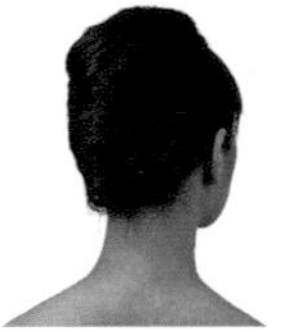

French twist
french jūṛā | फ़्रेंच जूड़ा

bun
jūṛā | जूड़ा

pigtails
do choṭī | दो चोटी

bob
bob | बॉब

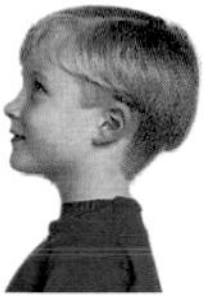

crop
crop | क्रॉप

curly
ghuṅghrāle | घुंघराले

perm
parm | पर्म

straight
sidhe bāl | सीधे बाल

roots
jareṃ
जड़ें

highlights
haīlāiṭ | हाइलाइट

bald
ganjā | गंजा

wig
vig | विग

vocabulary • śabdāvalī • शब्दावली

trim (v) chhāṃṭnā छांटना	**greasy** tailīya तैलीय
straighten (v) sīdhā karnā सीधा करना	**dry** rūkhe रूखे
barber nāī नाई	**normal** sāmānya सामान्य
dandruff rūsī रूसी	**scalp** śirovalk शिरोवल्क
split ends domuṃhe bāl दोमुंहे बाल	**hairband** bāloṃ kā fītā बालों का फ़ीता

colors • raṅg • रंग

blonde
sunahrā
सुनहरा

brunette
kālā-bhūrā
काला–भूरा

auburn
sunahrā bhūrā
सुनहरा भूरा

red
lāl bhūrā
लाल भूरा

black
kālā | काला

gray
sleṭī | स्लेटी

white
safed | सफ़ेद

dyed | raṅge
hue | रंगे हुए

beauty • saundarya • सौंदर्य

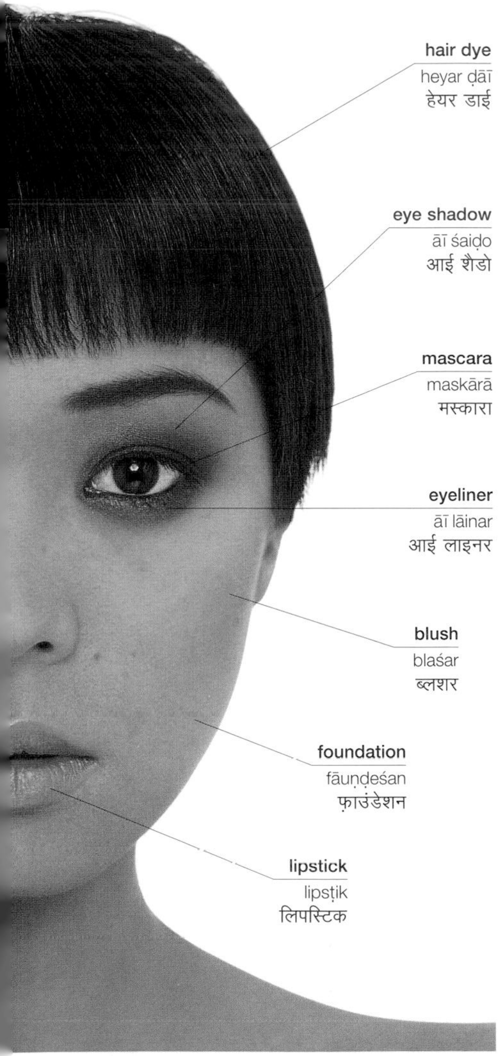
hair dye
heyar ḍāī
हेयर डाई
eye shadow
āī śaiḍo
आई शैडो
mascara
maskārā
मस्कारा
eyeliner
āī lāinar
आई लाइनर
blush
blaśar
ब्लशर
foundation
fāunḍeśan
फ़ाउंडेशन
lipstick
lipsṭik
लिपस्टिक

makeup • sāj-śṛṅgār • साज–श्रृंगार

eyebrow pencil
āī bro pensil | आई ब्रो पेंसिल
eyebrow brush
āī bro braś | आई ब्रो ब्रश
tweezers
chimṭī | चिमटी
lip gloss
lip gloss
लिप ग्लॉस
lip brush
lip braś
लिप ब्रश
lip liner
lip lāinar | लिप लाइनर
brush
braś | ब्रश
concealer
kansīlar | कंसीलर
mirror
śīśā
शीशा
face powder
fes pāuḍar
फ़ेस पाउडर
powder puff
paf
पफ़

compact | pāuḍar | पाउडर

beauty treatments • sundarya upchār • सौंदर्य उपचार

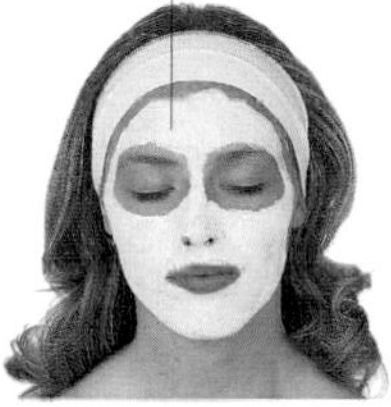

facial mask
fes paik
फ़ेस पैक

facial
feśiyal | फ़ेशियल

sunbed
san baiḍ | सन बैड

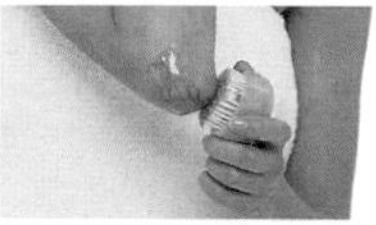

exfoliate (v)
mṛt tvachā utārnā
मृत त्वचा उतारना

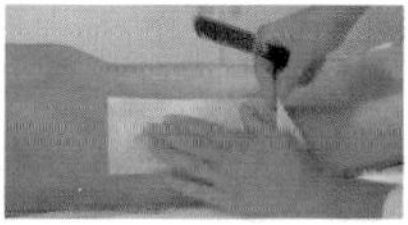

wax
vaiks | वैक्स

pedicure
pairoṃ kī safāī
पैरों की सफ़ाई

manicure • hāthoṃ kī safāī • हाथों की सफ़ाई

nail file
nel fāilar
नेल फ़ाइलर

nail polish remover
nel polish rimūvar
नेल पॉलिश रिमूवर

nail polish
nel polish
नेल पॉलिश

nail scissors
nakh kaiṃchī
नख क़ैंची

nail clippers
nel kaṭar
नेल कटर

toiletries • saundarya prasādhan • सौंदर्य प्रसाधन

cleanser
klīnzar
क्लींज़र

toner
ṭonar
टोनर

moisturizer
moisturizer
मॉइश्चराइज़र

self-tanning cream
ṭain karne kī krīm
टैन करने की क्रीम

perfume
itr
इत्र

cologne
parfyūm spre
परफ़्यूम स्प्रे

vocabulary • śabdāvalī • शब्दावली

complexion raṅg rūp रंग–रूप	**oily** tailīya तैलीय	**dark** kālī काली
fair gorī गोरी	**sensitive** saṃvedanśīl संवेदनशील	**tattoo** gudnā गुदना
dry rūkhī रूखी	**shade** raṅg रंग	**cotton balls** rūī ke phāhe रूई के फाहे
antiwrinkle jhurrī-nivārak झुर्री–निवारक	**hypoallergenic** elarjī rodhak एलर्जी रोधक	**tan** bhūre raṅg kā honā भूरे रंग का होना

health
svāsthya
स्वास्थ्य

illness • bīmārī • बीमारी

fever
bukhār | बुख़ार

headache
sirdard
सिरदर्द

nosebleed
naksīr
नकसीर

cough
khāṃsī
खांसी

sneeze
chhīṃk | छींक

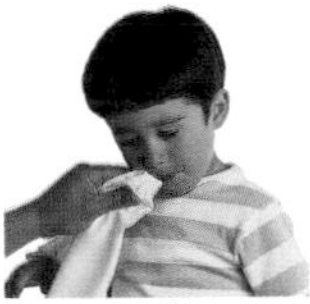

cold
zukām | जुकाम

flu
flū | फ़्लू

inhaler
inhelar
इनहेलर

asthma
damā | दमा

cramps
maroṛ | मरोड़

nausea
mitlī | मितली

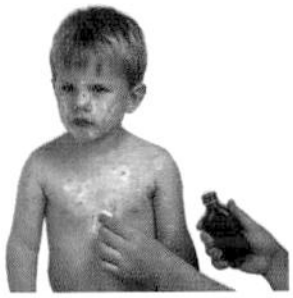

chickenpox
chhoṭī chechak | छोटी चेचक

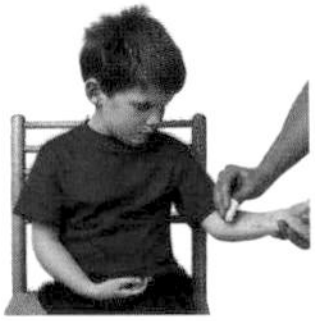

rash
funsī | फुंसी

vocabulary • śabdāvalī • शब्दावली

stroke pakṣāghāt पक्षाघात	**diabetes** madhumeh मधुमेह	**eczema** khāj खाज	**chill** sardī सर्दी	**vomit (v)** ulṭī karnā उल्टी करना	**diarrhea** dast दस्त
blood pressure raktchāp रक्तचाप	**allergy** elarjī एलर्जी	**infection** saṅkramaṇ संक्रमण	**stomachache** peṭ dard पेट दर्द	**epilepsy** mirgī मिरगी	**measles** khasrā खसरा
heart attack dil kā daurā दिल का दौरा	**hayfever** parāgaj jvar परागज ज्वर	**virus** viṣāṇu विषाणु	**faint (v)** behoś honā बेहोश होना	**migraine** ādhāsīsī आधासीसी	**mumps** kanpeṛā कनपेड़ा

doctor • chikitsak • चिकित्सक

consultation • parāmarś • परामर्श

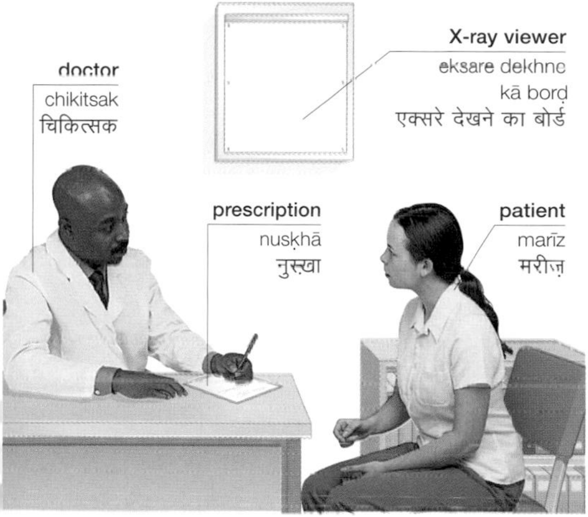
X-ray viewer
eksare dekhne kā borḍ
एक्सरे देखने का बोर्ड
doctor
chikitsak
चिकित्सक
prescription
nusḳhā
नुस्ख़ा
patient
marīz
मरीज़

nurse
nars
नर्स
scale
vazan-māpī
वज़न–मापी

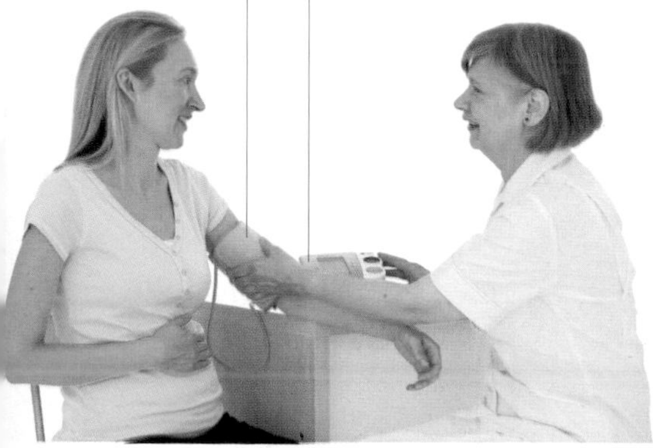
cuff
kalāī paṭṭī
कलाई पट्टी
electric blood pressure gauge
bijlī se chalne vālā raktchāp māpak
बिजली से चलने वाला रक्तचाप मापक

vocabulary • śabdāvalī • शब्दावली

appointment
milne kā samaya
मिलने का समय

surgery
śalya chikitsā
शल्य चिकित्सा

waiting room
pratīkṣā kakṣ
प्रतीक्षा कक्ष

inoculation
ṭīkā
टीका

thermometer
tharmāmīṭar
थर्मामीटर

medical examination
śārīrik jāṃch
शारीरिक जांच

I need to see a doctor.
mujhe doctor ko dikhānā hai
मुझे डॉक्टर को दिखाना है।

It hurts here.
yahāṃ dard ho rahā hai
यहां दर्द हो रहा है।

injury • choṭ • चोट

sprain | moch | मोच

sling
sliṅg paṭṭī
स्लिंग पट्टी

fracture | haḍḍī ṭūṭnā
हड्डी टूटना

neck brace
gardan kā
paṭṭā
गर्दन का पट्टा

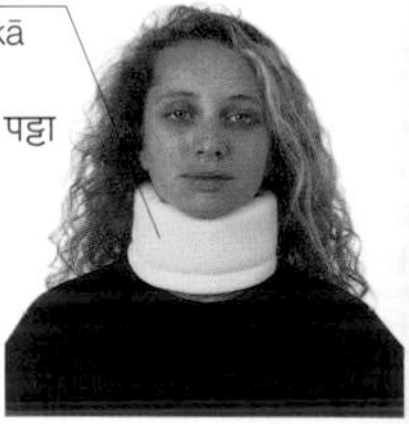

whiplash | gale kī moch
गले की मोच

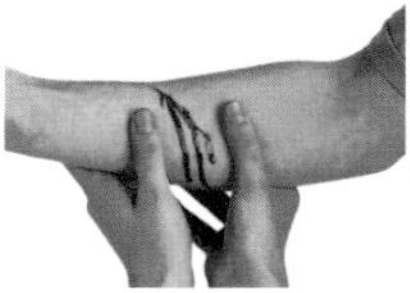

cut
kaṭnā | कटना

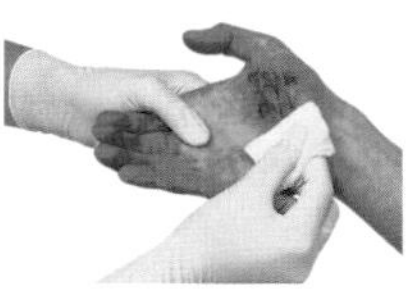

graze
ragaṛ | रगड़

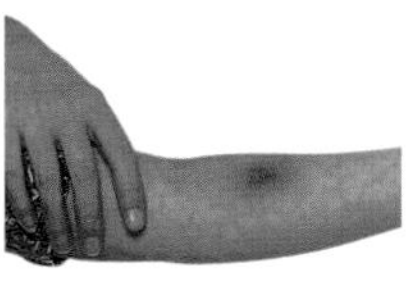

bruise
kharoṃch | खरोंच

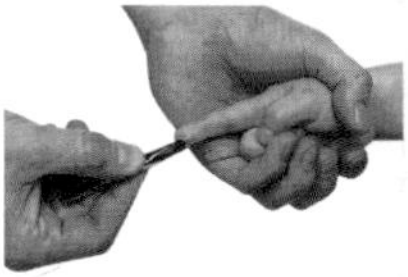

splinter
khapchī | खपची

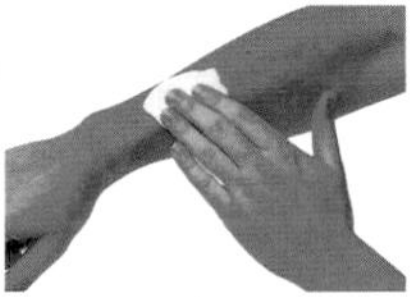

sunburn
dhūp se jalnā
धूप से जलना

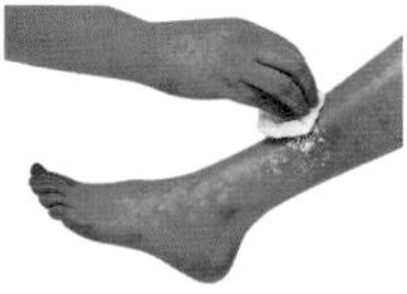

burn
jalnā
जलना

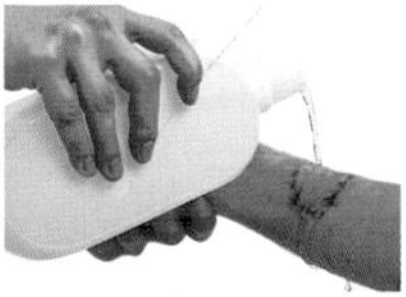

bite
kāṭā huā
काटा हुआ

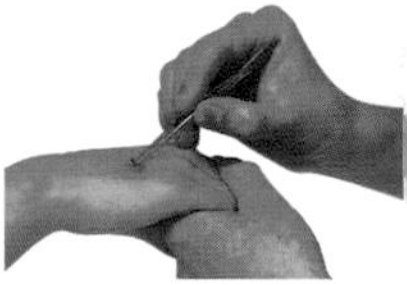

sting
ḍaṅk
डंक

vocabulary • śabdāvalī • शब्दावली

accident durghaṭnā दुर्घटना	**hemorrhage** raktsrāv रक्तस्राव	**poisoning** viṣpān विषपान	**Will he be all right?** kyā vah ṭhīk ho jāegā? क्या वह ठीक हो जाएगा?
emergency āpātkāl आपातकाल	**blister** chhālā छाला	**electric shock** bijlī kā jhaṭkā बिजली का झटका	**Where does it hurt?** kahāṃ dard ho rahā hai? कहां दर्द हो रहा है?
wound ghāv घाव	**concussion** āghāt आघात	**head injury** sir kī choṭ सिर की चोट	**Please call an ambulance!** kṛpyā embulens bulāie! कृपया एंबुलेंस बुलाइए!

first aid • prāthmik chikitsā • प्राथमिक चिकित्सा

ointment
marham
मरहम

bandage
palastar
पलस्तर

safety pin
sefṭī pin
सेफ़्टी पिन

bandage
paṭṭī
पट्टी

painkillers
dardnāśak davā
दर्दनाशक दवा

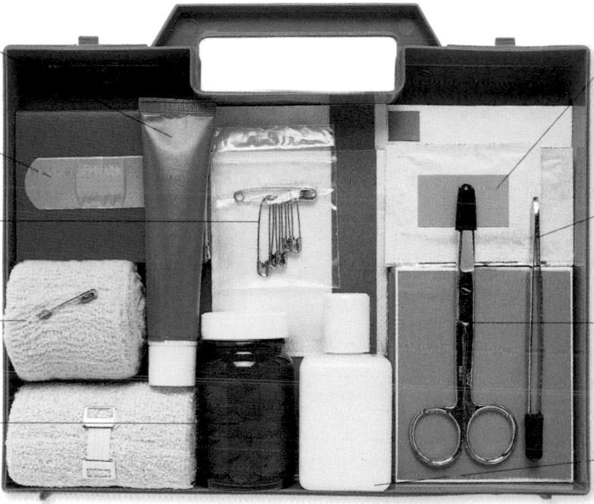

antiseptic wipe
kīṭāṇunāśak paṭṭī
कीटाणुनाशक पट्टी

tweezers
chimṭī
चिमटी

scissors
kaiṃchī
कैंची

antiseptic
kīṭāṇunāśak
कीटाणुनाशक

first-aid box | prāthmik chikitsā peṭī | प्राथमिक चिकित्सा पेटी

gauze
gauze
गॉज़

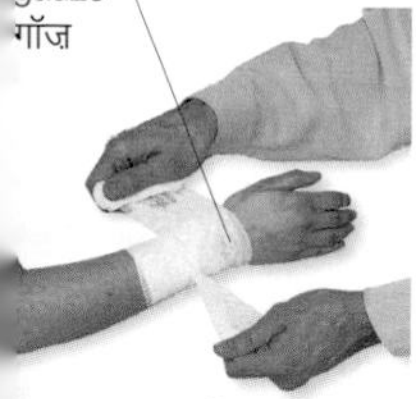

dressing
marham paṭṭī | मरहम पट्टी

splint | khapachī | खपची

adhesive tape
chipakne vālā ṭep
चिपकने वाला टेप

resuscitation
śvasan kriyā | श्वसन क्रिया

vocabulary • śabdāvalī • शब्दावली

shock
sadmā
सदमा

pulse
nāṛī
नाड़ी

choke (v)
dam ghuṭnā
दम घुटना

unconscious
behoś
बेहोश

breathing
sāṃs
सांस

sterile
saṅkramaṇ rahit
संक्रमण रहित

Can you help?
kyā āp madad kar sakte haiṃ?
क्या आप मदद कर सकते हैं?

Do you know first aid?
kyā āp prāthmik chikitsā jānte haiṃ?
क्या आप प्राथमिक चिकित्सा जानते हैं?

hospital • aspatāl • अस्पताल

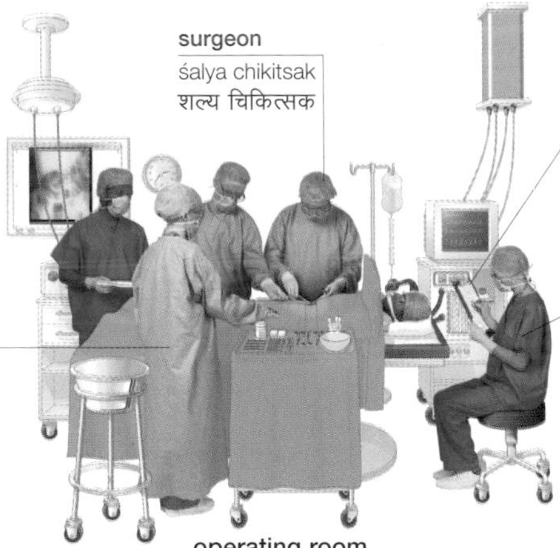

surgeon
śalya chikitsak
शल्य चिकित्सक

chart
chārṭ
चार्ट

anesthetist
niśchetan chikitsak
निश्चेतन चिकित्सक

nurse
nars
नर्स

operating room
śalya kakṣ | शल्य कक्ष

blood test
k̲hūn kī jāṃch
ख़ून की जांच

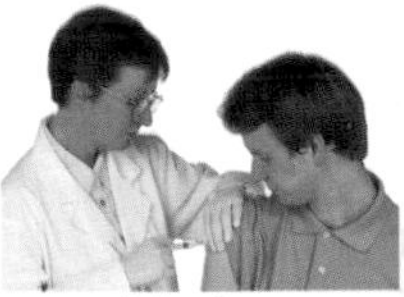

injection
ṭīkākaraṇ | टीकाकरण

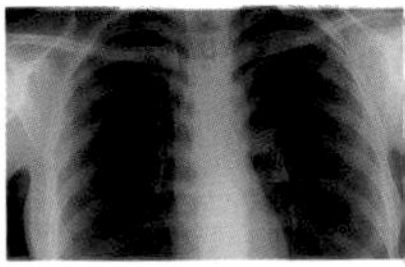

X-ray
eks-re | एक्स–रे

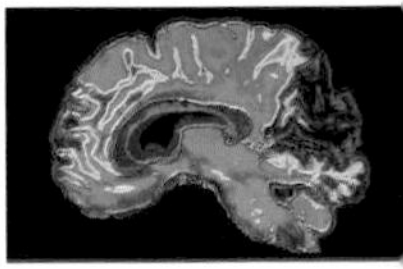

scan
skain | स्कैन

gurney
trolley
ट्रॉली

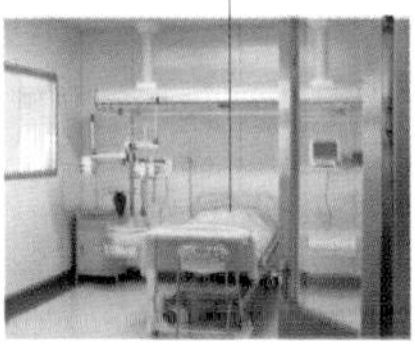

emergency room
āpātkālīn kakṣ
आपातकालीन कक्ष

call button
call baṭan
कॉल बटन

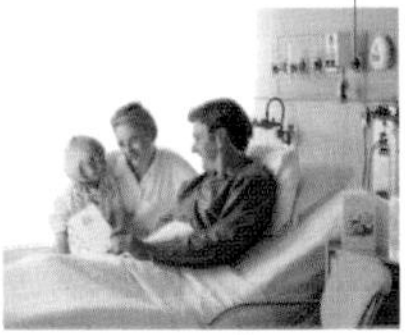

ward
kakṣ | कक्ष

wheelchair
vhīlcheyar | व्हीलचेयर

vocabulary • śabdāvalī • शब्दावली

operation
śalya chikitsā
शल्य चिकित्सा

discharged
chhuṭṭī denā
छुट्टी देना

visiting hours
milne kā samaya
मिलने का समय

children's ward
bacchoṃ kā ward
बच्चों का वॉर्ड

intensive care unit
gahan chikitsā kakṣ
गहन चिकित्सा कक्ष

admitted
bhartī
भर्ती

clinic
chikitsālaya
चिकित्सालय

maternity ward
prasūti kakṣ
प्रसूति कक्ष

private room
nijī kamrā
निजी कमरा

outpatient
bāhya rogī
बाह्य रोगी

departments • vibhāg • विभाग

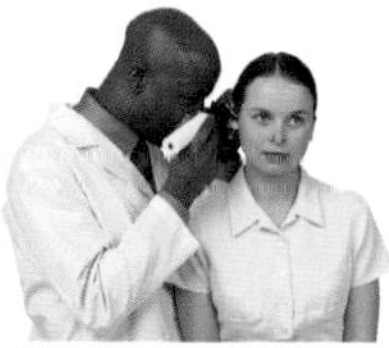

Ear, Nose, and Throat
kān, nāk, evam galā chikitsā
कान, नाक एवं गला चिकित्सा

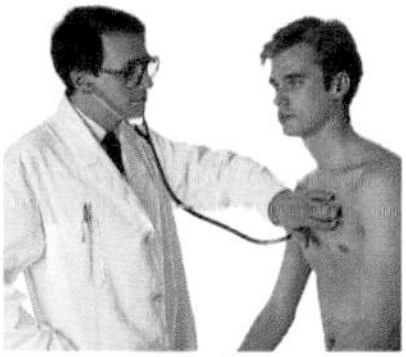

cardiology
hṛdaya chikitsā
हृदय चिकित्सा

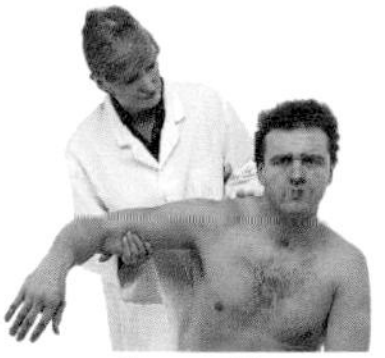

orthopedics
asthi chikitsā
अस्थि चिकित्सा

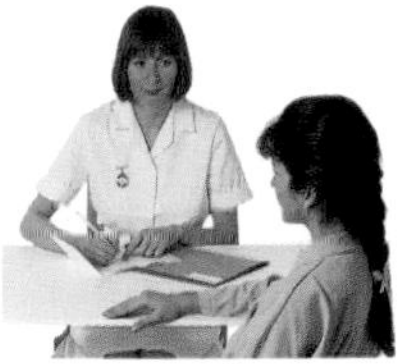

gynecology
strī rog chikitsā
स्त्री–रोग चिकित्सा

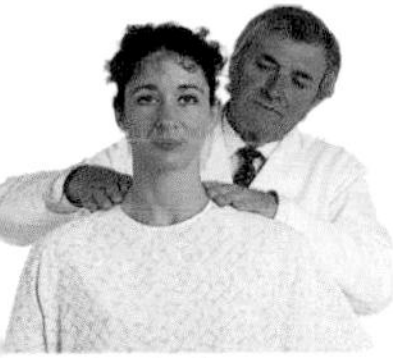

physiotherapy
vyāyām chikitsā
व्यायाम चिकित्सा

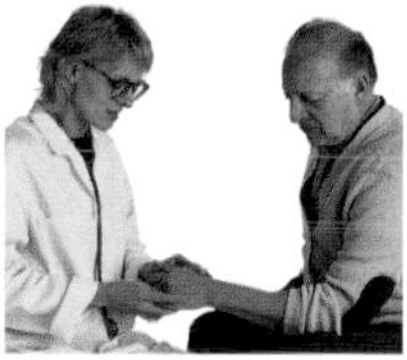

dermatology
tvachā chikitsā
त्वचा चिकित्सा

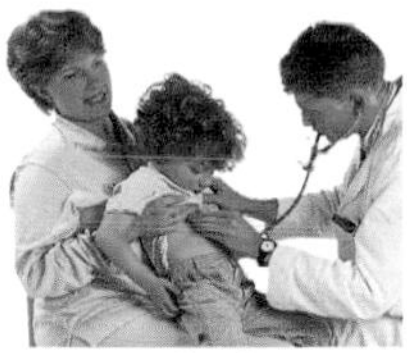

pediatrics
bāl chikitsā
बाल चिकित्सा

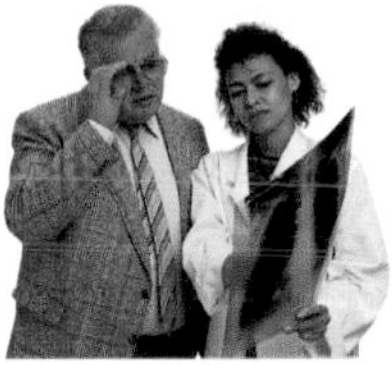

radiology
vikiraṇ chikitsā
विकिरण चिकित्सा

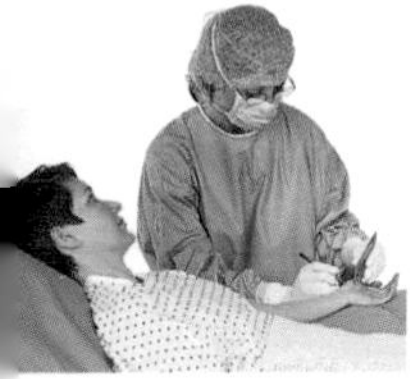

surgery
śalya chikitsā
शल्य चिकित्सा

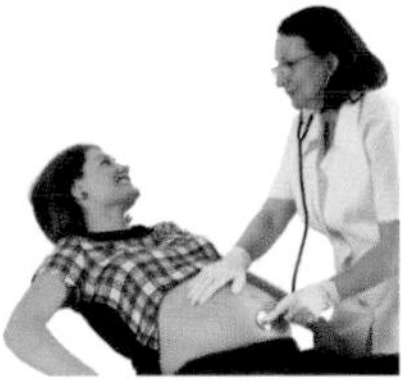

maternity
prasūti
प्रसूति

psychiatry
manochikitsā
मनोचिकित्सा

ophthalmology
netr chikitsā
नेत्र चिकित्सा

vocabulary • śabdāvalī • शब्दावली

neurology
snāyu vijñān
स्नायु विज्ञान

oncology
kainsar vijñān
कैंसर विज्ञान

urology
mūtr vijñān
मूत्र विज्ञान

plastic surgery
plāsṭik sarjarī
प्लास्टिक सर्जरी

endocrinology
antaḥ srāvīkī
अंत: स्त्रावीकी

referral
sifāriś
सिफ़ारिश

pathology
rog nidān
रोग निदान

test
jāṃch
जांच

result
pariṇām
परिणाम

consultant
parāmarśdātā
परामर्शदाता

dentist • dant chikitsak • दंत चिकित्सक

tooth • dāṃt • दांत

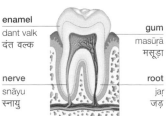

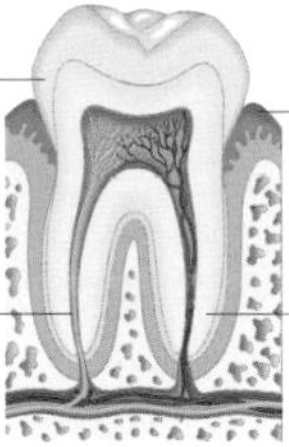
enamel
dant valk
दंत वल्क
gum
masūṛā
मसूड़ा
nerve
snāyu
स्नायु
root
jaṛ
जड़

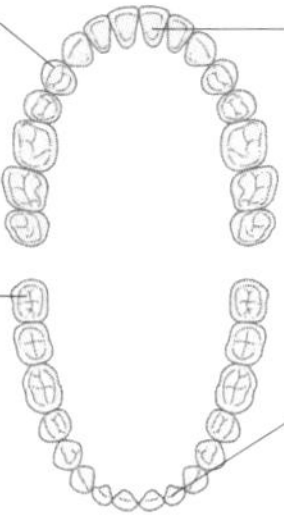
premolar
chhoṭī dāṛh
छोटी दाढ़
incisor
karttan
dāṃt
कर्त्तन
दांत
molar
dāṛh
दाढ़
canine
kīlā
कीला

vocabulary • śabdāvalī • शब्दावली

toothache
dāṃt kā dard
दांत का दर्द

plaque
plāk
प्लाक

decay
saṛan
सड़न

filling
bharāvan
भरावन

drill
chhed karnā
छेद करना

extraction
dāṃt ukhāṛnā
दांत उखाड़ना

crown
upri dant
उपरि दंत

checkup • jāṃch • जांच

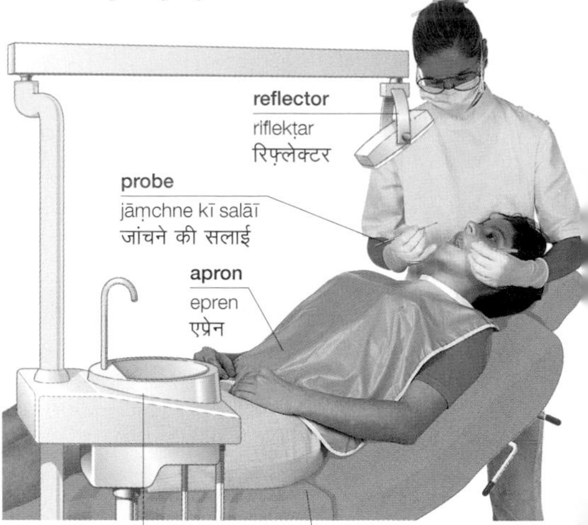
reflector
riflekṭar
रिफ़्लेक्टर
probe
jāṃchne kī salāī
जांचने की सलाई
apron
epren
एप्रेन
sink
besin
बेसिन
dentist's chair
dant chikitsā kursī
दंत चिकित्सा–कुर्सी

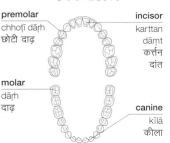

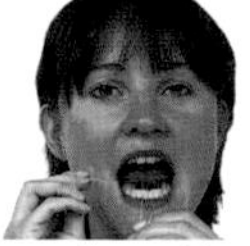
floss (v)
dhāge se safāī karnā
धागे से सफ़ाई करना

brush
braś karnā
ब्रश करना

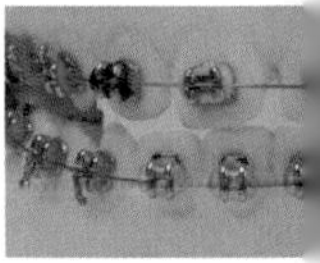
brace
tār kasnā
तार कसना

dental X-ray
dāṃtoṃ kā eksare
दांतों का एक्सरे

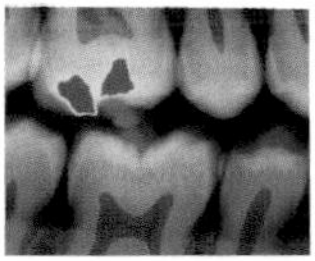
X-ray film
eksare film
एक्सरे फ़िल्म

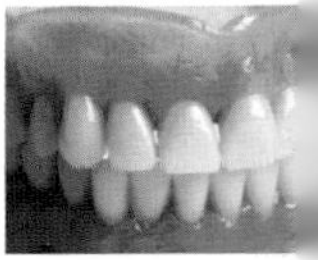
dentures
naklī battīsī
नक़ली बत्तीसी

optometrist • dṛṣṭi parīkṣak • दृष्टि परीक्षक

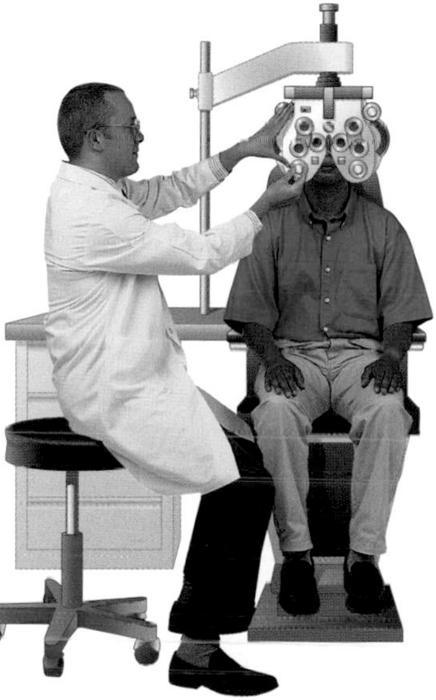

eye test | āṃkhoṃ kī jāṃch | आंखों की जांच

case
kavar
कवर

lens
lains
लैंस

glasses
chaśmā | चश्मा

frame
frem
फ़्रेम

sunglasses
dhūp kā chaśmā | धूप का चश्मा

cleaning fluid
lains sāf karne
kā dravya
लैंस साफ़ करने का द्रव्य

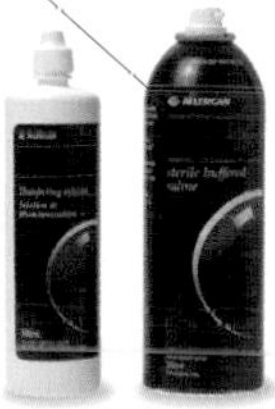

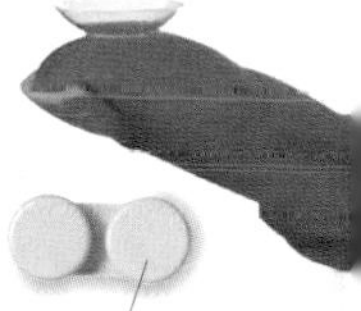

lens case
lains kavar
लैंस कवर

contact lenses | contact lains | कॉन्टेक्ट लैंस

eye • āṃkh • आंख

eyebrow
bhauṃh
भौंह

eyelid
palak
पलक

pupil
putlī
पुतली

eyelash
baraunī
बरौनी

iris
uptārā
उपतारा

retina
dṛṣṭi paṭal
दृष्टि पटल

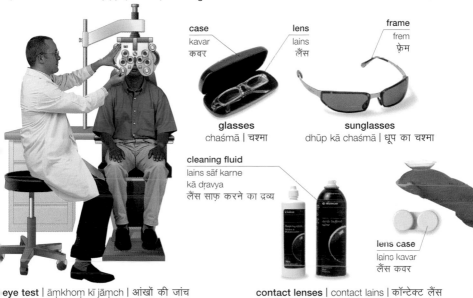

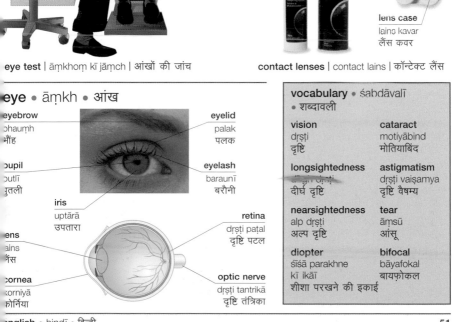

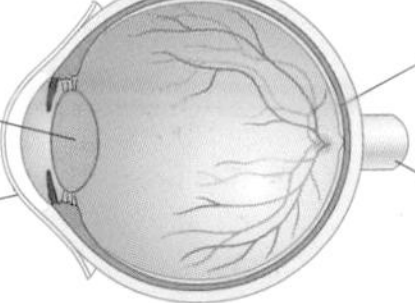

lens
lains
लैंस

cornea
korniyā
कोर्निया

optic nerve
dṛṣṭi tantrikā
दृष्टि तंत्रिका

vocabulary • śabdāvalī • शब्दावली

vision
dṛṣṭi
दृष्टि

longsightedness
dīrgh dṛṣṭi
दीर्घ दृष्टि

nearsightedness
alp dṛṣṭi
अल्प दृष्टि

diopter
śīśā parakhne
kī ikāī
शीशा परखने की इकाई

cataract
motiyābind
मोतियाबिंद

astigmatism
dṛṣṭi vaiṣamya
दृष्टि वैषम्य

tear
āṃsū
आंसू

bifocal
bāyafokal
बायफ़ोकल

pregnancy • garbhāvasthā • गर्भावस्था

pregnancy test
garbhāvasthā jāṃch
गर्भावस्था जांच

scan
skain
स्कैन

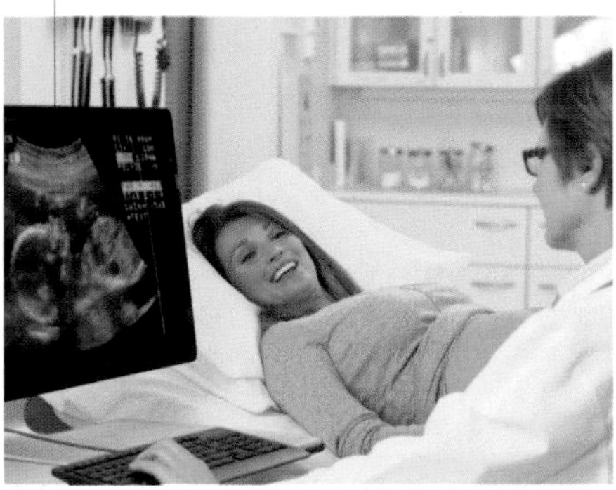

ultrasound
alṭrāsāunḍ | अल्ट्रासाउंड

umbilical cord
nābhi-rajju
नाभि–रज्जु

placenta
garbhnāl
गर्भनाल

cervix
garbhaśaya dvār
गर्भाशय द्वार

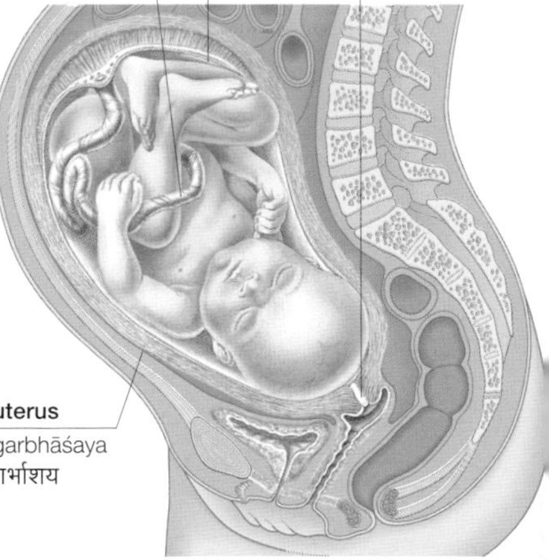

uterus
garbhāśaya
गर्भाशय

fetus
bhrūṇ | भ्रूण

vocabulary • śabdāvalī • शब्दावली

ovulation bījjanan बीजजनन	**prenatal** janm pūrv जन्म पूर्व	**contraction** saṇkuchan संकुचन	**dilation** phailāv फैलाव	**delivery** prasav प्रसव	**breech** ulṭā bhrūṇ उल्टा भ्रूण
conception garbhādhān गर्भाधान	**womb** bacchedānī बच्चेदानी	**break water (v)** pānī jānā पानी जाना	**epidural** epiḍyūral एपिड्यूरल	**birth** janm जन्म	**premature** samaya pūrv समय पूर्व
pregnant garbhvatī गर्भवती	**trimester** trimās त्रिमास	**amniotic fluid** ulv drav उल्व द्रव	**episiotomy** bhagacchhedan भगच्छेदन	**miscarriage** garbhpāt गर्भपात	**gynecologist** strī rog viśeṣajñ स्त्री–रोग विशेषज्ञ
expecting garbhvatī गर्भवती	**embryo** aviksit bhrūṇ अविकसित भ्रूण	**amniocentesis** sīrinj se ulv drav nikālnā सीरिंज से उल्व–द्रव निकालना	**cesarean section** operation prasav ऑपरेशन प्रसव	**stitches** ṭāṃke टांके	**obstetrician** prasav viśeṣajñ प्रसव विशेषज्ञ

childbirth • śiśu janm • शिशु जन्म

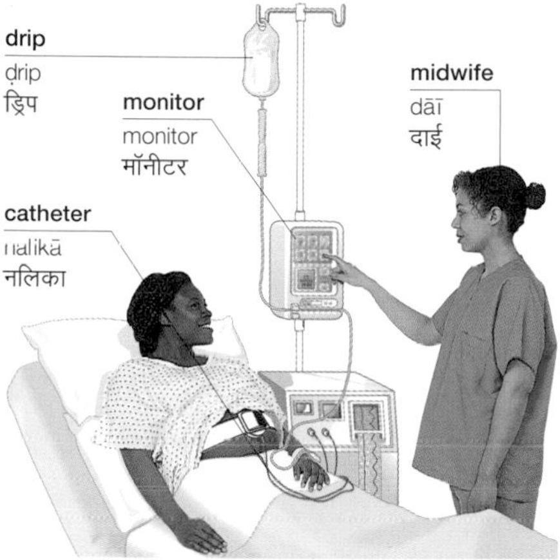
drip
drip
ड्रिप
monitor
monitor
मॉनीटर
catheter
nalikā
नलिका
midwife
dāī
दाई

induce labor (v)
kṛtrim prasav karānā | कृत्रिम प्रसव कराना

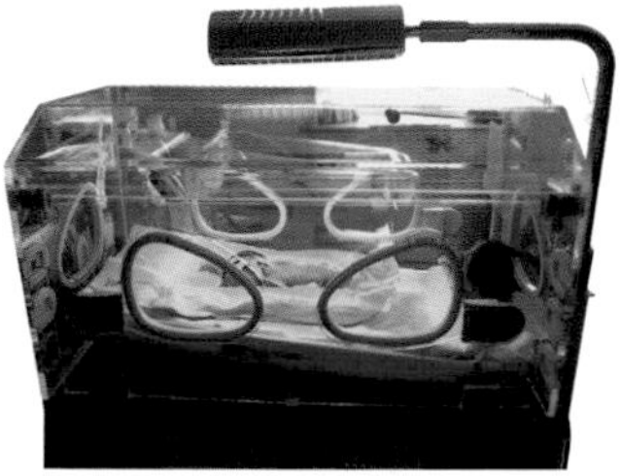

incubator | ūṣmak | ऊष्मक

birth weight
janm bhār | जन्म भार

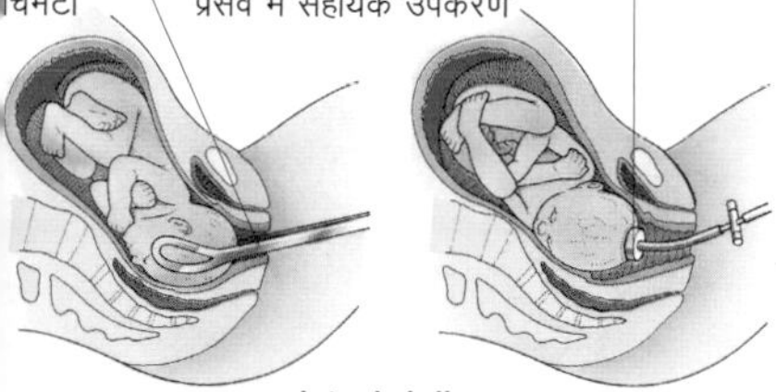
forceps
chimṭī
चिमटी
ventouse cup
prasav meṃ sahāyak upkaraṇ
प्रसव में सहायक उपकरण

assisted delivery
upkaraṇ dvārā prasav | उपकरण द्वारा प्रसव

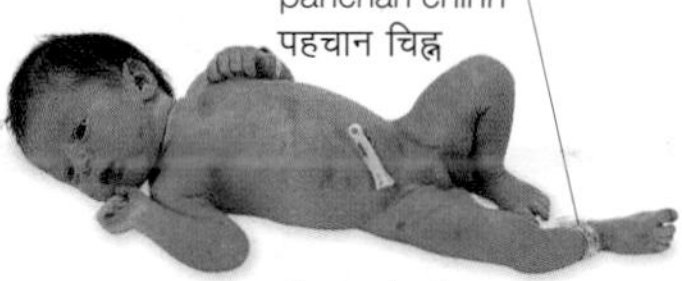
identity tag
pahchān chihn
पहचान चिह्न

newborn baby
navjāt śiśu | नवजात शिशु

nursing • stanpān • स्तनपान

breast pump
stan pamp
स्तन पंप

nursing bra
narsiṅg brā
नर्सिंग ब्रा

breastfeed (v)
stanpān karānā
स्तनपान कराना

pads
paid
पैड

complementary therapy • vaikalpik chikitsā • वैकल्पिक चिकित्सा

t-shirt
ṭī śarṭ
टी शर्ट
mat
chaṭāī
चटाई

yoga
yog | योग

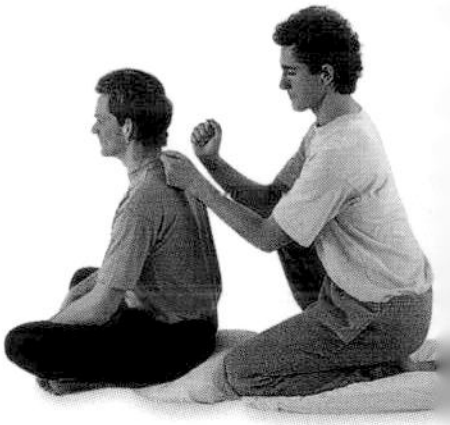

massage
māliś | मालिश

shiatsu
śiyātsu | शियात्सु

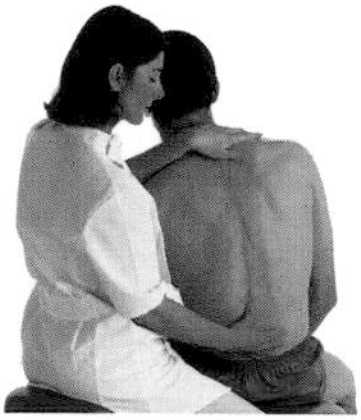

chiropractic
merudaṇḍ upchār
मेरुदंड उपचार

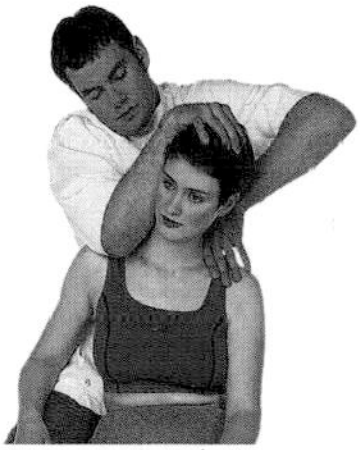

osteopathy | asthi chikitsā | अस्थि चिकित्सा

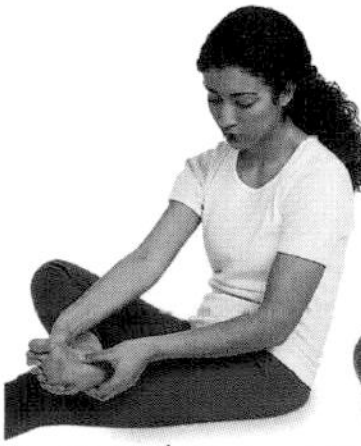

reflexology | rifleksolojī
रिफ़्लेक्सोलॉजी

meditation
dhyān | ध्यान

counselor
parāmarśdātā
परामर्शदाता

group therapy
samūh chikitsā | समूह चिकित्सा

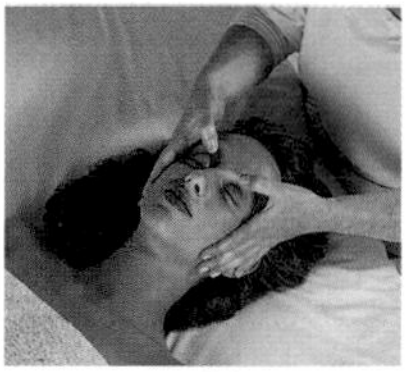

reiki
rekī | रेकी

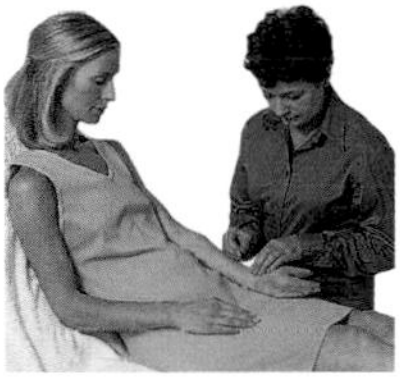

acupuncture
ekyūpaṅkchar
एक्यूपंक्चर

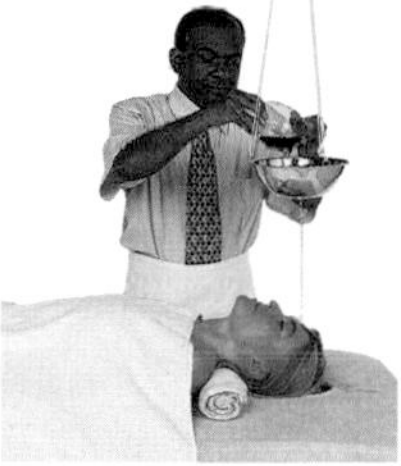

ayurveda
āyurved | आयुर्वेद

hypnotherapy
sammohan chikitsā
सम्मोहन चिकित्सा

herbalism | jaṛī-būṭī sevan | जड़ी–बूटी सेवन

essential oils
sugandhit tel
सुगंधित तेल

aromatherapy
sugandh chikitsā
सुगंध चिकित्सा

homeopathy
homyopaithī
होम्योपैथी

acupressure therapy
ekyūpraiśar
एक्यूप्रैशर

therapist
chikitsak
चिकित्सक

psychotherapy
manochikitsā | मनोचिकित्सा

vocabulary • śabdāvalī • शब्दावली

supplement pūrak पूरक	**feng shui** feṅg śuī फ़ेंग शुई	**relaxation** tanāv mukti तनाव मुक्ति	**naturopathy** prākṛtik chikitsā प्राकृतिक चिकित्सा
hydrotherapy jal chikitsā जल चिकित्सा	**herb** jaṛī-būṭī जड़ी–बूटी	**stress** tanāv तनाव	**crystal healing** kristal chikitsā क्रिस्टल चिकित्सा

home
ghar
घर

house • makān • मकान

gutter
gaṭar
गटर
roof
chhat
छत
chimney
chimnī
चिमनी
wall
dīvār
दीवार
eaves
chhajjā
छज्जा
shingle
ṭāil
टाइल
shutter
kapāṭ
कपाट
porch
dvārmaṇḍap
द्वारमंडप
window
khiṛkī
खिड़की
extension
atirikt bhāg
अतिरिक्त भाग
sidewalk
rāstā
रास्ता
front door
mukhyadvār
मुख्यद्वार

vocabulary • śabdāvalī • शब्दावली

single-family ekal ghar एकल घर	**tenant** kirāedār किराएदार	**garage** gairej गैरेज	**mailbox** laiṭar box लैटर बॉक्स	**burglar alarm** chor ghanṭī चोर घंटी	**rent (v)** kirāe par lenā किराए पर लेना
townhouse śahrī makān शहरी मकान	**ranch house** baṅglā बंगला	**attic** aṭārī अटारी	**landlord** makān mālik मकान मालिक	**courtyard** āṅgan आंगन	**rent** kirāyā किराया
duplex saṭā huā ghar सटा हुआ घर	**basement** tahkhānā तहख़ाना	**room** kamrā कमरा	**porch light** dvārmaṇḍap battī द्वारमंडप बत्ती	**floor** manzil मंज़िल	**row house** chhat vālā छत वाला

entrance • praveś dvār • प्रवेश द्वार

hand rail
reliṅg
रेलिंग

staircase
zīnā
ज़ीना

landing
chauṛī sīṛhī
चौड़ी सीढ़ी

banister
sīṛhiyoṃ kā jaṅglā
सीढ़ियों का जंगला

hallway
galiyārā | गलियारा

doorbell
darvāze kī ghaṇṭī
दरवाज़े की घंटी

doormat
pāyadān
पायदान

door knocker
kuṇḍā
कुंडा

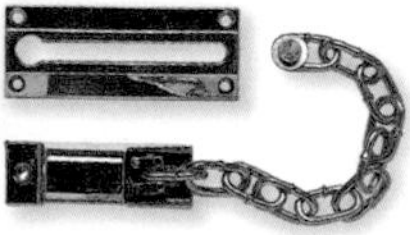

door chain | darvāze kī kaṛī | दरवाजे की कड़ी

key
chābī
चाबी

lock
tālā | ताला

bolt
chaṭkhanī | चटख़नी

apartment • flaiṭ • फ़्लैट

balcony
bālkanī
बालकनी

apartment building
apārṭmenṭ | अपार्टमेंट

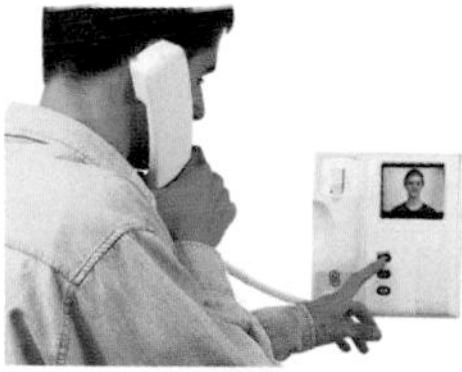

intercom
antaḥ sanchār | अंतः संचार

elevator
lifṭ | लिफ़्ट

internal systems • gharelū upkaraṇ • घरेलू उपकरण

radiator | reḍieṭar | रेडिएटर

space heater
hīṭar | हीटर

blade
paṅkh | पंख

fan | paṅkhā | पंखा

portable heater
bloar | ब्लोअर

electricity • bijlī • बिजली

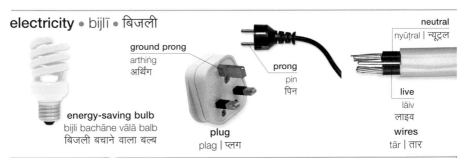

energy-saving bulb
bijli bachāne vālā balb
बिजली बचाने वाला बल्ब

ground prong
arthiṅg
अर्थिंग

plug
plag | प्लग

prong
pin
पिन

neutral
nyūṭral | न्यूट्रल

live
lāiv
लाइव

wires
tār | तार

vocabulary • śabdāvalī • शब्दावली

voltage volṭej वोल्टेज	**fuse** fyūz फ़्यूज़	**outlet** socket सॉकेट	**household current** men saplāī मेन सप्लाई	**direct current** ḍāyarekṭ karanṭ डायरेक्ट करंट
amp empīyar एम्पियर	**fuse box** fyūz box फ़्यूज़ बॉक्स	**switch** svich स्विच	**transformer** transformer ट्रांसफ़ॉर्मर	**alternating current** alternating karanṭ ऑल्टरनेटिंग करंट
power ūrjā ऊर्जा	**generator** jenreṭar जेनरेटर	**power outage** bijlī kaṭautī बिजली कटौती	**electricity meter** bijlī kā mīṭar बिजली का मीटर	

plumbing • nalsāzī • नलसाज़ी

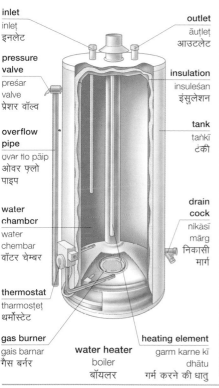

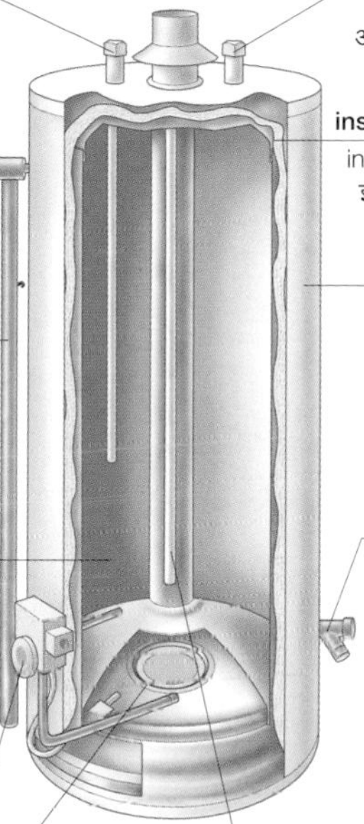
inlet
inleṭ
इनलेट
outlet
āuṭleṭ
आउटलेट
pressure valve
preśar valve
प्रेशर वॉल्व
insulation
insuleśan
इंसुलेशन
tank
ṭaṅkī
टंकी
overflow pipe
ovar flo pāip
ओवर फ़्लो पाइप
water chamber
water chembar
वॉटर चेम्बर
drain cock
nikāsī mārg
निकासी मार्ग
thermostat
tharmosṭeṭ
थर्मोस्टेट
gas burner
gais barnar
गैस बर्नर
heating element
garm karne kī dhātu
गर्म करने की धातु

water heater
boiler
बॉयलर

sink • siṅk • सिंक

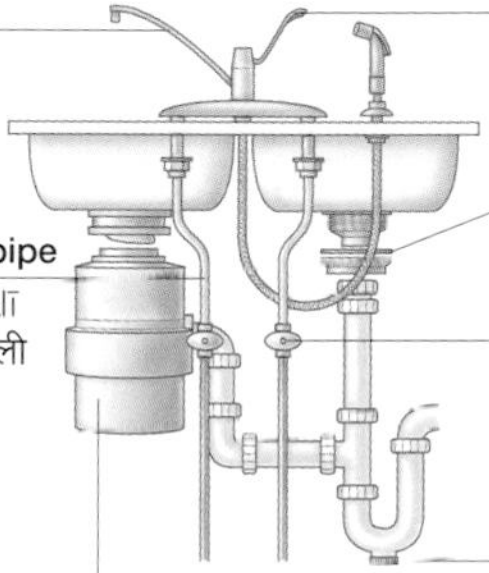
faucet
nal
नल
lever
līvar
लीवर
gasket
gāskeṭ
गास्केट
supply pipe
āpurti nalī
आपूर्ति नली
shutoff valve
shutoff valve
शटऑफ़ वॉल्व
drain
nikās
निकास
waste disposal unit
kūṛā nikās ikāī
कूड़ा निकास इकाई

water closet • śauchālaya • शौचालय

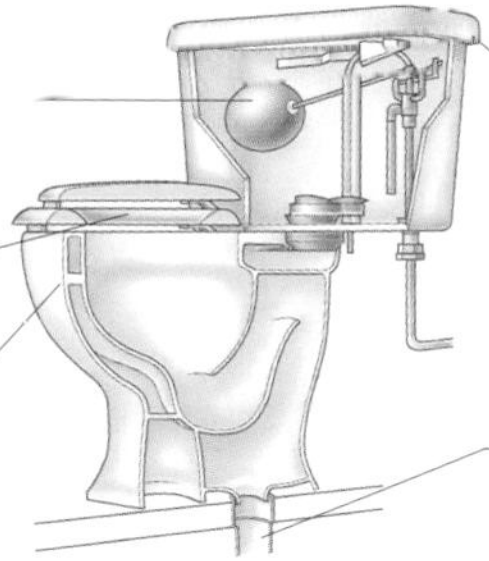
float ball
floṭ ball
फ़्लोट बॉल
tank
ṭaṅkī
टंकी
seat
sīṭ
सीट
bowl
bāul
बाउल
drain
nikās pāip
निकास पाइप

waste disposal • kūṛe kā nipṭān • कूड़े का निपटान

bottle
botal
बोतल

recycling bin
punarchakraṇ pātr
पुनर्चक्रण पात्र

lid
ḍhakkan
ढक्कन
pedal
paiḍal
पैडल

trash can
kūṛedān
कूड़ेदान

sorting unit
chhaṃṭāī yūniṭ
छंटाई यूनिट

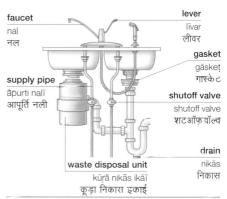

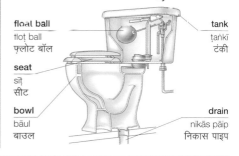

organic waste
jaivik kūṛā
जैविक कूड़ा

living room • baiṭhak • बैठक

lamp
laimp
लैंप

wall light
lāiṭ
लाइट

fireplace
fāyarples
फ़ायरप्लेस

ceiling
chhat
छत

vase
guldān
गुलदान

cushion
gaddī
गद्दी

coffee table
coffee ṭebal
कॉफ़ी टेबल

sofa
sofā
सोफ़ा

floor
farś
फ़र्श

frame
frem
फ़्रेम

painting
chitr
चित्र

curtain
pardā | पर्दा

sheer curtain
jālīdār pardā
जालीदार पर्दा

venetian blind
veneśiyan blāinḍ
वेनेशियन ब्लाइंड

roller blind | rolar blāinḍ | रोलर ब्लाइंड

molding
paṭṭī | पट्टी

armchair
kursī
कुर्सी

bookshelf
kitāboṃ kī almārī
किताबों की अलमारी

sofa bed
sofā-kam-beḍ
सोफ़ा–कम–बेड

rug
darī
दरी

study | paṛhne kā kamrā | पढ़ने का कमरा

dining room • bhojan kakṣ • भोजन कक्ष

pepper
kālī mirch
काली मिर्च
salt
namak
नमक
table
mez
मेज़
crockery
chīnī miṭṭī ke bartan
चीनी मिट्टी के बर्तन
cutlery
chhurī-kāṃṭe
छुरी–कांटे
chair
kursī
कुर्सी
back
pīṭh
पीठ
seat
sīṭ
सीट
leg
pāyā
पाया

vocabulary • śabdāvalī • शब्दावली

serve (v) parosnā परोसना	**hungry** bhūkhā भूखा	**dinner** rāt kā bhojan रात का भोजन	**full** bharā huā भरा हुआ	**host** mezbān मेज़बान
eat (v) khānā खाना	**tablecloth** mezpoś मेज़पोश	**hostess** mahilā mezbān महिला मेज़बान	**portion** hissā हिस्सा	**guest** mehmān मेहमान
set the table (v) mez lagānā मेज़ लगाना	**breakfast** nāśtā नाश्ता	**lunch** dopahar kā bhojan दोपहर का भोजन	**meal** bhojan भोजन	**placemat** ṭebal maiṭ टेबल मैट

Can I have some more, please?
kyā maiṃ aur le saktā hūṃ?
क्या मैं और ले सकता हूं?

I've had enough, thank you.
aur nahīṃ chāhie, dhanyavād.
और नहीं चाहिए धन्यवाद।

That was delicious.
khānā svādiṣṭ thā.
खाना स्वादिष्ट था।

crockery and cutlery • bartan aur chhurī-kāṃṭe • बर्तन और छुरी–कांटे

mug
mag
मग

coffee cup
coffee kā pyālā
कॉफ़ी का प्याला

teaspoon
chhoṭā chammach
छोटा चम्मच

teacup
chāya kā pyālā
चाय का प्याला

plate
pleṭ
प्लेट

bowl
kaṭorā
कटोरा

cafetière
coffee kī ketlī
कॉफ़ी की केतली

teapot
ketlī
केतली

pitcher
jag
जग

egg cup
aṇḍe kā kap
अंडे का कप

wine glass
vāin gilās
वाइन गिलास

tumbler
gilas
गिलास

glassware
kāṃch ke gilās
कांच के गिलास

napkin ring
naipkin ring
नैपकिन रिंग

side plate
chhoṭī pleṭ
छोटी प्लेट

dinner plate
baṛī pleṭ
बड़ी प्लेट

soup bowl
sūp kī pleṭ
सूप की प्लेट

soup spoon
sūp kā chammach
सूप का चम्मच

napkin
naipkin
नैपकिन

fork
kāṃṭā
कांटा

place setting
bartan lagāne kā tarīḳā
बर्तन लगाने का तरीक़ा

spoon
chammach
चम्मच

knife
chhurī
छुरी

kitchen • rasoī • रसोई

shelves
khāne
ख़ाने

faucet
nal
नल

sink
siṅk
सिंक

drawer
darāz
दराज़

extractor fan
chimnī
चिमनी

stovetop
range
sṭov
स्टोव

countertop
khānā banāne
kī jagah
खाना बनाने
की जगह

oven
ovan
ओवन

cabinet
almārī
अलमारी

appliances • upkaraṇ • उपकरण

microwave oven
māikrovev ovan | माइक्रोवेव ओवन

electric kettle
ketlī
केतली

toaster
ṭosṭar
टोस्टर

mixing bowl
miksiṅg bāul
मिक्सिंग बाउल

blade
bleḍ
ब्लेड

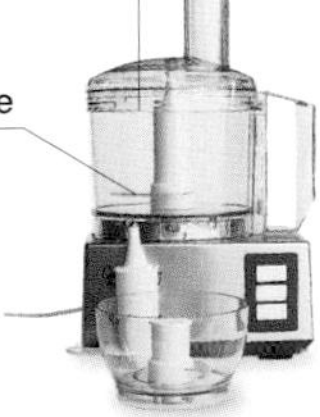

food processor
fūḍ prosesar
फ़ूड प्रोसेसर

lid
ḍhakkan
ढक्कन

blender
blenḍar
ब्लेंडर

dishwasher
bartan dhone kī maśīn
बर्तन धोने की मशीन

icemaker
baraf jamāne kī jagah
बर्फ़ जमाने की जगह
freezer
frīzar
फ़्रीज़र
refrigerator
refrījareṭar
रेफ़्रीजरेटर
shelf
ḳhānā
ख़ाना
crisper
krispar
क्रिस्पर

fridge-freezer
frij | फ़्रिज

vocabulary • śabdāvalī • शब्दावली

burner
barnar
बर्नर

stovetop
sṭov
स्टोव

trash can
kūṛedān
कूड़ेदान

draining board
ḍreniṅg borḍ
ड्रेनिंग बोर्ड

freeze (v)
jamānā
जमाना

defrost (v)
pighlānā
पिघलाना

sauté (v)
halkā bhūnnā
हल्का भूनना

steam (v)
bhāp se pakānā
भाप से पकाना

cooking • khānā pakānā • खाना पकाना

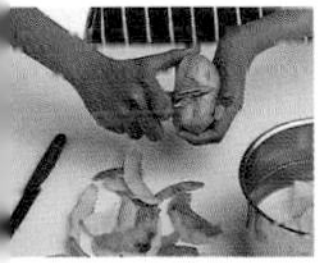

peel (v)
chhīlnā | छीलना

slice (v)
kāṭnā | काटना

grate (v)
ghisnā | घिसना

pour (v)
uṛelnā | उड़ेलना

mix (v)
milānā | मिलाना

whisk (v)
pheṃṭnā | फेंटना

boil (v)
ubālnā | उबालना

fry (v)
talnā | तलना

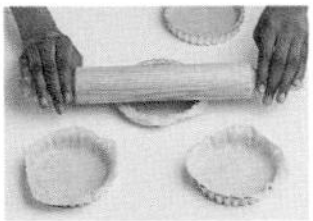

roll (v)
belnā | बेलना

stir (v)
chalānā | चलाना

simmer (v)
khadaknā
खदकना

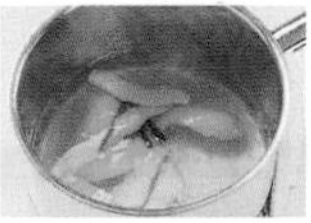

poach (v)
pānī meṃ pakānā
पानी में पकाना

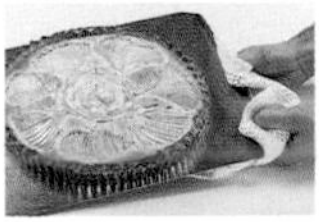

bake (v)
bek karnā
बेक करना

roast (v)
bhūnnā
भूनना

grill (v) | tandūr meṃ bhūnnā
तंदूर में भूनना

kitchenware • rasoī upkaraṇ • रसोई उपकरण

cutting board
sabzī kāṭne kā takhtā | सब्ज़ी काटने का तख़्ता

bread knife
breḍ kāṭne kī chhurī
ब्रेड काटने की छुरी

kitchen knife
chākū
चाकू

cleaver
chāpaṛ
चापड़

knife sharpener
chāḳū tez karne vālā
चाक़ू तेज़ करने वाला

meat tenderizer
māṃs kūṭne kā auzār | मांस कूटने का औज़ार

skewer
sīkh | सीख

grater
kaddūkas
कद्दूकस

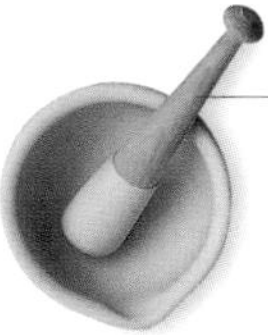

pestle
mūsal
मूसल

mortar
kharal | खरल

potato masher
meśar | मेशर

vegetable peeler
chhīlne vālā chākū
छीलने वाला चाकू

apple corer | bīj nikālne kī salāī
बीज निकालने की सलाई

can opener
kain opnar
कैन ओपनर

bottle opener
botal opnar
बोतल ओपनर

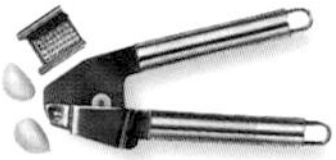

garlic press
lahsun kūṭne vālā
लहसुन कूटने वाला

serving spoon
parosne kā chammach
परोसने का चम्मच

food turner
palṭā | पलटा

colander
chhalnā | छलना

spatula
speṭulā | स्पेटुला

wooden spoon
lakṛī kā chammach
लकड़ी का चम्मच

slotted spoon
kalchhī | कलछी

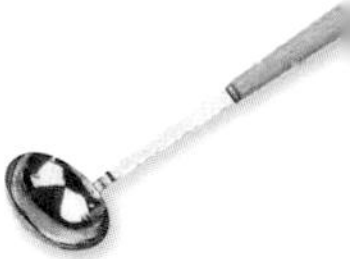

ladle
chamchā | चमचा

carving fork | ghumāvdār kāṃṭā | घुमावदार कांटा

ice-cream scoop
chammach | चम्मच

whisk
pheṃṭnī | फेंटनी

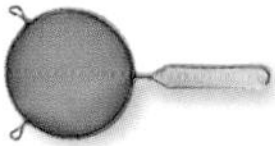

strainer
chhannī | छन्नी

lid
ḍhakkan | ढक्कन

non-stick
non stick | नॉनस्टिक

frying pan
frāiṅg pain
फ़्राइंग पैन

saucepan
ḍegchī
डेगची

grill pan
gril pain
ग्रिल पैन

wok
kaṛāhī
कड़ाही

earthenware dish
miṭṭī kā bartan
मिट्टी का बर्तन

glass
kāṃch
कांच

ovenproof
ovan rodhī | ओवन रोधी

mixing bowl
miksiṅg bāul
मिक्सिंग बाउल

soufflé dish
sūfle bartan
सूफ़ले बर्तन

gratin dish
grātin ḍiś
ग्राटिन डिश

ramekin
remikīn
रेमिकीन

casserole dish
kaisrol
कैसरोल

baking cakes • kek banānā • केक बनाना

scale
tarāzū
तराज़ू

measuring cup
māpak jag
मापक जग

cake pan | kek banāne kā sāṃchā
केक बनाने का सांचा

pie pan | pāī banāne kā sāṃchā
पाई बनाने का सांचा

flan pan | flain banāne kā sāṃchā
फ़्लैन बनाने का सांचा

pastry brush
pesṭrī braś | पेस्ट्री ब्रश

rolling pin
belan | बेलन

piping bag | pāipiṅg baig | पाइपिंग बैग

muffin tray
muffin ṭre
मॅफ़िन ट्रे

baking tray
bekiṅg ṭre
बेकिंग ट्रे

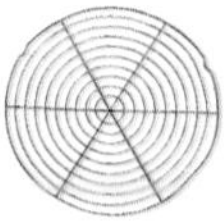

cooling rack
kūliṅg raik
कूलिंग रैक

oven gloves
ovan ke dastāne
ओवन के दस्ताने

apron
epren
एप्रेन

bedroom • śayan kakṣ • शयन कक्ष

wardrobe
almārī
अलमारी

bedside lamp
sāiḍ laimp
साइड लैम्प

headboard
palaṅg kā sirhānā
पलंग का सिरहाना

nightstand
sāiḍ ṭebal
साइड टेबल

chest of drawers
darāzoṃ kī almārī
दराज़ों की अलमारी

drawer
darāz
दराज़

bed
palaṅg
पलंग

mattress
gaddā
गद्दा

bedspread
palaṅgpoś
पलंगपोश

pillow
takiyā
तकिया

hot-water bottle | garm panī kī thailī
गर्म पानी की थैली

clock radio
reḍiyo ghaṛī
रेडियो घड़ी

alarm clock
alārm ghaṛī
अलार्म घड़ी

box of tissues
ṭiśyū box
टिश्यू बॉक्स

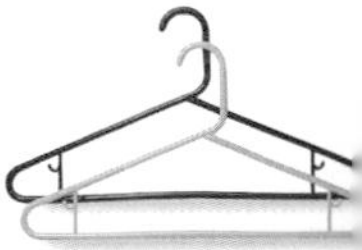

coathanger
koṭ kā haiṅgar
कोट का हैंगर

bed linen • chādar va takiyā gilāf ādi • चादर व तकिया गिलाफ़ आदि

mirror
śīśā
शीशा

dressing table
śṛaṅgār mez
शृंगार मेज़

floor
farś
फ़र्श

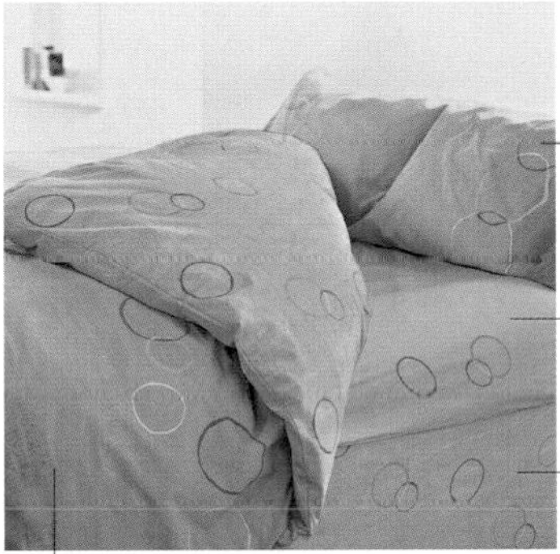

pillowcase
gilāf
गिलाफ़

sheet
chādar
चादर

dust ruffle
jhālar
झालर

comforter
roeṃ se banī razāī
रोएं से बनी रज़ाई

quilt
razāī
रज़ाई

blanket
kambal
कंबल

vocabulary • śabdāvalī • शब्दावली

twin bed
siṅgal palaṅg
सिंगल पलंग

full bed
ḍabal palaṅg
डबल पलंग

electric blanket
vidyut kambal
विद्युत कंबल

footboard
pāyadān
पायदान

spring
spriṅg
स्प्रिंग

carpet
ḳālīn
क़ालीनड्ड

insomnia
anidrā
अनिद्रा

go to bed (v)
sone jānā
सोने जाना

go to sleep (v)
sonā
सोना

wake up (v)
jāgnā
जागना

get up (v)
uṭhnā
उठना

set the alarm (v)
alārm lagānā
अलार्म लगाना

make the bed (v)
bistar lagānā
बिस्तर लगाना

snore (v)
ḳharrāṭe lenā
ख़र्राटे लेना

closet
antarnirmit almārī
अंतर्निर्मित अलमारी

bathroom • snānghar • स्नानघर

towel bar
tauliyā haiṅgar
तौलिया हैंगर

shower door
śāvar darvāzā
शॉवर दरवाज़ा

cold faucet
ṭhaṇḍe pānī kā nal
ठंडे पानी का नल

hot faucet
garm pānī kā nal
गर्म पानी का नल

shower head
phuhārā
फुहारा

sink
washbasin
वॉशबेसिन

shower
shower
शॉवर

plug
ḍāṭ
डाट

drain
nālī
नाली

toilet seat
toilet sīṭ
टॉयलेट सीट

toilet
toilet
टॉयलेट

toilet brush
toilet braś
टॉयलेट ब्रश

bathtub
bāth ṭab | बाथ टब

bidet
biḍe | बिडे

vocabulary • śabdāvalī • शब्दावली

medicine cabinet davāī kī almārī दवाई की अलमारी	**bath mat** snānghar kī chaṭāī स्नानघर की चटाई
toilet paper toilet rol टॉयलेट रोल	**shower curtain** shower kā pardā शॉवर का पर्दा
take a shower (v) phuhāre meṃ nahānā फुहारे में नहाना	**take a bath (v)** nahānā नहाना

dental hygiene • dāṃtoṃ kī safāī • दांतों की सफ़ाई

toothbrush
ṭūthbraś | टूथब्रश

toothpaste
ṭūthpesṭ | टूथपेस्ट

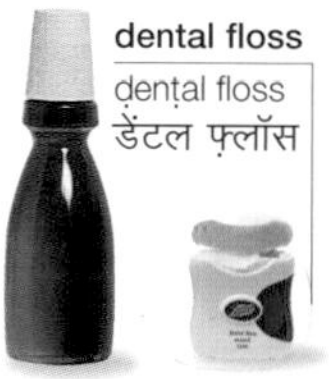

dental floss
denṭal floss
डेंटल फ़्लॉस

mouthwash
mouthwash | माउथवॉश

sponge
spañj | स्पंज

pumice stone
jhāmak | झामक

back brush | pīṭh kā braś | पीठ का ब्रश

deodorant
ḍiyoḍrenṭ | डियोडरेंट

soap dish
sābundānī
साबुनदानी

soap
sābun
साबुन

face cream
krīm
क्रीम

shower gel
shower jail
शॉवर जैल

bubble bath
babbal bāth
बब्बल बाथ

hand towel
chhoṭā tauliyā
छोटा तौलिया

bath towel
tauliyā
तौलिया

towels
taulie | तौलिए

body lotion
body lośan | बॉडी लोशन

talcum powder
ṭelkam pāuḍar
टेल्कम पाउडर

bathrobe | ḍresiṅg gāun | ड्रेसिंग गाउन

shaving • hajāmat • हजामत

electric razor
ilekṭrik rezar
इलेक्ट्रिक रेज़र

shaving foam
śeviṅg fom
शेविंग फ़ोम

disposable razor
ḍispozebal rezar
डिस्पोज़ेबल रेज़र

razor blade
rezar bleḍ
रेज़र ब्लेड

aftershave
āfṭar śev
आफ़्टर शेव

baby's room • śiśugṛh • शिशुगृह

baby care • śiśu dekhbhāl • शिशु देखभाल

sponge
spañj
स्पंज

baby bath
śiśu snān | शिशु स्नान

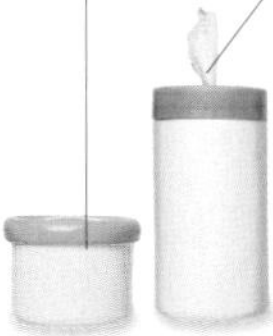

diaper rash cream
naipī raiś krīm
नैपी रैश क्रीम

wet wipe
nam ṭiśyu
नम टिश्यु

potty
potty | पॉटी

changing mat | kapṛe badalne kī gaddī | कपड़े बदलने की गद्दी

sleeping • sonā • सोना

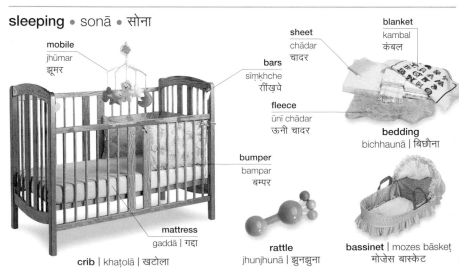

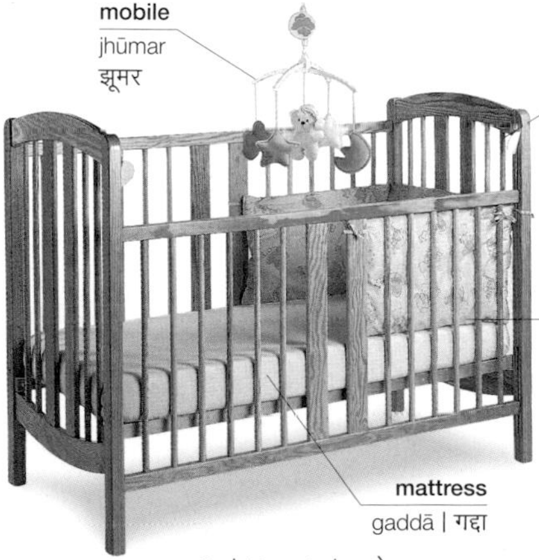

mobile
jhūmar
झूमर

bars
sīṃkhche
सींख़चे

bumper
bampar
बम्पर

mattress
gaddā | गद्दा

crib | khaṭolā | खटोला

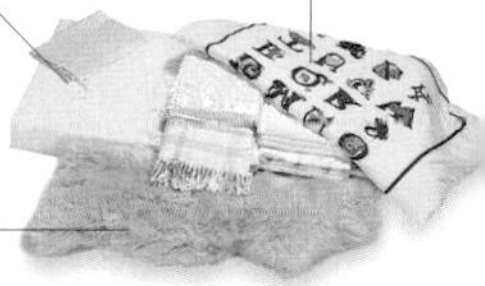

sheet
chādar
चादर

blanket
kambal
कंबल

fleece
ūnī chādar
ऊनी चादर

bedding
bichhaunā | बिछौना

rattle
jhunjhunā | झुनझुना

bassinet | mozes bāskeṭ
मोज़ेस बास्केट

playing • khelnā • खेलना

doll
guṛiyā
गुड़िया

soft toy
mulāyam khilaune
मुलायम खिलौने

dollhouse
guṛiyā ghar
गुड़िया घर

playhouse
khel ghar | खेल घर

teddy bear
khilaunā bhālū
टेडी बेयर

toy
khilaunā
खिलौना

toy basket | khilaune kī ṭokrī | खिलौने की टोकरी

ball
gend
गेंद

playpen
khel bāṛā | खेल बाड़ा

safety • surakṣā • सुरक्षा

child lock
bacchoṃ kā tālā
बच्चों का ताला

baby monitor
bebī monitor
बेबी मॉनीटर

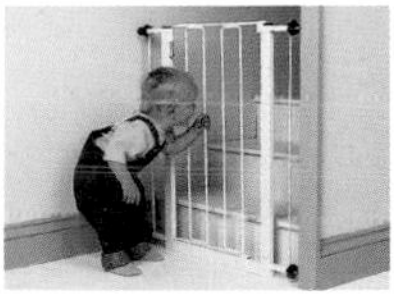

stair gate
siṛhiyoṃ kā geṭ
सीढ़ियों का गेट

eating • khānā • खाना

high chair
ūṃchī kursī | ऊंची कुर्सी

nipple
nippal
निप्पल

drinking cup
pīne kā kap
पीने का कप

bottle
botal | बोतल

going out • bāhar jānā • बाहर जाना

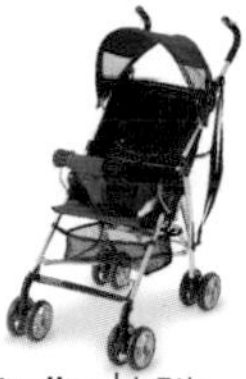

stroller | hāth gāṛī | हाथ गाड़ी

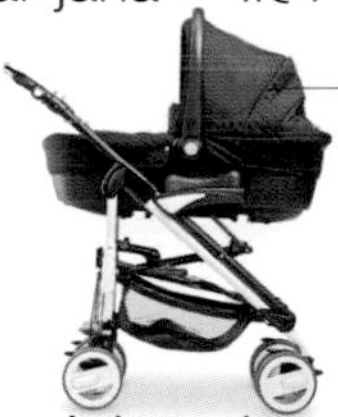

hood
chhatrī
छतरी

baby carriage
bagghī | बग्घी

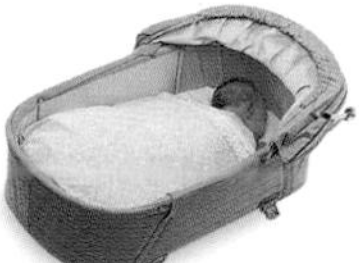

carrier
pālnā | पालना

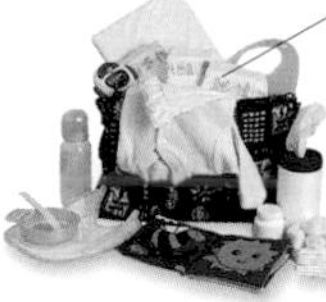

diaper
laṅgoṭī
लंगोटी

diaper bag | bacchoṃkā thailā | बच्चों का थैला

baby sling | śiśu paṭṭā
शिशु पट्टा

utility room • gharelū kārya kakṣ • घरेलू कार्य कक्ष

laundry • laundry • लॉन्ड्री

dirty laundry
gande kapṛe
गंदे कपड़े

clean clothes
dhule kapṛe
धुले कपड़े

laundry basket
gande kapṛoṃ kī ṭokrī | गंदे कपड़ों की टोकरी

washing machine
kapṛe dhone kī maśīn | कपड़े धोने की मशीन

washer-dryer
washer ḍrāyar
वॉशर–ड्रायर

tumble dryer
ḍrāyar
ड्रायर

linen basket
kapṛoṃ kī ṭokrī
कपड़ों की टोकरी

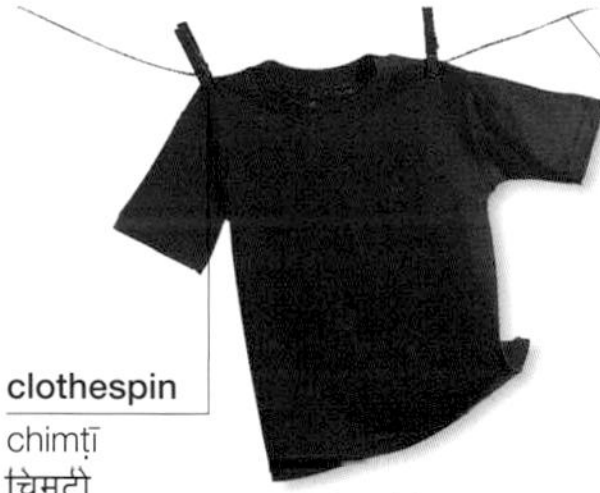

clothesline
alganī
अलगनी

clothespin
chimṭī
चिमटी

dry (v)
sukhānā | सुखाना

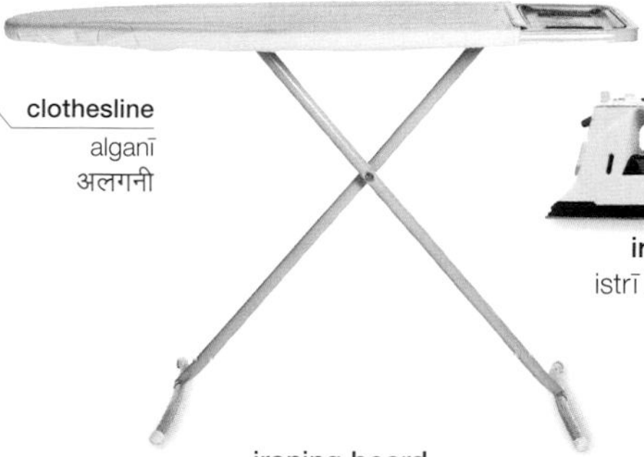

ironing board
istrī kā taḳhtā | इस्त्री का तख़्ता

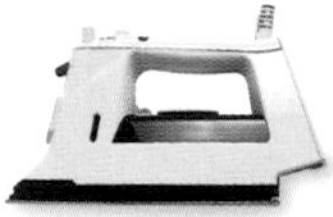

iron
istrī | इस्त्री

vocabulary • śabdāvalī • शब्दावली

rinse (v)
khaṅgālnā
खंगालना

load (v)
kapṛe maśīn meṃ ḍālnā
कपड़े मशीन में डालना

spin (v)
kapṛe nichoṛnā
कपड़े निचोड़ना

spin-dryer
kapṛe nichoṛne vālā
कपड़े निचोड़ने वाला

iron (v)
istrī karnā
इस्त्री करना

fabric softener
kanḍīśnar
कंडीशनर

How do I operate the washing machine?
washing maśīn kaise chalānī hai?
वॉशिंग मशीन कैसे चलानी है?

cleaning equipment • safāī upkaraṇ • सफ़ाई उपकरण

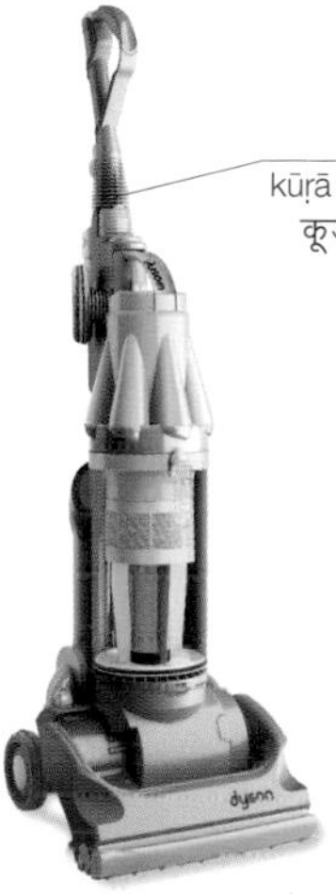

suction hose
kūṛā khīṃchne kī nalī
कूड़ा खींचने की नली

vacuum cleaner | vekyūm klīnar | वेक्यूम क्लीनर

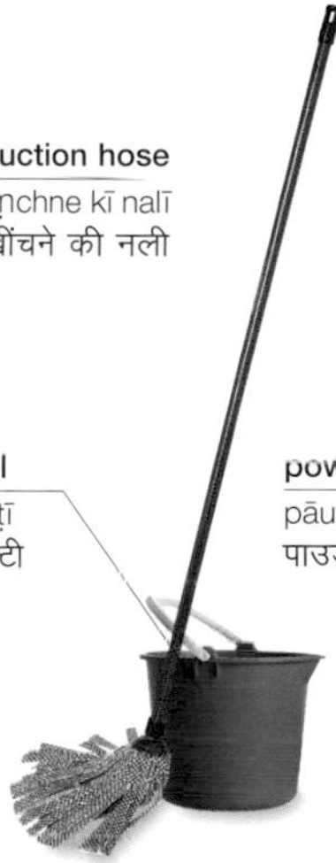

pail
bālṭī
बाल्टी

mop
pochhā | पोछा

brush
braś
ब्रश

dustpan | kūṛe kā paṅjā | कूड़े का पंजा

bleach
blīch | ब्लीच

powder
pāuḍar
पाउडर

liquid
dravya
द्रव्य

detergent
ḍiṭarjenṭ | डिटर्जेंट

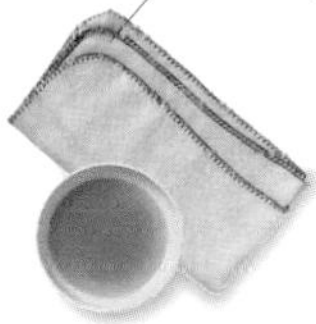

dustcloth
jhāṛan
झाड़न

polish
polish | पॉलिश

activities • gatividhiyāṃ • गतिविधियां

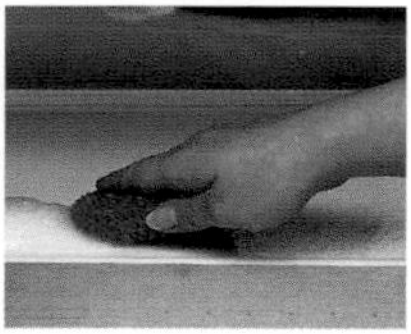

clean (v)
safāī karnā | सफ़ाई करना

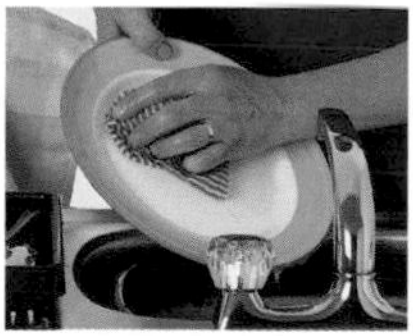

wash (v)
dhonā | धोना

wipe (v)
poṃchhnā | पोंछना

scrub (v)
ghisnā | घिसना

scrape (v)
khurachnā | खुरचना

broom
jhāṛū
झाड़ू

sweep (v)
jhāṛū lagānā | झाड़ू लगाना

dust (v)
dhūl jhāṛnā | धूल झाड़ना

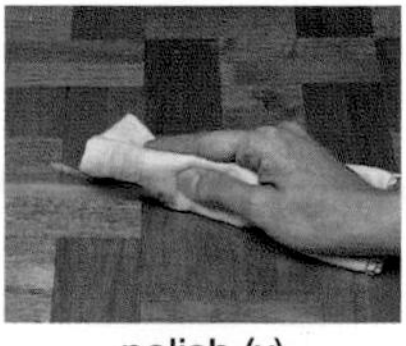

polish (v)
chamkānā | चमकाना

workshop • kārḳhānā • कारख़ाना

chuck
chakkā
चक्का

drill bit
chhed karne kī sūī
छेद करने की सूई

jigsaw
chhoṭā ārā
छोटा आरा

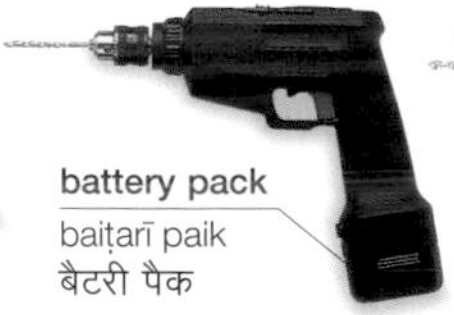

battery pack
baiṭarī paik
बैटरी पैक

cordless drill
richārjebal ḍril
रिचार्जेबल ड्रिल

electric drill
vidyut ḍril/vedhnī
विद्युत ड्रिल/वेधनी

glue gun
gond gan | गोंद गन

clamp
śikanjā/paṭṭī
शिकंजा/पट्टी

vise
śikanjā | शिकंजा

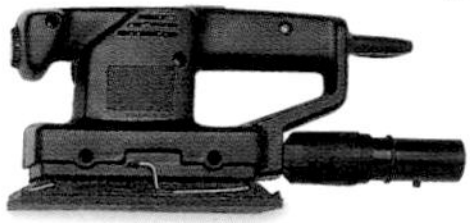

sander
senḍar | सेंडर

blade
bleḍ
ब्लेड

circular saw
vṛttākār ārī | वृत्ताकार आरी

workbench
kām karne kī mez
काम करने की मेज़

wood glue
lakṛī kā gond
लकड़ी का गोंद

router
rūṭar
रूटर

wood shavings
lakṛī kī chhīlan
लकड़ी की छीलन

tool rack
auzār raik
औज़ार रैक

bit brace
biṭ bres
बिट ब्रेस

extension cord
atirikt tār
अतिरिक्त तार

techniques • vidhiyāṃ • विधियां

cut (v)
kāṭnā | काटना

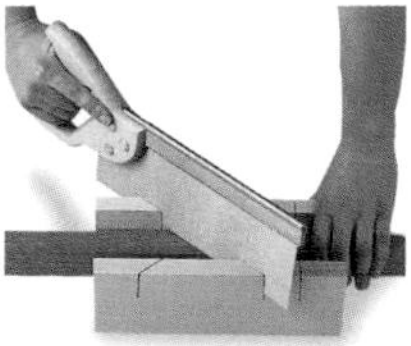

saw (v)
chīrnā | चीरना

drill (v)
chhed karnā | छेद करना

hammer (v)
ṭhoknā | ठोकना

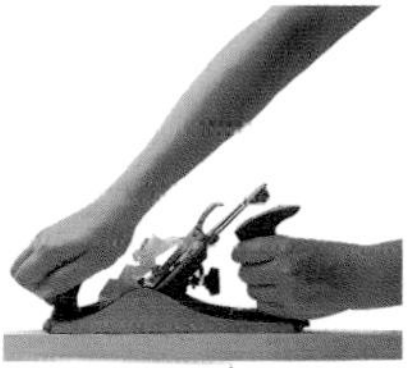

plane (v) | randā karnā | रंदा करना

turn (v)
kharādnā | खरादना

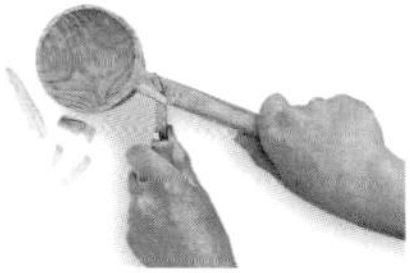

carve (v)
nakkāśī karnā | नक्काशी करना

solder
solḍar karne kā tār
सोल्डर करने का तार

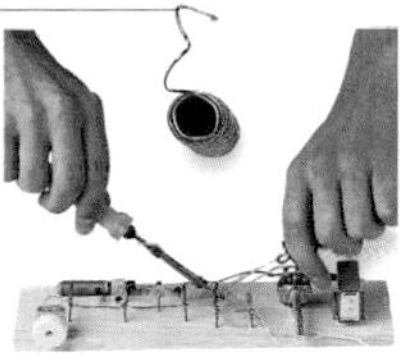

solder (v) | ṭāṃka lagānā | टांका लगाना

materials • sāmān • सामान

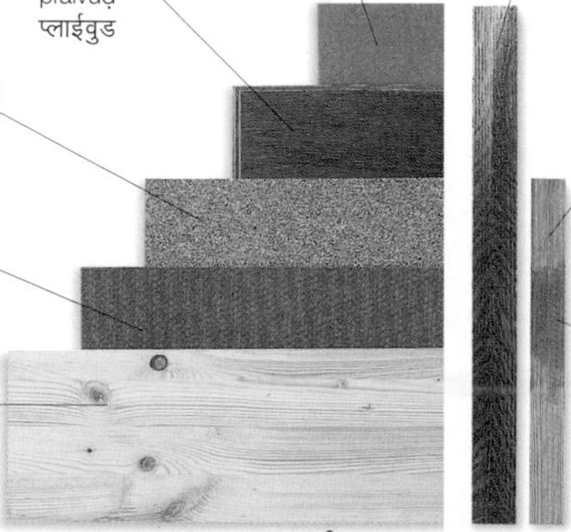

MDF
em ḍī ef
एम डी एफ़

plywood
plāīvuḍ
प्लाईवुड

particle board
chip borḍ
चिप बोर्ड

hardboard
hārḍ borḍ
हार्ड बोर्ड

softwood
mulāyam lakṛī
मुलायम लकड़ी

hardwood
kaṭhor lakṛī
कठोर लकड़ी

varnish
rogan
रोग़न

wood stain
lakṛī ke dāg
लकड़ी के दाग़

wood | lakṛī | लकड़ी

wire
tār
तार

cable
kebal | केबल

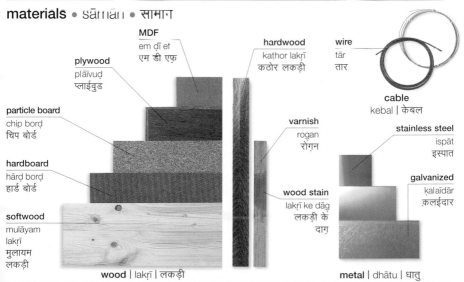

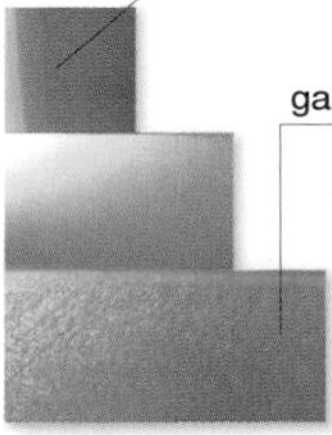

stainless steel
ispāt
इस्पात

galvanized
ḳalaīdār
क़लईदार

metal | dhātu | धातु

toolbox • auzār peṭī • औज़ार पेटी

wrench
pānā
पाना

adjustable wrench
parivartnīya pānā
परिवर्तनीय पाना

hammer
hathauṛā
हथौड़ा

needle-nose pliers
bārīk plās
बारीक प्लास

socket wrench
socket rinch
सॉकेट रिंच

screwdriver bits
pechkas vajr
पेचकस वज्र

level
spiriṭ leval
स्पिरिट लेवल

washer
wāśar
वाशर

screwdriver
pechkas
पेचकस

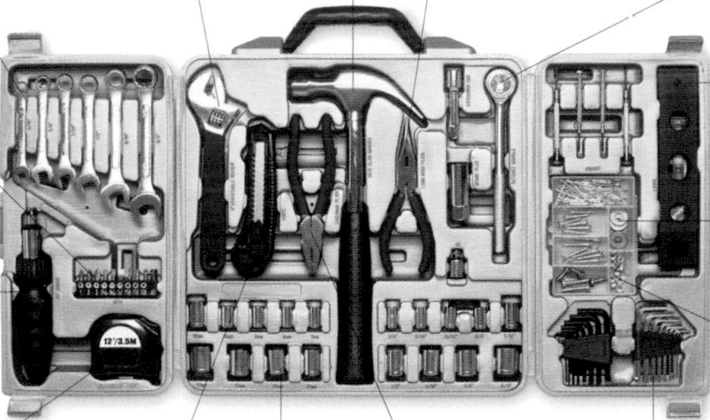

nut
purzā
पुर्ज़ा

tape measure
inch ṭep
इंच टेप

utility knife
chākū
चाकू

socket
socket
सॉकेट

bull-nose pliers
moṭā plās
मोटा प्लास

Allen wrench
chābī
चाबी

drill bits • ḍriliṅg maśīn ke vajr • ड्रिलिंग मशीन के वज्र

flat wood bit
samtal takhtā vajr | समतल तख़्ता वज्र

metal bit
dhātu vajr
धातु वज्र

reamer
barmā
बरमा

carpentry bits
baṛhaīgirī ke vajr
बढ़ईगिरी के वज्र

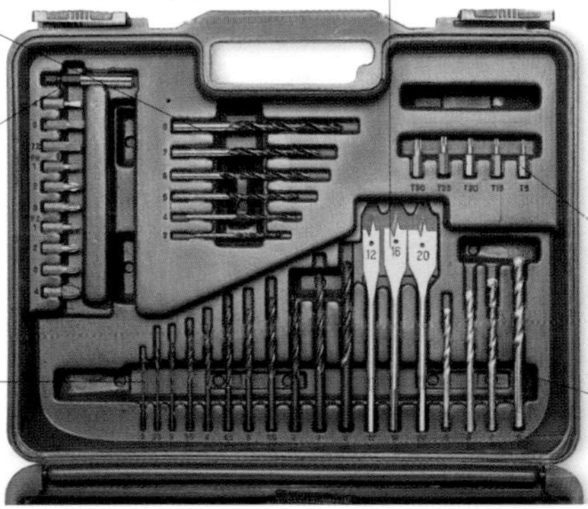

security bit
surakṣā vajr
सुरक्षा वज्र

masonry bit
rājgirī ke vajr
राजगिरी के वज्र

Phillips screwdriver
filips pechkas
फ़िलिप्स पेचकस

head
sirā
सिरा

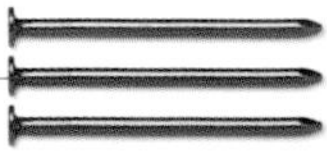

nail
kīl | कील

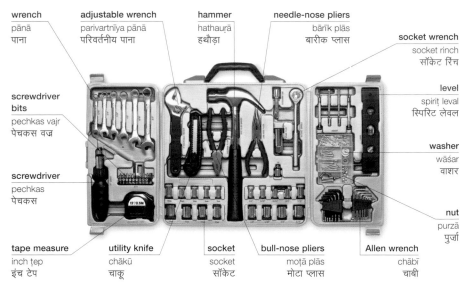

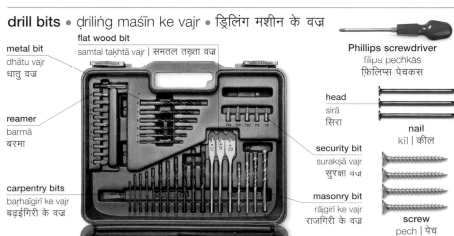

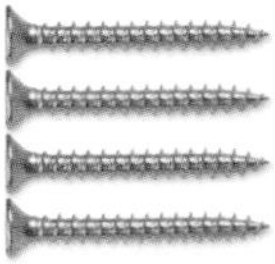

screw
pech | पेच

wire strippers
tār chhīlne kā plās
तार छीलने का प्लास

wire cutters
tār kāṭne kā yantr
तार काटने का यंत्र

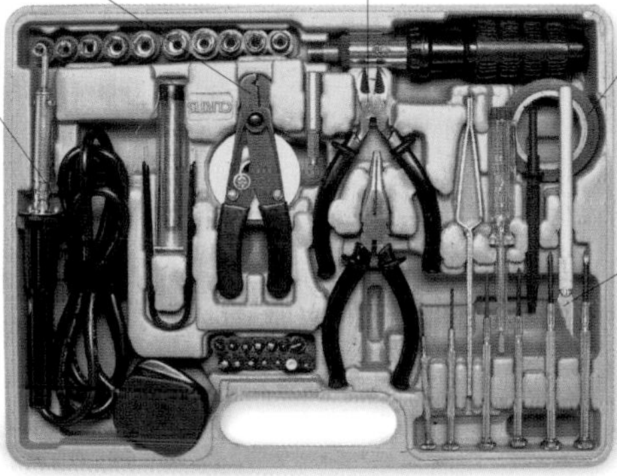

insulating tape
bijlī kā ṭep
बिजली का टेप

soldering iron
ṭāṃke kā upkaraṇ
टांके का उपकरण

craft knife
chhurī
छुरी

fretsaw
patlī ārī
पतली आरी

solder
ṭāṃkā lagāne kā tār
टांका लगाने का तार

tenon saw | chul ārā | चुल आरा

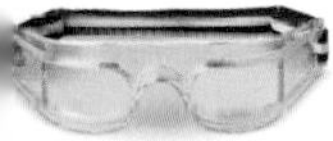

safety goggles
surakṣā chaśmā
सुरक्षा–चश्मा

plane
randā | रंदा

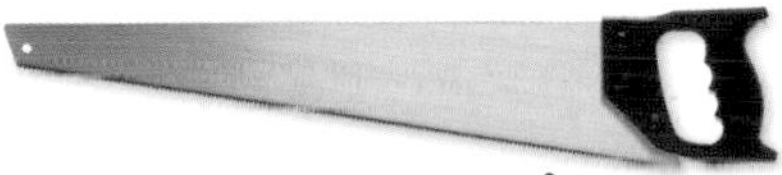

handsaw | ārī | आरी

miter block
mīṭar block
मीटर ब्लॉक

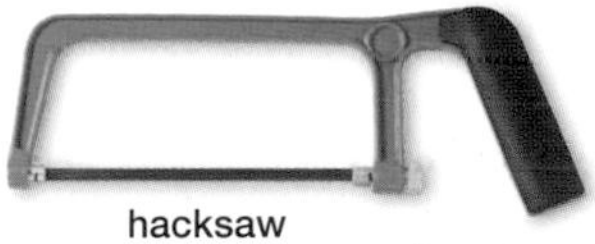

hacksaw
dāṃtedār ārī | दांतेदार आरी

hand drill
haiṇḍ ḍril
हैंड ड्रिल

steel wool
tār
तार

sandpaper
regmāl
रेगमाल

wrench
rinch
रिंच

chisel
chhenī | छेनी

whetstone
sān | सान

pipe cutter | pāip kaṭar | पाइप कटर

file
retī | रेती

plunger
ḍaṭṭā
डट्टा

decorating • gṛh sajjā • गृह सज्जा

scissors
kaiṃchī | कैंची

utility knife
chhurī | छुरी

plumb line
sāhul ḍorī | साहुल डोरी

scraper
khurachnī | खुरचनी

decorator
prasādhak
प्रसाधक

wallpaper
wallpaper
वॉलपेपर

stepladder
sīṛhī
सीढ़ी

wallpaper brush
wallpaper
braś
वॉलपेपर ब्रश

pasting table
pesṭiṅg ṭebal
पेस्टिंग टेबल

pasting brush
pesṭiṅg braś
पेस्टिंग ब्रश

wallpaper paste
wallpaper pesṭ
वॉलपेपर पेस्ट

pail
ṭokrī
टोकरी

wallpaper (v) | wallpaper lagānā | वॉलपेपर लगाना

strip (v) | khurachnā | खुरचना

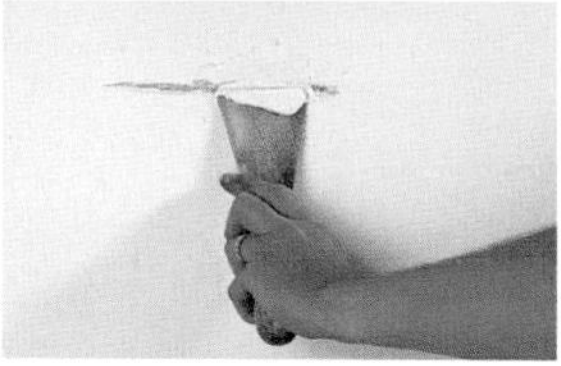

fill (v) | bharnā | भरना

sand (v)
ghisāī karnā | घिसाई करना

plaster (v)
plastar karnā | प्लस्तर करना

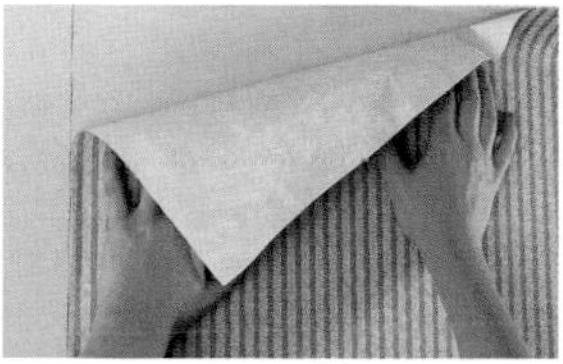

hang (v)
laṭkānā | लटकाना

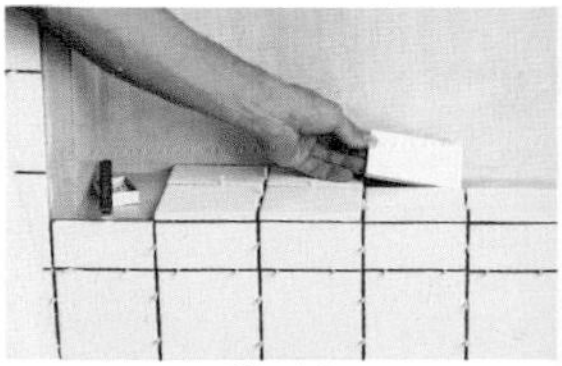

tile (v)
ṭāil lagānā | टाइल लगाना

brush
braś
ब्रश

paint can
penṭ kā ḍibbā
पेंट का डिब्बा

coveralls
ūprī vastr
ऊपरी वस्त्र

drop cloth
gandī darī
गंदी दरी

paint (v)
raṅgnā | रंगना

roller
rolar
रोलर

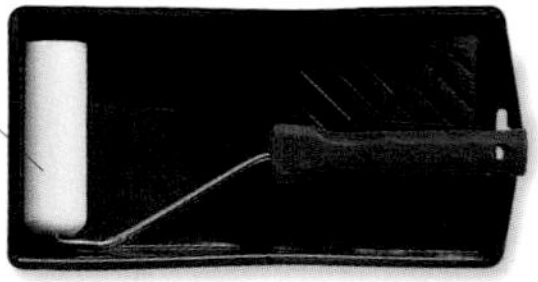

paint tray
penṭ ṭre | पेंट ट्रे

paint
penṭ | पेंट

sponge
spañj
स्पंज

masking tape
apārdarśī ṭep
अपारदर्शी टेप

sandpaper
regmāl
रेगमाल

filler
filar | फ़िलर

turpentine
tarpin
तारपीन

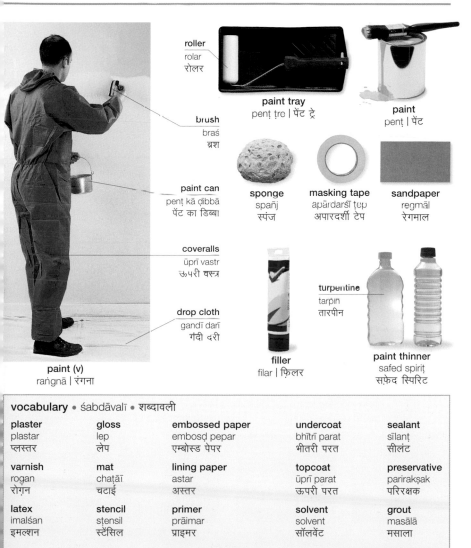

paint thinner
safed spiriṭ
सफ़ेद स्पिरिट

vocabulary • śabdāvalī • शब्दावली

plaster
plastar
प्लस्तर

varnish
rogan
रोग़न

latex
imalśan
इमल्शन

gloss
lep
लेप

mat
chaṭāī
चटाई

stencil
sṭensil
स्टेंसिल

embossed paper
embosḍ pepar
एम्बोस्ड पेपर

lining paper
astar
अस्तर

primer
prāimar
प्राइमर

undercoat
bhītrī parat
भीतरी परत

topcoat
ūprī parat
ऊपरी परत

solvent
solvent
सॉलवेंट

sealant
sīlanṭ
सीलंट

preservative
parirakṣak
परिरक्षक

grout
masālā
मसाला

garden • bag̣īchā • बग़ीचा

garden styles • bag̣īche kī śailiyāṃ • बग़ीचे की शैलियां

patio garden | upvan/bag̣īchī | उपवन/बग़ीची

roof garden
chhat bag̣īchī
छत बग़ीची

rock garden
pathrīlā bāg̣ | पथरीला बाग़

formal garden | bag̣īchā | बग़ीचा

courtyard | āṅgan | आंगन

cottage garden
kuṭīr udyān
कुटीर उद्यान

herb garden
auṣadhi udyān
औषधि उद्यान

water garden
jal udyān
जल उद्यान

garden features • bag̣īche kī rūp sajjā • बग़ीचे की रूप सज्जा

hanging basket
jhūltī ṭokrī | झूलती टोकरी

trellis
bāṛā/jālī | बाड़ा/जाली

pergola
latāmaṇḍap
लतामंडप

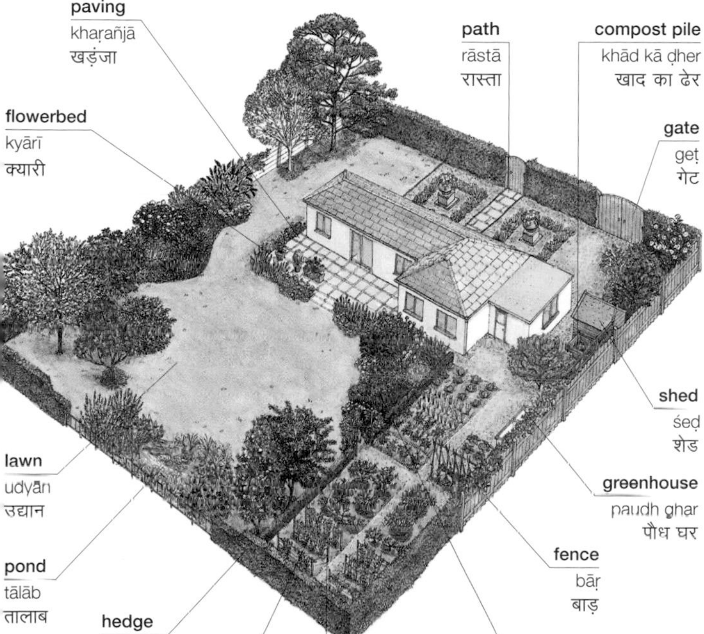
paving
kharañjā
खड़ंजा
flowerbed
kyārī
क्यारी
lawn
udyān
उद्यान
pond
tālāb
तालाब
hedge
bāṛ/meṛ
बाड़/मेड़
arch
ārch
आर्च
vegetable garden
sabziyoṃ kā bagīchā
सब्ज़ियों का बग़ीचा
path
rāstā
रास्ता
compost pile
khād kā ḍher
खाद का ढेर
gate
geṭ
गेट
shed
śeḍ
शेड
greenhouse
paudh ghar
पौध घर
fence
bāṛ
बाड़
herbaceous border
hare-bhare paudhoṃ se banā gherā
हरे–भरे पौधों से बना घेरा

deck
chabūtrā | चबूतरा

fountain | favvārā | फ़व्वारा

soil • miṭṭī • मिट्टी

topsoil
ūprī miṭṭī | ऊपरी मिट्टी

sand
ret | रेत

chalk
khaṛiyā | खड़िया

silt
gād | गाद

clay | miṭṭī | मिट्टी

garden plants • bagīche ke paudhe • बग़ीचे के पौधे

types of plants • paudhoṃ ke prakār • पौधों के प्रकार

annual | vārṣikī paudh
वार्षिकी पौध

biennial | dvivārṣik paudh | द्विवार्षिक पौध

perennial
bārahmāsī | बारहमासी

bulb
balb | बल्ब

fern
parṇāṅg | पर्णाङ्ग

rush
jalbeṃt | जलबेंत

bamboo
bāṃs | बांस

weeds
ghās-pāt | घास–पात

herb
jaṛī-būṭī | जड़ी–बूटी

water plant
jalīya paudh | जलीय पौध

tree
peṛ | पेड़

palm
tāṛ | ताड़

conifer
śaṅku vṛkṣ | शंकु वृक्ष

evergreen
sadābahār | सदाबहार

deciduous
parṇpātī | पर्णपाती

topiary
kaṭāī-chhaṃṭāī
कटाई–छंटाई

alpine
parvatīya paudhe
पर्वतीय पौधे

succulent
ārdr paudh
आर्द्र पौध

cactus
kaikṭas
कैक्टस

potted plant
gamle ke paudhe
गमले के पौधे
shade plant
chhāyādār paudhe
छायादार पौधे
climber
latā
लता
flowering shrub
phūloṃ kī jhāṛī
फूलों की झाड़ी
ground cover
grāuṇḍ kavar
ग्राउंड कवर
creeper
bel
बेल
ornamental
sajāvaṭī
सजावटी
grass
ghās
घास

garden tools • bagīche ke upkaraṇ • बग़ीचे के उपकरण

compost
khād | खाद

seeds
bīj | बीज

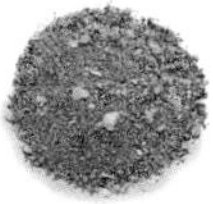

bone meal
asthi chūrṇ
अस्थि चूर्ण

gravel
bajrī | बजरी

spade
phāvṛā
फावड़ा

fork
kāṃṭā auzār
कांटा औज़ार

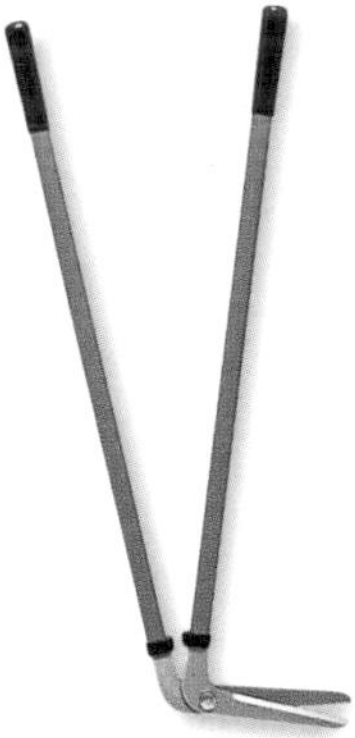

long-handled shears
lambe hatthe kī ḳaiṃchī
लंबे हत्थे की क़ैंची

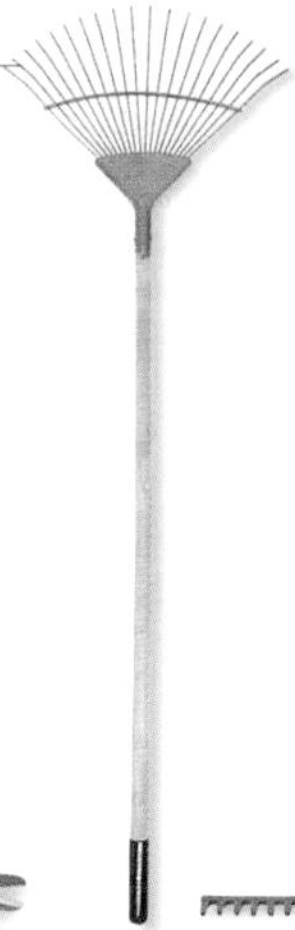

lawn rake
jhāṛū
झाड़ू

rake
pāñchā
पांचा

hoe
khurpā | खुरपा

tote | ṭre/ṭokrī | ट्रे/टोकरी

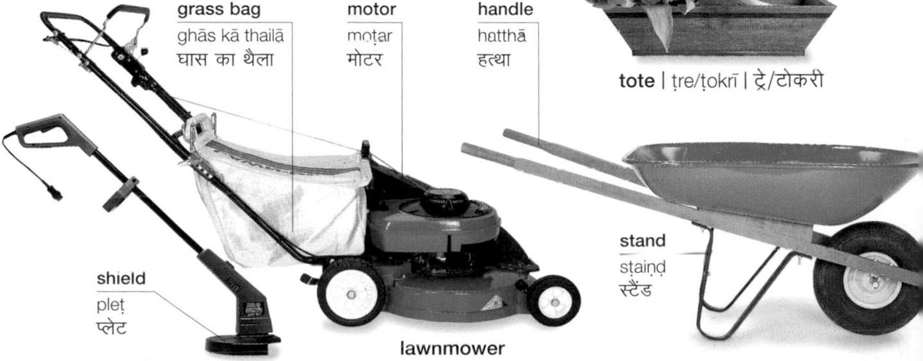

grass bag
ghās kā thailā
घास का थैला

motor
moṭar
मोटर

handle
hatthā
हत्था

shield
pleṭ
प्लेट

stand
staiṇḍ
स्टैंड

trimmer | katarne kā auzār
कतरने का औज़ार

lawnmower
ghās kāṭne kī maśīn
घास काटने की मशीन

wheelbarrow
ṭhelā gāṛī | ठेला गाड़ी

hand fork
kurednī | कुरेदनी

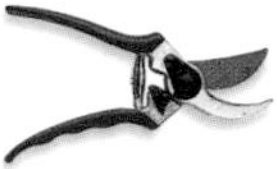
pruners
kaṭar | कटर

gardening gloves
bāgbānī ke dastāne
बाग़बानी के दस्ताने

trowel
khurpī | खुरपी

seed tray
bīj ṭre | बीज ट्रे

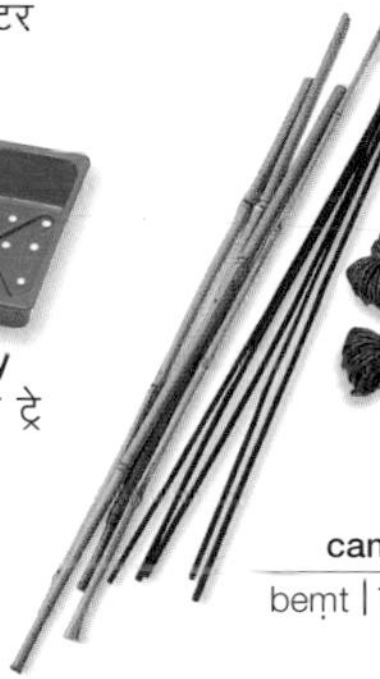

twine
ḍorī
डोरी

labels
lebal
लेबल

twist ties
chimṭiyāṃ
चिमटियां

blade
phal
फल
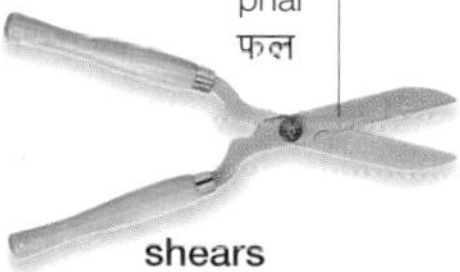
shears
baṛī kaiṃchī
बड़ी कैंची

ring ties
chhalle
छल्ले

canes
beṃt | बेंत

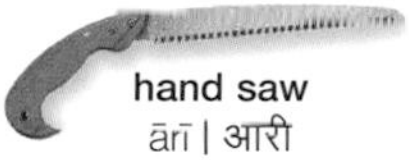
hand saw
ārī | आरी

pesticide
kīṭnāśak
कीटनाशक

sieve
chhalnī
छलनी

plant pot
gamlā
गमला

rubber boots | rabaṛ ke jūte | रबड़ के जूते

watering • sīṃchnā • सींचना

watering can
phuhārā
फुहारा

spray bottle
pichkārī | पिचकारी

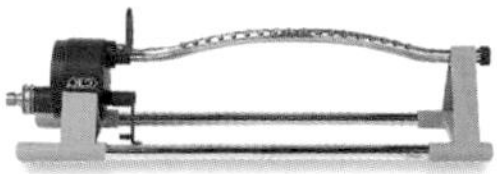
sprinkler
hazārā
हज़ारा

nozzle
ṭoṃṭī
टोंटी

hose
rabaṛ nalī
रबड़ नली

hose reel | huchkā | हुचका

gardening • bāġbānī • बाग़बानी

lawn
udyān
उद्यान

flowerbed
kyārī | क्यारी

lawnmower
ghās kāṭne kī maśīn
घास काटने की मशीन

hedge
bāṛ
बाड़

stake
khūṃṭā
खूंटा

mow (v) | ghās kāṭnā | घास काटना

sod (v)
ghās bichhānā
घास बिछाना

spike (v)
khūṃṭā ṭhoknā
खूंटा ठोकना

rake (v)
buhārnā
बुहारना

trim (v)
chhāṃṭnā
छांटना

dig (v)
khodnā | खोदना

sow (v)
bonā | बोना

top-dress (v)
khād ḍālnā | खाद डालना

water (v)
sīṃchnā | सींचना

train (v) | ākār denā
आकार देना

deadhead (v) | sūkhe patte nikālnā | सूखे पत्ते निकालना

spray (v)
chhiṛaknā | छिड़कना

stake (v) | khūṃṭī se bāṃdhnā | खूंटी से बांधना

graft (v) | ḳalam bāṃdhnā | क़लम बांधना

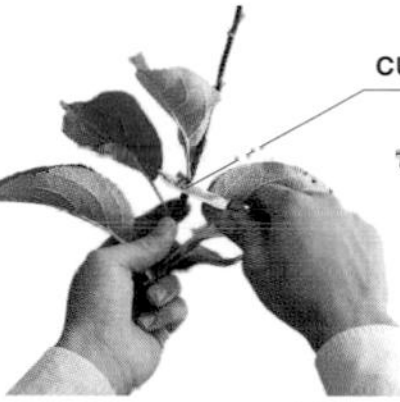

propagate (v)
baṛhana | बढ़ाना

prune (v)
chhaṃṭna | छांटना

transplant (v)
pratiropit karnā
प्रतिरोपित करना

weed (v)
nirānā
निराना

mulch (v)
ghās-pāt se ḍhaknā
घास–पात से ढकना

harvest (v)
fasal kāṭnā
फ़सल काटना

vocabulary • śabdāvalī • शब्दावली

cultivate (v) khetī karnā खेती करना	**fertilize (v)** urvar banānā उर्वर बनाना	**sift (v)** chhānnā छानना	**organic** jaiv जैव	**seedling** paud पौद	**pot (v)** gamle meṃ ḍālnā गमले में डालना	**subsoil** avmṛdā अवमृदा
tend (v) dekhbhāl karnā देखभाल करना	**pick (v)** chunnā/toṛnā चुनना/तोड़ना	**aerate (v)** havā lagānā हवा लगाना	**drainage** morī मोरी	**fertilizer** urvarak उर्वरक	**weedkiller** kharpatvār nāśak खरपतवार नाशक	

2
JKL
5
TUV
8
7
0

services
sevāeṃ
सेवाएं

emergency services • āpātkālīn sevāeṃ • आपातकालीन सेवाएं

ambulance • embulens • एंबुलेंस

ambulance | embulens | एंबुलेंस

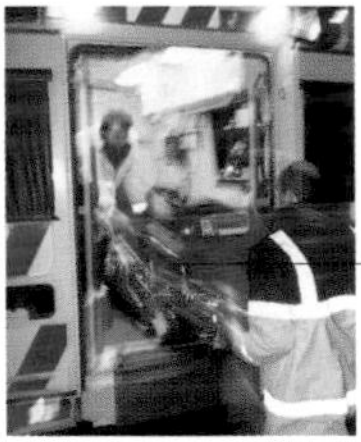

paramedic
parāchikitsak | पराचिकित्सक

police • pulis • पुलिस

badge
billā
बिल्ला
uniform
vardī
वर्दी
nightstick
beṃt
बेंत
gun
bandūḳ
बंदूक़
police officer
pulis adhikārī | पुलिस अधिकारी

handcuffs
hathkaṛī
हथकड़ी

siren
sāyaran
सायरन
lights
battīyan
बत्तीयां
POLICE
police car
pulis kār | पुलिस कार

police station
pulis chaukī
पुलिस चौकी

vocabulary • śabdāvalī • शब्दावली

captain darogā दरोगा	**suspect** saṃdigdh संदिग्ध	**complaint** śikāyat शिकायत	**arrest** giraftār गिरफ़्तार
crime jurm जुर्म	**assault** hamlā हमला	**investigation** jāṃch जांच	**cell** havālāt हवालात
detective jāsūs जासूस	**fingerprint** uṃgliyoṃ kī chhāp उंगलियों की छाप	**burglary** chorī चोरी	**charge** ārop आरोप

fire department • damkal dastā • दमकल दस्ता

smoke
dhuāṃ
धुआं

basket
pālnā
पालना

boom
pāl daṇḍ
पाल दंड

fire | āg | आग

helmet
helmeṭ
हेलमेट

hose
pānī kī nalī
पानी की नली

water jet
pānī kī dhār
पानी की धार

firefighters
agniśāmak karmī
अग्निशामक कर्मी

fire station
damkal kendr
दमकल केंद्र

fire escape
āpātkālīn rakṣā mārg
आपातकालीन रक्षा मार्ग

ladder
sīṛhī
सीढ़ी

cab
gāṛī
गाड़ी

fire engine
damkal | दमकल

smoke alarm
smok alārm
स्मोक अलार्म

fire alarm
fāyar alārm
फ़ायर अलार्म

ax
kulhāṛī
कुल्हाड़ी

fire extinguisher
agniśāmak upkaraṇ
अग्निशामक उपकरण

hydrant
pānī kā nal
पानी का नल

I need the ambulance.
mujhe embulens bulānī hai.
मुझे एंबुलेंस बुलानी है।

There's a fire at…
...meṃ āg lagī hai.
... में आग लगी है।

There's been an accident.
ek durghaṭnā huī hai.
एक दुर्घटना हुई है।

Call the police!
pulis ko bulāo!
पुलिस को बुलाओ!

bank • baink • बैंक

customer
grāhak
ग्राहक

window
khiṛkī
खिड़की

teller
ḳhazānchī
ख़ज़ांची

brochures
parchī
पर्ची

counter
kāunṭar
काउंटर

deposit slips
jamā parchī
जमा पर्ची

bank manager
baink prabandhak
बैंक प्रबंधक

debit card
ḍebiṭ kārḍ
डेबिट कार्ड

credit card
kreḍiṭ kārḍ
क्रेडिट कार्ड

stub
parchī
पर्ची

account number
khātā sankhyā
खाता संख्या

signature
hastākṣar
हस्ताक्षर

amount
raḳam
रक़म

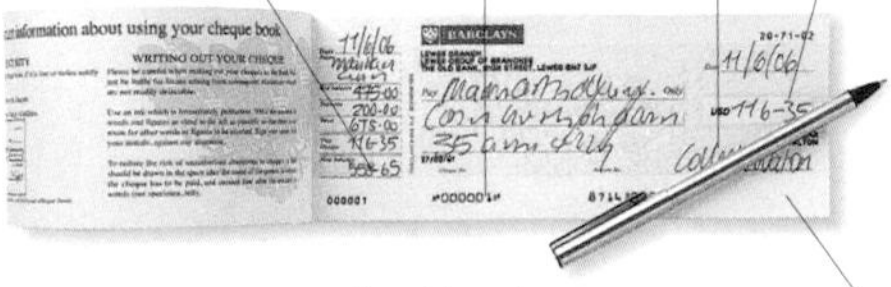

checkbook
chek buk
चेक बुक

check
chek
चेक

vocabulary • śabdāvalī • शब्दावली

savings bachat बचत	**mortgage** bandhak बंधक	**payment** bhugtān भुगतान	**deposit (v)** jamā karnā जमा करना	**checking account** chālū khātā चालू खाता
tax kar कर	**overdraft** ovar ḍrāfṭ ओवर ड्राफ़्ट	**automatic payment** pratyakṣ bhugtān प्रत्यक्ष भुगतान	**bank charge** baink prabhār बैंक प्रभार	**savings account** bachat khātā बचत खाता
loan ṛiṇ ऋण	**interest rate** byāj dar ब्याज दर	**withdrawal slip** āharaṇ parchī आहरण पर्ची	**electronic transfer** baink antraṇ बैंक अंतरण	**PIN** pin nambar पिन नंबर

coin
sikkā
सिक्का
bill
noṭ
नोट

money
dhan | धन

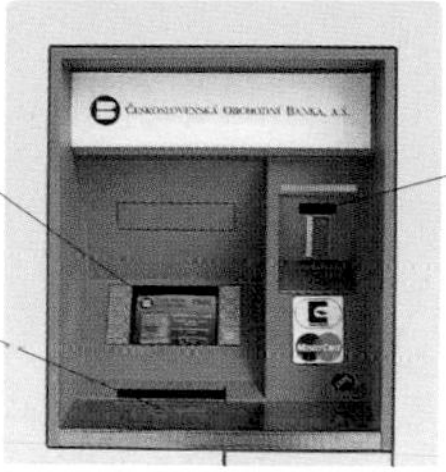
screen
skrīn
स्क्रीन
keypad
kuñjī paṭal
कुंजी पटल
card slot
kārḍ ḍālne kī jagah
कार्ड डालने की जगह

ATM
ATM | एटीएम

currency • mudrā • मुद्रा

bureau de change
videśī mudrā vinimaya kendr
विदेशी मुद्रा विनिमय केंद्र

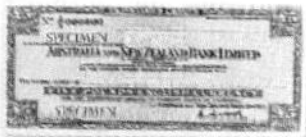

traveler's check
yātrī chek | यात्री चेक

exchange rate
vinimaya dar
विनिमय दर

finance • vitt • वित्त

financial advisor
vittīya salāhkār
वित्तीय सलाहकार

share price
śeyar mūlya
शेयर मूल्य
stockbroker
śeyar dalāl
शेयर दलाल

stock exchange
śeyar bāzār | शेयर बाज़ार

vocabulary • śabdāvalī • शब्दावली

cash (v)
nakad nikālnā
नक़द निकालना

denomination
mūlyavarg
मूल्यवर्ग

commission
dalālī
दलाली

investment
niveś
निवेश

stocks
stock
स्टॉक

shares
śeyar
शेयर

dividends
lābhānś
लाभांश

accountant
lekhākār
लेखाकार

portfolio
niveś sūchī
निवेश सूची

equity
śeyar pūñjī
शेयर पूंजी

Can I change this, please?
kyā maiṃ ise badal saktā hūṃ?
क्या मैं इसे बदल सकता हूं?

What's today's exchange rate?
vartmān vinimaya dar kyā hai?
वर्तमान विनिमय दर क्या है?

communications • sañchār • संचार

postal worker
ḍāk karmī
डाक कर्मी
window
khiṛkī
खिड़की
scale
vazan-māpī
वज़न–मापी
counter
kāunṭar
काउंटर

post office
ḍākghar | डाकघर

postmark
mohar
मोहर
stamp
ḍāk ṭikaṭ
डाक टिकट
address
patā
पता
ZIP code
ḍāk koḍ
डाक कोड

envelope | lifāfā | लिफ़ाफ़ा

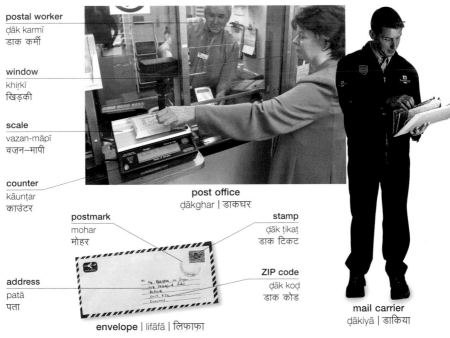

mail carrier
ḍākiyā | डाकिया

vocabulary • śabdāvalī • शब्दावली

letter patr पत्र	**return address** vāpsī kā patā वापसी का पता	**delivery** vitraṇ वितरण	**fragile** nāzuk vastu नाजुक वस्तु	**do not bend (v)** kripyā moreṃ nahīṃ कृपया मोड़ें नहीं
by airmail havāī ḍāk dvārā हवाई डाक द्वारा	**signature** hastākśar हस्ताक्षर	**money order** posṭal order पोस्टल ऑर्डर	**mailbag** ḍāk thailā डाक थैला	**this way up** is prakār rakheṃ इस प्रकार रखें।
registered mail rajisṭarḍ ḍāk रजिस्टर्ड डाक	**pickup** saṅgrah संग्रह	**postage** ḍāk vyaya डाक व्यय	**telegram** tār तार	**fax** faiks फ़ैक्स

mailbox
ḍākpeṭī | डाकपेटी

letterslot
patrpeṭī | पत्रपेटी

package
pārsal | पार्सल

courier
kūriyar | कूरियर

telephone • dūrbhāṣ • दूरभाष

handset
haiṇḍ seṭ
हैंडसेट

base station
fon staiṇḍ
फ़ोन स्टैंड

answering machine
āṇsariṅg maśīn
आंसरिंग मशीन

cordless phone
kordles fon
कॉर्डलेस फ़ोन

video phone
vīḍiyo fon | वीडियो फ़ोन

telephone booth
ṭelifon box
टेलिफ़ोन बॉक्स

smartphone
smārṭfon
स्मार्टफ़ोन

keypad
kī paiḍ
की–पैड

cell phone
mobāil fon
मोबाइल फ़ोन

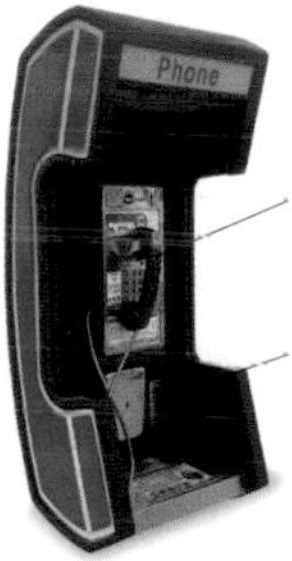

receiver
risīvar
रिसीवर

coin return
sikkā vāpsī
सिक्का वापसी

payphone
PCO fon
पी सी ओ फ़ोन

vocabulary • śabdāvalī • शब्दावली

dial (v)
nambar milānā
नंबर मिलाना

collect call
revars chārj call
रिवर्स चार्ज कॉल

directory assistance
ḍāyarekṭarī pūchhtāchh
डायरेक्टरी पूछताछ

app
aip
ऐप

answer (v)
uttar denā
उत्तर देना

text
SMS
एस एम एस

voice message
dhvani sandeś
ध्वनि संदेश

passcode
pāskoḍ
पासकोड

operator
prachālak
प्रचालक

busy
vyast
व्यस्त

disconnected
sampark ṭūṭnā
संपर्क टूटना

Can you give me the number for...?
kyā āp mujhe … kā nambar de sakte haiṃ.?
क्या आप मुझे... का नंबर दे सकते हैं?

What is the area code for...?
… ke lie ḍāyaliṅg koḍ kyā hai?
... के लिए डायलिंग कोड क्या है?

Text me!
mujhe es em es bhejeṃ!
मुझे एस एम एस भेजें!

hotel • hoṭal • होटल

lobby • lobby • लॉबी

messages
sandeś
संदेश

guest
mehmān
मेहमान

room key
kamre kī chābī
कमरे की चाबी

pigeonhole
koṣṭh
कोष्ठ

receptionist
svāgat adhikārī
स्वागत अधिकारी

register
rajisṭar
रजिस्टर

counter
kāunṭar
काउंटर

reception | svāgat | स्वागत

luggage
sāmān
सामान

cart
trolley
ट्रॉली

porter | darbān | दरबान

elevator | lifṭ | लिफ़्ट

room number
kamrā nambar
कमरा नंबर

rooms • kamre • कमरे

single room
siṅgal kamrā
सिंगल कमरा

double room
ḍabal kamrā
डबल कमरा

twin room
ṭvin kamrā
ट्विन कमरा

private bathroom
nijī snānghar
निजी स्नानघर

services • sevāeṃ • सेवाएं

maid service
parichārikā sevā
परिचारिका सेवा

laundry service
laundry sevā
लॉन्ड्री सेवा

breakfast tray
nāśte kī ṭre | नाश्ते की ट्रे

room service | rūm sarvis | रूम सर्विस

minibar
minī bār | मिनी बार

restaurant
restrāṃ
रेस्तरां

gym
vyāyāmśālā
व्यायामशाला

swimming pool
taraṇtāl
तरणताल

vocabulary • śabdāvalī • शब्दावली

bed and breakfast
rahnā aur nāśtā
रहना और नाश्ता

full board
ful borḍ
फुल बोर्ड

half-board
hāf borḍ
हाफ़ बोर्ड

Do you have any vacancies?
kyā āpke yahāṃ kamrā ḳhālī hai?
क्या आपके यहां कमरा ख़ाली है?

I have a reservation.
maiṃne kamrā ārakṣit karāyā huā hai
मैंने कमरा आरक्षित कराया हुआ है।

I'd like a single room.
mujhe ek siṅgal kamrā chāhie
मुझे एक सिंगल कमरा चाहिए।

I'd like a room for three nights.
mujhe tīn rātoṃ ke lie ek kamrā chāhie
मुझे तीन रातों के लिए एक कमरा चाहिए।

What is the charge per night?
ek rāt kā kirāyā kitnā hai?
एक रात का किराया कितना है?

When do I have to check out?
mujhe kab kamrā ḳhālī karnā hai?
मुझे कब कमरा ख़ाली करना है?

shopping
ḳharīdārī
ख़रीदारी

shopping center • ḳharīdārī kendr • ख़रीदारी केंद्र

atrium
prāṅgaṇ
प्रांगण

sign
nām
नाम

elevator
lifṭ
लिफ़्ट

third floor
dūsrī mañzil
दूसरी मंज़िल

second floor
pahlī mañzil
पहली मंज़िल

escalator
svachālit sīṛhiyāṃ
स्वचालित सीढ़ियां

ground floor
bhūtal
भूतल

customer
grāhak
ग्राहक

vocabulary • śabdāvalī • शब्दावली

luggage department
sāmān vibhāg
सामान विभाग

shoe department
jūtā chappal vibhāg
जूता चप्पल विभाग

children's department
bāl vibhāg
बाल विभाग

store directory
sṭor nirdeśikā
स्टोर निर्देशिका

sales clerk
bikrī sahāyak
बिक्री सहायक

customer services
grāhak sevāeṃ
ग्राहक सेवाएं

changing rooms
chenjiṅg rūm
चेंजिंग रूम

restrooms
prasādhan
प्रसाधन

baby changing facilities
bāl suvidhā kendr
बाल–सुविधा केंद्र

How much is this?
iskī kyā ḳīmat hai?
इसकी क्या क़ीमत है?

May I exchange this?
kyā maiṃ ise badal saktā hūṃ?
क्या मैं इसे बदल सकता हूं?

department store • ḍepārṭmenṭal sṭor • डिपार्टमेंटल स्टोर

menswear
puruṣ paridhān
पुरुष परिधान

women's clothing
mahilā paridhān
महिला परिधान

lingerie
adhovastr
अधोवस्त्र

perfume
itr ityādi
इत्र इत्यादि

beauty
saundarya
सौंदर्य

linen
chādar takiyā ādi
चादर तकिया आदि

home furnishings
gṛh sāj-sajjā
गृह साज–सज्जा

notions
bisāt
बिसात

kitchenware
bartan
बर्तन

china
chīnī miṭṭī ke bartan
चीनी मिट्टी के बर्तन

electrical goods
bijlī kā sāmān
बिजली का सामान

lighting
lāiṭiṅg
लाइटिंग

sports
sporṭs | स्पोर्ट्स

toys
khilaune | खिलौने

stationery | lekhan sāmagrī | लेखन सामग्री

food
fūḍ hall | फ़ूड हॉल

supermarket • supar bāzār • सुपर बाज़ार

aisle | galiyārā | गलियारा

shelf | śelf | शेल्फ़

conveyer belt | chal paṭṭī | चल पट्टी

checker | ḳhazānchī | ख़ज़ांची

specials | chhūṭ | छूट

checkout | bhugatān sthal | भुगतान स्थल

customer | grāhak | ग्राहक

cash register | tijorī | तिजोरी

shopping bag | ḳharīdārī kā thailā | ख़रीदारी का थैला

groceries | kirānā vastueṃ | किराना वस्तुएं

cart | trolley | ट्रॉली

handle | haiṇḍal | हैंडल

basket | ṭokrī | टोकरी

780863 185779

bar code | bār koḍ | बार कोड

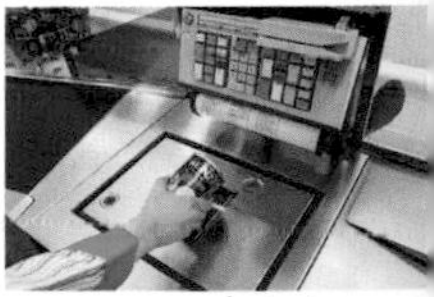

scanner | skainar | स्कैनर

bakery
bekrī
बेकरी

dairy
dugdh utpād
दुग्ध उत्पाद

cereals
anāj
अनाज

canned food
ḍibbāband khādya padārth
डिब्बाबंद खाद्य पदार्थ

candy
mīṭhe khādya
मीठे खाद्य

vegetables
sāg-sabzī
साग–सब्ज़ी

fruit
phal
फल

meat and poultry
māṃsāhārī khādya padārth
मांसाहारी खाद्य पदार्थ

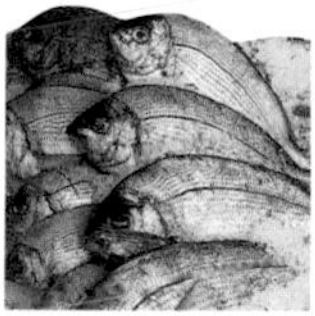

fish
machhlī
मछली

deli
delī
डेली

frozen food
frozan āhār
फ़्रोज़न आहार

convenience food
suvidhājanak bhojan
सुविधाजनक भोजन

drinks
peya padārth
पेय पदार्थ

household products
gharelū vastueṃ
घरेलू वस्तुएं

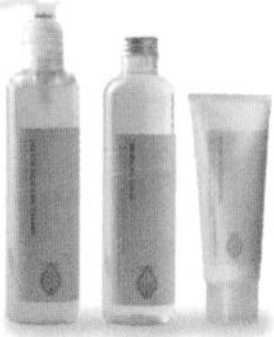

toiletries
saundarya prasādhan
सौंदर्य प्रसाधन

baby products
śiśu utpād
शिशु उत्पाद

electrical goods
bijlī kī vastueṃ
बिजली की वस्तुएं

pet food
paśu āhār
पशु आहार

magazines | patrikāeṃ | पत्रिकाएं

drugstore • davāī vikretā • दवाई विक्रेता

dental care
dant surakṣā
दंत सुरक्षा

feminine hygiene
strī svacchhatā sāmān
स्त्री–स्वच्छता सामान

vitamins
viṭāmin
विटामिन

pharmacy
davāḳhānā
दवाख़ाना

pharmacist
auṣadh vitrak
औषध वितरक

cough medicine
khāṃsī kī davāī
खांसी की दवाई

herbal remedies
jaṛī-būṭī auṣadh
जड़ी–बूटी औषध

skin care
tvachā surakṣā
त्वचा सुरक्षा

aftersun
āfṭarsan
आफ़्टरसन

sunscreen
sanskrīn | सनस्क्रीन

sunblock
sunblock
सनब्लॉक

insect repellent
macchhar avrodhak
मच्छर अवरोधक

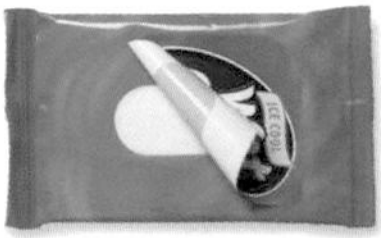

wet wipe
namīyukt ṭiśyū
नमीयुक्त टिश्यू

tissue
ṭiśyū | टिश्यू

sanitary napkin | sainiṭ arī paid | सैनिटरी पैड

tampon
ṭempon | टेम्पोन

panty liner | painṭī lāinar | पैंटी लाइनर

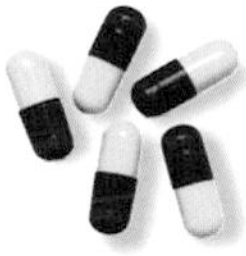

capsule
kaipsūl | कैप्सूल

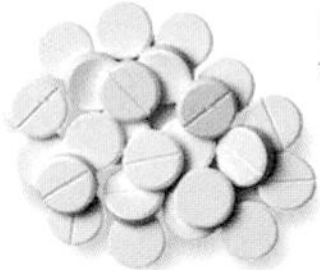

pill
goliyāṃ | गोलियां

measuring spoon
māpak chammach
मापक चम्मच

syrup
sirap | सिरप

instructions
nirdeś
निर्देश

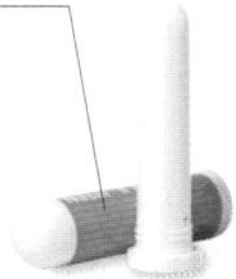

inhaler | śvās yantr
श्वास यंत्र

cream
krīm | क्रीम

ointment
marham | मरहम

gel
jail | जैल

suppository
guhyavarti | गुह्यवर्ति

dropper
dropper
ड्रॉपर

drops | drops
ड्रॉप्स

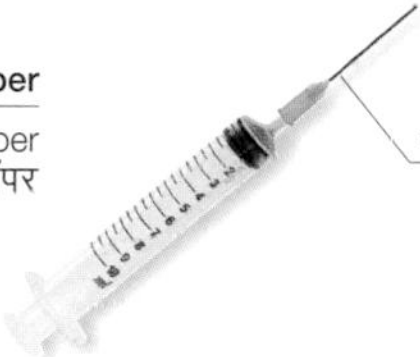

needle
sūī
सूई

syringe
siriṅj | सिरिंज

spray
spre | स्प्रे

powder
pauḍar | पाउडर

vocabulary • śabdāvalī • शब्दावली

iron āyaran आयरन	**insulin** insulin इंसुलिन	**disposable** ḍispozebal डिस्पोज़ेबल	**medicine** davāī दवाई	**painkiller** dardnāśak दर्दनाशक
calcium kailśiyam कैल्शियम	**side effects** viprīt prabhāv विपरीत प्रभाव	**soluble** ghulanśīl घुलनशील	**laxative** ḳabzḳuśā क़ब्ज़कुशा	**sedative** praśāmak प्रशामक
magnesium maignīśiyam मैग्नीशियम	**expiration date** samāpti tithi समाप्ति तिथि	**dosage** ḳhurāk ख़ुराक	**diarrhea** dast दस्त	**sleeping pill** nīṃd kī golīyāṃ नींद की गोलियां
multivitamins bahu viṭāmin बहु विटामिन	**travel sickness pills** mitlī kī davā मितली की दवा	**medication** upchār उपचार	**cough drop** ḳharāś kī davā ख़राश की दवा	**anti-inflammatory** sūjan rodhī सूजन रोधी

florist • phūl vikretā • फूल विक्रेता

flowers
phūl
फूल
lily
lilī
लिली
acacia
babūl
बबूल
carnation
kārneśan
कार्नेशन
pot plant
gamle kā paudhā
गमले का पौधा
gladiolus
gleḍiyolas
ग्लेडियोलस
iris
āyaris
आयरिस
daisy
ḍezī
डेज़ी
chrysanthemum
guldāūdī
गुलदाऊदी
gypsophila
jipsofilā
जिप्सोफ़िला

stocks
stocks | स्टॉक्स

gerbera
jarberā | जरबेरा

foliage
phūl-patte | फूल–पत्ते

rose
gulāb | गुलाब

freesia
frīziyā | फ़्रीज़िया

vase
phūldān
फूलदान

orchid
orchid | ऑरकिड

peony
piyoni | पियोनि

bunch
gucchhā
गुच्छा

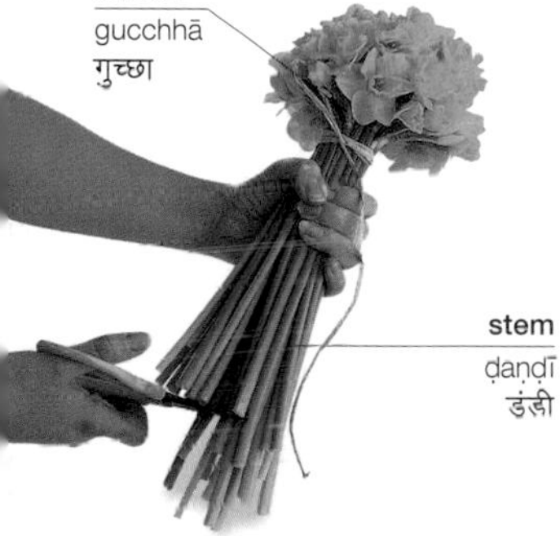

stem
ḍaṇḍī
डंडी

daffodil
ḍaifoḍil
डैफ़ोडिल

bud
kalī
कली

wrapping
gifṭ pepar
गिफ़्ट पेपर

tulip | ṭyulip | ट्यूलिप

arrangements • sajāvaṭ • सजावट

ribbon
riban
रिबन

bouquet
guldasta | गुलदस्ता

dried flowers | sūkhe phūl | सूखे फूल

potpourri
sūkhe phūl | सूखे फूल

wreath
puṣp chakr | पुष्प चक्र

garland
phūlmālā
फूलमाला

vocabulary • śabdāvalī • शब्दावली

Can I have them wrapped?
āp inheṃ kagaz meṃ lapeṭ deṇge?
आप इन्हें काग़ज़ में लपेट देंगे?

Can I have a bunch of…, please.
kyā mujhe … kā gucchhā mil saktā hai?
क्या मुझे... का गुच्छा मिल सकता है?

Can I attach a message?
kyā maiṃ ek sandeś lagā saktā hūṃ?
क्या मैं एक संदेश लगा सकता हूं?

Can you send them to…?
kyā āp unheṃ … ko bhej sakte haiṃ?
क्या आप उन्हें... को भेज सकते हैं?

newsstand • samāchār patr vikretā • समाचार पत्र विक्रेता

cigarettes
sigreṭ
सिगरेट

packet of cigarettes
sigreṭ kī ḍibbī
सिगरेट की डिब्बी

stamps
ḍāk ṭikaṭ
डाक टिकट

postcard
posṭ kārḍ | पोस्ट कार्ड

comic book
chitrkathā | चित्रकथा

magazine
patrikā | पत्रिका

newspaper
samāchār patr | समाचार पत्र

smoking • dhūmrpān • धूम्रपान

tobacco
tambāḳū | तंबाक़ू

lighter
lāiṭar | लाइटर

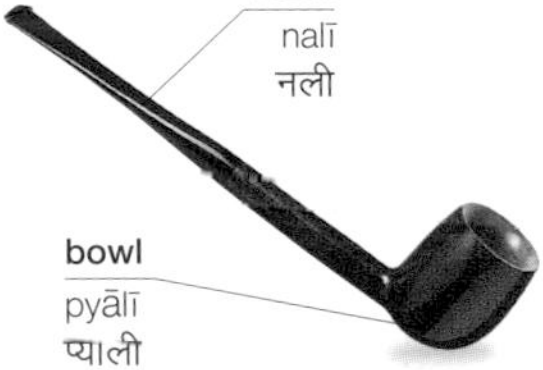

stem
nalī
नली

bowl
pyālī
प्याली

pipe
pāip | पाइप

cigar
sigār | सिगार

confectionery • kanfekśnar • कन्फेक्शनर

box of chocolates
chocolate box
चॉकलेट बॉक्स

snack bar
snaiks bār
स्नैक्स बार

crisps
krisps
क्रिस्प्स

candy store | toffee kī dukān | टॉफ़ी की दुकान

vocabulary • śabdāvalī • शब्दावली

milk chocolate
dūdh kī chocolate
दूध की चॉकलेट

semisweet chocolate
sādī chocolate
सादी चॉकलेट

white chocolate
safed chocolate
सफ़ेद चॉकलेट

pick and mix
milī-julī goliyāṃ
मिली-जुली गोलियां

caramel
kairāmal
कैरामल

truffle
ṭrafal
ट्रफ़ल

cookie
biskuṭ
बिस्कुट

hard candy
mīṭhī goliyāṃ
मीठी गोलियां

confectionery • kanfekśnarī • कन्फेक्शनरी

chocolate
chocolate | चॉकलेट

chocolate bar
chocolate kī paṭṭī
चॉकलेट की पट्टी

candies
kaiṇḍī | कैंडी

lollipop
lollipop | लॉलीपॉप

toffee | toffee | टॉफ़ी

nougat | girī kī chocolate | गिरी की चॉकलेट

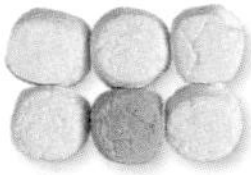

marshmallow
mārśmailo
मार्शमैलो

mint
minṭ toffee | मिंट टॉफ़ी

chewing gum
chuing gam | च्यूइंग गम

jellybean
jailībīn | जैलीबीन

gumdrop
frūṭ gam | फ़्रूट गम

licorice
mulethī kaiṇḍī
मुलेठी कैंडी

other stores • anya dukānem̩ • अन्य दुकानें

bread shop
bekrī
बेकरी

bakery
kek kī dukān
केक की दुकान

butcher shop
ḳasāī kī dukān
क़साई की दुकान

fish-seller
machhlī kī dukān
मछली की दुकान

produce stand | phal evam sabziyom̩ kī dukān
फल एवं सब्ज़ियों की दुकान

grocery store
pansārī kī dukān
पंसारी की दुकान

shoe store
jūte kī dukān
जूते की दुकान

hardware store
hārḍveyar shop
हार्डवेयर शॉप

antique store | prāchīn vastuom̩ kī dukān
प्राचीन वस्तुओं की दुकान

gift shop
uphārom̩ kī dukān
उपहारों की दुकान

travel agent
ṭreval ejensī
ट्रेवल एजेंसी

jewelry store
sunār kī dukān
सुनार की दुकान

bookstore
kitāboṃ kī dukān
किताबों की दुकान

record store
record kī dukān
रिकॉर्ड की दुकान

liquor store
śarāb kī dukān
शराब की दुकान

pet store
pāltū jānvaroṃ kī dukān
पालतू जानवरों की दुकान

furniture store
farnīchar kī dukān
फ़र्नीचर की दुकान

boutique
buṭīk
बुटीक

vocabulary • śabdāvalī • शब्दावली

realtor
property ḍīlar
प्रॉपर्टी डीलर

garden center
bagbānī kī dukān
बाग़बानी की दुकान

dry-cleaner
ḍraī klīnar
ड्राई क्लीनर

laundromat
laundry
लॉन्ड्री

camera store
kaimre kī dukān
कैमरे की दुकान

art store
ārṭ shop
आर्ट शॉप

second-hand store
saikaṇḍ haiṇḍ shop
सैकंड हैंड शॉप

health food store
svāsthya āhār kī dukān
स्वास्थ्य आहार की दुकान

tailor shop | darzī kī dukān | दर्ज़ी की दुकान

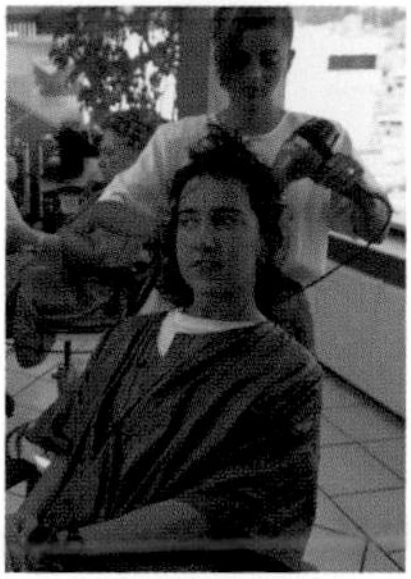

beauty salon | nāī kī dukān | नाई की दुकान

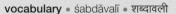

market | bāzār | बाज़ार

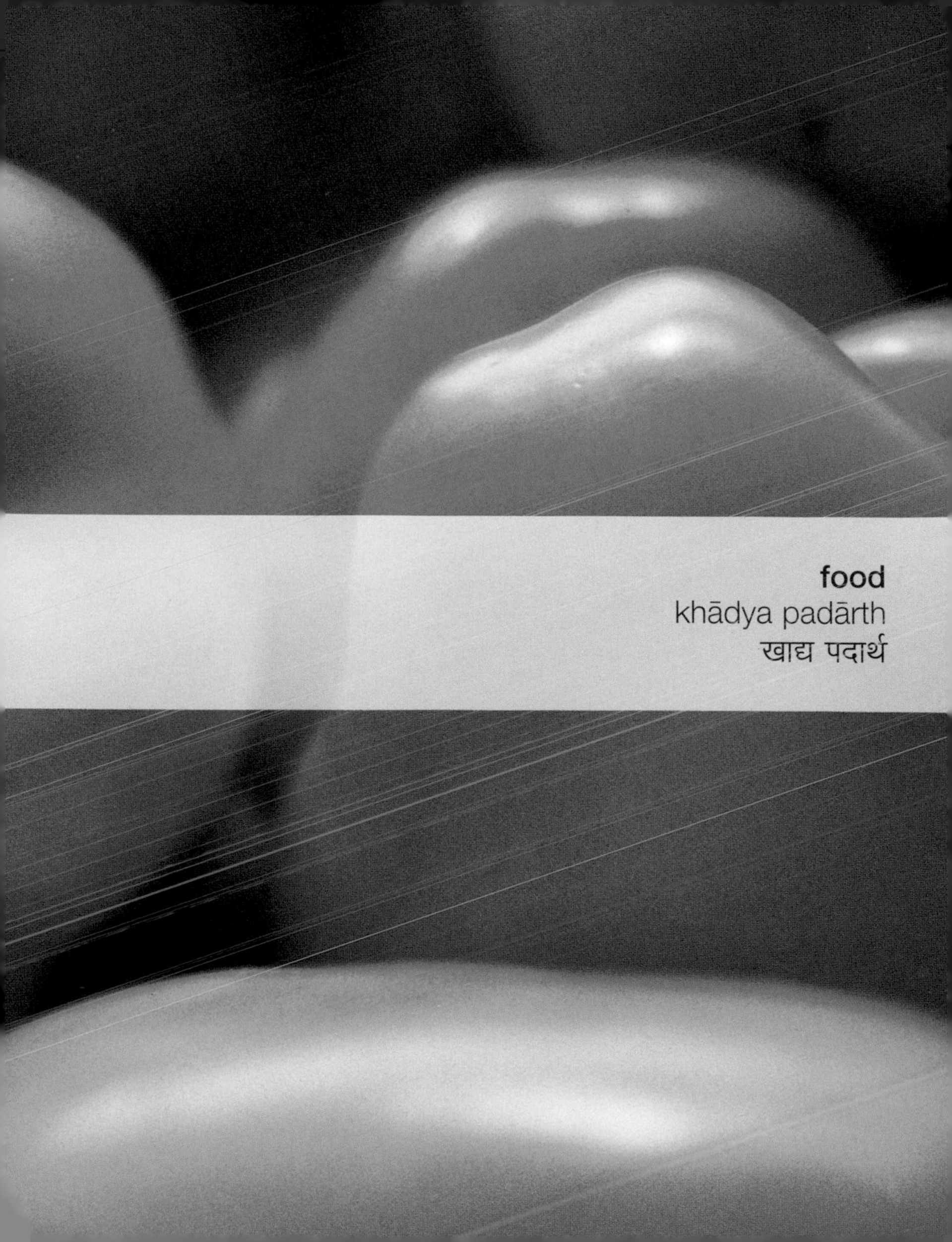

food
khādya padārth
खाद्य पदार्थ

meat • māṃs • मांस

butcher
kasāī
क़साई
knife sharpener
chākū/chhurī tez karne kā upkaraṇ
चाकू/छुरी तेज़ करने का उपकरण
meat hook
mīṭ huk
मीट हुक
scale
tarāzū
तराजू
lamb
maṭan | मटन
bacon
bekan | बेकन
sausages
sausages | सॉसेजेस
liver
kalejī | कलेजी

vocabulary • śabdāvalī • शब्दावली

pork
sūar kā māṃs
सूअर का मांस

beef
go māṃs
गो मांस

veal
bachhṛe kā māṃs
बछड़े का मांस

venison
mṛg māṃs
मृग मांस

rabbit
khargoś
ख़रगोश

tongue
jībh
जीभ

offal
chhīchhṛe
छीछड़े

cured
saṃrakṣit
संरक्षित

smoked
dhūmrit
धूम्रित

free range
jaṅglī
जंगली

organic
jaivik
जैविक

white meat
safed māṃs
सफ़ेद मांस

red meat
lāl māṃs
लाल मांस

lean meat
binā charbī kā māṃs
बिना चर्बी का मांस

cooked meat
pakā huā māṃs
पका हुआ मांस

cuts • māṃs ke ṭukṛe • मांस के टुकड़े

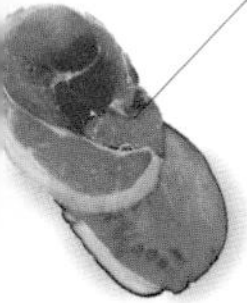
ham
haim
हैम

slice
ḳatlā | क़तला

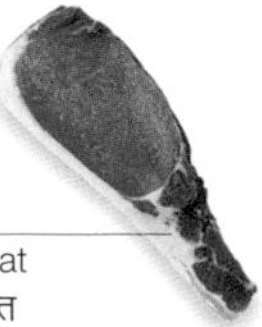
rind
bāhrī parat
बाहरी परत

bacon strip
jaṅghā kā māṃs
जंघा का मांस

ground meat
ḳīmā | क़ीमा

fillet
machhlī kā ṭukṛā
मछली का टुकड़ा

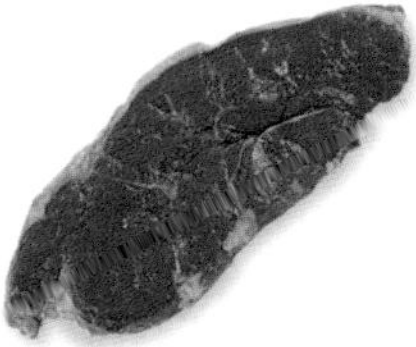
rump steak | kamar kā māṃs | कमर का मांस

sirloin steak | puṭṭhe kā māṃs | पुट्ठे का मांस

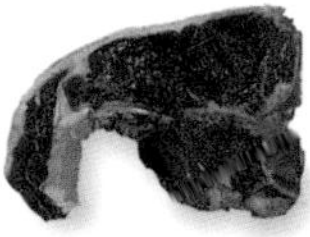
rib
paslī | पसली

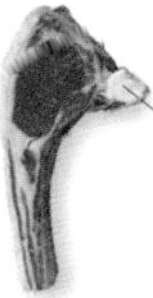
fat
vasā
वसा

bone
haḍḍī
हड्डी

chop
chop | चॉप

joint
joṛ | जोड़

kidney
gurdā
गुर्दा

heart
dil | दिल

poultry • pakṣī-māṃs • पक्षी-मांस

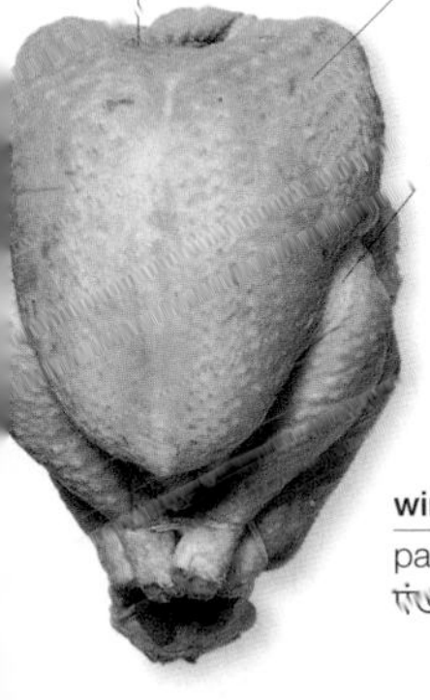
skin
khāl
खाल

breast
chhātī
छाती

thigh
jaṅgh
जांघ

turkey | ṭarkī | टर्की

dressed chicken
pakāne ke lie
taiyār murg
पकाने के लिए
तैयार मुर्ग़

wing
paṅkh
पंख

chicken | murg | मुर्ग़

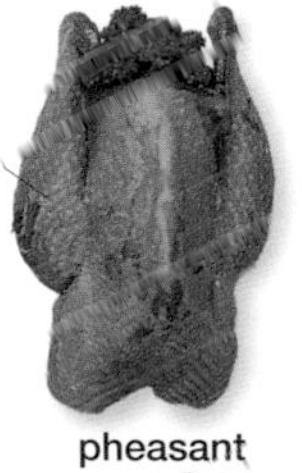
game
śikār | शिकार

pheasant
tītar | तीतर

leg
ṭāṅg
टांग

quail | baṭer | बटेर

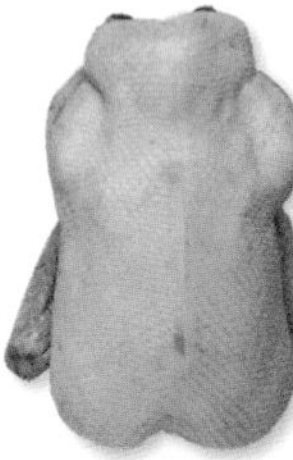
duck | batakh | बतख़

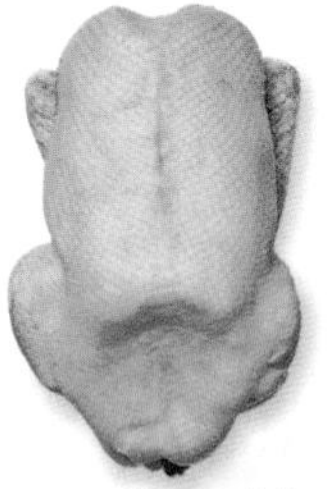
goose | hans | हंस

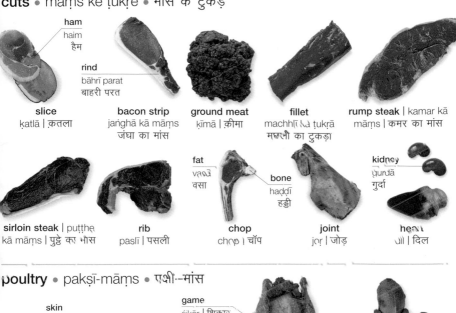

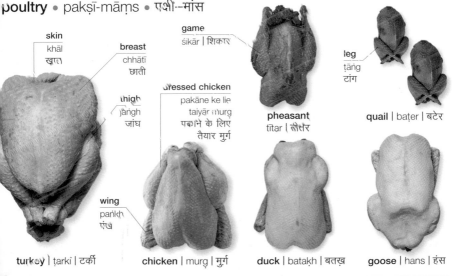

fish • machhlī • मछली

peeled shrimp
chhile hue jhīṅge
छिले हुए झींगे

ice
baraf
बर्फ़

red mullet
chhoṭī machhlī
छोटी मछली

halibut fillets
hailibaṭ ḳatlī
हैलिबट क़तली

rainbow trout
renbo ṭrāuṭ machhlī
रेनबो ट्राउट मछली

skate wings
skeṭ machhlī
स्केट मछली

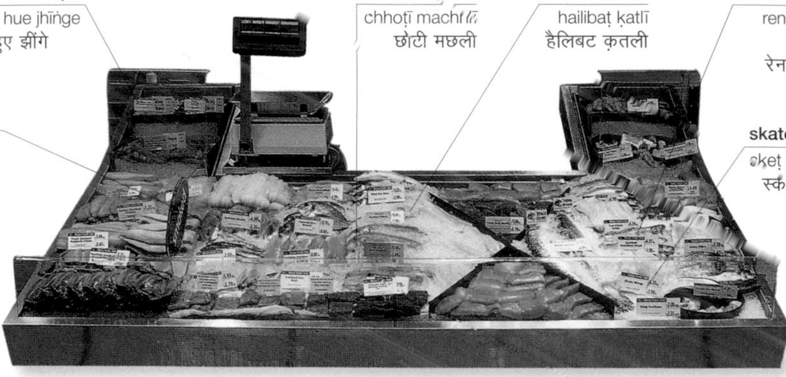

fish counter
machhlī kī dukān | मछली की दुकान

monkfish
maṅk fiś | मंक फ़िश

mackerel | maikral machhlī | मैकरल मछली

trout | ṭrāuṭ machhlī
ट्राउट मछली

swordfish
khaṅg mīn
खंग मीन

Dover sole
sol machhlī
सोल मछली

lemon sole
laiman sol
लैमन सोल

haddock
haddock | हैडॉक

sardine
sārḍin | सार्डिन

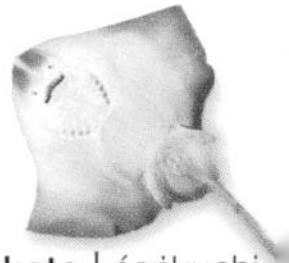

skate | śaṅkuchi machhlī | शंकुचि मछली

whiting | viṭiṅg | विटिंग

sea bass | sī bās | सी बास

salmon | sāman machhlī | सामन मछली

cod | cod machhlī
कॉड मछली

sea bream
sī brīm | सी ब्रीम

tuna | ṭyūnā machhlī
ट्यूना मछली

seafood • samudrī bhojan • समुद्री भोजन

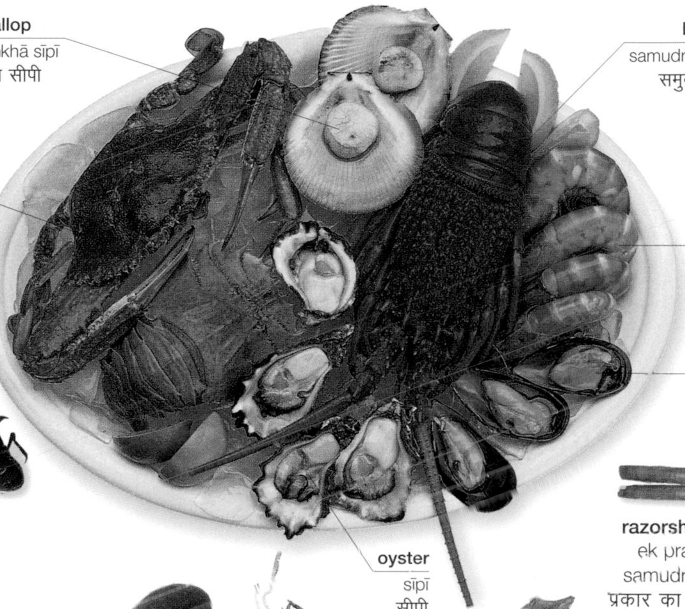

scallop
paṅkhā sīpī
पंखा सीपी

lobster
samudrī jhīṅgā
समुद्री झींगा

crab
kekṛā
केकड़ा

jumbo shrimp
jhīṅgā
झींगा

mussel
śaṃbūk
शंबूक

crayfish
krefiś
क्रेफ़िश

razorshell clam
ek prakār kā samudrī jīv | एक प्रकार का समुद्री जीव

oyster
sīpī
सीपी

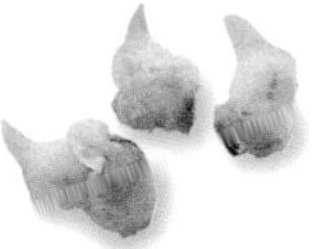

cockle | cockle sīpī | कॉकल सीपी

octopus
aṣṭbhuj | अष्टभुज

cuttlefish
kaṭal fiś | कटल फ़िश

squid
skivaḍ | स्किवड

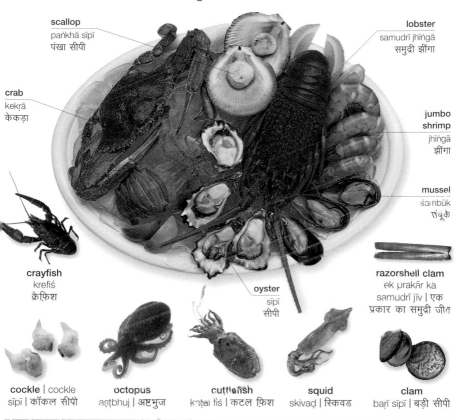

clam
baṛī sīpī | बड़ी सीपी

vocabulary • śabdāvalī • शब्दावली

fresh tāzā ताज़ा	**cleaned** svacchh स्वच्छ	**smoked** dhūmrit धूम्रित	**tail** pūñchh पूंछ	**fillet** ḳatlā क़तला	**salted** lavaṇit लवणित	**loin** śroṇik māṃs श्रोणिक मांस
frozen saṃśītit संशीतित	**filleted** ḳatle kiyā huā क़तले किया हुआ	**skinned** khāl rahit खाल रहित	**bone** kāṃṭe कांटे	**scale** mīn śalk मीन शल्क		

Will you clean it for me?
kyā āp ise sāf kar deṅge?
क्या आप इसे साफ़ कर देंगे?

vegetables 1 • sabziyāṃ • सब्ज़ियां

fava bean
bāklā
बाकला

green bean
guār kī phalī
गुआर की फली

french bean
frānsbīn
फ़्रांसबीन

garden pea
maṭar
मटर

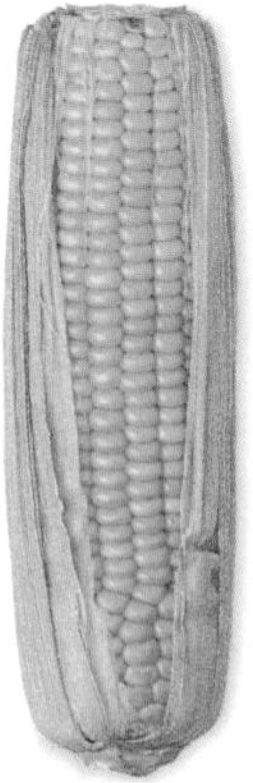

corn
mīṭhī makaī
मीठी मकई

bean sprout
aṅkurit phalī
अंकुरित फली

bamboo
bāṃs
बांस

pod
phalī
फली

okra
bhiṇḍī
भिंडी

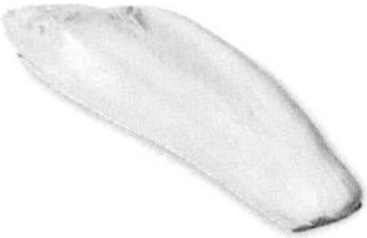

chicory
chikorī
चिकोरी

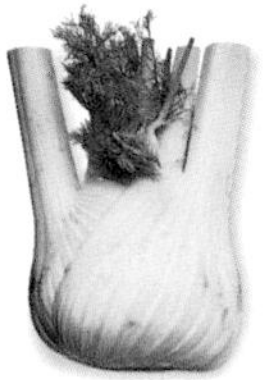

fennel
soā
सोआ

palm hearts
tāṛ kī gāṃṭheṃ
ताड़ की गांठें

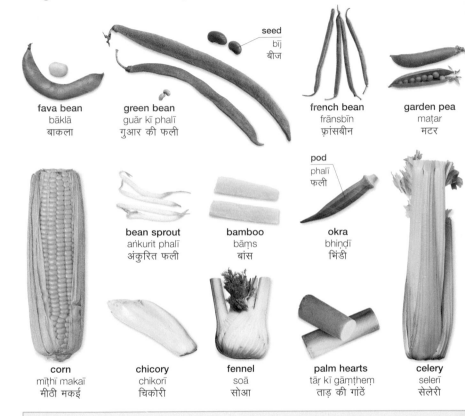

celery
selerī
सेलेरी

vocabulary • śabdāvalī • शब्दावली

leaf pattī पत्ती	**floret** chhoṭā phūl छोटा फूल	**tip** nok नोक	**organic** jaivik जैविक	**Do you sell organic vegetables?** āp jaivik sabziyāṃ bechte haiṃ? आप जैविक सब्ज़ियां बेचते हैं?
stalk ḍanṭhal डंठल	**kernel** girī गिरी	**heart** bhītrī gāṃṭh भीतरी गांठ	**plastic bag** plāsṭik baig प्लास्टिक बैग	**Are these grown locally?** kyā ye āspās ugāī jātī haiṃ? क्या ये आसपास उगाई जाती हैं?

arugula
rocket salād
रॉकेट सलाद

watercress
watercress
वॉटरक्रेस

radicchio
lāl pattāgobhī
लाल पत्तागोभी

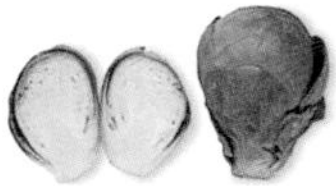

Brussels sprout
gāṃṭh gobhī
गांठ गोभी

Swiss chard
svis chārḍ | स्विस चार्ड

kale
kel pattī | केल पत्ती

sorrel
sorrel pattī | सॉरेल पत्ती

endive | enḍāiv pattī | एनडाइव पत्ती

dandelion
ḍenḍiliyan
डेंडिलियन

spinach
pālak
पालक

kohlrabi
śalgam
शलगम

pak-choi
pāk-choī
पाक–चोई

lettuce
salād pattā | सलाद पत्ता

broccoli
broklī | ब्रोकली

cabbage
bandgobhī | बंदगोभी

spring greens
harā salād pattā | हरा सलाद पत्ता

vegetables 2 • sabziyāṃ • सब्ज़ियां

turnip
śalgam
शलग़म
artichoke
artichoke
आर्टीचॉक
radish
chhoṭī mūlī
छोटी मूली
cauliflower
phūlgobhī
फूलगोभी
asparagus
nāgadaun sāg
नागदौन साग
potato
ālū
आलू
squash
harā kaddū
हरा कद्दू
onion
pyāz
प्याज़
pepper
śimlā mirch
शिमला मिर्च
chili pepper
lāl mirch
लाल मिर्च
sweetcorn
mīṭhī makaī
मीठी मकई

vocabulary • śabdāvalī • शब्दावली

cherry tomato
bebī ṭamāṭar
बेबी टमाटर

carrot
gājar
गाजर

breadfruit
breḍfrūṭ
ब्रेडफ्रूट

new potato
nayā ālū
नया आलू

celeriac
ek prakār kā kand
एक प्रकार का कंद

taro root
kachālū
कचालू

cassava
kasāvā
कसावा

water chestnut
siṅghāṛā
सिंघाड़ा

frozen
frozan
फ़्रोज़न

raw
kacchā
कच्चा

hot (spicy)
tīkhā
तीखा

sweet
mīṭhā
मीठा

bitter
kaṛvā
कड़वा

firm
sakht
सख़्त

flesh
gūdā
गूदा

root
jaṛ
जड़

Can I have one kilo of potatoes please?
kyā mujhe ek kilo ālū deṇge?
क्या मुझे एक किलो आलू देंगे?

What's the price per kilo?
ek kilo kitne kā hai?
एक किलो कितने का है?

What are those called?
inheṃ kyā kahte haiṃ?
इन्हें क्या कहते हैं?

sweet potato
śakarkandī
शकरकंदी

yam
zimīkand
ज़िमीकंद

beet
chukandar
चुकंदर

rutabaga
svīḍan kā śalgam
स्वीडन का शलग़म

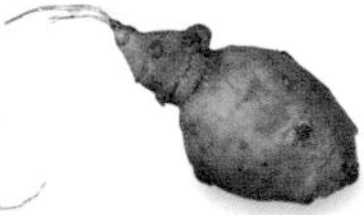

Jerusalem artichoke
yerūśalam artichoke
येरूशलम आर्टीचॉक

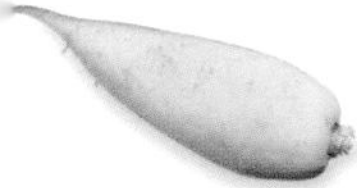

horseradish
nāgarmothā
नागरमोथा

parsnip
pīlī gājar
पीली गाजर

ginger
adrak
अदरक

eggplant
baiṅgan
बैंगन

tomato
ṭamāṭar
टमाटर

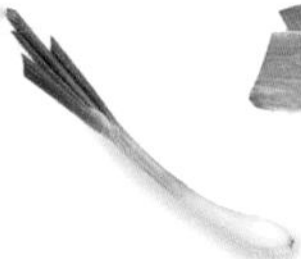

green onion
harā pyāz
हरा प्याज़

leek
līk
लीक

shallot
pyāz
प्याज़

clove
kalī
कली

garlic
lahsun
लहसुन

truffle
gucchhī
गुच्छी

mushroom
maśrūm
मशरूम

cucumber
khīrā
खीरा

zucchini
toraī
तोरई

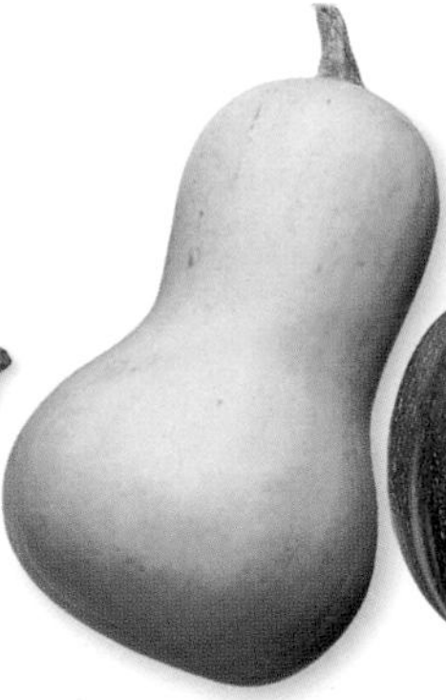

butternut squash
peṭhā
पेठा

acorn squash
banjuphal
बंजुफल

pumpkin
kaddū
कद्दू

fruit 1 • phal • फल

citrus fruit • khaṭṭe phal • खट्टे फल

orange
santrā | संतरा

clementine
māltā | माल्टा

ugli fruit
aglī frūṭ | अगली फ़्रूट

pith
bhītrī
chhilkā
भीतरी
छिलका

grapefruit
chakotrā | चकोतरा

tangerine
nāraṅgī | नारंगी

segment
phāṃk
फांक

satsuma
jāpānī santrā
जापानी संतरा

zest
chhilkā
छिलका

lime
nībū | नीबू

lemon
khaṭṭā | खट्टा

kumquat
kummkāṭ | कुम्मकाट

stone fruit • guṭhlīdār phal • गुठलीदार फल

peach
āṛū | आड़ू

nectarine
śaftālū | शफ़तालू

apricot
ḳhubānī
ख़ुबानी

plum
ālū buḳhārā
आलू बुख़ारा

cherry
cherī
चेरी

pear
nāśpātī
नाशपाती

apple
seb | सेब

basket of fruit
phaloṃ kī ṭokrī | फलों की टोकरी

berries and melons • ber aur sardā • बेर और सर्दा

strawberry
strawberry | स्ट्रॉबेरी

raspberry
rasbharī | रसभरी

melon
sardā
सर्दा

blackberry
blaikberi | ब्लैकबेरी

red currant
reḍ karanṭ | रेड करंट

grapes
āmgūr | अंगूर

cranberry
krainberi
क्रैनबेरी

black currant
blaik karanṭ
ब्लैक करंट

rind
chhilkā
छिलका

seed
bīj
बीज

blueberry
jāmun | जामुन

white currant
vhāiṭ karanṭ
व्हाइट करंट

flesh
gūdā
गूदा

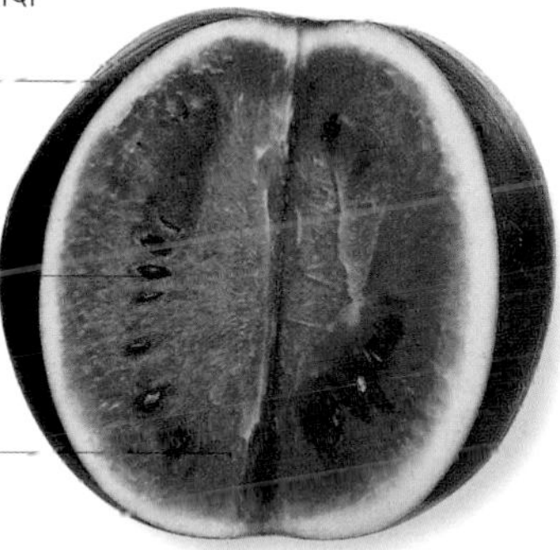

watermelon
tarbūz
तरबूज़

loganberry
loganberī
लोगनबेरी

gooseberry
jharberī
झरबेरी

vocabulary • śabdāvalī • शब्दावली

rhubarb	sour	crisp	juice	Are they ripe?
revāchīnī	khaṭ.ṭā	kurkurā	jūs	kyā ye pake hue haim.?
रेवाचीनी	खट्टा	कुरकुरा	जूस	क्या ये पके हुए हैं?
fiber	fresh	rotten	core	Can I try one?
reśedār	tāzā	sar.ā huā	bīj	kyā maim. ek chakh lūm. ?
रेशेदार	ताज़ा	सड़ा हुआ	बीज	क्या मैं एक चख लूं?
sweet	juicy	pulp	seedless	How long will they keep?
mīṭ.hā	rasīlā	gūdā	bīj rahit	ye kab tak t.hīk rahen.ge?
मीठा	रसीला	गूदा	बीज रहित	ये कब तक ठीक रहेंगे?

fruit 2 • phal 2 • फल 2

mango
ām | आम
pineapple
anannās
अनन्नास
avocado
avokāḍo
अवोकाडो
papaya
papītā
पपीता
peach
āṛū
आड़ू
lychee
līchī
लीची
kiwifruit
kīvī | कीवी
cape gooseberry
rasbharī
रसभरी

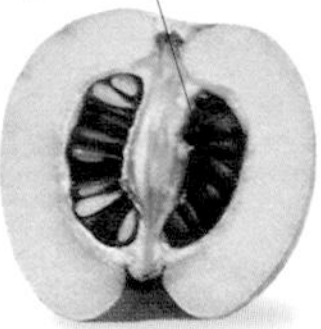
pip
bīj | बीज

quince
kīns | कीन्स

passion fruit
paiśan frūṭ
पैशन फ़्रूट

skin
chhilkā
छिलका

banana
kelā | केला

guava
amrūd | अमरूद

pomegranate
anār | अनार

persimmon
tendū phal
तेंदू फल

feijoa
fehoā | फ़ेहोआ

prickly pear
nākh | नाख

starfruit
kamrakh
कमरख

mangosteen
maṅguṣṭh
मंगुष्ठ

nuts and dried fruit • meve aur girī • मेवे और गिरी

pine nut
chilgozā | चिलगोज़ा

pistachio
pistā | पिस्ता

cashew
kājū | काजू

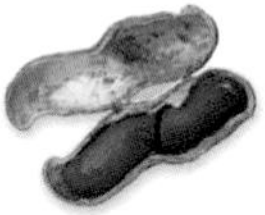

peanut
mūṅgphalī | मूंगफली

hazelnut
pahāṛī bādām
पहाड़ी बादाम

Brazil nut
brāzīlnaṭ | ब्राज़ीलनट

pecan
pīkan | पीकन

almond
bādām | बादाम

walnut
akhroṭ | अख़रोट

chestnut
chesṭnaṭ | चेस्टनट

macadamia
maikāḍemiyā
मैकाडेमिया

fig
añjīr | अंजीर

date
khajūr | खजूर

prune
sūkhā alūchā
सूखा अलूचा

sultana raisin
bījrahit kiśmiś
बीजरहित किशमिश

raisin
kiśmiś
किशमिश

currant
munakkā
मुनक्का

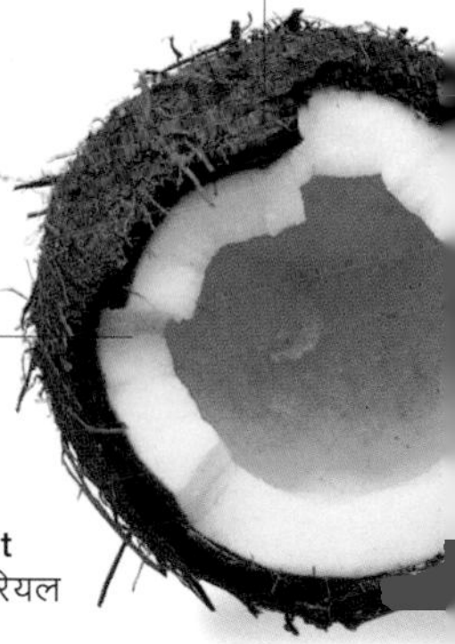

shell
khol
ख़ोल

flesh
girī
गिरी

coconut
nāriyal | नारियल

vocabulary • śabdāvalī • शब्दावली

green harā हरा	**hard** sak.ht सख़्त	**kernel** girī गिरी	**salted** lavan.it लवणित	**roasted** bhunā भुना	**tropical fruit** us.n.deśīya phal उष्णदेशीय फल	**shelled** chhilkā rahit छिलका रहित
ripe pakā पका	**soft** narm नर्म	**desiccated** sukhāyā huā सुखाया हुआ	**raw** kacchā कच्चा	**seasonal** mausmī मौसमी	**candied fruit** page phal पगे फल	**whole** sābut साबुत

grains and legumes • anāj evam dāleṃ • अनाज एवं दालें

grains • anāj • अनाज

wheat
gehūṃ | गेहूं

oats
jaī | जई

barley
jau | जौ

millet
jvār | ज्वार

corn
makkā | मक्का

quinoa
kinoyā | किनोया

vocabulary • śabdāvalī • शब्दावली

seed bīj बीज	**fragranced** ḳhuśbūdār ख़ुशबूदार	**long-grain** baṛā dānā बड़ा दाना
husk bhūsī भूसी	**cereal** khādyānn खाद्यान्न	**short-grain** chhoṭā dānā छोटा दाना
kernel girī गिरी	**whole-grain** sābut साबुत	**fresh** tāzā ताज़ा
dry sukhā सूखा	**soak (v)** bhigonā भिगोना	**easy-cook** jaldī pakne vālā जल्दी पकने वाला

rice • chāval • चावल

white rice | safed chāval | सफ़ेद चावल

brown rice | brāun rāis | ब्राउन राइस

wild rice | jaṅglī chāval | जंगली चावल

pudding rice | puḍiṅg rāis | पुडिंग राइस

processed grains • saṅsādhit anāj • संसाधित अनाज

couscous
khaskhas | खसखस

cracked wheat
daliyā | दलिया

semolina
sūjī | सूजी

bran
chokar | चोकर

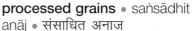

beans and peas • dāleṃ • दालें

butter beans
sem
सेम

haricot beans
safed rājmā
सफ़ेद राजमा

red kidney beans
rājmā
राजमा

aduki beans
aḍukī bīn
अडुकी बीन

fava beans
bāklā
बाकला

soybeans
soyābīn
सोयाबीन

black-eyed beans
lobiyā
लोबिया

pinto beans
chitrā rājmā
चितरा राजमा

mung beans
sābut mūṅg
साबुत मूंग

flageolet beans
sūkhī frānsbīn
सूखी फ़्रांसबीन

brown lentils
kālī masūr
काली मसूर

red lentils
lāl masūr
लाल मसूर

green peas
maṭar
मटर

garbanzos
kābulī chane
काबुली चने

split peas
maṭrā
मटरा

seeds • bīj • बीज

pumpkin seed
kaddū ke bīj
कद्दू के बीज

mustard seed
rāī | राई

caraway
safed zīrā
सफ़ेद ज़ीरा

sesame seed
til | तिल

sunflower seed
sūrajmukhī ke bīj
सूरजमुखी के बीज

herbs and spices • auṣadhi evam masāle • औषधि एवं मसाले

spices • masāle • मसाले

vanilla | vainilā (paudhā) | वैनिला (पौधा)

nutmeg
jāyaphal
जायफल

mace
jāvitrī | जावित्री

turmeric
haldī | हल्दी

cumin
zīrā | ज़ीरा

bouquet garni
masālom̐ kī poṭlī
मसालों की पोटली

allspice
lavaṅg badar
लवंग बदर

peppercorn | kālī mirch | काली मिर्च

fenugreek
methī | मेथी

chili powder
mirch | मिर्च

saffron
kesar | केसर

cardamom
ilāyachī | इलायची

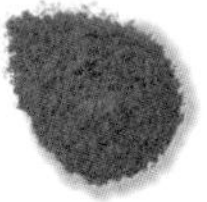
curry powder
śorbe kā masālā
शोरबे का मसाला

whole
sābut
साबुत
crushed
kuṭā
कुटा
ground
pisā
पिसा
flakes
dardarā
दरदरा

paprika
pisī mirch
पिसी मिर्च

garlic
lahsun | लहसुन

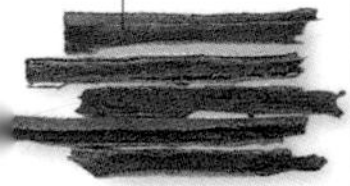
sticks
chhāl
छाल

cinnamon
dālchīnī | दालचीनी

lemon grass
leman grās
लेमन ग्रास

cloves
lauṅg
लौंग

star anise
sṭār enīs
स्टार एनीस

ginger
adrak
अदरक

herbs • auṣadhi • औषधि

fennel | soā | सोआ

fennel seeds
moṭī sauṃf
मोटी सौंफ़

bay leaf
tezpattā | तेज़पत्ता

parsley
pārsli | पारस्लि

chives
jambū | जंबू

mint
pudīnā | पुदीना

thyme
ajvāyan | अजवायन

sage | kapūr kā pattā | कपूर का पत्ता

tarragon
ṭairāgan | टैरागन

marjoram
marūvā | मरूवा

basil
tulsī | तुलसी

oregano
oregano | ऑरिगानो

cilantro
dhaniyā | धनिया

dill
śatpuṣpikā
शतपुष्पिका

rosemary
rozmerī | रोज़मेरी

bottled foods • botalband khādya padārth • बोतलबंद खाद्य पदार्थ

cork
ḍhakkan
ढक्कन
sunflower oil
sūrajmukhī kā tel
सूरजमुखी का तेल
walnut oil
akhroṭ kā tel
अख़रोट का तेल
grapeseed oil
aṃgūr ke bīj kā tel
अंगूर के बीज का तेल
almond oil
bādām kā tel
बादाम का तेल
sesame oil
til kā tel
तिल का तेल
hazelnut oil
hezalnaṭ tel
हेज़लनट तेल
olive oil
zaitūn kā tel
ज़ैतून का तेल
herbs
jaṛī-būṭī
जड़ी–बूटी
flavored oil
sugandhit tel
सुगंधित तेल

oils | tel | तेल

sweet spreads • jaim, śahad ityādi • जैम, शहद इत्यादि

jar
jār | जार
honeycomb
chhattā | छत्ता
candied honey
kārtik śahad
कार्तिक शहद
lemon curd
leman karḍ
लेमन कर्ड
raspberry jam
rasbharī jaim
रसभरी जैम
marmalade
mārmleḍ
मार्मलेड
clear honey
śahad
शहद
maple syrup
mepal sirap
मेपल सिरप

condiments and spreads • chaṭnī sauce ityādi • चटनी, सॉस इत्यादि

mayonnaise
myonīz
म्योनीज़

cider vinegar
seb sirkā
सेब सिरका

balsamic vinegar
bolsam sirkā
बॉल्सम सिरका

malt vinegar
mālṭ kā sirkā
माल्ट का सिरका

wine vinegar
vāin sirkā
वाइन सिरका

vinegar | sirkā | सिरका

bottle
botal
बोतल

ketchup
ṭamāṭar sauce
टमाटर सॉस

english mustard
iṅgliś masṭarḍ
इंगलिश मस्टर्ड

french mustard
french masṭarḍ
फ्रेंच मस्टर्ड

chutney
chaṭnī
चटनी

sauce
sauce
सॉस

whole-grain mustard
sābut sarsoṃ
साबुत सरसों

peanut butter
pīnaṭ baṭar
पीनट बटर

chocolate spread
chocolate spraiḍ
चॉकलेट स्प्रैड

sealed jar
sīlband jār
सीलबंद जार

preserved fruit
sanrakṣit phal
संरक्षित फल

vocabulary • śabdāvalī • शब्दावली

corn oil
makaī kā tel
मकई का तेल

peanut oil
mūn'gphalī kā tel
मूंगफली का तेल

vegetable oil
vanaspati tel
वनस्पति तेल

canola oil
tilhan kā tel
तिलहन का तेल

cold-pressed oil
kold.-praisd. tel
कोल्ड–प्रैस्ड तेल

dairy products • ḍeyarī utpād • डेयरी उत्पाद

cheese • chīz • चीज़

rind
paprī
पपड़ी

semi-hard cheese
ardh sakht chīz
अर्ध सख़्त चीज़

semi-soft cheese
ardh mulāyam chīz
अर्ध मुलायम चीज़

blue cheese
blū chīz
ब्लू चीज़

soft cheese
mulāyam chīz
मुलायम चीज़

grated cheese
kaddūkas kiyā chīz
कद्दूकस किया चीज़

hard cheese
ṭhos chīz | ठोस चीज़

cottage cheese
panīr
पनीर

cream cheese
krīm chīz
क्रीम चीज़

fresh cheese | tāzā chīz | ताज़ा चीज़

milk • dūdh • दूध

whole milk
ful krīm dūdh
फुल क्रीम दूध

reduced-fat milk
ardha-malāīrahit dūdh
अर्ध-मलाईरहित दूध

skim milk
krīm rahit dūdh
क्रीम रहित दूध

cow's milk | gāya kā dūdh | गाय का दूध

milk carton
dūdh kā ḍibbā
दूध का डिब्बा

goat's milk
bakrī kā dūdh
बकरी का दूध

condensed milk
kanḍensḍ milk
कंडेंस्ड मिल्क

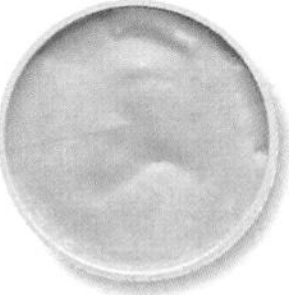

butter
makkhan | मक्खन

margarine
kṛtrim makkhan
कृत्रिम मक्खन

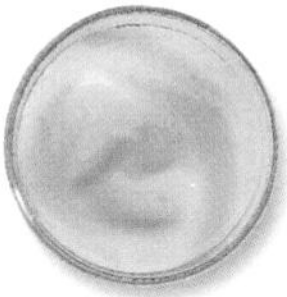

cream
krīm | क्रीम

light cream
patlī krīm | पतली क्रीम

heavy cream
gaṛhī krīm
गाढ़ी क्रीम

whipped cream
phemṭī huī krīm
फेंटी हुई क्रीम

sour cream
khaṭṭī krīm
खट्टी क्रीम

yoghurt
dahī
दही

ice cream
āīskrīm
आइसक्रीम

eggs • aṇḍe • अंडे

yolk
zardī
ज़र्दी

white
safed bhāg
सफ़ेद भाग

shell
chhilkā
छिलका

egg cup
aṇḍā
kap
अंडा कप

boiled egg | ublā aṇḍā | उबला अंडा

hen's egg
murgī kā aṇḍā
मुर्गी का अंडा

duck egg
batakh kā aṇḍā
बतख़ का अंडा

goose egg
hans kā aṇḍā
हंस का अंडा

quail egg
baṭer kā aṇḍā
बटेर का अंडा

vocabulary • śabdāvalī • शब्दावली

pasteurized
pāscharīkṛt
पास्चरीकृत

unpasteurized
apāscharīkṛt
अपास्चरीकृत

milkshake
milkśek
मिल्कशेक

frozen yogurt
ṭhaṇḍā dahī
ठंडा दही

salted
namkīn
नमकीन

unsalted
namak rahit
नमक रहित

sheep's milk
bheṛ kā dūdh
भेड़ का दूध

buttermilk
chhāchh
छाछ

lactose
dugdh śarkarā
दुग्ध शर्करा

fat-free
vasā rahit
वसा रहित

homogenised
samāṅgīkṛt dūdh
समांगीकृत दूध

powdered milk
pāuḍar dūdh
पाउडर दूध

breads and flours • breḍ evam āṭā • ब्रेड एवं आटा

sliced bread
breḍ slāis
ब्रेड स्लाइस
poppy seeds
khaskhas
खसखस
rye bread
rāī breḍ
राई ब्रेड
baguette
french breḍ
फ़्रेंच ब्रेड

bakery | bekrī | बेकरी

making bread • breḍ banānā • ब्रेड बनाना

white flour
maidā | मैदा

brown flour
gehūṃ kā āṭā | गेहूं का आटा

wholemeal flour
āṭā | आटा

yeast
khamīr | खमीर

sift (v)
chhānnā | छानना

mix (v)
milānā | मिलाना

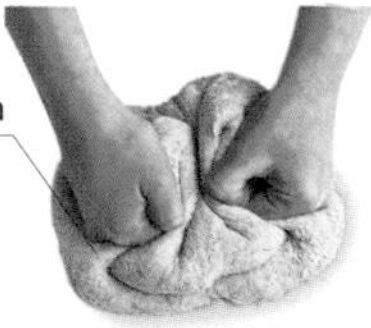
dough
loī
लोई

knead (v)
gūṃdhnā | गूंधना

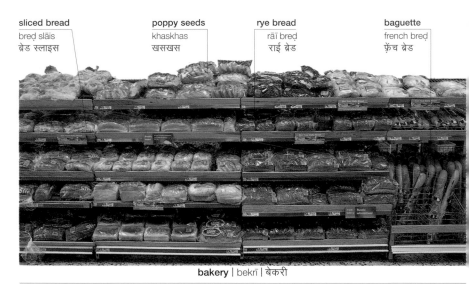

bake (v)
bek karnā | बेक करना

crust
kinārā
किनारा

white bread
maidā breḍ | मैदा ब्रेड

loaf
sābut
breḍ
साबुत ब्रेड

brown bread
brāun breḍ | ब्राउन ब्रेड

whole-wheat bread
āṭe kī breḍ | आटे की ब्रेड

slice
ṭukṛā
टुकड़ा

multigrain bread
miśrit anāj breḍ
मिश्रित अनाज ब्रेड

corn bread
makaī breḍ | मकई ब्रेड

soda bread
soḍā breḍ | सोडा ब्रेड

sourdough bread
khamīrī breḍ
खमीरी ब्रेड

flatbread
chupṭī breḍ | चपटी ब्रेड

bagel
begal ban | बेगल बन

bun
safed ban | सफ़ेद बन

roll
rol | रोल

fruit bread
frūṭ breḍ | फ्रूट ब्रेड

seeded bread
bījyukt breḍ | बीजयुक्त ब्रेड

naan bread
nān | नान

pitta bread
piṭā breḍ | पीटा ब्रेड

crispbread
kurkurī breḍ | कुरकुरी ब्रेड

vocabulary • śabdāvalī • शब्दावली

bread flour mot.ā āt.ā मोटा आटा	**ṛise (v)** phūlnā फूलना	**prove (v)** ūpar ut.hnā ऊपर उठना	**breadcrumbs** bred. kā chūrā ब्रेड का चूरा	**slicer** slāisar स्लाइसर
self-rising flour mahīn āt.ā महीन आटा	**all-purpose flour** āt.ā आटा	**glaze (v)** chamak ānā चमक आना	**flute** flūt. फ़्लूट	**baker** bekar बेकर

cakes and desserts • kek aur miṣṭānn • केक और मिष्टान्न

éclair
ekleyar
एक्लेयर
cream
krīm
क्रीम
filling
bharāv
भराव
choux pastry
śūz pesṭrī
शूज़ पेस्ट्री
puff pastry
paf pesṭrī
पफ़ पेस्ट्री
filo pastry
phyllo pesṭrī
फ़िलो पेस्ट्री

fruitcake
frūṭ kek
फ्रूट केक
fruit tart
frūṭ ṭārṭ
फ्रूट टार्ट
meringue
mīraiṅg
मिरैंग
chocolate coated
chocolate parat
चॉकलेट परत
muffin
mafin
मफ़िन
sponge cake
spañj kek
स्पंज केक

cakes | kek | केक

vocabulary • śabdāvalī • शब्दावली

rice pudding
khīr
खीर

celebration
samāroh
समारोह

sweet bun
ban
बन

custard
kast.ard.
कस्टर्ड

pastry
pest.rī
पेस्ट्री

slice
tukr.ā
टुकड़ा

crème patisserie
krīm pest.rī
क्रीम पेस्ट्री

chocolate cake
chocolate kek
चॉकलेट केक

May I have a slice, please?
kyā maim. ek t.ukr.ā le saktā hūm.?
क्या मैं एक टुकड़ा ले सकता हूं?

chocolate chip
chocolate chip biskuṭ
चॉकलेट चिप बिस्कुट

florentine
florenṭāin
फ़्लोरेन्टाइन

cookies | biskuṭ | बिस्कुट

lady fingers
spañj fiṅgar
स्पंज फ़िंगर

trifle
ṭrāifal
ट्राइ.फ़ल

mousse
mūs puḍiṅg | मूस पुडिंग

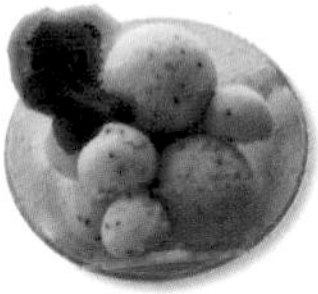

sherbet
sorbet | सॉर्बेट

cream pie
krīm pāī | क्रीम गाई

crème caramel | krīm kairāmal | क्रीम कैरामल

celebration cakes • samāroh kek • समारोह केक

top tier
ūprī chakr
ऊपरी चक्र

decoration
sajāvaṭ
सजावट

ribbon
riban
रिबन

bottom tier
nichlā chakr
निचला चक्र

frosting
āisiṅg
आइसिंग

marzipan
bādām parat
बादाम परत

wedding cake | śādī kā kek | शादी का केक

birthday candles
mombattī
मोमबत्ती

blow out (v)
phūṃk se bujhānā
फूंक से बुझाना

birthday cake | janmdin kā kek | जन्मदिन का केक

delicatessen • pake bhojan ki dukān • पके भोजन की दुकान

spicy sausage
masāledār sausage
मसालेदार सॉसेज

oil
tel
तेल

vinegar
sirkā
सिरका

salami
salāmī
सलामी

pepperoni
tīkhī sausages
तीखी सॉसेजेस

flan
flain kek
फ़्लैन केक

uncooked meat
kacchā māṃs
कच्चा मांस

counter
kāunṭar
काउंटर

pâté
paiṭī
पैटी

mozzarella
mozerelā | मोज़ेरेला

brie
brī chīz | ब्री चीज

goat's cheese | bakrī ke dūdh kā chīz | बकरी के दूध का चीज़

cheddar
cheḍar chīz | चेडर चीज़

parmesan | ek prakār kā iṭeliyan chīz | एक प्रकार का इटेलियन चीज

camembert | ek prakār kā french chīz | एक प्रकार का फ्रेंच चीज़

rind
papṛī
पपड़ी

edam | eḍām chīz | एडाम चीज़

manchego | manchego chīz | मनचेगो चीज़

meat pies
pāī
पाई

cooked meat
pakā huā māṃs
पका हुआ मांस

ham
haim
हैम

black olive
kālā zaitūn
काला ज़ैतून

chili pepper
mirch
मिर्च

sauce
chaṭnī
चटनी

bread roll
breḍ rol
ब्रेड रोल

green olive
harā zaitūn
हरा ज़ैतून

sandwich counter
sainḍvich kāunṭar | सैंडविच काउंटर

smoked fish
dhūmit machhlī
धूमित मछली

capers
kaipars
कैपर्स

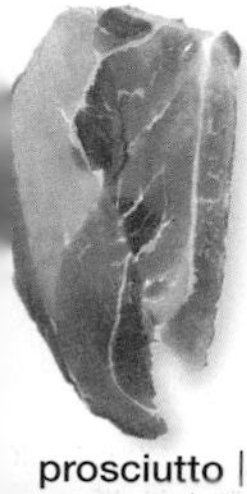

prosciutto | iṭeliyan haim | इटेलियन हैम

chorizo
speniś sausage
स्पेनिश सॉसेज

stuffed olive | bharvāṃ zaitūn | भरवां ज़ैतून

vocabulary • śabdāvalī • शब्दावली

in oil tel mem. pakā तेल में पका	**marinated** masāle mem. lipt.ā मसाले मैं लिपटा	**in brine** namkīn pānī meṃ rakhā नमकीन पानी में रखा
smoked dhūmrit धूम्रित	**salted** namkīn नमकीन	**cured** sanraks.it संरक्षित

Take a number please.
kr.pyā nambar le lem.
कृपया नंबर ले लें।

Can I try some of that, please?
kyā maim. ise chakh saktā hūm. ?
क्या मैं इसे चख सकता हूं?

May I have six slices of that, please?
kyā mujhe iske chhah pīs den.ge?
क्या मुझे इसके छह पीस देंगे?

drinks • peya • पेय

water • pānī • पानी

bottled water
botalband pānī
बोतलबंद पानी

sparkling
bulbuledār
बुलबुलेदार

still
sthir
स्थिर

mineral water
minral water | मिनरल वॉटर

tap water | nal kā pānī | नल का पानी

tonic water
tonic water
टॉनिक वॉटर

soda water
soḍā water
सोडा वॉटर

hot drinks • garm peya • गर्म पेय

teabag
ṭī baig
टी बैग

loose tea
khulī chāya pattī
खुली चाय पत्ती

tea | chāya | चाय

beans
coffee ke bīj
कॉफ़ी के बीज

ground coffee
pisī coffee
पिसी कॉफ़ी

coffee | coffee | कॉफ़ी

hot chocolate
hot chocolate
हॉट चॉकलेट

malted drink
mālṭ vālā peya
माल्ट वाला पेय

soft drinks • śītal peya • शीतल पेय

tomato juice
ṭamāṭar kā jūs
टमाटर का जूस

straw
straw
स्ट्रॉ

grape juice
aṃgūr kā jūs
अंगूर का जूस

lemonade
śikanjī
शिकंजी

orangeade
santare kā jūs
संतरे का जूस

cola
kolā
कोला

alcoholic drinks • madya peya • मद्य पेय

gin
jin | जिन

beer
bīyar | बीयर

can
kain
कैन

cider | seb kī vain | सेब की वाइन

bitter
charparā | चरपरा

stout
sṭāuṭ | स्टाउट

vodka
vodkā | वोदका

whisky
vhiskī | व्हिस्की

rum
ram | रम

brandy
brānḍī | ब्रांडी

port
porṭ | पोर्ट

sherry
śerī | शेरी

dry
sādī
सादी

campari
kampārī | कमपारी

rosé
gulābī
गुलाबी

white
safed
सफ़ेद

red
lāl
लाल

wine
vāin | वाइन

liqueur
likar | लिकर

tequila
ṭakīlā | टकीला

champagne
śaimpen | शैम्पेन

eating out
bāhar khānā
बाहर खाना

café • kaife • कैफ़े

awning
sāyabān
सायबान

menu
vyañjan sūchī
व्यंजन सूची

sidewalk café | roḍ sāiḍ kaife | रोड साइड कैफ़े

umbrella
chhātā
छाता

terrace café | khulā kaife | खुला कैफ़े

waiter
bairā
बैरा

coffee machine
coffee maśīn
कॉफ़ी मशीन

table
mez
मेज़

snack bar | snaik bār | स्नैक बार

coffee • coffee • कॉफ़ी

coffee with milk
coffee
कॉफ़ी

black coffee
blaik coffee
ब्लैक कॉफ़ी

filter coffee
filṭar coffee | फ़िल्टर कॉफ़ी

espresso
espraiso | एस्प्रैसो

cocoa powder
koko pāuḍar
कोको पाउडर

froth
jhāg
झाग

cappuccino
kepyūchino | केप्यूचिनो

iced coffee
āisḍ coffee | आइस्ड कॉफ़ी

tea • chāya • चाय

herbal tea
auṣadhīya chāya
औषधीय चाय

chamomile tea | babūnā kī chāya
बबूना की चाय

green tea | harī chāya
हरी चाय

tea with milk
dudh valī chāya
दूध वाली चाय

plain tea
kālī chāya
काली चाय

tea with lemon
nībū vālī chāya
नीबू वाली चाय

mint tea
pudīne kī chāya
पुदीने की चाय

iced tea
ṭhaṇḍī chāya
ठंडी चाय

juices and milkshakes • jūs evam milkśek • जूस एवं मिल्कशेक

chocolate milkshake
chocolate milkśek
चॉकलेट मिल्कशेक

strawberry milkshake
strawberry milkśek
स्ट्रॉबेरी मिल्कशेक

orange juice
santare kā jūs
संतरे का जूस

apple juice
seb kā jūs
सेब का जूस

pineapple juice
anannās kā jūs
अनन्नास का जूस

tomato juice
ṭamāṭar kā jūs
टमाटर का जूस

coffee milkshake
coffee milkśek
कॉफ़ी मिल्कशेक

food • khādya padārth • खाद्य पदार्थ

brown bread
brāun breḍ
ब्राउन ब्रेड

scoop
skūp
स्कूप

toasted sandwich | ṭosṭeḍ saiṇḍvich | टोस्टेड सैंडविच

salad
salād | सलाद

ice cream
āiskrīm | आइसक्रीम

pastry
pesṭrī | पेस्ट्री

bar • bār • बार

glasses
gilās
गिलास

optic
opṭik
ऑप्टिक

cash register
tijorī
तिजोरी

bartender
bārṭenḍar
बारटेंडर

beer tap
bīyar ṭaip
बीयर टैप

coffee machine
coffee maśīn
कॉफ़ी मशीन

ice bucket
āis bakeṭ
आइस बकेट

bar stool
bār kursī
बार कुर्सी

ashtray
aiśṭre
ऐशट्रे

coaster
kosṭar
कोस्टर

bar counter
bār kāunṭar
बार काउंटर

bottle opener
botal opnar
बोतल ओपनर

lever
līvar
लीवर

corkscrew | corkscrew | कॉर्कस्क्रू

tongs
chimṭā
चिमटा

stirre
peya hilāne kī ḍanḍ
पेय हिलाने की डंडी

measure
māpak
मापक

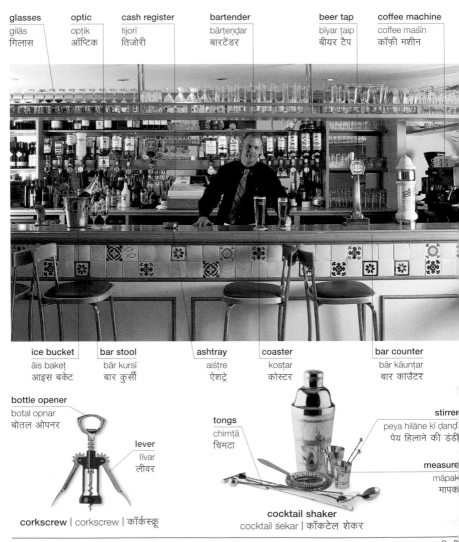

cocktail shaker
cocktail śekar | कॉकटेल शेकर

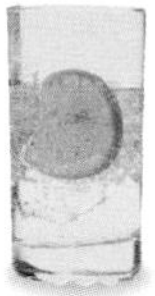

gin and tonic
jin aur tonic
जिन और टॉनिक

pitcher
jag
जग

scotch and water
scotch aur pānī
स्कॉच और पानी

ice cube
baraf
बर्फ़

rum and cola
ram aur kok
रम और कोक

screwdriver
vodkā aur santrā
वोदका और संतरा

martini
mārṭinī | मार्टिनी

cocktail
cocktail | कॉकटेल

wine
vāin | वाइन

beer
bīyar | बीयर

shot
ek shot | एक शॉट

single
singal
सिंगल

double
ḍabal
डबल

measure
māp | माप

without ice | baraf rahit | बर्फ़ रहित

ice and lemon
baraf va nīmbū
बर्फ़ व नींबू

with ice | baraf ke sāth | बर्फ़ के साथ

bar snacks • bār snaiks • बार स्नैक्स

crisps | kurkurā namkīn | कुरकुरा नमकीन

cashews
kājū
काजू

peanuts
mūngfalī
मूंगफ़ली

almonds
bādām
बादाम

nuts | meve | मेवे

olives | zaitūn | ज़ैतून

restaurant • restrām. • रेस्तरां

table setting
mez sajjā
मेज़ सज्जा

commis chef
sahāyak rasoiyā
सहायक रसोइया

chef
rasoiyā
रसोइया

kitchen
rasoī | रसोई

glass
gilās
गिलास

tray
ṭre
ट्रे

waiter
bairā | बैरा

vocabulary • śabdāvalī • शब्दावली

receipt rasīd रसीद	**specials** viśeṣ विशेष	**price** mūlya मूल्य	**customer** grāhak ग्राहक	**service included** sevā sammilit सेवा सम्मिलित	**à la carte** menū ke anusār मेनू के अनुसार
wine list vāin sūchī वाइन सूची	**dessert cart** pesṭrī trolley पेस्ट्री ट्रॉली	**check** bil बिल	**salt** namak नमक	**service not included** sevā sammilit nahīṃ सेवा सम्मिलित नहीं	**smoking section** dhūmrapān kṣetr धूम्रपान क्षेत्र
tip bakhśīś बख़्शीश	**pepper** kālī mirch काली मिर्च	**bar** bār बार	**buffet** bufe बुफ़े	**evening menu** sandhyākālīn menū संध्याकालीन मेनू	**lunch menu** dopahar kā menū दोपहर का मेनू

menu
vyañjan suchi
व्यंजन सूची

child's meal
bāl āhār | बाल–आहार

order (v)
order denā | ऑर्डर देना

pay (v)
dām chukānā | दाम चुकाना

courses • bhojan ke daur • भोजन के दौर

apéritif
ārambh peya
आरंभ पेय

appetizer
sṭārṭar | स्टार्टर

soup
sūp | सूप

entrée
men kors | मेन कोर्स

side order
sāiḍ order | साइड ऑर्डर

dessert | miṣṭānn | मिष्टान्न

coffee | coffee | कॉफ़ी

vocabulary • śabdavalı • शब्दावली

A table for two, please.
kr.pyā do logom. ke lie t.ebal batāem.
कृपया दो लोगों के लिए टेबल बताएं।

Can I see the menu/winelist, please?
kyā menū/vāin list. dikhāen'ge?
क्या मेनू/वाइन लिस्ट दिखाएंगे?

Is there a fixed-price menu?
kyā yah ek dām menū hai?
क्या यह एक दाम मेनू है?

Do you have any vegetarian dishes?
kyā yahām. śākāhārī khānā hai?
क्या यहां शाकाहारी खाना है?

Could I have the check/a receipt, please?
kyā mujhe bil/rasīd mil saktī hai?
क्या मुझे बिल/रसीद मिल सकती है?

Can we pay separately?
kyā ham alag-alag bil de sakte haim.?
क्या हम अलग–अलग बिल दे सकते हैं?

Where are the restrooms, please?
śauchālaya kahām. hain'?
शौचालय कहाँ हैं?

fast food • fāsṭ fūḍ • फ़ास्ट फ़ूड

burger
bargar
बर्गर

straw
straw
स्ट्रॉ

soft drink
śītal peya
शीतल पेय

french fries
french frāī
फ्रेंच फ़्राई

paper napkin
pepar naipkin
पेपर नैपकिन

tray
ṭre
ट्रे

burger meal | bargar mīl | बर्गर मील

pizza
pītsā
पीत्सा

price list
mūlya sūchī
मूल्य सूची

canned drink
ḍibbāband peya
डिब्बाबंद पेय

home delivery
hom ḍilīvarī | होम डिलीवरी

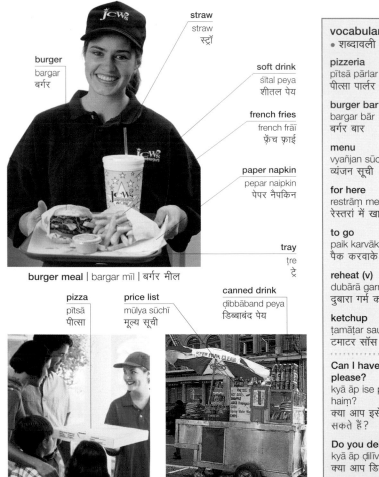

hot dog vendor
sṭrīṭ stall | स्ट्रीट स्टॉल

vocabulary • śabdāvalī • शब्दावली

pizzeria
pītsā pārlar
पीत्सा पार्लर

burger bar
bargar bār
बर्गर बार

menu
vyañjan sūchī
व्यंजन सूची

for here
restrāṃ meṃ khānā
रेस्तरां में खाना

to go
paik karvāke le jānā
पैक करवाके ले जाना

reheat (v)
dubārā garm karnā
दुबारा गर्म करना

ketchup
ṭamāṭar sauce
टमाटर सॉस

Can I have that to go, please?
kyā āp ise paik kar sakte haiṃ?
क्या आप इसे पैक कर सकते हैं?

Do you deliver?
kyā āp ḍilīvar karte haiṃ?
क्या आप डिलीवर करते हैं?

hamburger
haim bargar
हैम बर्गर

bun
ban
बन

chicken burger
chikan bargar
चिकन बर्गर

veggie burger
vej bargar
वेज बर्गर

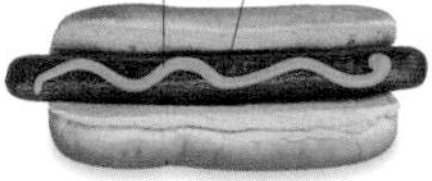
mustard
mastarḍ
मस्टर्ड
sausage
sausage
सॉसेज

hot dog
hot dog | हॉट डॉग

sandwich
saiṇḍvich
सैंडविच

club sandwich
klab saiṇḍvich
क्लब सैंडविच

open sandwich
khulā saiṇḍvich
खुला सैंडविच

filling
bharāvan
भरावन

wrap
rol | रोल

sauce
sauce
सॉस

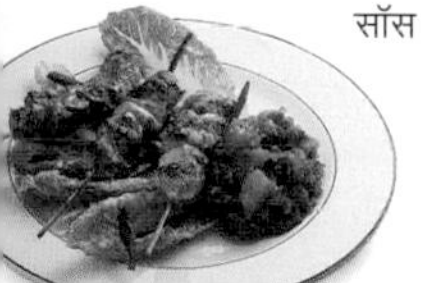

kebab
kabāb | कबाब

chicken nuggets | chikan nageṭs | चिकन नगेट्स

savory
namkīn
नमकीन
sweet
mīṭhā
मीठा

crêpes
maide kā chīlā
मैदे का चीला

fish and chips
talī machhlī aur chips
तली मछली और चिप्स

ribs
chāṃp
चांप

fried chicken
frāiḍ chikan
फ़्राइड चिकन

topping
topping
टॉपिंग

pizza
pītsā
पीत्सा

breakfast • subah kā nāśtā • सुबह का नाश्ता

milk
dūdh
दूध

cereal
sīriyal
सीरियल

jam
jaim
जैम

dried fruit
meve
मेवे

ham
haim
हैम

cheese
chīz
चीज़

crispbread
kurkurī breḍ
कुरकुरी ब्रेड

breakfast buffet
brekfāsṭ bufe | ब्रेकफ़ास्ट बुफ़े

marmalade
mārmleḍ
मार्मलेड

pâté
mīṭ kā pesṭ
मीट का पेस्ट

butter
makkhan
मक्खन

fruit juice
phaloṃ kā ras
फलों का रस

coffee
coffee
कॉफ़ी

breakfast table
nāśte kī mez | नाश्ते की मेज़

hot chocolate
hot chocolate
हॉट चॉकलेट

croissant
krosāṃ ban
क्रोसां बन

tea
chāya
चाय

drinks
peya padārth | पेय पदार्थ

brioche
mīṭhe ban | मीठे बन

bread
breḍ | ब्रेड

tomato
ṭamāṭar
टमाटर

black pudding
blaik puḍiṅg
ब्लैक पुडिंग

toast
ṭosṭ
टोस्ट

sausage
sausage
सॉसेज

fried egg
frāiḍ aṇḍā
फ़्राइड अंडा

bacon
bekan
बेकन

English breakfast
aṅgrezī nāśtā | अंग्रेज़ी नाश्ता

kippers
kipars | किपर्स

French toast
french ṭosṭ
फ़्रेंच टोस्ट

yolk
zardī
ज़र्दी

boiled egg
ublā aṇḍā
उबला अंडा

scrambled eggs
aṇḍe kī bhurjī | अंडे की भुर्जी

fruit yogurt
frūṭ dahī
फ़्रूट दही

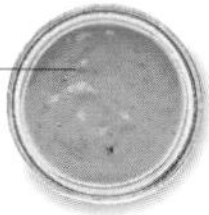

crêpes
painkek | पैनकेक

cream
krīm
क्रीम

waffles
waffles | वॉफ़ल्स

oatmeal
daliyā | दलिया

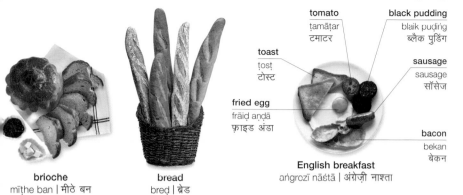

fresh fruit
tāze phal | ताज़े फल

dinner • d.inar • डिनर

soup
sūp | सूप

broth
śorbā | शोरबा

stew
dampuḳht | दमपुख़्त

curry
rasedār | रसेदार

roast
bhunā | भुना

pie
pāī | पाई

soufflé
sūfle | सूफ़्ले

kebab
kabāb | कबाब

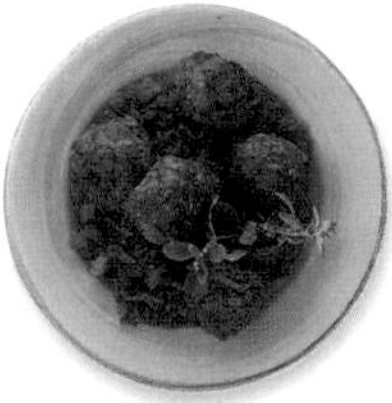

meatballs
kofte | कोफ़्ते

omelet
omelette | ऑमलेट

noodles
nūḍals
नूडल्स

stir fry | kam tel meṃ bhunā | कम तेल में भुना

pasta
pāstā | पास्ता

rice
chāval | चावल

tossed salad | miśrit salād | मिश्रित सलाद

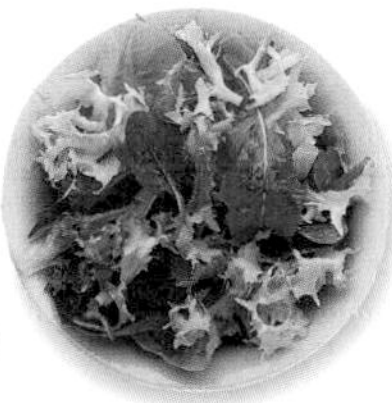

green salad
harā salād | हरा सलाद

dressing
ḍresiṅg | ड्रेसिंग

techniques • vidhiyāṃ • विधियां

stuffed
bharvāṃ | भरवां

in sauce | sauce meṃ
सॉस में

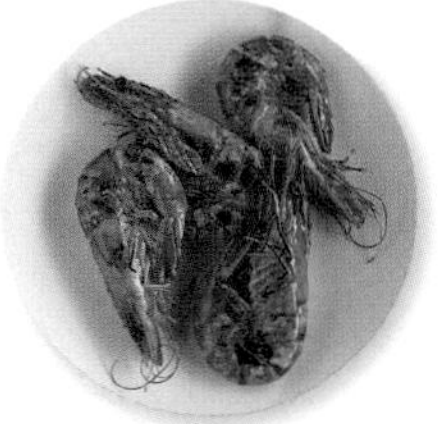

grilled
bhunā huā | भुना हुआ

marinated | masāle meṃ
lipṭā | मसाले में लिपटा

poached
pochaḍ | पोच्ड

mashed
maslā huā | मसला हुआ

baked | bek kiyā
huā | बेक किया हुआ

pan-fried | kam tel meṃ
pakā | कम तेल में पका

fried
talā huā | तला हुआ

pickled
achārit | अचारित

smoked
dhūmrit | धूम्रित

deep fried
talā huā | तला हुआ

syrup | sirap meṃ
banā | सिरप में बना

dressed | ḍresiṅg kiyā
huā | ड्रेसिंग किया हुआ

steamed | bhāp meṃ
pakā | भाप में पका

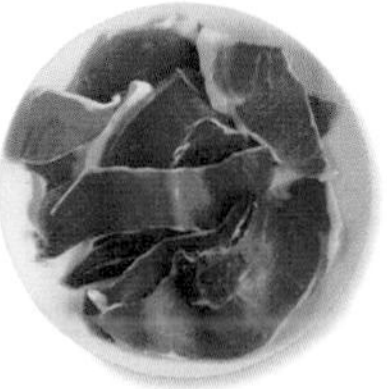

cured
sanrakṣit | संरक्षित

study
adhyayan
अध्ययन

school • vidyālaya • विद्यालय

blackboard | śyāmpaṭṭ | श्यामपट्ट

student | chhātr | छात्र

teacher | adhyāpikā | अध्यापिका

desk | beñch | बेंच

chalk | chalk | चॉक

classroom | kakṣā | कक्षा

schoolbag | skūl bastā | स्कूल बस्ता

schoolgirl | skūl chhātrā | स्कूल छात्रा

schoolboy | skūl chhātra | स्कूल छात्

vocabulary • śabdāvalī • शब्दावली

history itihās इतिहास	**science** vijñān विज्ञान	**physics** bhautikī भौतिकी
languages bhāṣāeṃ भाषाएं	**art** kalā कला	**chemistry** rasāyan śāstr रसायन शास्त्र
literature sāhitya साहित्य	**music** saṅgīt संगीत	**biology** jīv vijñān जीव विज्ञान
geography bhūgol भूगोल	**math** gaṇit गणित	**physical education** vyāyām śikṣā व्यायाम शिक्षा

activities • gatividhiyāṃ • गतिविधिय

read (v) | paṛhnā | पढ़ना

write (v) | likhnā | लिखन

spell (v) | uchchāraṇ karnā | उच्चारण करना

draw (v) | chitr banānā | चित्र बनाना

digital projector
ḍijiṭal projekṭar
डिजिटल प्रोजेक्टर

nib
nib
निब

pen
pen | पेन

colored pencil
raṅgīn pensil
रंगीन पेंसिल

pencil
pensil | पेंसिल

pencil sharpener
pensil śārpnar
पेंसिल शार्पनर

eraser
rabaṛ | रबड़

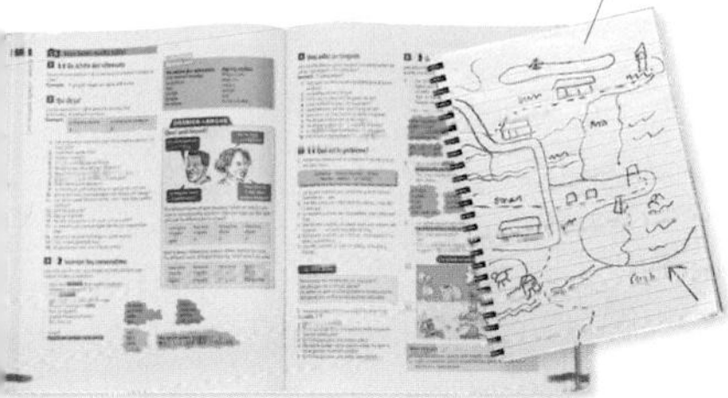

notebook
copy | कॉपी

textbook | pāṭhya pustak | पाठ्य पुस्तक

pencil case
pensil kes | पेंसिल केस

ruler
paimānā | पैमाना

question (v) | praśan pūchhnā | प्रश्न पूछना

answer (v)
uttar denā | उत्तर देना

discuss (v) | vichār-vimarś karnā | विचार–विमर्श करना

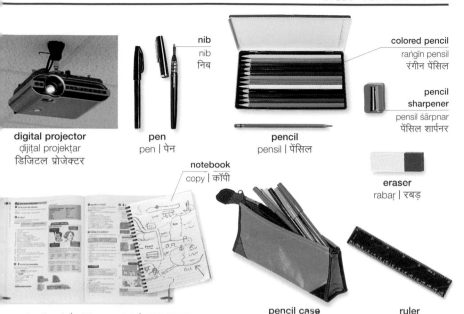

learn (v)
sīkhnā | सीखना

vocabulary • śabdāvalī • शब्दावली

principal
mukhyādhyāpak/ mukhyādhyāpikā
मुख्याध्यापक / मुख्याध्यापिका

lesson
adhyāya
अध्याय

question
praśan
प्रश्न

take notes (v)
noṭs lenā
नोट्स लेना

answer
uttar
उत्तर

homework
gṛhkārya
गृहकार्य

test
parīkṣā
परीक्षा

essay
nibandh
निबंध

grade
śreṇī
श्रेणी

year
varṣ
वर्ष

dictionary
śabdkoś
शब्दकोश

encyclopaedia
viśvakoś
विश्वकोश

math • gaṇit • गणित

shapes • ākṛtiyāṃ • आकृतियां

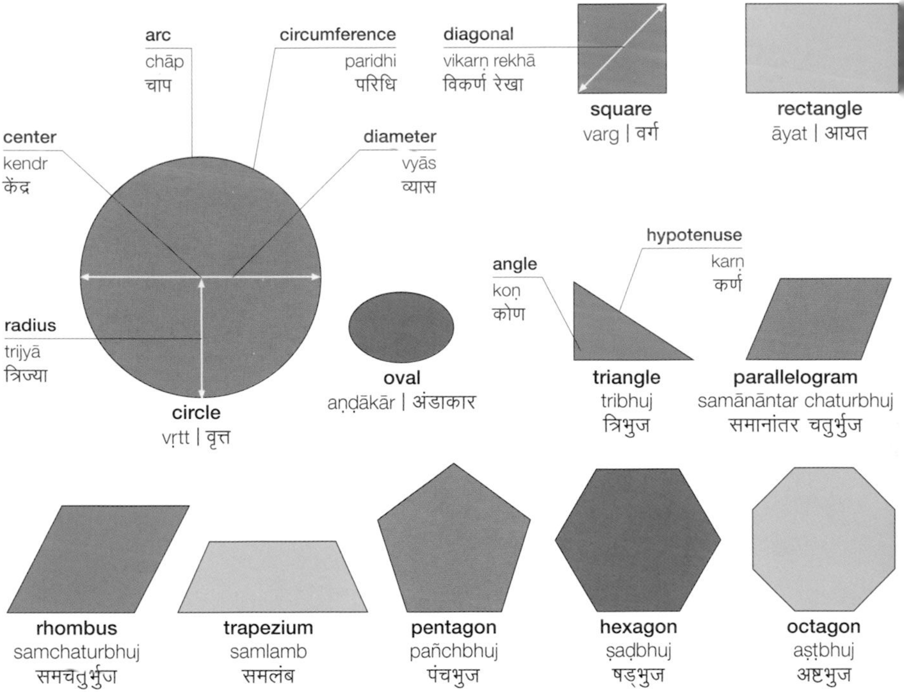
arc
chāp
चाप
circumference
paridhi
परिधि
diagonal
vikarṇ rekhā
विकर्ण रेखा
square
varg | वर्ग
rectangle
āyat | आयत
center
kendr
केंद्र
diameter
vyās
व्यास
radius
trijyā
त्रिज्या
circle
vṛtt | वृत्त
oval
aṇḍākār | अंडाकार
hypotenuse
karṇ
कर्ण
angle
koṇ
कोण
triangle
tribhuj
त्रिभुज
parallelogram
samānāntar chaturbhuj
समानांतर चतुर्भुज
rhombus
samchaturbhuj
समचतुर्भुज
trapezium
samlamb
समलंब
pentagon
pañchbhuj
पंचभुज
hexagon
ṣaḍbhuj
षड्भुज
octagon
aṣṭbhuj
अष्टभुज

solids • ghanākṛtiyāṃ • घनाकृतियां

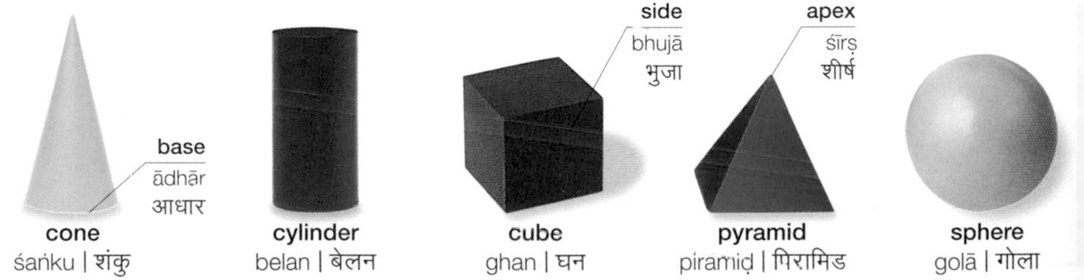
side
bhujā
भुजा
apex
śīrṣ
शीर्ष
base
ādhār
आधार
cone
śaṅku | शंकु
cylinder
belan | बेलन
cube
ghan | घन
pyramid
piramiḍ | पिरामिड
sphere
golā | गोला

lines • rekhāeṃ • रेखाएं

straight	parallel	perpendicular	curved
sīdhī | सीधी	samānāntar | समानांतर	lamb | लंब	vakr | वक्र

measurements • māpak • मापक

numerator
aṃś
अंश

denominator
har
हर

width
chauṛāī
चौड़ाई

length
lambāī
लंबाई

height
ūṃchāī
ऊंचाई

depth
gahrāī
गहराई

volume	fraction	dimensions	area
parimāṇ | परिमाण	bhinn | भिन्न	āyām | आयाम	kṣetraphal | क्षेत्रफल

equipment • upkaraṇ • उपकरण

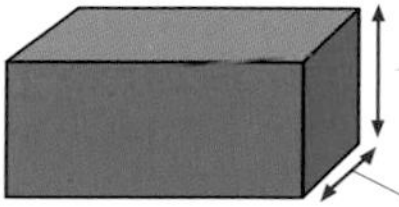

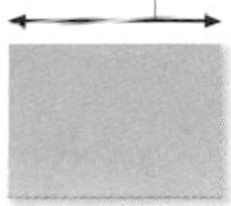

square	protractor	ruler	compass	calculator
samkoṇak	koṇmāpak/ḍī	paimānā	parkār	kailkyuleṭar
समकोणक	कोणमापक/डी	पैमाना	परकार	कैलक्युलेटर

vocabulary • śabdāvalī • शब्दावली

geometry	plus	times	equals	add (v)	multiply (v)	equation
rekhāgaṇit	jamā	gunā	barābar	jornā	gunā karnā	samīkaraṇ
रेखागणित	जमा	गुना	बराबर	जोड़ना	गुणा करना	समीकरण

arithmetic	minus	divided by	count (v)	subtract (v)	divide (v)	percentage
aṅkgaṇit	ghaṭā	bhājak	ginnā	ghaṭānā	bhāg denā	pratiśat
अंकगणित	घटा	भाजक	गिनना	घटाना	भाग देना	प्रतिशत

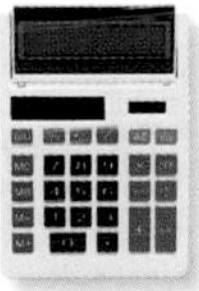

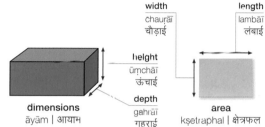

science • vijñān • विज्ञान

laboratory
prayogśālā | प्रयोगशाला

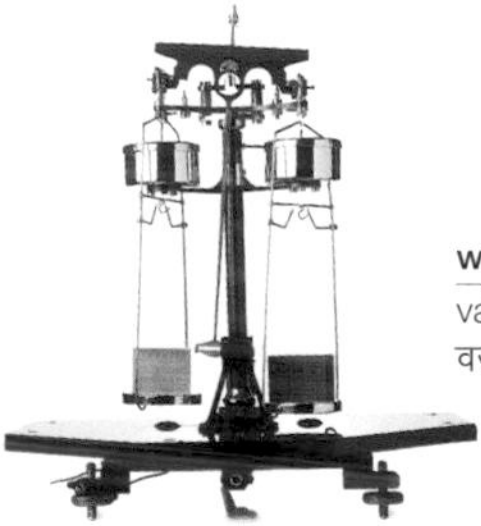

scales
tarāzū | तराज़ू

weight
vazan
वज़न

spring balance
spriṅg tulā | स्प्रिंग तुला

crucible
kuṭhālī
कुठाली
bunsen burner
bansan barnar
बनसन बर्नर

tripod
tipāī | तिपाई

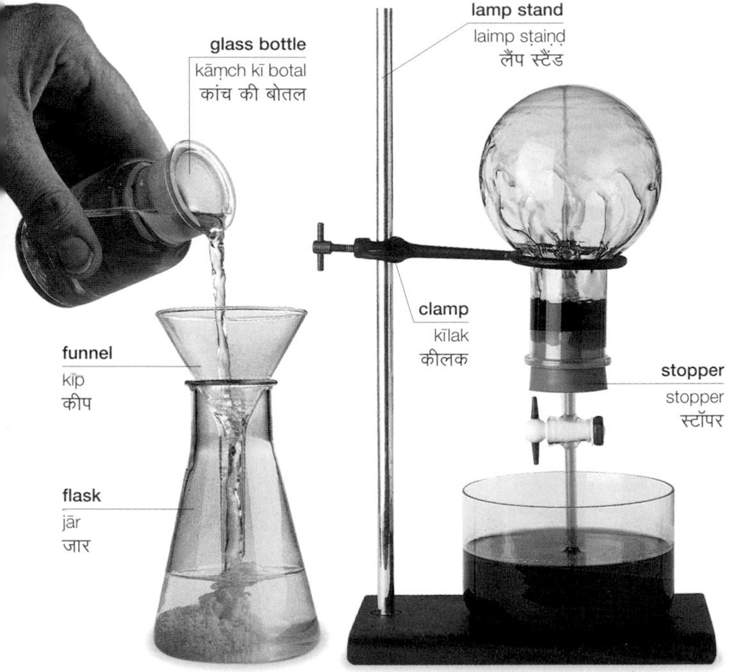
glass bottle
kāṃch kī botal
कांच की बोतल
lamp stand
laimp sṭaiṇḍ
लैंप स्टैंड
funnel
kīp
कीप
clamp
kīlak
कीलक
stopper
stopper
स्टॉपर
flask
jār
जार

experiment | prayog | प्रयोग

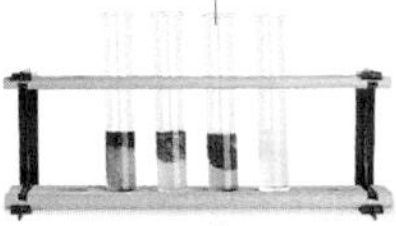
test tube
parakhnalī
परखनली

rack
raik | रैक

timer
ṭāimar | टाइमर

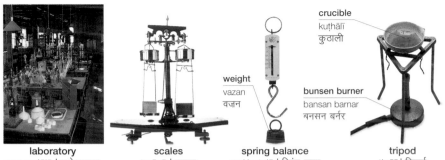

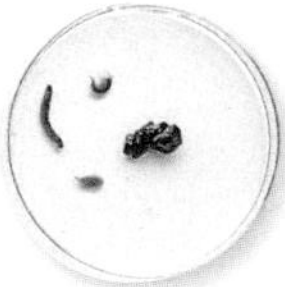

petri dish
peṭrī ḍiś | पेट्री ङिश

thermometer
tharmāmīṭar | थर्मामीटर

syringe
siriṅj | सिरिंज

tweezers
chhoṭī chimṭī | छोटी चिमटी

scalpel
chākū | चाकू

dropper
dropper | ड्रॉपर

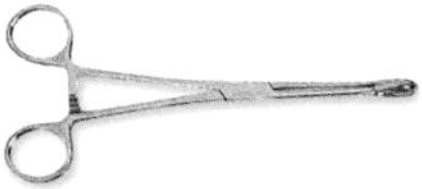
forceps
forceps | फ़ॉरसेप

tongs
baṛī chimṭī | बड़ी चिमटी

spatula
spaiṭyūlā | स्पैट्यूला

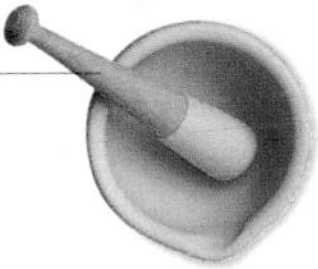
pestle
mūsal
मूसल

mortar
kharal | खरल

filter paper
filṭar pepar | फिल्टर पेपर

safety goggles | surakṣā chaśmā | सुरक्षा चश्मा

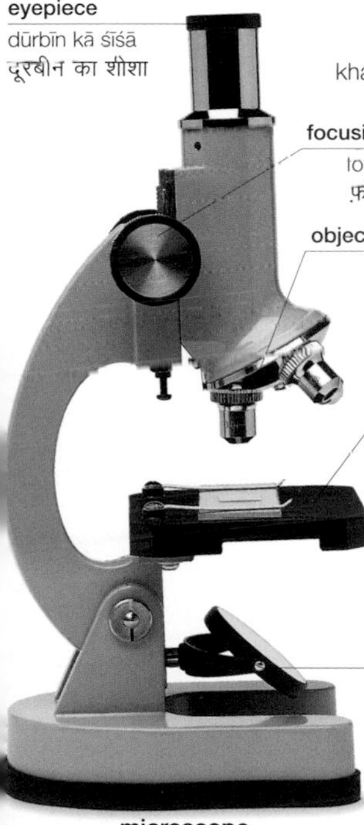
eyepiece
dūrbīn kā śīśā
दूरबीन का शीशा

focusing knob
fokas knob
फ़ोकस नॉब

objective lens
lains
लैंस

stage
tal
तल

slide
slāiḍ
स्लाइड

mirror
śīśā
शीशा

microscope
sūkṣamdarśī | सूक्ष्मदर्शी

pipette
nalikā | नलिका

glass stirrer
kāṃch kī chhaṛ
कांच की छड़

beaker
bīkar | बीकर

magnet
chumbak
चुंबक

alligator clip
daṃtedār chimṭī
दांतेदार चिमटी

negative electrode
negeṭiv electrode
नेगेटिव इलेक्ट्रॉड

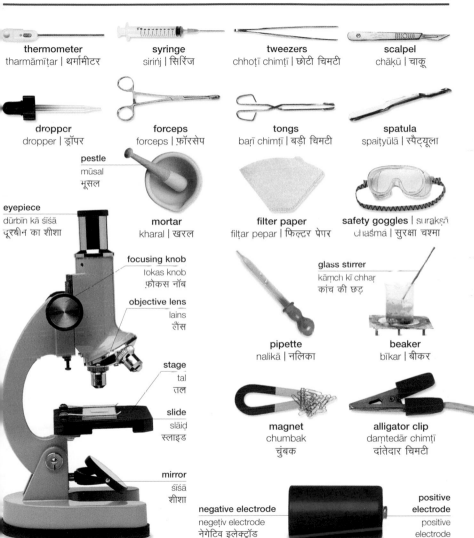

positive electrode
positive electrode
पॉज़ीटिव इलेक्ट्रॉड

battery
baiṭrī | बैटरी

college • mahāvidyālaya • महाविद्यालय

office
praveś
प्रवेश
cafeteria
bhojan kakṣ
भोजन कक्ष
clinic
svāsthya kendr
स्वास्थ्य केंद्र
sports field
khel kā
maidān
खेल का मैदान
residence hall
chhātrāvās
छात्रावास

campus | parisar | परिसर

librarian
pustakālaya adhyakṣ
पुस्तकालय अध्यक्ष
circulation desk
pustak prāpti
पुस्तक प्राप्ति
bookshelves
pustakoṃ
kī almārī
पुस्तकों की
अलमारी
periodical
patrikāeṃ
पत्रिकाएं
journal
patrikāeṃ
पत्रिकाएं

library | pustakālaya | पुस्तकालय

vocabulary • śabdāvalī • शब्दावली

library card pustakālaya kārḍ पुस्तकालय कार्ड	**help desk** pūchhtāchh पूछताछ	**loan** udhār उधार
reading room adhyayan kakṣ अध्ययन कक्ष	**borrow (v)** udhār lenā उधार लेना	**book** pustak पुस्तक
reading list adhyayan sūchī अध्ययन सूची	**reserve (v)** surakṣit karnā सुरक्षित करना	**title** śīrṣak शीर्षक
due date deya tithi देय तिथि	**renew (v)** navīkṛt karvānā नवीकृत करवाना	**aisle** galiyārā गलियारा

undergraduate
pūrvsnātak
पूर्वस्नातक
professor
prādhyāpak
प्राध्यापक

lecture hall
lekchar thiyeṭar | लेक्चर थियेटर

graduate
snātak
स्नातक
robe
chogā | चोग़ा

graduation ceremony
snātak samāroh | स्नातक समारोह

schools • vidyālaya • विद्यालय

model
model
मॉडल

art college | kalā mahāvidyālaya | कला महाविद्यालय

music school
saṅgīt vidyālaya | संगीत विद्यालय

dance academy
nṛtya akādmī | नृत्य अकादमी

vocabulary • śabdāvalī • शब्दावली

scholarship chhātrvṛtti छात्रवृत्ति	**research** anusandhān अनुसंधान	**dissertation** śodh nibandh शोध निबंध	**medicine** āyurvijñān आयुर्विज्ञान	**philosophy** darśan śāstr दर्शन शास्त्र
diploma ḍiplomā डिप्लोमा	**master's degree** viśārad विशारद	**department** vibhāg विभाग	**zoology** prāṇī vijñān प्राणी विज्ञान	**literature** sāhitya साहित्य
degree upādhi उपाधि	**doctorate** doctorate डॉक्ट्रेट	**law** ḳānūn क़ानून	**physics** bhautikī भौतिकी	**art history** kalā kā itihās कला का इतिहास
postgraduate snātakottar स्नातकोत्तर	**thesis** śodh prabandh शोध प्रबंध	**engineering** abhiyāntrikī अभियांत्रिकी	**politics** rājnīti राजनीति	**economics** arthśāstr अर्थशास्त्र

work
kārya
कार्य

office 1 • kāryālaya • कार्यालय

desktop organizer
desktop organizer
डेस्कटॉप ऑर्गेनाइज़र
laptop
laptop
लैपटॉप
monitor
monitor
मॉनीटर
in-tray
in-ṭre
इन–ट्रे
out-tray
āuṭ-ṭre
आउट–ट्रे
drawer
darāz
दराज़
notebook
copy
कॉपी
desk
mez
मेज़
swivel chair
ghumāū kursī
घुमाऊ कुर्सी
wastebasket
raddī kī ṭokrī
रद्दी की टोकरी
filing cabinet
fāil-darāz
फ़ाइल–दराज़

office equipment • kāryālayī upkaraṇ • कार्यालयी उपकरण

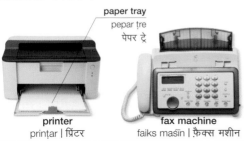

paper tray
pepar ṭre
पेपर ट्रे

printer
prinṭar | प्रिंटर

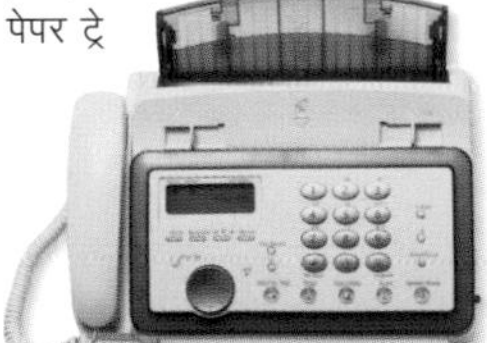

fax machine
faiks maśīn | फ़ैक्स मशीन

vocabulary • śabdāvalī • शब्दावली

print (v)
prinṭ lenā
प्रिंट लेना

enlarge (v)
baṛā karnā
बड़ा करना

copy (v)
prati banānā
प्रति बनाना

reduce (v)
chhoṭā karnā
छोटा करना

I need to make some copies
mujhe kuchh pratiyāṃ banānī haiṃ.
मुझे कुछ प्रतियां बनानी हैं।

office supplies • kāryālayī vastueṃ • कार्यालयी वस्तुएं

compliments slip
preṣak parchī
प्रेषक पर्ची

letterhead
laiṭar haiḍ
लैटर हैड

envelope
lifāfā | लिफ़ाफ़ा

box file
box fāil
बॉक्स फ़ाइल

ring binder
līvar ārch fail
लीवर आर्च फ़ाइल

clipboard
klip borḍ
क्लिप बोर्ड

notepad
noṭ paiḍ
नोट पैड

tab
ṭaib
टैब

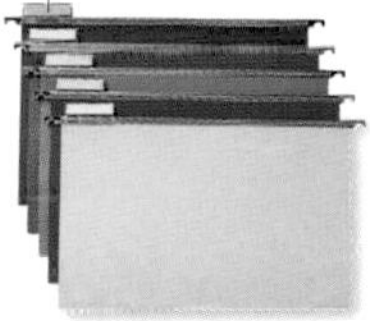

hanging file
hainging fāil
हैंगिंग फ़ाइल

divider
vibhājak
विभाजक

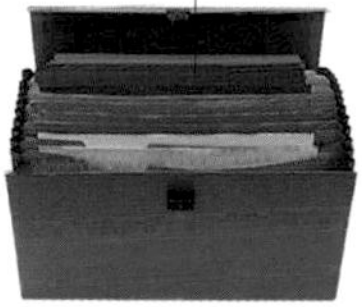

accordion file
concertina fāil
कॉनसर्टीना फ़ाइल

personal organizer
nijī organizer
निजी ऑर्गेनाइज़र

staples
sṭepals
स्टेपल्स

stapler
sṭeplar
स्टेप्लर

adhesive tape
ṭep
टेप

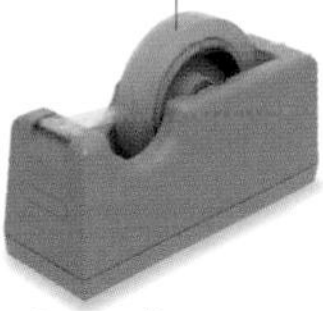

tape dispenser
ṭep ḍispensar
टेप डिस्पेंसर

hole punch
hol pañch
होल पंच

ink pad
syāhī paiḍ
स्याही पैड

rubber stamp
rabaṛ kī mohar
रबड़ की मोहर

rubber band
rabaṛ bainḍ
रबड़ बैंड

bulldog clip
baṛī klip
बड़ी क्लिप

paper clip
pepar klip
पेपर क्लिप

drawing pin
thumbtack
ड्रॉइंग पिन

notice board
sūchanā paṭṭ | सूचना पट्ट

office 2 • kāryālaya • कार्यालय

flipchart
flip chārṭ
फ़्लिप चार्ट
minutes
kāryavṛtt
कार्यवृत्त
easel
chitrādhār
चित्राधार
report
prativedan
प्रतिवेदन
manager
prabandhak
प्रबंधक
proposal
prastāv
प्रस्ताव
executive
ekzīkyūṭi
एक्ज़ीक्यूटि

meeting | sabhā/mīṭiṅg | सभा/मीटिंग

vocabulary • śabdāvalī • शब्दावली

meeting room
sabhā kakṣ
सभा कक्ष

agenda
kāryasūchī
कार्यसूची

attend (v)
upasthit rahnā
उपस्थित रहना

chair (v)
adhyakṣtā karnā
अध्यक्षता करना

What time is the meeting?
mīṭiṅg kis samaya hai?
मीटिंग किस समय है?

What are your office hours?
āpake kāryālay kā samay kyā hai?
आपके कार्यालय का समय क्या है?

speaker
vaktā
वक्ता

presentation | prastutīkaraṇ | प्रस्तुतीकरण

business • vyavsāya • व्यवसाय

businessman
vyavsāyī
व्यवसायी

businesswoman
mahilā vyavsāyī
महिला व्यवसायी

business lunch | biznes lanch | बिज़नेस लंच

business trip | biznes ṭrip | बिज़नेस ट्रिप

appointment
milne kā samaya
मिलने का समय

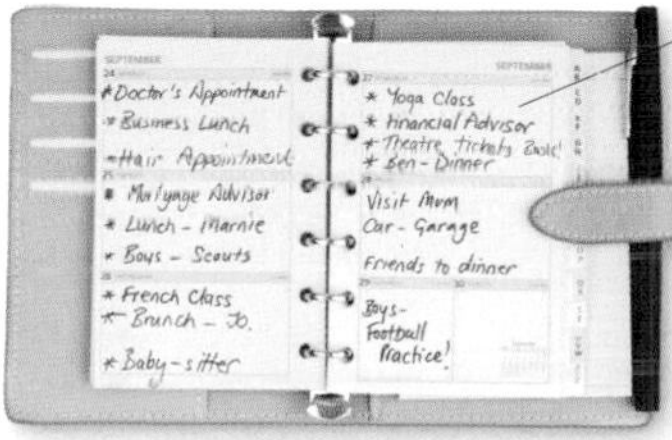

organizer | ḍāyarī | डायरी

client
grāhak
ग्राहक

CEO
prabandh nideśak
प्रबंध निदेशक

business deal
vyāvsāyik saudā | व्यावसायिक सौदा

vocabulary • śabdāvalī • शब्दावली

company
kampnī
कंपनी

headquarters
pradhān kāryālaya
प्रधान कार्यालय

regional office
śākhā
शाखा

staff
karmchārī varg
कर्मचारी वर्ग

salary
vetan
वेतन

payroll
vetansūchī
वेतनसूची

accounts department
lekhā vibhāg
लेखा विभाग

marketing department
vipṇan vibhāg
विपणन विभाग

sales department
bikrī vibhāg
बिक्री विभाग

legal department
ḳānūnī vibhāg
क़ानूनी विभाग

customer service department
grāhak sevā vibhāg
ग्राहक सेवा विभाग

human resources department
kārmik vibhāg
कार्मिक विभाग

computer • kampyūṭar • कंप्यूटर

printer
prinṭar
प्रिंटर

scanner
skainar
स्कैनर

screen
skrīn
स्क्रीन

laptop
laptop | लैपटॉप

speaker
spīkar | स्पीकर

key
kī | की

keyboard
kunjīpaṭal
कुंजीपटल

mouse
māus | माउस

hardware | hārḍveyar | हार्डवेयर

memory stick
memorī sṭik | मेमोरी स्टिक

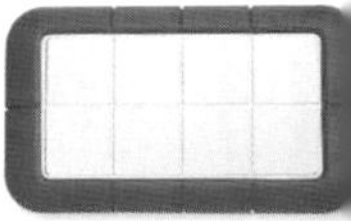

external hard drive
bāharī hārḍ ḍrāiv
बाहरी हार्ड ड्राइव

vocabulary • śabdāvalī • शब्दावली

memory memorī मेमोरी	**software** software सॉफ़्टवेयर	**server** sarvar सर्वर
RAM raim रैम	**application** eplīkeśan एप्लीकेशन	**port** porṭ पोर्ट
bytes bāiṭs बाइट्स	**program** progrām प्रोग्राम	**processor** prosesar प्रोसेसर
system sisṭam सिस्टम	**network** neṭvark नेटवर्क	**power cord** vidyut tār विद्युत तार

iPad©
āī paiḍ | आई पैड

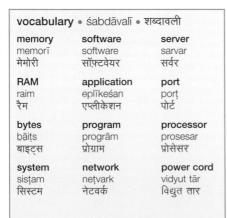

smartphone
smārṭfon | स्मार्टफ़ोन

desktop • desktop • डेस्कटॉप

font
font
फ़ॉन्ट

menu bar
menū bār
मेनू बार

toolbar
ṭūlbār
टूलबार

wallpaper
wallpaper
वॉलपेपर

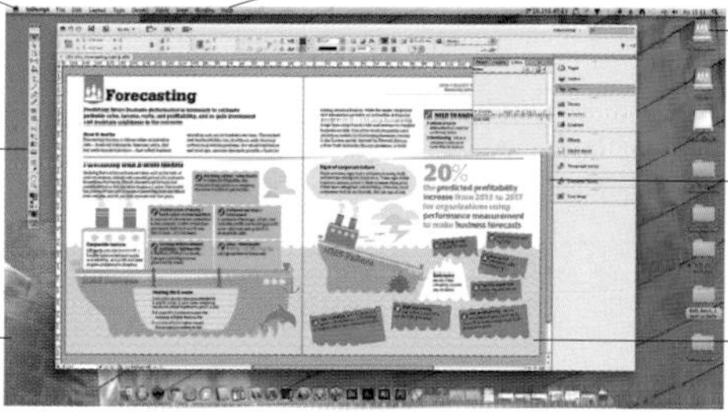

icon
āikan
आइकन

scrollbar
skrolbār
स्क्रोलबार

window
vinḍo
विंडो

file
fāil | फ़ाइल

folder
folḍar | फ़ोल्डर

trash | ṭraiś | ट्रैश

internet • inṭarneṭ • इंटरनेट

browser
brāuzar
ब्राउज़र

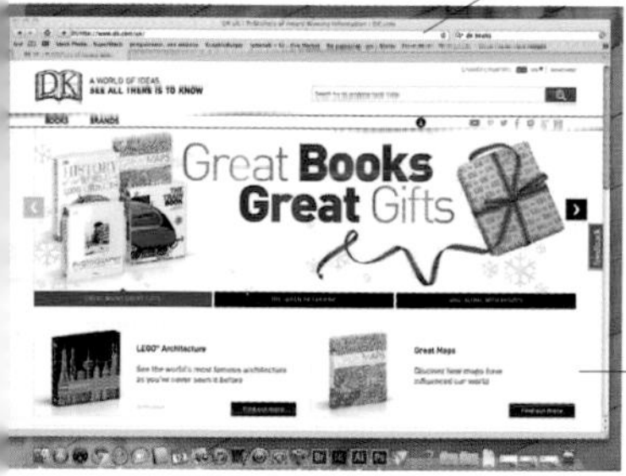

website
vebsāiṭ
वेबसाइट

browse (v)
brāuz | ब्राउज़

email • ī-mel • ई–मेल

email address
ī-mel patā
ई–मेल पता

inbox
inbox
इनबॉक्स

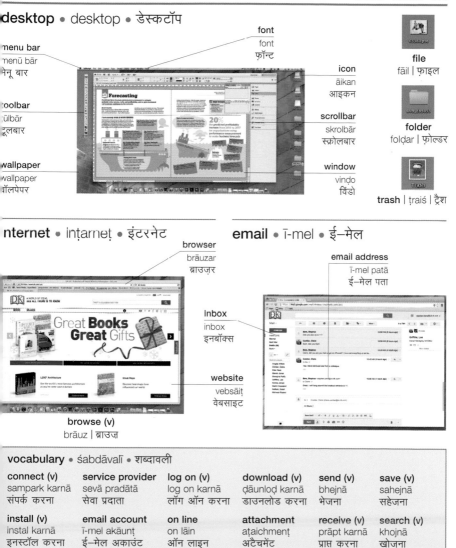

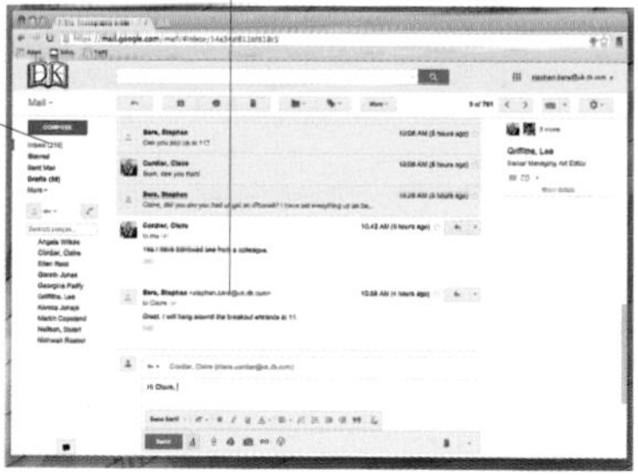

vocabulary • śabdāvalī • शब्दावली

connect (v) sampark karnā संपर्क करना	**service provider** sevā pradātā सेवा प्रदाता	**log on (v)** log on karnā लॉग ऑन करना	**download (v)** ḍāunloḍ karnā डाउनलोड करना	**send (v)** bhejnā भेजना	**save (v)** sahejnā सहेजना
install (v) instal karnā इनस्टॉल करना	**email account** ī-mel akāunṭ ई–मेल अकाउंट	**on line** on lāin ऑन लाइन	**attachment** aṭaichmenṭ अटैचमेंट	**receive (v)** prāpt karnā प्राप्त करना	**search (v)** khojnā खोजना

media • mīḍiyā • मीडिया

television studio • ṭelīvizan stūḍiyo • टेलीविज़न स्टूडियो

set	presenter	light
seṭ	prastutkartā	lāiṭ
सेट	प्रस्तुतकर्ता	लाइट

camera	camera crane	cameraman
kaimrā	kaimrā kren	kaimrāmain
कैमरा	कैमरा क्रेन	कैमरामैन

vocabulary • śabdāvalī • शब्दावली

channel	news	press	soap opera	cartoon	live
chainal	samāchār	prais	nāṭak	kārṭūn	sīdhā prasāraṇ
चैनल	समाचार	प्रैस	नाटक	कार्टून	सीधा प्रसारण

programming	documentary	television series	game show	prerecorded	broadcast (v)
progrāming	vṛttchitr	ṭelīvizan śriṅkhlā	gem śo	pūrv recorded	prasārit karnā
प्रोग्रामिंग	वृत्तचित्र	टेलीविज़न शृंखला	गेम शो	पूर्व रिकॉर्डेड	प्रसारित करना

interviewer
sākṣātkārkartā
साक्षात्कारकर्ता

reporter
patrakār | पत्रकार

teleprompter
ṭelī prompṭar
टेली प्रॉम्प्टर

anchor | samāchār vāchak | समाचार वाचक

actors
abhinetā | अभिनेता

sound boom
sāuṇḍ būm | साउंड बूम

clapper board | klaipar borḍ | क्लैपर बोर्ड

movie set
film seṭ | फ़िल्म सेट

radio • reḍiyo • रेडियो

sound technician
sāuṇḍ taknīśiyan
साउंड तकनीशियन

mixing desk
miksiṅg ḍesk
मिक्सिंग डेस्क

microphone
māikrofon
माइक्रोफ़ोन

recording studio | recording sṭūḍiyo | रिकॉर्डिंग स्टूडियो

vocabulary • śabdāvalī • शब्दावली

radio station reḍiyo sṭeśan रेडियो स्टेशन	**frequency** āvṛtti आवृत्ति
broadcast prasāraṇ प्रसारण	**volume** dhvani star ध्वनि स्तर
wavelength vevlenth वेवलैंथ	**DJ** ḍīje डीजे
long wave long vev लॉन्ग वेव	**short wave** short vev शॉर्ट वेव
tune (v) chainal seṭ karnā चैनल सेट करना	**medium wave** mīḍiyam vev मीडियम वेव
analog enālog एनालॉग	**digital** ḍijiṭal डिजिटल

law • ḳānūn • क़ानून

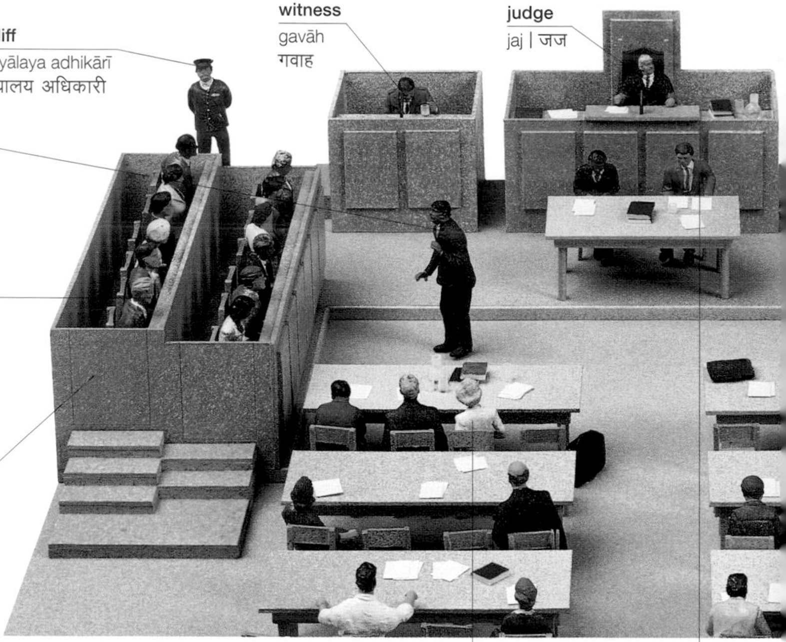
witness
gavāh
गवाह
judge
jaj | जज
bailiff
nyāyālaya adhikārī
न्यायालय अधिकारी
lawyer
vakīl
वकील
jury
jūrī
जूरी
jury box
jūrī box
जूरी बॉक्स
courtroom
nyāyālaya | न्यायालय
prosecution
abhiyojan
अभियोजन
clerk
nyāyālaya karmchārī
न्यायालय कर्मचारी

vocabulary • śabdāvalī • शब्दावली

lawyer's office
vakīl kā kāryālaya
वकील का कार्यालय

legal advice
ḳānūnī salāh
क़ानूनी सलाह

client
muvakkil
मुवक्किल

summons
saman
समन

statement
bayān
बयान

warrant
vāran.t.
वारंट

writ
rit.
रिट

court date
nyāyālaya kī tārīḳh
न्यायालय की तारीख़

plea
pairavī
पैरवी

court case
muḳaddmā
मुक़द्दमा

charge
abhiyog
अभियोग

accused
abhiyukt
अभियुक्त

defendant
prativādī
प्रतिवादी

stenographer
āśulipik
आशुलिपिक

defense
bachāv pakṣ
बचाव पक्ष

suspect
sandigdh
संदिग्ध

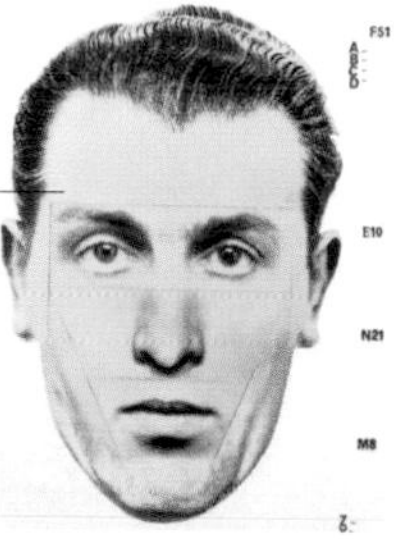

composite
anumānit tasvīr
अनुमानित तस्वीर

criminal
aprādhī
अपराधी

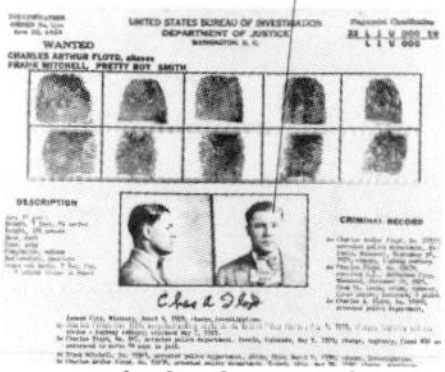

criminal record
āprādhik record
आपराधिक रिकॉर्ड

prison guard | jel kā pahredār | जेल का पहरेदार

cell | jel kī koṭhrī | जेल की कोठरी

prison
jel | जेल

vocabulary • śabdāvalī • शब्दावली

evidence
sabūt
सबूत

verdict
faislā
फ़ैसला

innocent
bek.asūr
बेक़सूर

guilty
dos.ī
दोषी

acquitted
abhimukt
अभिमुक्त

sentence
dan.d.ādeś
दंडादेश

bail
zamānat
ज़मानत

appeal
apīl
अपील

parole
pairol
पैरोल

I want to see a lawyer.
mujhe ek vakīl chāhie.
मुझे एक वकील चाहिए

Where is the courthouse?
nyāyālaya kahām. hai?
न्यायालय कहां है?

Can I post bail?
kyā maim. zamānat bhar saktā hūm.?
क्या मैं ज़मानत भर सकता हूं?

farm • khet • खेत

farmer
kisān
किसान

farmland kṛṣi bhūmi कृषि भूमि
farmyard ahātā अहाता
outbuilding āuṭ hāus आउट हाउस
farmhouse fārm hāus फ़ार्म हाउस
field khet खेत
barn khalihān खलिहान
vegetable garden śāk khet शाक खेत
gate darvāzā दरवाज़ा
hedge meṛ मेड़
fence bāṛ बाड़
pasture charāgāh चरागाह
livestock paśudhan पशुधन

cultivator phāl फाल

tractor
ṭrekṭar | ट्रेक्टर

combine
kaṭāī maśīn | कटाई मशीन

types of farm • khetoṃ ke prakār • खेतों के प्रकार

crop farm
khetī yogya bhūmi
खेती योग्य भूमि

dairy farm
deyarī fārm
डेयरी फ़ार्म

sheep farm
bheṛoṃ kā bāṛā
भेड़ों का बाड़ा

poultry farm
murgī pālan kendr
मुर्गी पालन केंद्र

pig farm
śūar pālan kendr
सूअर पालन केंद्र

fish farm
machhlī pālan kṣetr
मछली पालन क्षेत्र

fruit farm
phaloṃ kā bāġ
फलों का बाग़

vineyard
aṃgūr kā bāġ
अंगूर का बाग़

actions • khetoṃ ke kāmkāj • खेतों के कामकाज

plow (v)
jotnā | जोतना

sow (v)
bonā | बोना

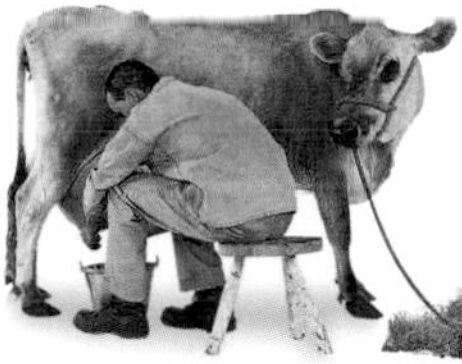

milk (v)
dūdh duhnā | दूध दुहना

feed (v)
charnā | चरना

water (v)
sīṃchnā | सींचना

harvest (v)
fasal kāṭnā | फ़सल काटना

vocabulary • śabdāvalī • शब्दावली

herbicide
vanaspatināśak
वनस्पतिनाशक

herd
jhuṇḍ
झुंड

trough
nāṃd
नांद

pesticide
kīṭnāśak
कीटनाशक

silo
khattī
खत्ती

plant (v)
ropna
रोपना

farm • khet • खेत

crops • fasal • फ़सल

wheat
gehūṃ | गेहूं

corn
makaī | मकई

barley
jau | जौ

rapeseed | safed sarsoṃ | सफ़ेद सरसों

sunflower
sūrajmukhī | सूरजमुखी

bale
gaṭṭhā | गट्ठा

hay
sūkhī ghās | सूखी घास

alfalfa
alfālfā | अल्फ़ाल्फ़ा

tobacco
tambāḳū | तंबाक़ू

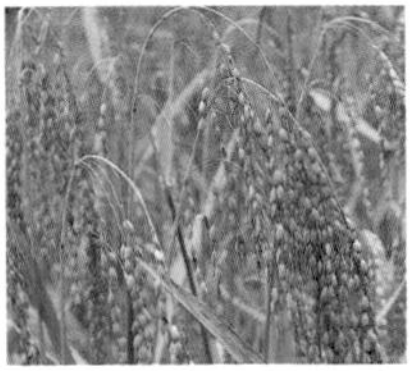

rice
dhān | धान

tea
chāya | चाय

coffee
coffee | कॉफ़ी

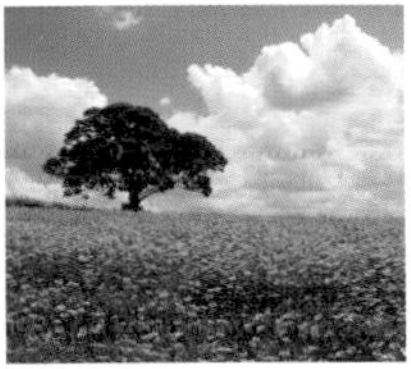

flax
alsī
अलसी

sugarcane
gannā
गन्ना

cotton
kapās
कपास

scarecrow
bijūkā
बिजूका

livestock • paśudhan • पशुधन

piglet
śiśu sūar
शिशु सूअर

pig
sūar | सूअर

calf
bachhṛā
बछड़ा

cow
gāya | गाय

bull
bail | बैल

sheep
bheṛ | भेड़

lamb
meṛhā | मेढ़ा

kid
memnā | मेमना

goat
bakrī | बकरी

foal
śiśu aśv
शिशु अश्व

horse
ghoṛā | घोड़ा

donkey
gadhā | गधा

chick
chūzā | चूज़ा

chicken
murgī | मुर्गी

rooster
murgā | मुर्गा

turkey
ṭarkī | टर्की

duckling
śiśu bataḳh
शिशु बतख़

duck
bataḳh | बतख़

stable
astabal | अस्तबल

pen
bāṛā | बाड़ा

chicken coop
daṛbā | दड़बा

pig sty
sūarbāṛā | सूअरबाड़ा

construction • nirmāṇ kārya • निर्माण कार्य

scaffolding
pāṛ | पाड़

pallet
taḳhte
तख़्ते

ladder
sīṛhī
सीढ़ी

window
khiṛkī
खिड़की

rafte
kaṛī/śahtī
कड़ी/शहतीर

forklift truck
kren
क्रेन

building site
nirmāṇ sthal
निर्माण स्थल

lintel
chaukhaṭ
चौखट

wa
dīvā
दीवार

girder
gardar
गर्डर

hard hat
ṭop
टोप

build (v)
nirmāṇ karnā | निर्माण करना

toolbelt
auzār peṭī
औज़ार पेटी

beam
śahtīr
शहतीर

construction worker
rājgīr | राजगीर

cement
sīmenṭ
सीमेंट

cement mixer | sīmenṭ miksar | सीमेंट मिक्सर

materials • sāmān • सामान

brick
īṃṭ | ईंट

lumber
imāratī lakṛī | इमारती लकड़ी

roof tile
paṭiyā | पटिया

concrete block
concrete block | कॉन्क्रीट ब्लॉक

tools • auzār • औज़ार

nortar
jara | गारा

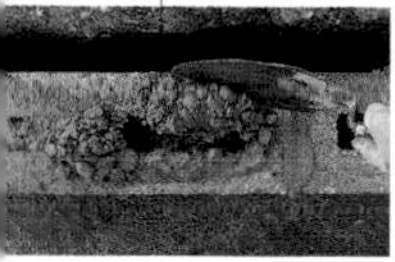

trowel
kannī | कन्नी

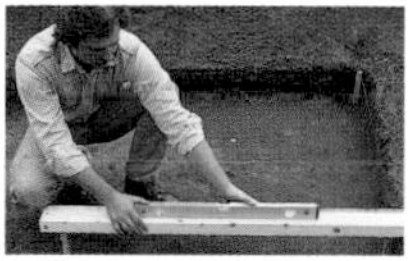

level
talmāpī | तलमापी

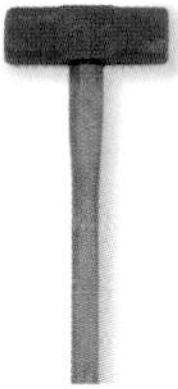

sledgehammer
hathauṛā | हथौड़ा

handle
hatthā
हत्था

pickax
kudāl | कुदाल

shovel
belcha | बेलचा

machinery • maśīnarī • मशीनरी

roller
rolar | रोलर

dump truck
ḍampar | डम्पर

support
ādhār stambh
आधार स्तंभ

ook
uk
क

crane | kren | क्रेन

roadworks • saṛak nirmāṇ kārya • सड़क निर्माण कार्य

asphalt
tārkol
तारकोल

cone
kon
कोन

jack hammer
nyūmaiṭik ḍril
न्यूमैटिक ड्रिल

resurfacing
punaḥ parat lagānā
पुनः परत लगाना

occupations 1 • vyavasāya 1 • व्यवसाय

carpenter
baṛhaī | बढ़ई

electrician | bijlī mistrī
बिजली मिस्त्री

plumber
nalsāz | नलसाज़

construction worker
rājgīr | राजगीर

gardener
mālī | माली

vacuum cleaner
vekyūm klīnar
वेक्यूम क्लीनर

cleaner
safaī karmī | सफ़ाई कर्मी

mechanic
mistrī | मिस्त्री

butcher
ḳasāī | क़साई

hairdresser | keś prasādhak | केश प्रसाधक

fish-seller
machhlī vikretā
मछली विक्रेता

produce-seller
sabzī vikretā
सब्ज़ी विक्रेता

florist
phool vikretā
फूल विक्रेता

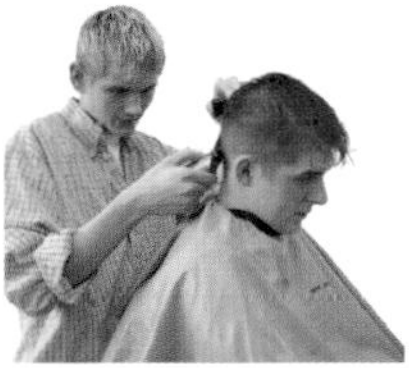

barber
nāī | नाई

jeweler
sunār | सुनार

sales clerk | dukān sahāyak | दुकान सहायक

realtor | bhūsam-
atti dalāl | भूसंपत्ति दलाल

optician | dṛṣṭi
parīkṣak | दृष्टि परीक्षक

mask
naqāb
नक़ाब

dentist | dant
chikitsak | दंत चिकित्सक

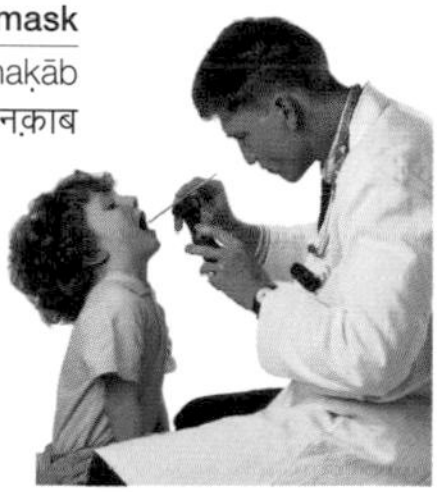

doctor
chikitsak | चिकित्सक

pharmacist
ṣadhkārak | औषधकारक

nurse
nars | नर्स

veterinarian | paśu
chikitsak | पशु चिकित्सक

farmer
kisān | किसान

fisherman
machhuārā | मछुआरा

machine gun
maśīn gan
मशीन गन

soldier
sainik | सैनिक

uniform
vardī
वर्दी

police officer | pulis
karmī | पुलिस कर्मी

badge
pahchān baij
पहचान बैज

security guard
surakṣā karmī | सुरक्षा
कर्मी

sailor
nāvik | नाविक

firefighter
fāyarmain | फ़ायरमैन

occupations 2 • vyavasāya 2 • व्यवसाय

lawyer
vakīl | वकील

accountant
lekhākār | लेखाकार

model
namūnā
नमूना

architect
vāstukār | वास्तुकार

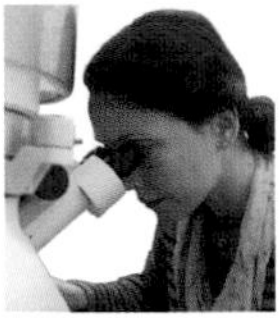

scientist
vaijñānik | वैज्ञानिक

teacher
adhyāpak | अध्यापक

librarian
pustakālaya adhyakṣ
पुस्तकालय अध्यक्ष

receptionist
svāgatkartā | स्वागतकर्ता

mailbag
ḍāk thailā
डाक–थैला

mail carrier
ḍākiyā | डाकिया

bus driver
bas chālak | बस चालक

truck driver
ṭrak chālak | ट्रक चालक

cab driver | ṭaiksī chālak | टैक्सी चालक

pilot | vimān chālak | विमान चालक

flight attendant | vimān parichārikā | विमान परिचारिका

travel agent | ṭraival ejenṭ | ट्रैवल एजेंट

chef's hat
rasoie kī ṭopī
रसोइए की टोपी

chef
rasoiyā | रसोइया

musician
saṅgītkār | संगीतकार

tutu
baile skarṭ
बैले स्कर्ट

dancer
nartakī | नर्तकी

actor
abhinetā | अभिनेता

singer
gāyikā | गायिका

waitress
parichārikā | परिचारिका

bartender
bārmain | बारमैन

sportsman
khilāṛī | खिलाड़ी

sculptor
mūrtikār | मूर्तिकार

painter
chitrakār | चित्रकार

photographer
chhāyākār | छायाकार

anchor | samāchār vāchak | समाचार वाचक

notes
noṭs
नोट्स

journalist
patrakār | पत्रकार

editor
sampādak | संपादक

designer
ḍizāinar | डिज़ाइनर

seamstress
darzin | दर्ज़िन

tailor
darzī | दर्ज़ी

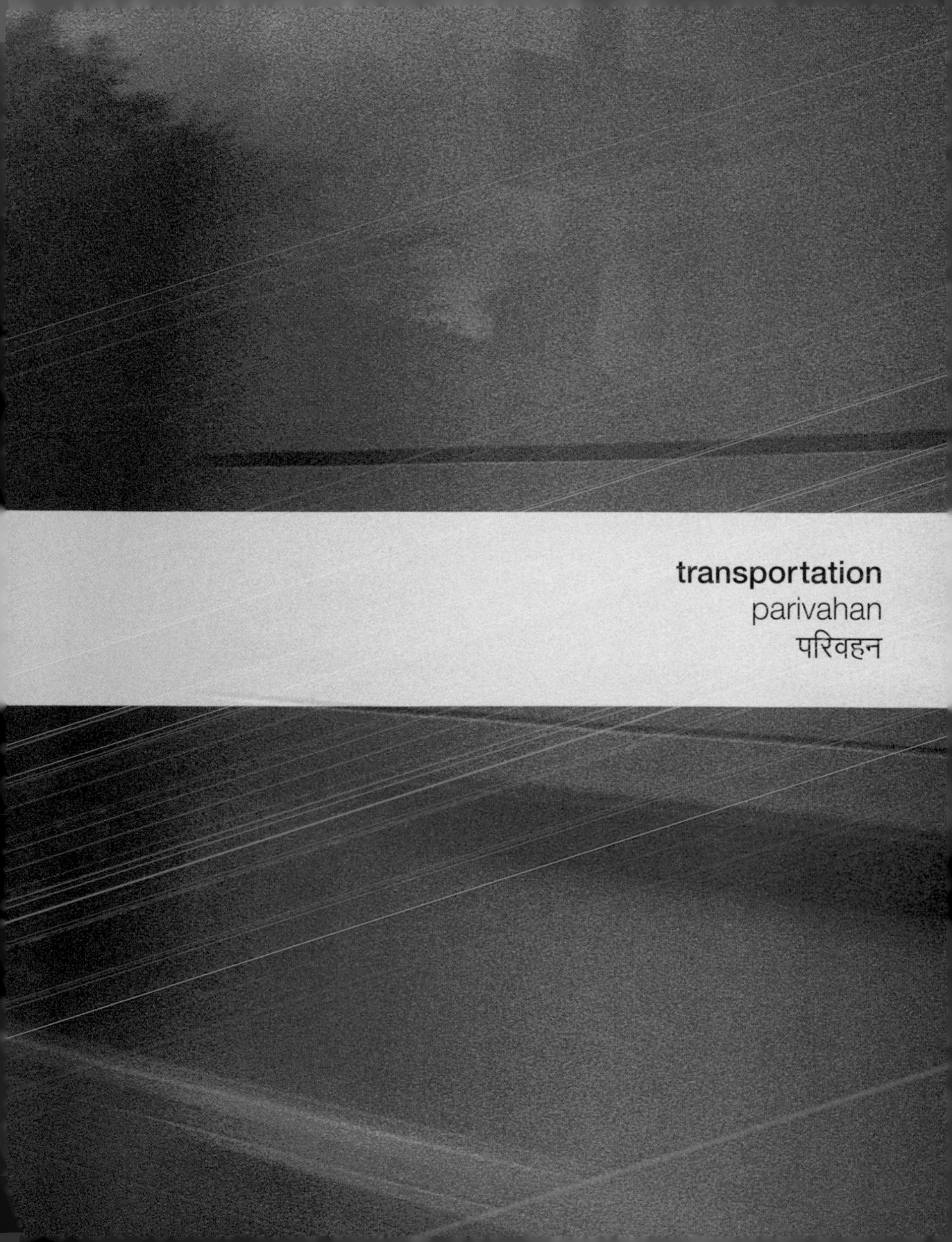

transportation

parivahan

परिवहन

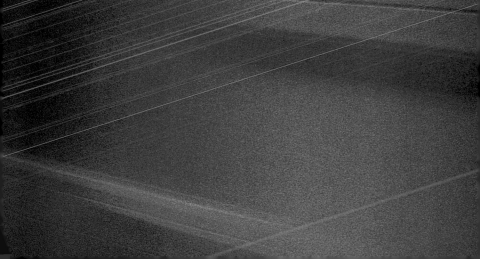

roads • saṛkeṃ • सड़कें

freeway
moṭar mārg
मोटर मार्ग
toll booth
ṭol būth
टोल बूथ
road markings
mārg chihn
मार्ग चिह्न
frontage road
sāiḍ kī saṛak
साइड की सड़क
one-way
ek diśā mārg
एक दिशा मार्ग
divider
vibhājak
विभाजक
interchange
jaṇkśan
जंक्शन
traffic light
yātāyāt battī
यातायात बत्ती
truck
ṭrak
ट्रक
median strip
kendrīya ārakṣaṇ
केंद्रीय आरक्षण
right lan
bhītrī le
भीतरी ले
center lan
madhya le
मध्य ले
passing lan
bāhrī le
बाहरी ले
exit ram
nikās ḍhalā
निकास ढला
traffi
yātāyā
याताया
overpas
flāī ova
फ़्लाईओव
shoulde
saṛak kā kinār
सड़क का किनार
underpas
bhūmigat mār
भूमिगत मा

crosswalk
paidal pārpath
पैदल पारपथ

emergency phone
āpātkālīn dūrbhāṣ
आपातकालीन दूरभाष

disabled parking
vikläṅg
pārkiṅg sthal
विकलांग
पार्किंग स्थल

traffic jam
yātāyāt jām | यातायात जाम

GPS
GPS | जीपीएस

traffic policeman
yātāyāt pulisakarmī
यातायात पुलिसकर्मी

parking meter
pārkiṅg mīṭar
पार्किंग मीटर

vocabulary • śabdāvalī • शब्दावली

roundabout
gol chakkar
गोल चक्कर

park (v)
pārk karnā
पार्क करना

road work
saṛak nirmāṇ kārya
सड़क निर्माण कार्य

tow away (v)
ṭo karnā
टो करना

pass (v)
āge nikālnā
आगे निकालना

detour
parivartit mārg
परिवर्तित मार्ग

drive (v)
gāṛī chalānā
गाड़ी चलाना

guard rail
ṭakkar avrodh
टक्कर अवरोध

back up (v)
pīchhe karnā
पीछे करना

Is this the road to...?
kyā... jāne kā yahī mārg hai?
क्या... जाने का यही मार्ग है?

divided highway
dvaya vāhan mārg
द्वय वाहन मार्ग

Where can I park?
maiṃ kahāṃ pārk kar saktā hūṃ?
मैं कहां पार्क कर सकता हूं?

road signs • yātāyāt saṅket • यातायात संकेत

do not enter
praveś niṣedh
प्रवेश निषेध

speed limit
gati sīmā
गति सीमा

hazard
khatrā
खतरा

no stopping
ruknā manā hai
रुकना मना है

no right turn
dāeṃ muṛnā niṣedh
दाएं मुड़ना निषेध

bus • bas • बस

driver's seat
chālak sīṭ
चालक सीट

handrail
haiṇḍrel
हैंडरेल

automatic door
svachālit darvāzā
स्वचालित दरवाज़ा

front wheel
āge kā pahiyā
आगे का पहिया

luggage hol
sāmān kak
सामान क

door | darvāzā | दरवाज़ा

long-distance bus | bas | बस

types of buses • basoṃ ke prakār • बसों के प्रकार

route number
rūṭ nambar
रूट नंबर

driver
chālak
चालक

double-decker bus
ḍabal-ḍekar bas
डबल-डेकर बस

tram
ṭrām | ट्राम

trolley bus
trolley bas | ट्रॉली बस

school bus | skūl bas | स्कूल बस

rear wheel
pichhlā pahiyā
पिछला पहिया

window
khiṛkī
खिड़की

bus ticket
bas ṭikaṭ | बस टिकट

stop button
stop baṭan
स्टॉप बटन

bell
ghaṇṭī | घंटी

bus station
bas aḍḍā | बस अड्डा

bus stop
bas stop
बस स्टॉप

vocabulary • śabdāvalī • शब्दावली

schedule
samaya sūchī
समय सूची

fare
kirāyā
किराया

wheelchair access
vhīlcheyar suvidhā
व्हीलचेयर सुविधा

bus stop
bas khaṛī karne kī jagah
बस खड़ी करने की जगह

Do you stop at...?
kyā āp ... par rokenge?
क्या आप ... पर रोकेंगे?

Which bus goes to...?
... ke lie kaun sī bas jātī hai?
... के लिए कौन सी बस जाती है?

minibus
minī bas | मिनी बस

tour bus | paryaṭak bas | पर्यटक बस

shuttle bus | śaṭal bas | शटल बस

car 1 • kār • कार

exterior • bāhrī svarūp • बाहरी स्वरूप

side mirror
viṅg mirar
विंग मिरर
windshield
vinḍskrīn
विंडस्क्रीन
rearview mirror
riyarvyū mirar
रियरव्यू मिरर
windshield wiper
vinḍskrīn vāipar
विंडस्क्रीन वाइपर
doo
darvāz
दरवाज
hood
bonaṭ
बोनट
trunk
ḍikk
डिक्की
turn signal
saṅketak
संकेतक
license plate
nambar pleṭ
नंबर प्लेट
bumper
bampar
बम्पर
headlight
āge kī battī
आगे की बत्ती
wheel
pahiyā
पहिया
tire
ṭāya
टायर
GG ZN 634

luggage
sāmān
सामान

roof rack
kairiyar | कैरियर

tailgate | ḍikkī kā darvāzā
डिक्की का दरवाज़ा

seat belt
sīṭ belṭ | सीट बेल्ट

car seat
bālak-sīṭ | बालक–सीट

types • prakār • प्रकार

electric car
bijlī se chalne vālī kār
बिजली से चलने वाली कार

hatchback
haichbaik | हैचबैक

sedan
salūn | सलून

station wagon
vaigan | वैगन

convertible
kanvarṭibal
कन्वर्टिबल

sports car
sporṭs kār
स्पोर्ट्स कार

minivan
pīpul kairiyar
पीपुल कैरियर

four-wheel drive
for-vhīl ḍrāiv
फ़ोर-व्हील ड्राइव

vintage
vinṭej kār | विंटेज कार

limousine
limozīn | लिमोज़ीन

gas station • peṭrol sṭeśan • पेट्रोल स्टेशन

gas pump
peṭrol pamp
पेट्रोल पंप

price
mūlya
मूल्य

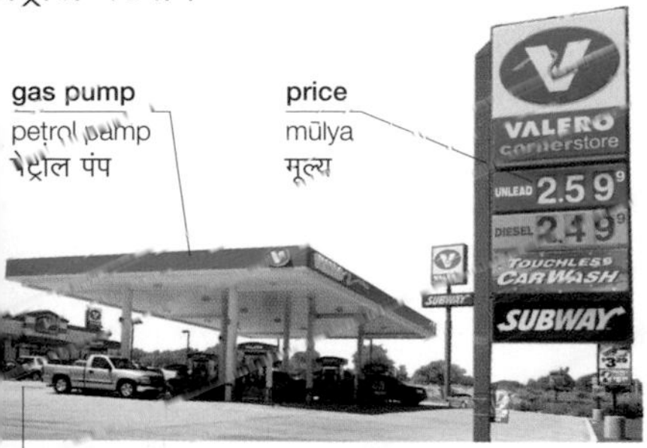

forecourt
dālān
दालान

vocabulary • śabdāvalī • शब्दावली

oil
tel
तेल

leaded
sīsā yukt
सीसा युक्त

car wash
kār dhulāī
कार धुलाई

gasoline
peṭrol
पेट्रोल

diesel
ḍīzal
डीज़ल

antifreeze
enṭī frīz
एंटी फ़्रीज़

unleaded
sīsā rahit
सीसा रहित

garage
gairej
गैरेज

washer fluid
screenwash
स्क्रीनवॉश

Fill it up, please.
kṛpyā pūrī ṭaṅkī bhar deṃ
कृपया पूरी टंकी भर दें।

car 2 • kār 2 • कार

interior • inṭīriyar • इंटीरियर

door lock
darvāze kā lock
दरवाज़े का लॉक

armrest
ārmresṭ
आर्मरेस्ट

handle
hainḍil
हैंडिल

back seat
pichhlī sīṭ | पिछली सीट

headrest
sirhānā | सिरहाना

vocabulary • śabdāvalī • शब्दावली

two-door	**four-door**	**automatic**	**brake**	**accelerator**
do-darvāzā	chār-darvāzā	svachālit	brek	aiksīlreṭar
दो–दरवाज़ा	चार–दरवाज़ा	स्वचालित	ब्रेक	ऐक्सीलरेटर
hatchback	**manual**	**ignition**	**clutch**	**air conditioning**
tīn-darvāzā	mānav-chālit	ignīśan	klach	vātānukūlan
तीन–दरवाज़ा	मानव–चालित	इग्नीशन	क्लच	वातानुकूलन

Can you tell me the way to...?
kyā āp mujhe... jāne kā rāstā
batāeṅge?
क्या आप मुझे... जाने का रास्ता बताएंगे?

**Where is the
parking lot?**
kār pārkiṅg kahāṃ hai?
कार पार्किंग कहां है?

Can I park here?
kyā maiṃ yahāṃ gāṛī khaṛī kar
saktā hūṃ?
क्या मैं यहां गाड़ी खड़ी कर सकता हूं?

controls • niyantraṇ • नियंत्रण

steering wheel
sṭīyariṅg
स्टीयरिंग

horn
horn
हॉर्न

dashboard
ḍaiśborḍ
डैशबोर्ड

hazard lights
saṅkaṭ sūchak battī
संकट सूचक बत्ती

satellite navigation
upgrah mārgdarśan
उपग्रह मार्गदर्शन

left-hand drive | bāīṃ or kī ḍrāiv | बाईं ओर की ड्राइव

temperature gauge
tāpmān māpak
तापमान मापक

tachometer
parikramaṇ gaṇak
परिक्रमण गणक

speedometer
spīḍ mīṭar
स्पीड मीटर

fuel gauge
īndhan māpī
ईंधन मापी

car stereo
sṭīriyo
स्टीरियो

light switch
lāiṭ baṭan
लाइट बटन

heater controls
hīṭar kanṭrol
हीटर कंट्रोल

odometer
pathmāpak yantr
पथमापक यंत्र

gearshift
gīyar
गीयर

air bag
eyar baig
एयर बैग

right-hand drive | dāīṃ or kī ḍrāiv | दाईं ओर की ड्राइव

car 3 • kār 3 • कार

mechanics • yāntrikī • यांत्रिकी

washer fluid reservoir
screen wash ḍibbā
स्क्रीन वॉश डिब्बा

dipstick
ḍipasṭik
डिपस्टिक

air filter
vāyu chhalnī
वायु छलनी

brake fluid reservoir
brek dravya ḍibbā
ब्रेक द्रव्य डिब्बा

battery
baiṭrī
बैटरी

bodywork
bodywork
बॉडीवर्क

coolant reservoir
kūlenṭ ḍibbā
कूलेंट डिब्बा

cylinder head
silenḍar
सिलेंडर

pipe
pāip
पाइप

sunroof
kār kī chhat
कार की छत

radiator
reḍieṭar
रेडिएटर

fan
paṅkhā
पंखा

engine
injan
इंजन

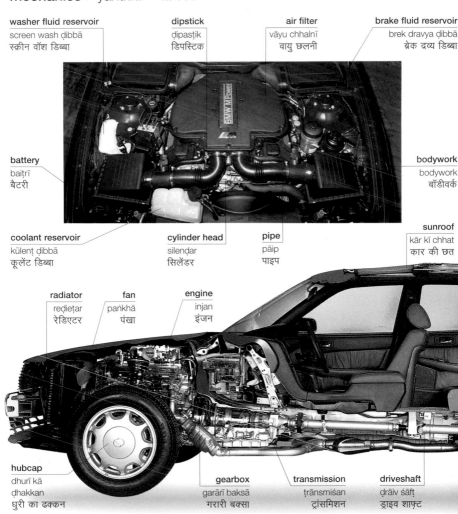

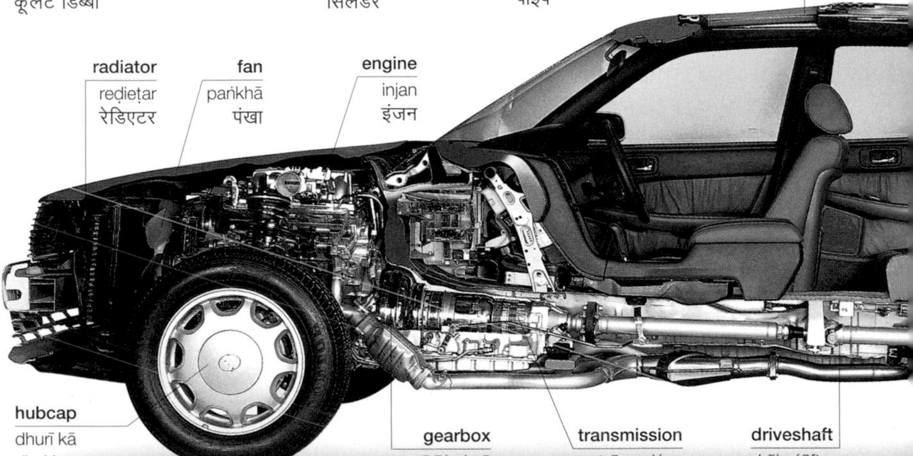

hubcap
dhurī kā ḍhakkan
धुरी का ढक्कन

gearbox
garārī baksā
गरारी बक्सा

transmission
ṭrānsmiśan
ट्रांसमिशन

driveshaft
ḍrāiv śāfṭ
ड्राइव शाफ़्ट

flat tire • paṅkchar • पंक्चर

spare tire
atirikt ṭāyar
अतिरिक्त टायर
tire iron
pānā
पाना
wheel nuts
ṭāyar ke pech
टायर के पेच
jack
jaik
जैक

change a tire (v)
ṭāyar badalnā | टायर बदलना

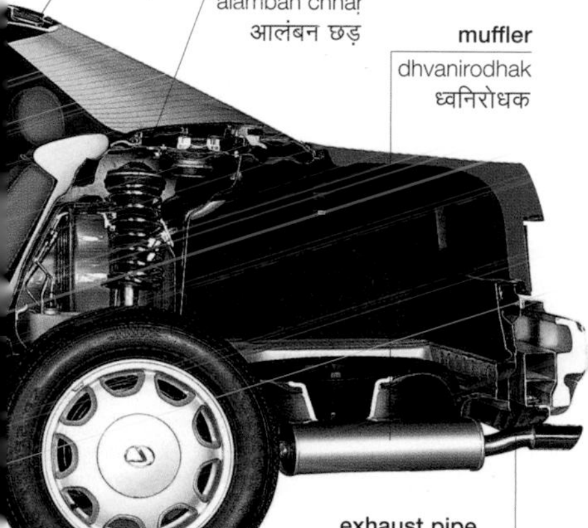
roof
chhat
छत
suspension
ālamban chhaṛ
आलंबन छड़
muffler
dhvanirodhak
ध्वनिरोधक
exhaust pipe
dhuāṃ nikās nalī
धुआं निकास नली

vocabulary • śabdāvalī • शब्दावली

car accident
kār durghaṭnā
कार दुर्घटना

breakdown
brek ḍāun
ब्रेक डाउन

insurance
bīmā
बीमा

towtruck
ṭo ṭrak
टो ट्रक

mechanic
maikenik
मैकेनिक

tire pressure
ṭāyar preśar
टायर प्रेशर

fuse box
fyūz baksā
फ़्यूज़ बक्सा

sparkplug
spārk plag
स्पार्क प्लग

fan belt
fain belṭ
फ़ैन बेल्ट

turbocharger
ṭarbo chārjar
टर्बो चार्जर

distributor
vitrak
वितरक

chassis
chesis
चेसिस

parking brake
haiṇḍ brek
हैंड ब्रेक

alternator
pratyāvartak
प्रत्यावर्तक

cam belt
kem belṭ
केम बेल्ट

timing
ṭāimiṅg
टाइमिंग

gas tank
peṭrol ṭaṅkī
पेट्रोल टंकी

My car won't start.
merī kār sṭārṭ nahīṃ ho rahī.
मेरी कार स्टार्ट नहीं हो रही।

My car has broken down.
merī gāṛī ḳharāb ho gaī hai.
मेरी गाड़ी ख़राब हो गई है।

motorcycle • moṭarbāik • मोटरबाइक

turn signal
saṅketak
संकेतक
speedometer
gatimāpak
गतिमापक
brake
brek
ब्रेक
clutch
klach
क्लच
horn
horn
हॉर्न
throttle
gati niyantrak
गति नियंत्रक

controls
niyantraṇ yantr | नियंत्रण यंत्र

helmet
hailmeṭ
हैलमेट

carrier
samvāhak
संवाहक

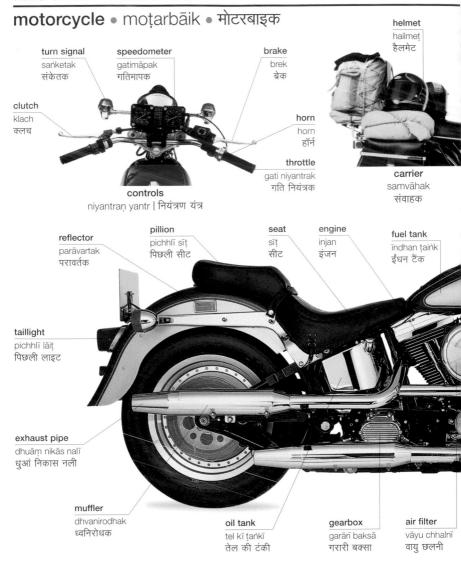

reflector
parāvartak
परावर्तक
pillion
pichhlī sīṭ
पिछली सीट
seat
sīṭ
सीट
engine
injan
इंजन
fuel tank
īndhan ṭaiṅk
ईंधन टैंक
taillight
pichhlī lāiṭ
पिछली लाइट
exhaust pipe
dhuāṃ nikās nalī
धुआं निकास नली
muffler
dhvanirodhak
ध्वनिरोधक
oil tank
tel kī ṭaṅkī
तेल की टंकी
gearbox
garārī baksā
गरारी बक्सा
air filter
vāyu chhalnī
वायु छलनी

visor
hailmeṭ kā śīśā
हैलमेट का शीशा
leathers
laidar vastr
लैदर वस्त्र
reflector strap
parāvartak paṭṭī
परावर्तक पट्टी
knee pad
nī paiḍ
नी पैड

clothing | vastr | वस्त्र

headlight
sāmne kī lāiṭ
सागने की लाइट
suspension
ālamban chhaṛ
आलंबन छड़
mudguard
miṭṭī rodhak
मिट्टी रोधक
brake pedal
brek paiḍal
ब्रेक पैडल
axle
dhurī
धुरी
tire
pahiyā
पहिया

types • prakār • प्रकार

racing bike | resiṅg bāik | रेसिंग बाइक

windshield
vinḍśīlaḍ
विंडशील्ड

tourer | moṭar sāikil | मोटर साइकिल

dirt bike | ḍarṭ bāik | डर्ट बाइक

stand
sṭainḍ | स्टैंड

scooter | skūṭar | स्कूटर

bicycle • sāikil • साइकिल

tandem | do sīṭoṃ vālī sāikil
दो सीटों वाली साइकिल

racing bike
resiṅg bāik
रेसिंग बाइक

mountain bike
māuṇṭen bāik
माउंटेन बाइक

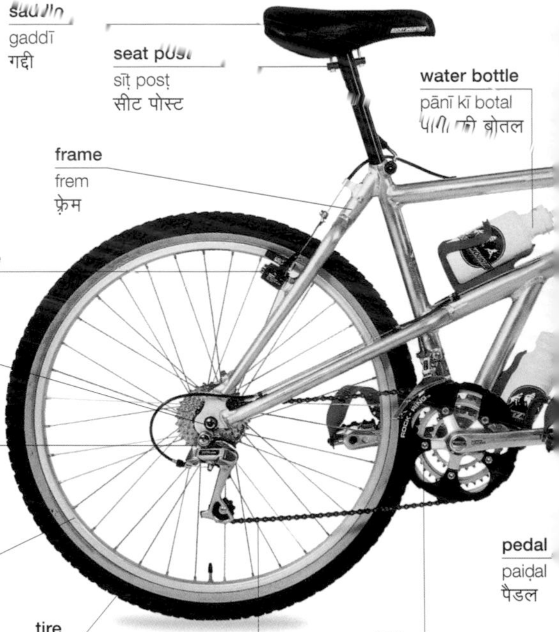
saddle
gaddī
गद्दी
seat post
sīṭ posṭ
सीट पोस्ट
water bottle
pānī kī botal
पानी की बोतल
frame
frem
फ़्रेम
brake
brek
ब्रेक
hub
dhurī
धुरी
gears
gīyar
गीयर
rim
rim
रिम
tire
ṭāyar
टायर
chain
chen
चेन
cog
dāṃtā
दांता
pedal
paiḍal
पैडल

touring bike
ṭūriṅg bāik | टूरिंग बाइक

helmet
hailmeṭ
हैलमेट

road bike
roḍ bāik | रोड बाइक

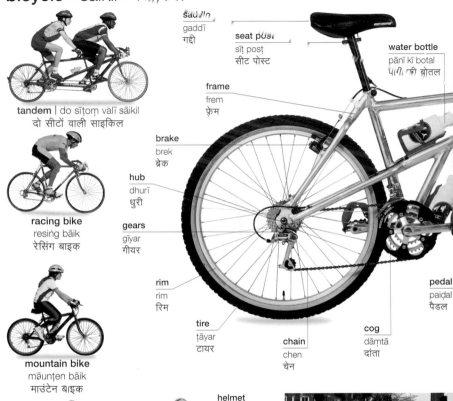

bike lane | sāikil len | साइकिल लेन

crossbar
crossbar
क्रॉसबार

handlebar
haiṇḍal
हैंडल

gear lever
gīyar līvar
गीयर लीवर

brake lever
brek līvar
ब्रेक लीवर

fork
chimṭā
चिमटा

spoke
tīlī
तीली

wheel
pahiyā
पहिया

valve
vālv
वाल्व

tread
ṭāyar par ḍizāin
टायर पर डिज़ाइन

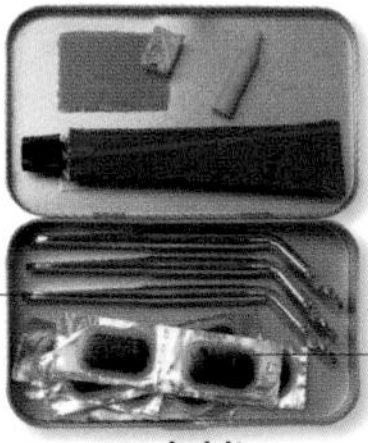

tire lever
ṭāyar līvar
टायर लीवर

patch
thiglī
थिगली

repair kit
marammat kā sāmān | मरम्मत का सामान

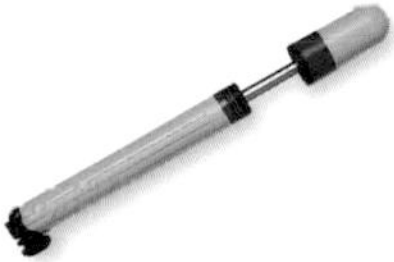

pump
pamp
पंप

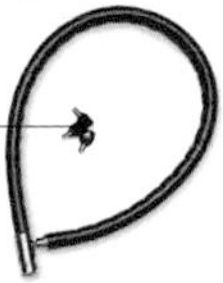

key
chābī
चाबी

lock
tālā
ताला

inner tube
bhītrī ṭyūb
भीतरी ट्यूब

child seat
bālak sīṭ
बालक–सीट

vocabulary • śabdāvalī • शब्दावली

headlight laimp लैंप	**kickstand** kiksṭaiṇḍ किकस्टैंड	**brake block** brek block ब्रेक ब्लॉक	**basket** ṭokrī टोकरी	**toe clip** ṭo klip टो क्लिप	**brake (v)** roknā रोकना
rear light pichhe kī lāiṭ पीछे की लाइट	**bike rack** bāik raik बाइक रैक	**cable** tār तार	**dynamo** ḍāyanemo डायनेमो	**toe strap** ṭo sṭrep टो स्ट्रेप	**cycle (v)** sāikil chalānā साइकिल चलाना
reflector parāvartak परावर्तक	**training wheels** sṭeblāizars स्टेबलाइज़र्स	**sprocket** chakradant चक्रदंत	**flat tire** paṅkchar पंक्चर	**pedal (v)** paiḍal mārnā पैडल मारना	**change gears (v)** gīyar badalnā गीयर बदलना

train • relgāṛī • रेलगाड़ी

car
relgāṛī ḍibbā
रेलगाड़ी डिब्बा

cart
trolley
ट्रॉली

platform number
platform saṃkhyā
प्लेटफ़ॉर्म संख्या

commuter
yātrī
यात्री

platform
platform
प्लेटफ़ॉर्म

train station | relve sṭeśan | रेलवे स्टेशन

types of train • relgaṛī ke prakār • रेलगाड़ी के प्रकार

steam train | bhāp chālit relgāṛī
भाप चालित रेलगाड़ी

engine
injan
इंजन

engineer's cab
chālak kakṣ
चालक कक्ष

rail
paṭrī
पटरी

diesel train | ḍīzal relgāṛī | डीज़ल रेलगाड़ी

electric train
vidyut relgāṛī | विद्युत रेलगाड़ी

high-speed train
tez gati relgāṛī | तेज़ गति रेलगाड़ी

monorail | ekpaṭrī relgāṛī
एकपटरी रेलगाड़ी

subway | bhūmigat relgāṛī
भूमिगत रेलगाड़ी

tram
ṭrām | ट्राम

freight train
mālgāṛī | मालगाड़ी

luggage rack
sāmān kī jagah
सामान की जगह

window
khiṛkī
खिड़की

track
paṭrī
पटरी

door
darvāzā
दरवाज़ा

seat
sīṭ
सीट

compartment | ḍibbā | डिब्बा

ticket gate
ṭikaṭ bairiyar | टिकट बैरियर

ticket
ṭikaṭ | टिकट

dining car | bhojanyān | भोजनयान

public address system
jan sūchnā praṇālī
जन सूचना प्रणाली

schedule
samaya sārṇī
समय-सारणी

concourse | relve parisar | रेलवे परिसर

sleeping compartment
śayan yān | शयन यान

vocabulary • śabdāvalī • शब्दावली

rail network
rel neṭvark
रेल नेटवर्क

express train
antar nagarīya relgāṛī
अंतर नगरीय रेलगाड़ी

rush hour
vyast samaya
व्यस्त समय

subway map
bhūmigat nakśā
भूमिगत नक़्शा

delay
vilamb
विलंब

fare
kirāyā
किराया

ticket office
ṭikaṭ ghar
टिकट घर

ticket inspector
ṭikaṭ nirīkṣak
टिकट निरीक्षक

change trains (v)
badalnā
बदलना

live rail
chālū paṭrī
चालू पटरी

signal
signal
सिग्नल

emergency lever
āpātkālīn līvar
आपातकालीन लीवर

aircraft • vāyuyān • वायुयान

airliner • yātrī vimān • यात्री विमान

cockpit
chālak kakṣ
चालक कक्ष
exit
nikās dvār
निकास द्वार
engine
injan
इंजन
fuselage
fyūzilej
फ़्यूज़िलेज
wing
paṅkh
पंख
tail
sirā
सिरा
AIR CANADA
rudder
raḍar | रडर
nose
agra bhāg
अग्र भाग
nosewheel
nāsā pahiyā
नासा पहिया
landing gear
laiṇḍiṅg giyar
लैंडिंग गियर
aileron
pichhlī patvār
पिछली पतवार
fin
paṅkh
पंख
tailplane
pichhlā samtal paṅkh
पिछला समतल पंख

cabin • kebin • केबिन

emergency exit
āpātkālīn nikās
आपातकालीन निकास
flight attendant
vimān parichārikā
विमान परिचारिका
overhead bi
ūprī locke
ऊपरी लॉक
air ven
vāyu chhic
वायु छि
window
khiṛkī
खिड़की
reading ligh
paṛhne kī bat
पढ़ने की बत्
seat
sīṭ
सीट
row
kaṭā
क़ता
tray-table
ṭre-ṭebal
ट्रे–टेबल
armrest
hatthā
हत्था
aisle
galiyārā
गलियारा
seat back
sīṭ kī pīṭh
सीट की पीठ

hot-air balloon
garm havā kā gubbārā
गर्म हवा का ग़ुब्बारा

ultralight
māikrolāiṭ
माइक्रोलाइट

glider
glāiḍar
ग्लाइडर

biplane
bāiplen
बाइप्लेन

propeller
chālak yantr
चालक यंत्र

light aircraft
halkā vayuyān
हल्का वायुयान

sea plane
naukā vimān
नौका विमान

private jet
nijī vimān | निजी विमान

fighter plane
laṛākū vimān | लड़ाकू विमान

missile
misāil | मिसाइल

rotor blade
rotar bleḍ
रोटर ब्लेड

helicopter
helicopter | हैलीकॉप्टर

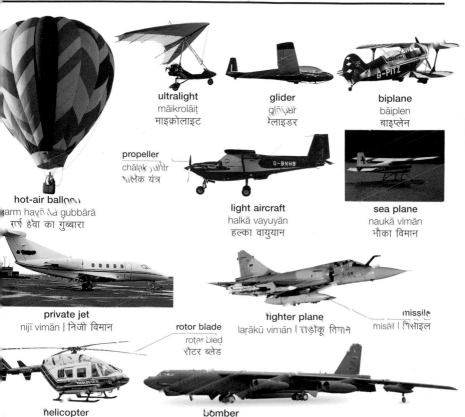

bomber
bamvarṣak | बमवर्षक

vocabulary • śabdāvalī • शब्दावली

pilot vimān chālak विमान चालक	**take off (v)** uṛān bharnā उड़ान भरना	**land (v)** utarnā उतरना	**economy class** sāmānya śreṇī सामान्य श्रेणी	**carry-on luggage** hāth kā sāmān हाथ क़ा सामान
copilot sah-vimān chālak सह–विमान चालक	**fly (v)** uṛnā उड़ना	**altitude** ūṃchāī उंचाई	**business class** vyāvasāyik śreṇī व्यावसायिक श्रेणी	**seat belt** sīṭ belṭ सीट बेल्ट

airport • havāī aḍḍā • हवाई अड्डा

apron
epran
एप्रन
baggage trailer
sāmān gāṛī
सामान गाड़ी
terminal
ṭarminal
टर्मिनल
service vehicle
sevā vāhan
सेवा वाहन
walkway
mārg
मार्ग

airliner | vāyuyān | वायुयान

vocabulary • śabdāvalī • शब्दावली

runway
havāī paṭṭī
हवाई पट्टी

international flight
antarrāṣṭrīya uṛān
अंतरराष्ट्रीय उड़ान

domestic flight
gharelū uṛān
घरेलू उड़ान

connection
sanyojan
संयोजन

flight number
uṛān nambar
उड़ान नंबर

immigration
āpravās
आप्रवास

customs
sīmā śulk
सीमा शुल्क

excess baggage
atirikt sāmān
अतिरिक्त सामान

carousel
sāmān kī chal paṭṭī
सामान की चल पट्टी

security
surakṣā
सुरक्षा

x-ray machine
eks-re maśīn
एक्स-रे मशीन

travel brochure
paryaṭan sūchnā pustikā
पर्यटन सूचना पुस्तिका

vacation
chhuṭṭiyāṃ
छुट्टियां

check in (v)
chek in
चेक इन

control tower
niyantraṇ tower
नियंत्रण टॉवर

make a flight reservation (v)
uṛān buk karnā
उड़ान बुक करना

arry-on
ıggage
āth kā sāmān
ाथ का सामान

ıggage
āmān
ामान

art
olley
ॉली

check-in desk
chek-in ḍesk
चेक-इन डेस्क

visa
vīzā
वीज़ा

passport | pāsporṭ | पासपोर्ट

passport control
pāsporṭ kanṭrol
पासपोर्ट कंट्रोल

boarding pass
borḍiṅg pās
बोर्डिंग पास

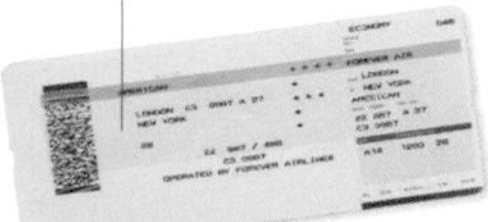

ticket
ṭikaṭ
टिकट

gate number
dvār saṃkhyā
द्वार संख्या

departures
prasthān
प्रस्थान

departure lounge
prasthān kakṣ | प्रस्थान कक्ष

destination
gantavya
sthān
गंतव्य स्थान

arrivals
āgman
आगमन

information screen
sūchnā skrīn | सूचना स्क्रीन

duty-free shop
śulk mukt dukān
शुल्क मुक्त दुकान

baggage claim
sāmān vāpsī
सामान वापसी

taxi stand
ṭaiksī ḳatār
टैक्सी–क़तार

car rental
kirāe kī kār
किराए की कार

ship • jahāz • जहाज़

radar
rāḍār
राडार
radio antenna
reḍiyo enṭīnā
रेडियो एंटीना
deck
ḍaik
डैक
funnel
chimnī
चिमनी
quarterdeck
kvārṭar ḍaik
क्वार्टर डैक
prow
potāgr
पोताग्र
Plimsoll mark
tal rekhā
तल रेखा
porthole
gavākṣ
गवाक्ष
hull
peṭā
पेटा
lifeboat
rakṣā naukā
रक्षा नौका
keel
nautal
नौतल
propeller
chālak yantr
चालक यंत्र

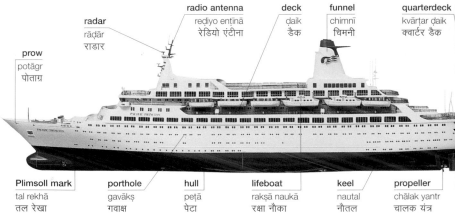

ocean liner | samudrī jahāz | समुद्री जहाज़

bridge
potādhikārī kakṣ
पोताधिकारी कक्ष

engine room
injan kakṣ
इंजन कक्ष

cabin
kaibin | कैबिन

galley
pot | पोत

vocabulary • śabdāvalī • शब्दावली

dock
dock
डॉक

port
bandargāh
बंदरगाह

gangway
mārgikā
मार्गिका

anchor
laṅgar
लंगर

bollard
rakṣā stambh
रक्षा–स्तंभ

windlass
charkhī
चरखी

captain
kaptān
कप्तान

speedboat
moṭar naukā
मोटर नौका

rowboat
chappū vālī nāv
चप्पू वाली नाव

canoe
ḍoṅgī
डोंगी

other ships • anya jahāz • अन्य जहाज़

ferry | yātrī vāhak jahāz | यात्री वाहक जहाज़

outboard motor
āuṭborḍ moṭar
आउटबोर्ड मोटर

inflatable dinghy | havā bharī ḍoṅgī | हवा भरी डोंगी

hydrofoil | jal patrak
जल पत्रक

yacht
krīṛā naukā | क्रीड़ा नौका

catamaran
donāvā | दोनावा

tugboat
karṣ naukā | कर्ष नौका

hovercraft
hover krāfṭ | हॉवर क्राफ़्ट

container ship
māl pot | माल पोत

rigging
sāj sāmān
साज सामान

sailboat
pāl naukā | पाल नौका

hold
māl kakṣ
माल कक्ष

freighter | mālvāhak
मालवाहक

oil tanker
tel pot | तेल पोत

aircraft carrier | vāyuyān vāhak | वायुयान वाहक

battleship
jaṅgī jahāz | जंगी जहाज़

conning tower
chālak kakṣ
चालक कक्ष

submarine
panḍubbī | पनडुब्बी

port • bandargāh • बंदरगाह

warehouse
mālgodām
मालगोदाम

crane
kren
क्रेन

forklift truck
kren
क्रेन

access road
praveś mārg
प्रवेश मार्ग

customs house
sīmā śulk chaukī
सीमा शुल्क चौकी

dock
godī
गोदी

container
māl ḍibbā
माल डिब्बा

quay
jahāz ghāṭ
जहाज़ घाट

cargo
kārgo
कार्गो

container port | māl vāhak bandargāh
माल वाहक बंदरगाह

ferry terminal
yātrī jahāz ṭarminal
यात्री जहाज़ टर्मिनल

ferr
yātrī jahā
यात्री जहा

ticket office
ṭikaṭ ghar
टिकट घर

passenge
yāt
यात्

passenger port
yātrī bandargāh | यात्री बंदरगाह

net
jāl
जाल

fishing boat
machhuārī nāv
मछुआरी नाव

mooring
laṅgargāh
लंगरगाह

fishing port | matsya bandargāh | मत्स्य बंदरगाह

marina | taṭvartī ḳasbā | तटवर्ती क़स्बा

harbor | bandargāh | बंदरगाह

pier | potghāṭ | पोतघाट

jetty | jeṭī | जेटी

shipyard | pot nirmāṇ ghāṭ
पोत निर्माण घाट

lamp
laimp
लैंप

lighthouse | prakāś stambh | प्रकाश स्तंभ

buoy
boyā | बोया

vocabulary • śabdāvalī • शब्दावली

coastguard
taṭrakṣak
तटरक्षक

harbor master
bandargāh pramukh
बंदरगाह प्रमुख

drop anchor (v)
laṅgar ḍālnā
लंगर डालना

dry dock
sūkhā bandargāh
सूखा बंदरगाह

moor (v)
nāv bāndhnā
नाव बांधना

dock (v)
bandargāh meṃ lānā
बंदरगाह में लाना

board (v)
chaṛhnā
चढ़ना

disembark (v)
jahāz se utarnā
जहाज़ से उतरना

set sail (v)
yātrā ārambh karnā
यात्रा आरंभ करना

ULTRA
3
DUNLOP
DDH
4
DUNLOP
TOUR
EDITION
1
ProStaff
4
GOLF CLUB
TOP-FLITE
HOT XL
4
ProStaff
4
RAM TOUR
1
MAXFLI
TOP-FLITE
STRATA
3
DISTANCE

sports
khelkūd
खेलकूद

football • amerikan fuṭball • अमेरिकन फ़ुटबॉल

goalpost
gol posṭ
गोल पोस्ट

sideline
sāiḍ lāin
साइड लाइन

line judge
lāin jaj
लाइन जज

goal line
gol lāin
गोल लाइन

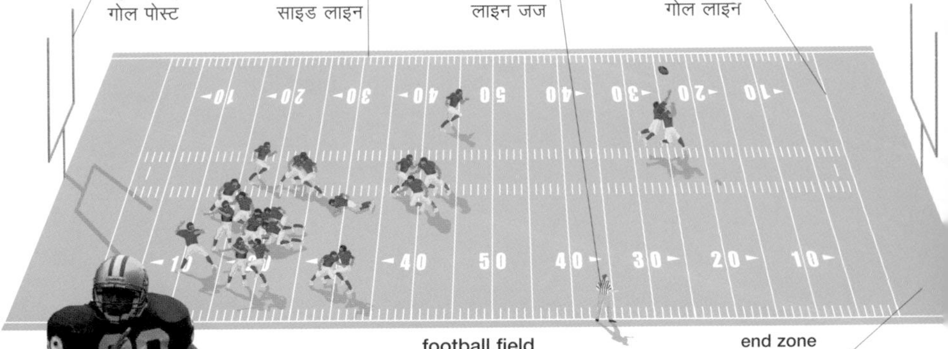

football field
fuṭball kā maidān | फ़ुटबॉल का मैदान

end zone
samāpti kṣetr
समाप्ति क्षेत्र

football
fuṭball | फ़ुटबॉल

pads
paid | पैड

helmet
hailmeṭ | हैलमेट

shoe
jūtā
जूता

football player
fuṭball khilāṛī
फ़ुटबॉल खिलाड़ी

tackle (v)
pratirodh karnā | प्रतिरोध करना

pass (v)
pās denā | पास देना

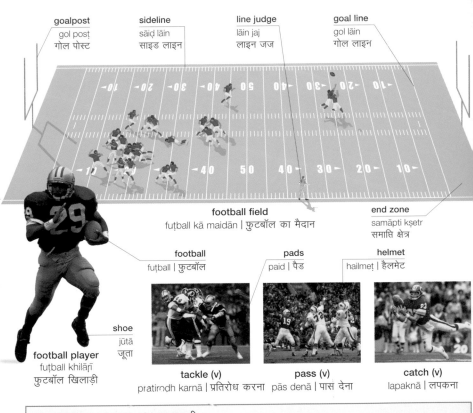

catch (v)
lapaknā | लपकना

vocabulary • śabdāvalī • शब्दावली

time out samaya samāpt समय समाप्त	**team** ṭīm टीम	**defense** bachāv बचाव	**cheerleader** protsāhak ṭīm netā प्रोत्साहक टीम नेता	**What is the score?** kyā skor huā hai? क्या स्कोर हुआ है?
fumble binā soche kik mārnā बिना सोचे किक मारना	**attack** hamlā हमला	**score** skor स्कोर	**touchdown** gend se zamīn chhūnā गेंद से ज़मीन छूना	**Who is winning?** kaun jīt rahā hai? कौन जीत रहा है?

rugby • ragbī • रग्बी

dead ball line
ḍed ball lāin
डेड बॉल लाइन

in-goal area
gol kā kṣetr
गोल का क्षेत्र

touch line
pārśv rekhā
पार्श्व रेखा

flag
jhaṇḍā
झंडा

goal
gol
गोल

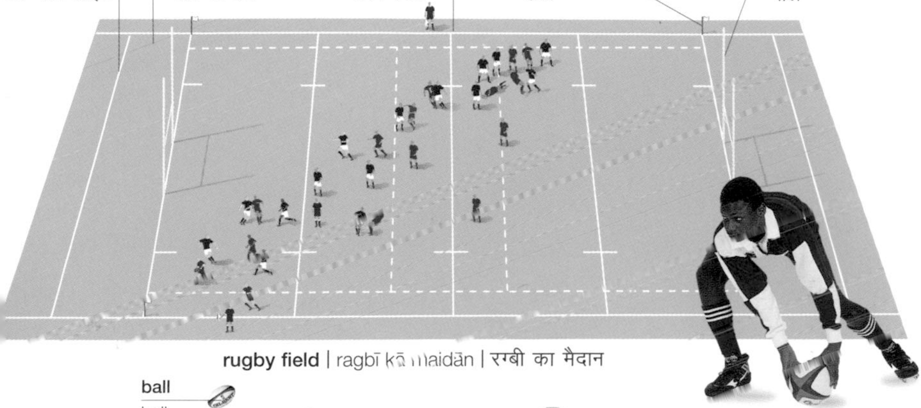

rugby field | ragbī kā maidān | रग्बी का मैदान

throw (v)
ball pheṃknā
बॉल फेंकना

ball
ball
बॉल

rugby uniform
ragbī sṭrip
रग्बी स्ट्रिप

kick (v)
kik mārnā
किक मारना

pass (v)
ball ek-dūsre ko denā
बॉल एक-दूसरे को देना

tackle (v)
pratirodh karnā
प्रतिरोध करना

try
ṭraī | ट्राई

player
khilāṛī
खिलाड़ी

ruck | khilāṛiyoṃ kā dal | खिलाड़ियों का दल

scrum | ball ko ghernā | बॉल को घेरना

soccer • soccer • सॉकर

football
fuṭball
फुटबॉल

soccer uniform
fuṭball sṭrip
फुटबॉल स्ट्रिप

soccer player
fuṭballer
फुटबॉलर

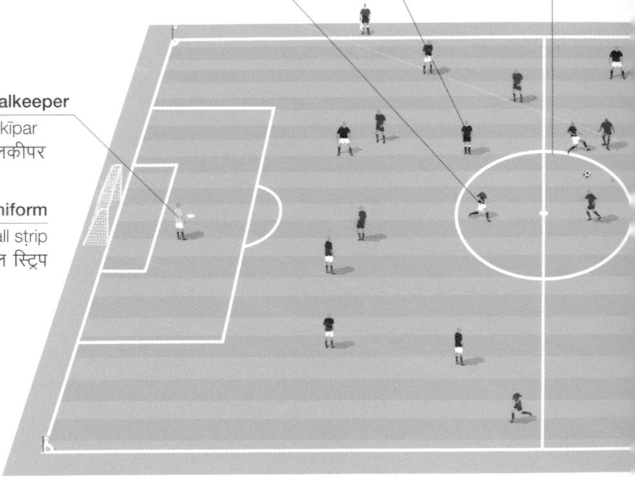

forward
agrim paṅkti kā khilāṛī
अग्रिम पंक्ति का खिलाड़ी

referee
refrī
रेफ़री

center circle
kendrīya gherā
केंद्रीय घेरा

goalkeeper
golkīpar
गोलकीपर

football field
fuṭball maidān | फुटबॉल मैदान

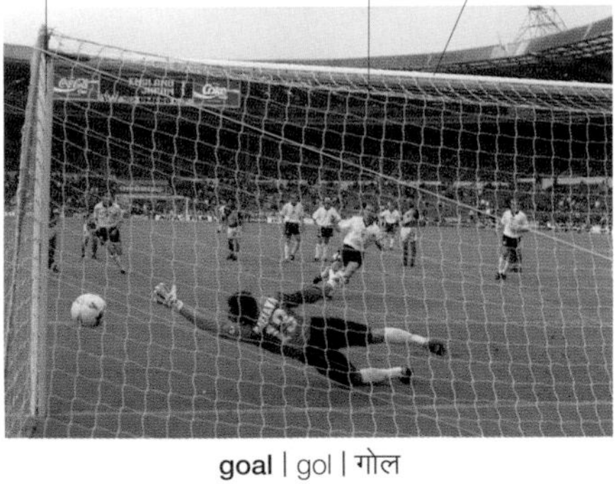

goalpost
gol posṭ
गोल पोस्ट

net
jāl
जाल

crossbar
crossbar
क्रॉसबार

goal | gol | गोल

dribble (v) | gend dhakelnā
गेंद धकेलना

head (v)
sir se mārnā | सिर से मार

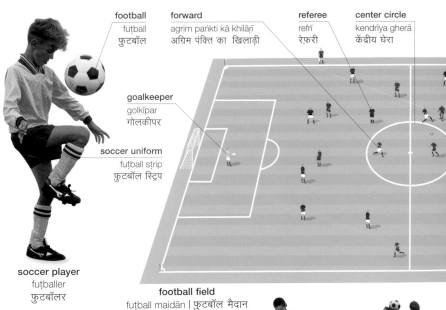

wall
pratirakṣak
paṅkti
प्रतिरक्षक पंक्ति

free kick | frī kik | फ़्री किक

penalty area
penaltī kṣetr
पेनल्टी क्षेत्र

goal line
gol sīmā
गोल सीमा

goal area
gol kṣetr
गोल क्षेत्र

goal
gol
गोल

defender
pratirakṣak
प्रतिरक्षक

linesman
lāins main
लाइन्स मैन

corner flag
corner jhaṇḍā
कॉर्नर–झंडा

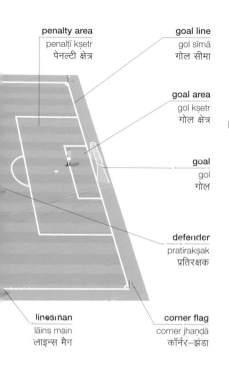

throw-in
ball pheṃknā | बॉल फेंकना

kick (v) | kik mārnā
किक मारना

shoe
jūtā
जूता

pass (v) | pāss denā
पास देना

shoot (v) | zor se
mārnā | ज़ोर से मारना

save (v)
gol roknā | गोल रोकना

tackle (v)
pratirodh karnā
प्रतिरोध करना

vocabulary • śabdāvalī • शब्दावली

stadium steḍiyam स्टेडियम	**foul** niyam ullaṅghan नियम उल्लंघन	**yellow card** pīlā kārḍ पीला कार्ड	**league** līg लीग	**extra time** atirikt samaya अतिरिक्त समय
score a goal (v) gol dāgnā गोल दाग़ना	**corner** corner कॉर्नर	**off-side** off - sāiḍ ऑफ़–साइड	**draw** anirṇit maich अनिर्णित मैच	**substitute** vaikalpik khilāṛī वैकल्पिक खिलाड़ी
penalty penaltī पेनल्टी	**red card** lāl kārḍ लाल कार्ड	**send off** saiṇḍ off सैंड ऑफ़	**half time** ādhā vakt आधा वक़्त	**substitution** vikalp bulānā विकल्प बुलाना

hockey • hockey • हॉकी

ice hockey • āis hockey • आइस हॉकी

defending zone
rakṣā kṣetr
रक्षा क्षेत्र
goal line
gol lāin
गोल लाइन
attack zone
ākramaṇ kṣetr
आक्रमण क्षेत्र
neutral zone
taṭasth kṣetr
तटस्थ क्षेत्र
goalkeeper
golkīpar
गोलकीपर
goal
gol
गोल
face-off circle
fes off sarkal
फ़ेस ऑफ़ सर्कल
center circle
kendrīya gherā
केंद्रीय घेरा

ice hockey rink
āis hockey kā maidān
आइस हॉकी का मैदान

pad
paiḍ
पैड
glove
dastānā
दस्ताना
ice-skat
āis ske
आइस स्के
stick
sṭik | स्टिक
puck
ḍisk | डिस्क

ice hockey player | āis hockey khilāṛī
आइस हॉकी खिलाड़ी

field hockey • fīlḍ hockey • फ़ील्ड हॉकी

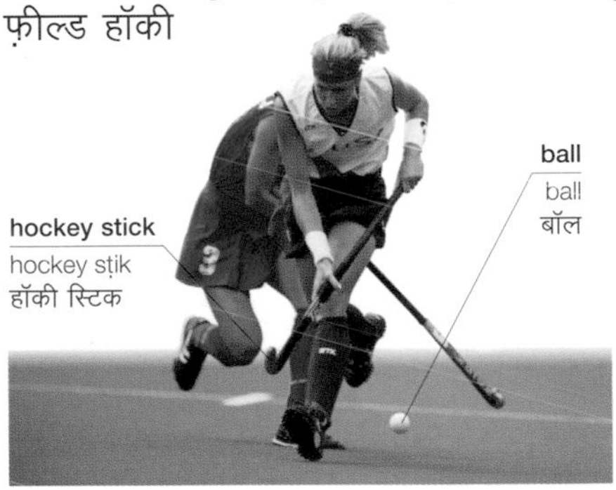
ball
ball
बॉल
hockey stick
hockey sṭik
हॉकी स्टिक

skate (v) | skeṭiṅg karnā | स्केटिंग करना

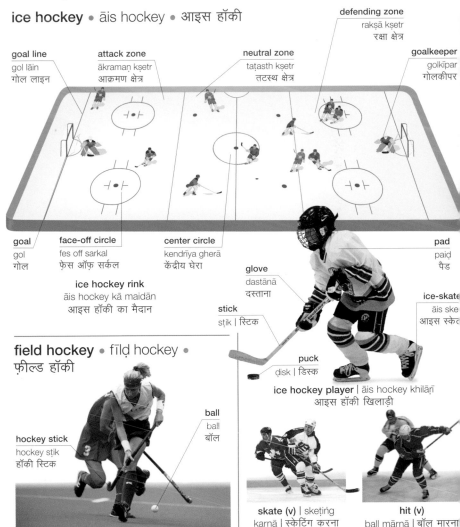

hit (v) | ball mārnā | बॉल मारना

cricket • kriketฺ • क्रिकेट

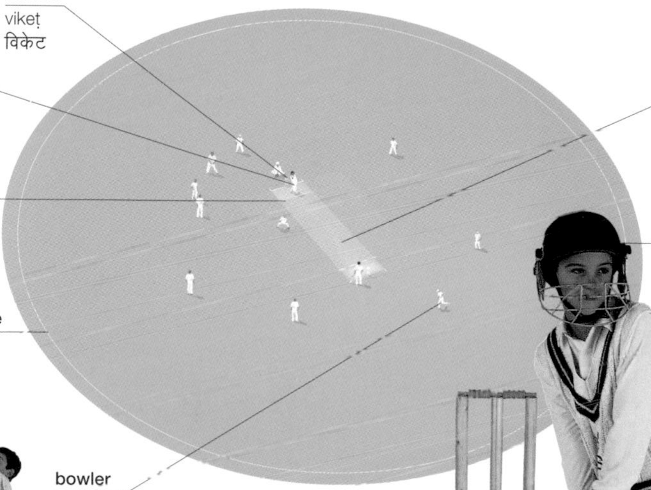
wicket
viketฺ
विकेट
batsman
ballebāz
बल्लेबाज़
crease
krīz
क्रीज़
boundary line
sīmā rekhā
सीमा रेखा
pitch
pich
पिच
face mask
hailmeṭ
हैलमेट
bowler
gendbāz
गेंदबाज़
stump
sṭamp
स्टंप
bat
ballā
बल्ला
leg pad
paiḍ
पैड

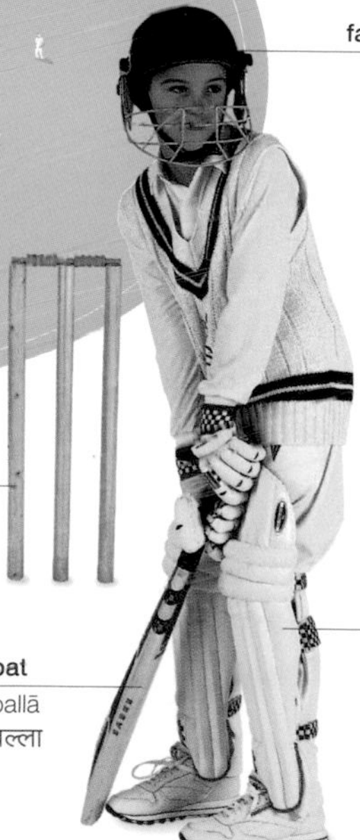

cricketer
kriketฺ khilāṛī | क्रिकेट खिलाड़ी

bowl (v)
gendbāzī karnā
गेंदबाज़ी करना

bat (v)
ballebāzī karnā | बल्लेबाज़ी करना

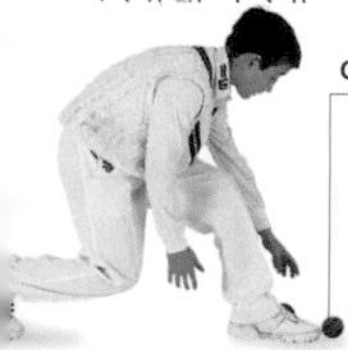
cricket ball
kriketฺ gend
क्रिकेट गेंद

field (v) | fīlḍiṅg karnā | फ़ील्डिंग करना

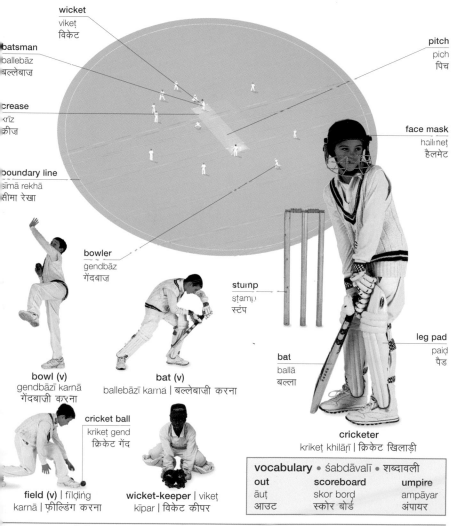

wicket-keeper | viketฺ kīpar | विकेट कीपर

vocabulary • śabdāvalī • शब्दावली

out	**scoreboard**	**umpire**
āuṭ	skor borḍ	ampāyar
आउट	स्कोर बोर्ड	अंपायर

basketball • bāskeṭ ball • बास्केट बॉल

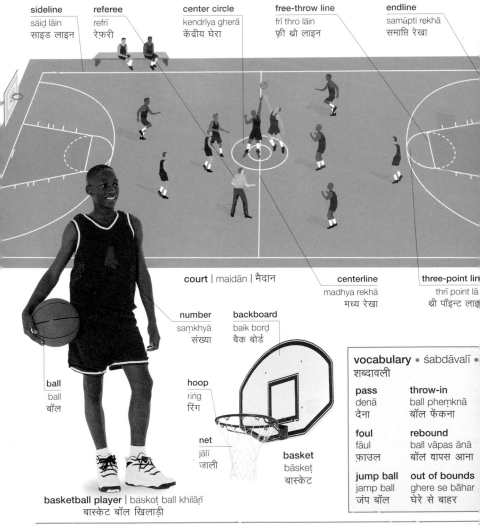

sideline
sāiḍ lāin
साइड लाइन
referee
refrī
रेफ़री
center circle
kendrīya gherā
केंद्रीय घेरा
free-throw line
frī thro lāin
फ़्री थ्रो लाइन
endline
samāpti rekhā
समाप्ति रेखा
court | maidān | मैदान
centerline
madhya rekhā
मध्य रेखा
three-point lin
thrī point lā
थ्री पॉइन्ट लाइ

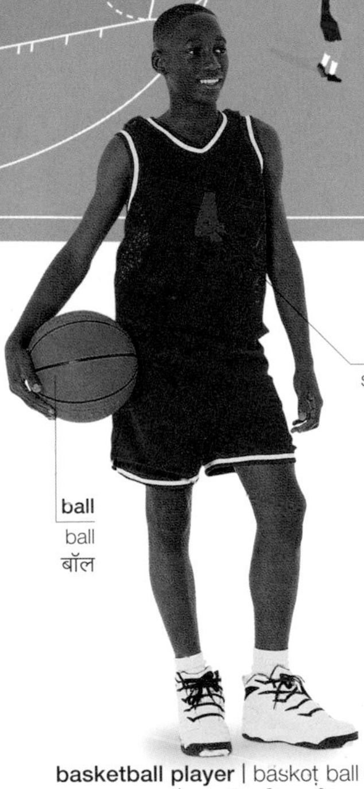
number
saṃkhyā
संख्या
ball
ball
बॉल
basketball player | bāskeṭ ball khilāṛī
बास्केट बॉल खिलाड़ी

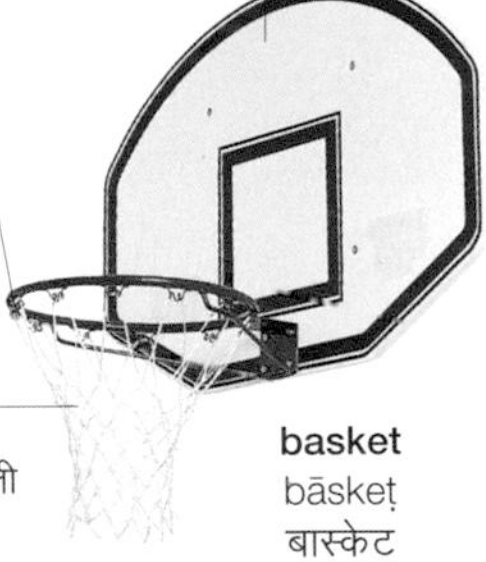
backboard
baik borḍ
बैक बोर्ड
hoop
ring
रिंग
net
jālī
जाली
basket
bāskeṭ
बास्केट

vocabulary • śabdāvalī • शब्दावली

pass denā देना	**throw-in** ball pheṃknā बॉल फेंकना
foul fāul फ़ाउल	**rebound** ball vāpas ānā बॉल वापस आना
jump ball jamp ball जंप बॉल	**out of bounds** ghere se bāhar घेरे से बाहर

actions • gatividhiyāṃ • गतिविधियां

throw (v)
ball pheṃknā
बॉल फेंकना

catch (v)
ball pakaṛnā
बॉल पकड़ना

shoot (v)
gol mārnā
गोल मारना

jump (v)
kūdnā
कूदना

mark (v) | ball niśāne par mārnā | बॉल निशाने पर मारना

block (v) | ball roknā | बॉल रोकना

dribble (v) | ṭappā mārnā | टप्पा मारना

dunk (v) | ball basketṭ meṃ ḍālnā | बॉल बास्केट में डालना

volleyball • volleyball • वॉलीबॉल

block (v)
ball roknā
बॉल रोकना

net
jāl
जाल

dig (v)
ball lapakne to taiyār rahnā
बॉल लपकने को तैयार रहना

referee
refrī
रेफ़री

knee support
nī saporṭ
नी सपोर्ट

court | maidān | मैदान

baseball • baseball • बेसबॉल

field • maidān • मैदान

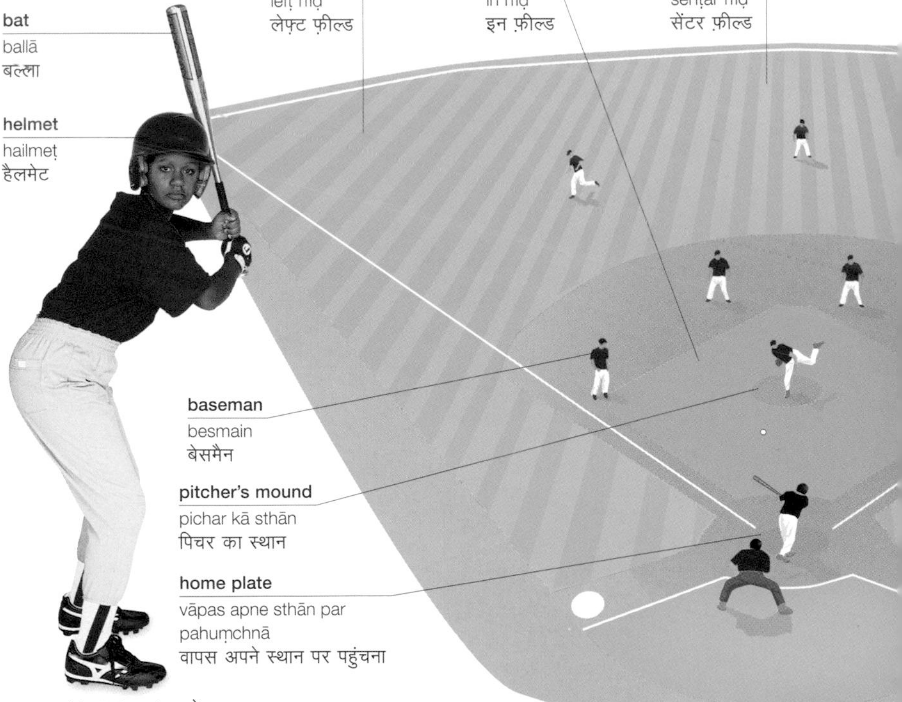
left field
left fīḍ
लेफ़्ट फ़ील्ड
infield
in fīlḍ
इन फ़ील्ड
center field
senṭar fīlḍ
सेंटर फ़ील्ड
bat
ballā
बल्ला
helmet
hailmeṭ
हैलमेट
baseman
besmain
बेसमैन
pitcher's mound
pichar kā sthān
पिचर का स्थान
home plate
vāpas apne sthān par
pahuṃchnā
वापस अपने स्थान पर पहुंचना

batter | ballebāz | बल्लेबाज़

vocabulary • śabdāvalī • शब्दावली

inning pārī पारी	**safe** surakṣit सुरक्षित	**foul ball** fāul gend फ़ाउल गेंद
run ran रन	**out** āuṭ आउट	**strike** sṭrāik स्ट्राइक

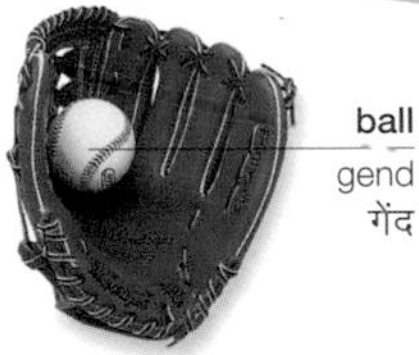
ball
gend
गेंद

mitt | dastānā
दस्ताना

mask | mukhauṭā
मुखौटा

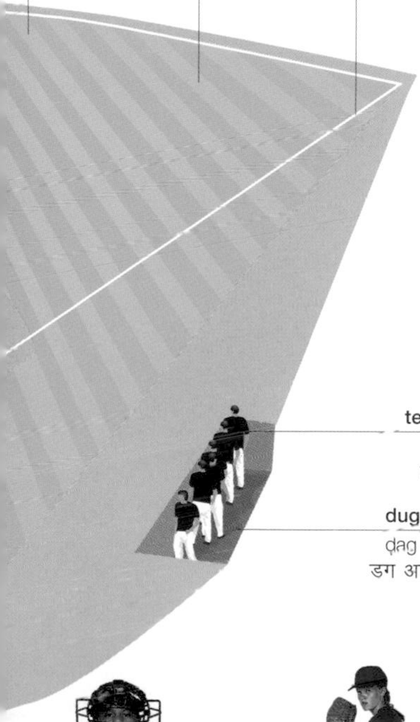
outfield
āuṭ fīlḍ
आउट फ़ील्ड
right field
rāiṭ fīlḍ
राइट फ़ील्ड
foul line
fāul lāin
फ़ाउल लाइन
team
ṭīm
टीम
dugout
ḍag āuṭ
डग आउट

catcher
kaichar | कैचर

pitcher
pichar | पिचर

actions • kriyāeṃ • क्रियाएं

throw (v) | ball pheṃknā
बॉल फेंकना

catch (v) | gend
pakaṛnā | गेंद पकड़ना

run (v)
dauṛnā | दौड़ना

field (v) | fīlḍiṅg karnā
फ़ील्डिंग करना

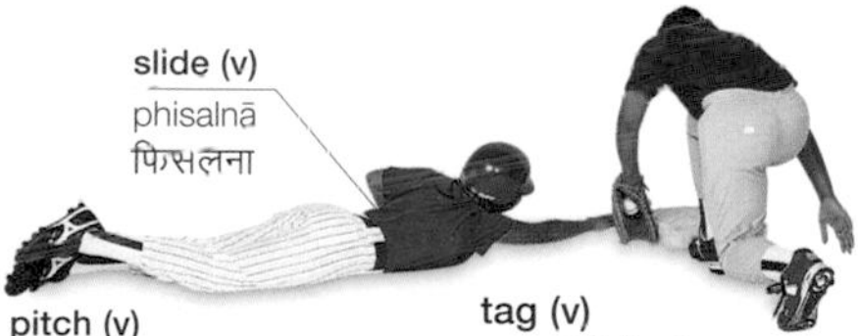
slide (v)
phisalnā
फिसलना
tag (v)
pīchhe dauṛnā | पीछे दौड़ना

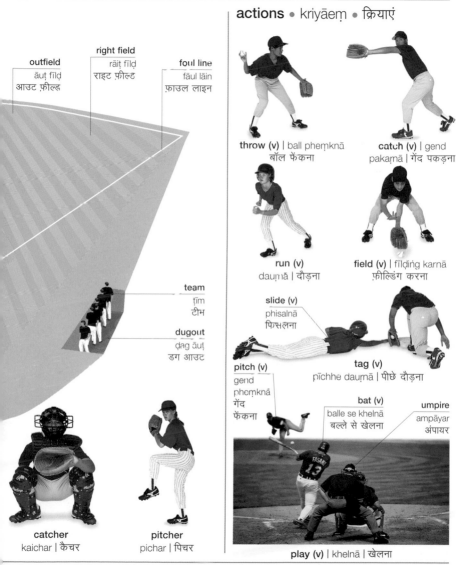

pitch (v)
gend
pheṃknā
गेंद
फेंकना
bat (v)
balle se khelnā
बल्ले से खेलना
umpire
ampāyar
अंपायर
play (v) | khelnā | खेलना

tennis • ṭenis • टेनिस

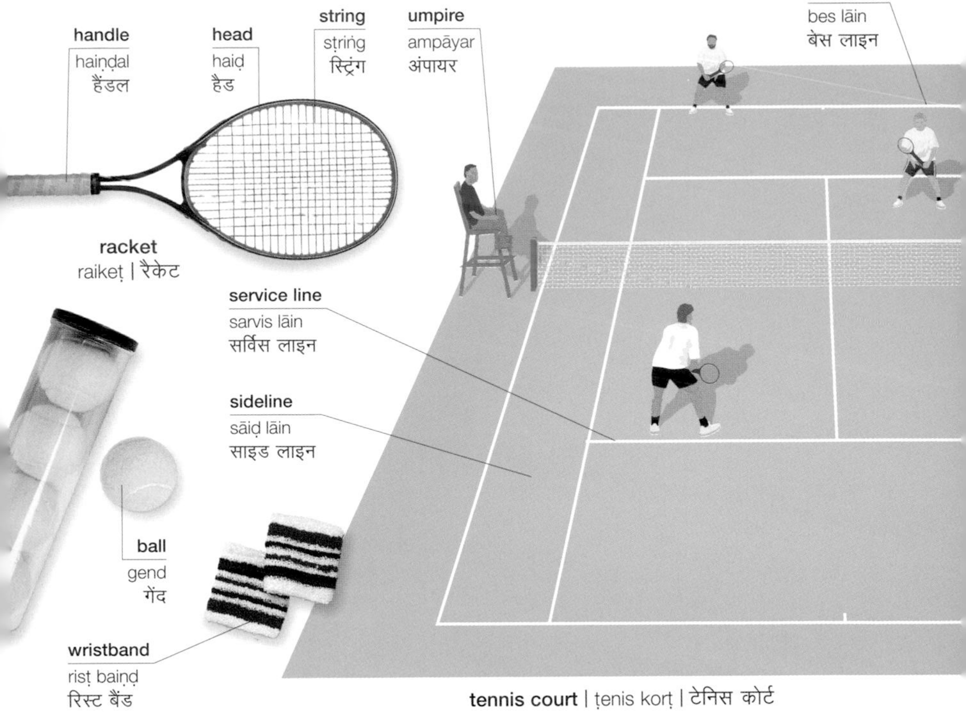
handle
haiṇḍal
हैंडल
head
haiḍ
हैड
string
string
स्ट्रिंग
umpire
ampāyar
अंपायर
baseline
bes lāin
बेस लाइन
racket
raikeṭ | रैकेट
service line
sarvis lāin
सर्विस लाइन
sideline
sāiḍ lāin
साइड लाइन
ball
gend
गेंद
wristband
risṭ baiṇḍ
रिस्ट बैंड

tennis court | ṭenis korṭ | टेनिस कोर्ट

vocabulary • śabdāvalī • शब्दावली

singles ekal एकल	**set** saiṭ सैट	**deuce** barābarī बराबरी	**fault** galat shot ग़लत शॉट	**slice** galat prahār ग़लत प्रहार	**let!** khilāṛī ko roknā खिलाड़ी को रोकना
doubles yugal युगल	**match** maich मैच	**love** śūnya शून्य	**dropshot** dropshot ड्रॉप शॉट	**rally** kaṛā pariśram कड़ा परिश्रम	**championship** chaimpiyanśip चैम्पियनशिप
game khel खेल	**spin** spin स्पिन	**tiebreaker** nirṇāyak aṃk निर्णायक अंक	**advantage** anukūl sthiti अनुकूल स्थिति	**linesman** lāins main लाइन्स मैन	**ace** pahlī sarvis se banā aṃk पहली सर्विस से बना अंक

net
neṭ
नेट
smash
zor se mārnā
ज़ोर से मारना
ball boy
ball boy
बॉल बॉय
serve (v)
sarvis karnā
सर्विस करना
tennis shoes
ṭenis jūte
टेनिस जूते

player
khilāṛī | खिलाड़ी

strokes • sṭroks • स्ट्रोक्स

serve
sarv | सर्व

volley
volley | वॉली

return
riṭarn | रिटर्न

lob | lob
लोब

forehand
forhaiṇḍ | फ़ोरहैंड

backhand
baikhaiṇḍ | बैकहैंड

racket games • raikeṭ ke khel • रैकेट के खेल

shuttlecock
chiṛiyā
चिड़िया

badminton
baiḍminṭan | बैडमिंटन

paddle
baiṭ
बैट

table tennis
ṭebal ṭenis | टेबल टेनिस

squash
skvaiś | स्क्वैश

racketball
raikeṭ ball | रैकेट बॉल

golf • golf • गोल्फ़

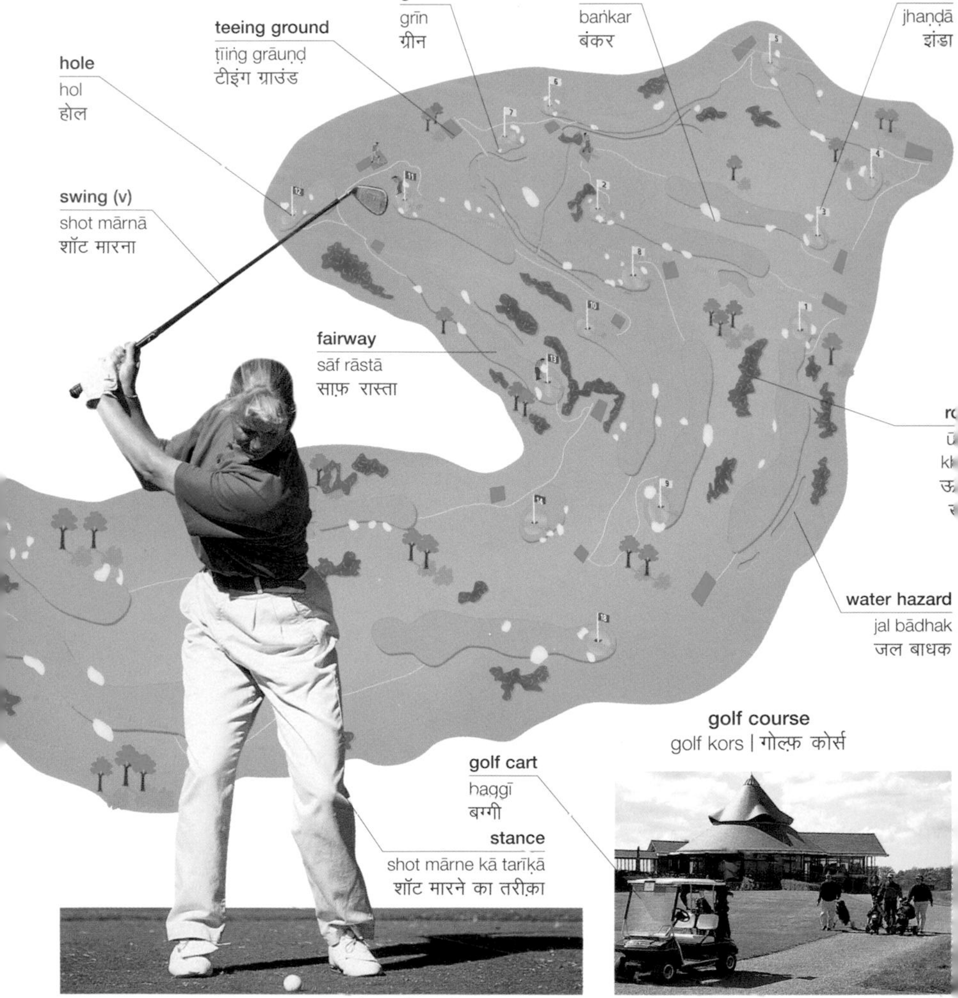
green
grīn
ग्रीन
bunker
baṅkar
बंकर
flag
jhaṇḍā
झंडा
teeing ground
ṭīiṅg grāuṇḍ
टीइंग ग्राउंड
hole
hol
होल
swing (v)
shot mārnā
शॉट मारना
fairway
sāf rāstā
साफ़ रास्ता
water hazard
jal bādhak
जल बाधक
golf cart
baggī
बग्गी
stance
shot mārne kā tarīķā
शॉट मारने का तरीक़ा

golf course
golf kors | गोल्फ़ कोर्स

golfer | golf khilāṛī | गोल्फ़ खिलाड़ी

clubhouse | klab hāus | क्लब हाउस

equipment • upkaraṇ • उपकरण

golf ball
golf ball
गोल्फ़ बॉल

tee | ṭī | टी

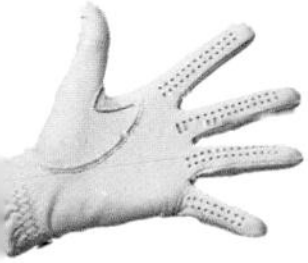

glove
dastānā | दस्ताना

golf bag
golf baig
गोल्फ़ बैग

cart
golf trolley | गोल्फ़ ट्रॉली

spikes
kīloṃ vāle jūte
कीलों वाले जूते

golf shoe
golf ke jūte | गोल्फ़ के जूते

golf clubs • golf klab • गोल्फ़ क्लब

wood
vuḍ | वुड

putter
paṭar | पटर

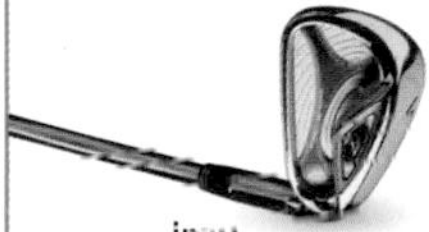

iron
āyaran | आयरन

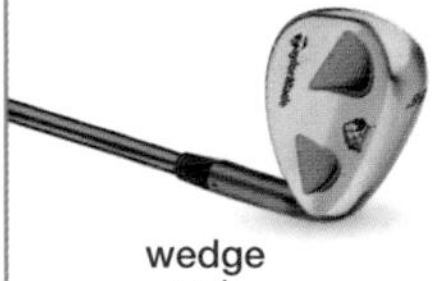

wedge
vej | वेज

actions • gatividhiyāṃ • गतिविधियां

tee-off (v) | khel ārambh karnā
खेल आरंभ करना

drive (v)
ḍrāiv mārnā
ड्राइव मारना

putt (v) | gend par prahār karnā
गेंद पर प्रहार करना

chip (v)
chip shot lenā
चिप शॉट लेना

vocabulary • śabdāvalī • शब्दावली

par
ausat khel
औसत खेल

over par
utkṛṣṭ khel
उत्कृष्ट खेल

handicap
haiṇḍīkaip
हैंडीकैप

caddy
golf sahāyak
गोल्फ़ सहायक

backswing
baiksviṅg
बैकस्विंग

stroke
sṭrok
स्ट्रोक

under par
nimn khel
निम्न खेल

hole in one
hol in van
होल इन वन

tournament
khel pratiyogitā
खेल प्रतियोगिता

spectators
darśak
दर्शक

practice swing
praikṭis shot
प्रैक्टिस शॉट

line of play
khel rekhā
खेल रेखा

track and field • ethleṭiks • एथलेटिक्स

lane
len
लेन

track
paṅkti
पंक्ति

finish line
samāpti rekhā
समाप्ति रेखा

starting line
prārambhik rekhā
प्रारंभिक रेखा

field
maidān | मैदान

starting blocks
ārambhik avrodh | आरंभिक अवरोध

sprinter
tez dhāvak
तेज़ धावक

discus
chakkā pheṃk
चक्का फेंक

athlete
ethlīṭ
एथलीट

shotput
golā pheṃk
गोला फेंक

javelin
bhālā pheṃk
भाला फेंक

vocabulary • śabdāvalī • शब्दावली

race dauṛ दौड़	**record** record रिकॉर्ड	**photo finish** barābarī kī dauṛ बराबरी की दौड़	**personal best** apnā viśeṣ pradarśan अपना विशेष प्रदर्शन
time samaya समय	**pole vault** bāṃs kūd बांस–कूद	**marathon** mairāthan मैराथन	**break a record (v)** record toṛnā रिकॉर्ड तोड़ना

stopwatch
virām ghaṛī | विराम घड़ी

baton
ḍaṇḍī
डंडी

relay race
rile dauṛ | रिले दौड़

crossbar
chhaṛ
छड़

high jump
ūṃchī kūd | ऊंची कूद

long jump
lambī kūd | लंबी कूद

hurdles | bādhā dauṛ | बाधा दौड़

gymnastics • jimnāsṭik • जिमनास्टिक

horse
horse
हॉर्स

vault
chhalāṅg mārnā
छलांग मारना

springboard
spriṅgborḍ
स्प्रिंगबोर्ड

somersault
kalābāzī | कलाबाज़ी

mat
chaṭāī | चटाई

floor exercises
zamīnī vyāyām
ज़मीनी व्यायाम

gymnast
jimnāsṭ
जिमनास्ट

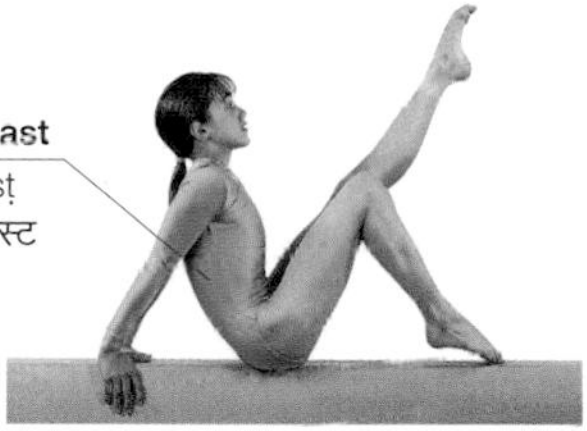

beam | bīm | बीम

tumble
kalābāzī
कलाबाज़ी

ribbon
fītā
फ़ीता

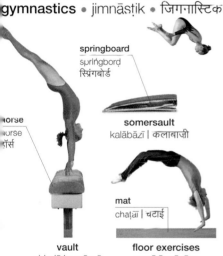

rhythmic gymnastics
saṅgītmaya jimnāsṭik
संगीतमय जिमनास्टिक

vocabulary • śabdāvalī • शब्दावली

horizontal bar
āṛī chhaṛ
आड़ी छड़

parallel bars
samānāntar chhaṛeṃ
समानांतर छड़ें

pommel horse
pommel horse
पॉमेल हॉर्स

asymmetric bars
asamān chhaṛeṃ
असमान छड़ें

rings
riṅg
रिंग

podium
poḍiyam
पोडियम

medals
padak
पदक

gold
svarṇ
स्वर्ण

silver
rajat
रजत

bronze
kāṃsya
कांस्य

combat sports • mall krīṛā • मल्ल क्रीड़ा

opponent
pratidvandī
प्रतिद्वंद्वी
guard
hailmeṭ
हैलमेट
glove
dastānā
दस्ताना
belt
peṭī
पेटी

tae kwon do | tāikvānḍo | ताइक्वांडो

karate | karāṭe | कराटे

judo | jūḍo | जूडो

aikido
ekāīḍo | एकाइडो

mask
mukhauṭā
मुखौटा
sword
talvār
तलवार

kendo
kenḍo | केनडो

kung fu
kuṅgfū | कुंगफ़ू

kickboxing
kik boxing | किक बॉक्सिंग

wrestling
kuśtī | कुश्ती

boxing
mukkebāzī | मुक्केबाज़ी

actions • daṅvpeṅch • दांवपेंच

fall
girnā | गिरना

hold
pakaṛnā | पकड़ना

throw
girānā | गिराना

pin | paṭkanī
denā | पटकनी देना

kick
klk | किक

punch
mukkā | मुक्का

strike
mukkā mārnā | मुक्का मारना

jump
kūdnā | कूदना

block
prahār roknā | प्रहार रोकना

chop | nīche vār
karnā | नीचे वार करना

vocabulary • śabdāvalī • शब्दावली

boxing ring boxing riṅg बॉक्सिंग रिंग	**round** charaṇ चरण	**fist** muṭṭhī मुट्ठी	**black belt** blaik belṭ ब्लैक बेल्ट	**capoeira** kepoirā केपोइरा
boxing gloves boxing dastāne बॉक्सिंग-दस्ताने	**bout** śakti parīkṣā शक्ति परीक्षा	**knockout** paṭkanī पटकनी	**self-defense** ātmrakṣā आत्मरक्षा	**sumo wrestling** sūmo kuśtī सूमो कुश्ती
mouth guard māuth gārḍ माउथ गार्ड	**sparring** paiṅtrebāzī पैंतरेबाज़ी	**punching bag** pañch baig पंच बैग	**martial arts** mārśal ārṭs मार्शल आर्ट्स	**tai chi** tāī chī ताई-ची

swimming • tairākī • तैराकी

equipment • upkaraṇ • उपकरण

armband
bāzū paṭṭī | बाजू पट्टी

nose clip
noz klip
नोज़ क्लिप

goggles
chaśmā | चश्मा

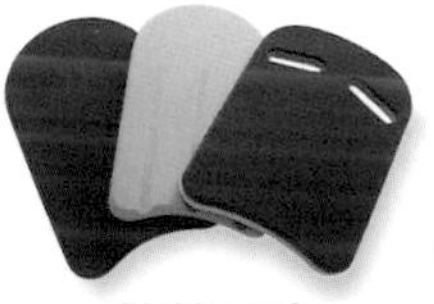

kickboard
floṭ | फ़्लोट

swimsuit
svimsūṭ | स्विमसूट

lane
len
लेन

water
pānī
पानी

starting block
ārambh sthal
आरंभ स्थल

swimming pool | taraṇtāl | तरणताल

ca
ṭop
टोप

trunk
jāṅghiy
जांघिय

swimmer | tairāk | तैराक

springboard
spriṅgborḍ
स्प्रिंगबोर्ड

diver
gotākhor
गोताख़ोर

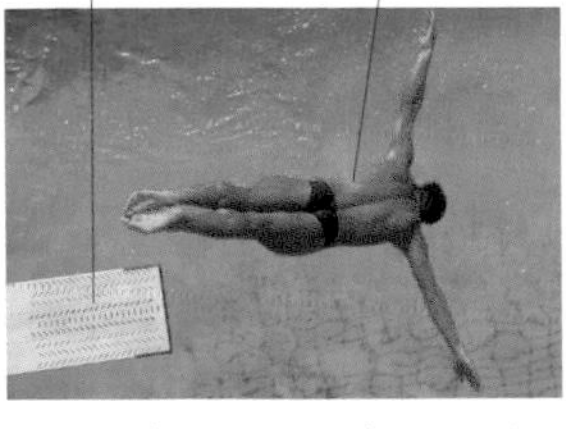

dive (v) | ḍāiv mārnā | डाइव मारना

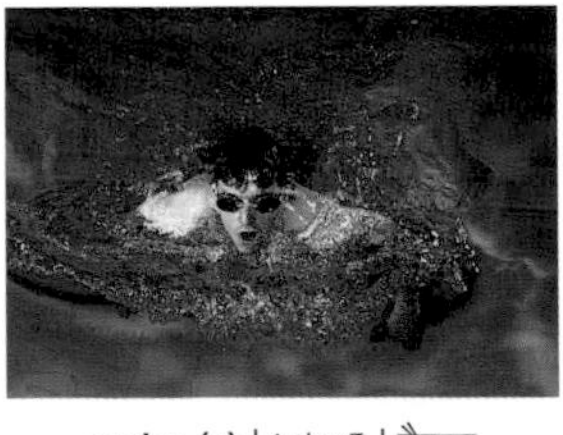

swim (v) | tairnā | तैरना

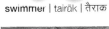

turn | palaṭnā | पलटना

styles • śailiyāṃ • शैलियां

front crawl | franṭ crawl | फ़्रंट क्रॉल

breaststroke | bresṭsṭrok | ब्रेस्टस्ट्रोक

stroke
sṭrok | स्ट्रोक

backstroke | baiksṭrok | बैकस्ट्रोक

kick
kik | किक

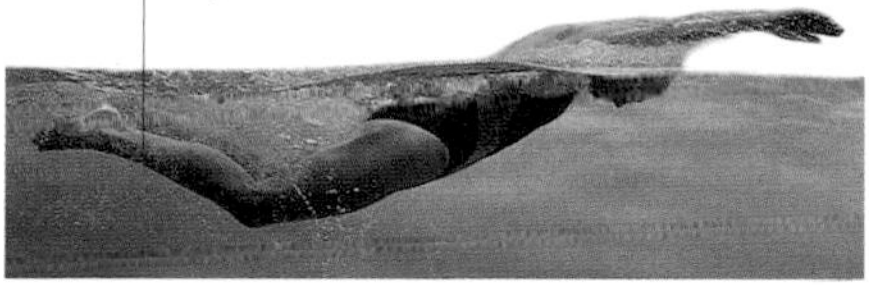

butterfly | baṭarflāī | बटरफ़्लाई

scuba diving • skūbā ḍāiviṅg • स्कूबा डाइविंग

vetsuit
et suṭ
ट सूट

lipper
ipar
फ़्लपर

veight belt
azanī peṭī
ज़नी पेटी

air cylinder
oksījan slienḍar
ऑक्सीजन सिलेंडर

mask
naḳāb
नक़ाब

regulator
regyūleṭar
रेग्यूलेटर

snorkel
śvās nalī
श्वास नली

vocabulary • śabdāvalī • शब्दावली

dive
ḍāiv
डाइव

high dive
ūṃchī ḍāiv
ऊंची डाइव

racing dive
resiṅg ḍāiv
रेसिंग डाइव

tread water (v)
pānī meṃ pair mārnā
पानी में पैर मारना

lockers
lokar
लॉकर

lifeguard
jīvan rakṣak
जीवन रक्षक

water polo
water polo
वॉटर पोलो

deep end
gahrā chhor
गहरा छोर

shallow end
uthlā chhor
उथला छोर

synchronized swimming
siṅkronāizḍ tairākī
सिंक्रोनाइज़्ड तैराकी

cramp
nas charhnā
नस चढ़ना

drown (v)
ḍūbnā
डूबना

sailing • pāl naukāyan • पाल नौकायन

compass
kampās | कंपास

anchor
laṅgar | लंगर

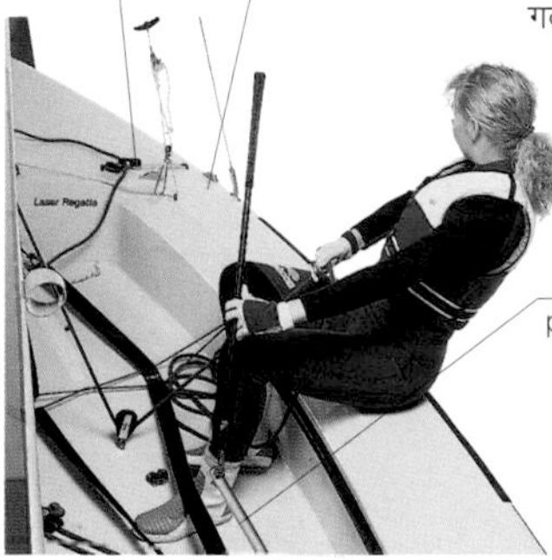
cleat
phannī
फन्नी
sidedeck
sāiḍ ḍek
साइड डेक
tiller
patvār hatthā
पतवार हत्था

navigate (v) | mārg nirdeśan karnā | मार्ग निर्देशन करना

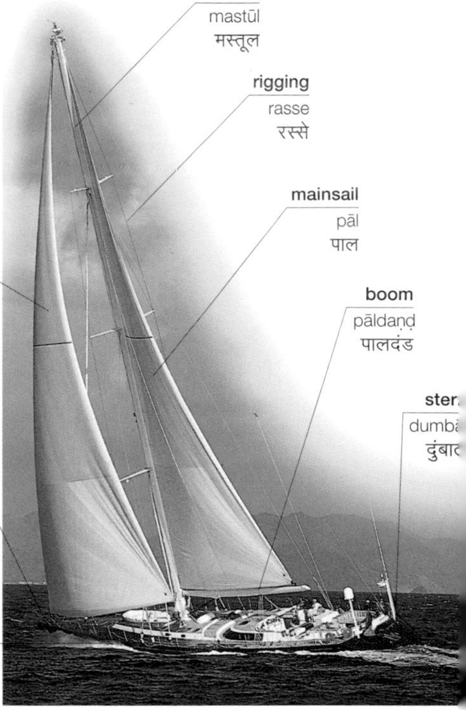
mast
mastūl
मस्तूल
rigging
rasse
रस्से
mainsail
pāl
पाल
headsail
aglā pāl
अगला पाल
boom
pāldaṇḍ
पालदंड
bow
galhī
गलही
ster
dumbā
दुंबा
hull
peṭā
पेटा

yacht | krīṛā naukā | क्रीड़ा–नौका

safety • surakṣā • सुरक्षा

flare
tīvr prakaś saṅketak
तीव्र प्रकाश संकेतक

life preserver
jīvan rakṣā ṭyūb
जीवन रक्षा ट्यूब

life jacket
rakṣā jaikeṭ
रक्षा जैकेट

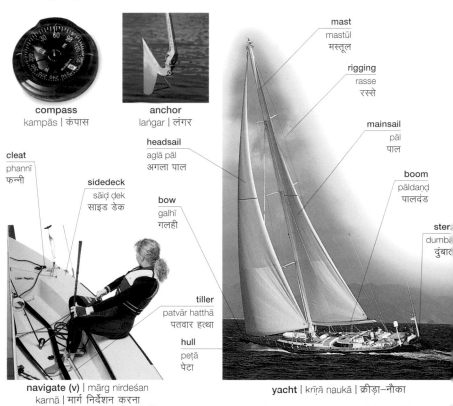

life raft
jīvan rakṣā naukā
जीवन रक्षा नौका

watersports • jalkrīṛā • जलक्रीड़ा

ower
āvik
ाविक

oar
chappū
चप्पू

kayak
pansuiyā
पनसुइया

paddle
chhoṭā chappū
छोटा चप्पू

row (v) | nāv khenā | नाव खेना

canoeing | naukā vihār | नौका विहार

ail
āl
ाल

indsurfer
ṇḍ sarfar
ाड सर्फ़र

oard
ord
ाई

surfboard
sarf borḍ
सर्फ़ बोर्ड

ski
skī | स्की

surfing
sarfiṅg | सर्फ़िंग

waterskiing | water
skiing | वॉटर स्कीइंग

speedboating | spīḍ
boṭiṅg | स्पीड बोटिंग

tootstrap
fuṭ strep
फ़ुट स्ट्रेप

rafting
naukāyan | नौकायन

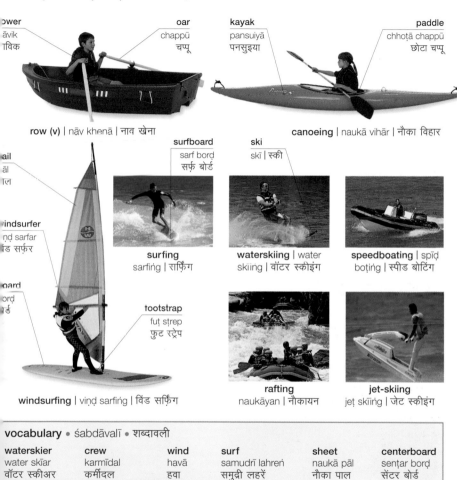

jet-skiing
jeṭ skīiṅg | जेट स्कीइंग

windsurfing | viṇḍ sarfiṅg | विंड सर्फ़िंग

vocabulary • śabdāvalī • शब्दावली

waterskier	**crew**	**wind**	**surf**	**sheet**	**centerboard**
water skīar	karmīdal	havā	samudrī lahreṅ	naukā pāl	senṭar borḍ
वॉटर स्कीअर	कर्मीदल	हवा	समुद्री लहरें	नौका पाल	सेंटर बोर्ड
surfer	**tack (v)**	**wave**	**rapids**	**rudder**	**capsize (v)**
sarfar	diśā badalnā	lahar	tīvr nadī	patvār	nāv ulaṭnā
सर्फ़र	दिशा बदलना	लहर	तीव्र नदी	पतवार	नाव उलटना

horseback riding • ghuṛsavārī • घुड़सवारी

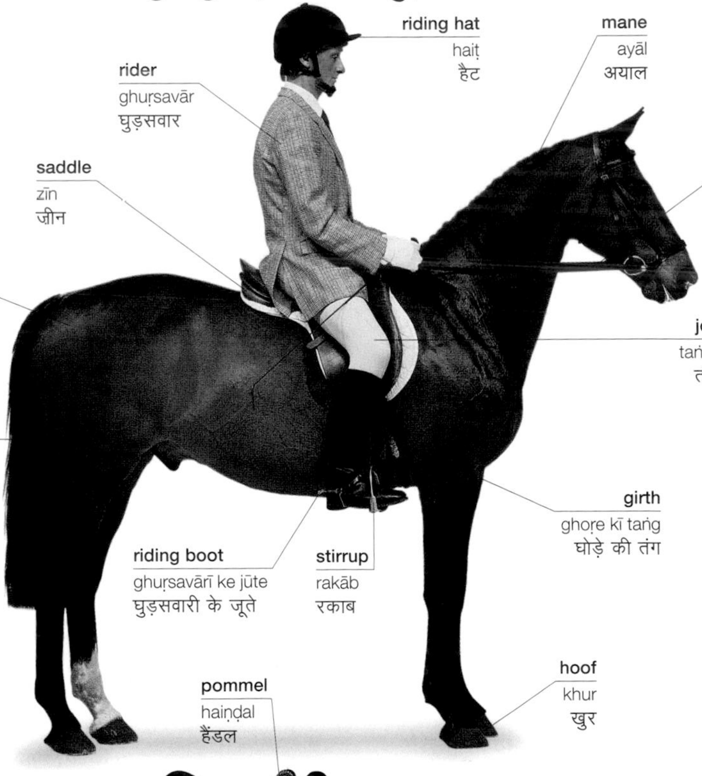
riding hat
haiṭ
हैट
mane
ayāl
अयाल
rider
ghuṛsavār
घुड़सवार
saddle
zīn
ज़ीन
rein
lagā
horse
ghoṛā
घोड़ा
jodhpurs
taṅg pajāmī
तंग पजामी
tail
pūṃchh
पूंछ
girth
ghoṛe kī taṅg
घोड़े की तंग
riding boot
ghuṛsavārī ke jūte
घुड़सवारी के जूते
stirrup
rakāb
रकाब
hoof
khur
खुर

pommel
haiṇḍal
हैंडल
seat
sīṭ
सीट

horseshoe
ghuṛnāl | घुड़नाल

side-saddle
sāiḍ zīn | साइड ज़ीन

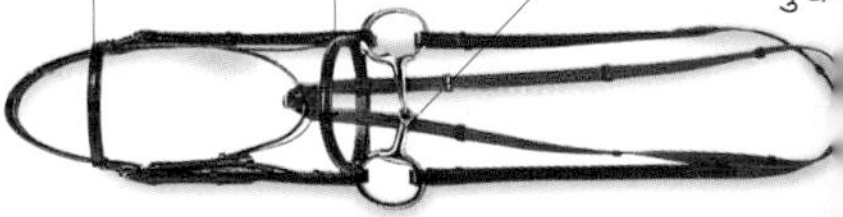
browband
sir paṭṭā
सिर–पट्टा
noseband
nakel
नकेल
lagām
मुख

bridle | lagām | लगाम

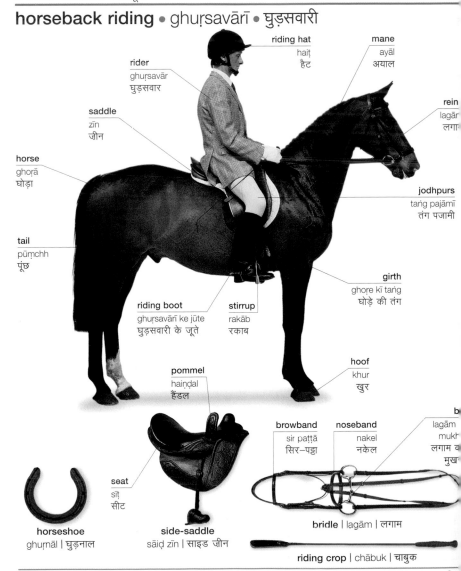

riding crop | chābuk | चाबुक

events • pratispardhā • प्रतिस्पर्धा

racehorse
dauṛ kā ghoṛā | दौड़ का घोड़ा

fence
bāṛ | बाड़

horse race
ghuṛdauṛ | घुड़दौड़

steeplechase
bādhā dauṛ | बाधा दौड़

harness race | ghoṛā gāṛī
dauṛ | घोड़ा गाड़ी दौड़

rodeo
ghuṛsavārī khel | घुड़सवारी खेल

showjumping
śo jampiṅg | शो जंपिंग

carriage race
baggī dauṛ | बग्गी दौड़

trail-riding
ṭraikiṅg | ट्रैकिंग

dressage
ghoṛā sadhānā | घोड़ा सधाना

polo
polo | पोलो

vocabulary • śabdāvalī • शब्दावली

walk	canter	jump	halter	paddock	flat race
chāl	ghoṛe kī mand chāl	kūd	rassī	ghoṛoṃ kā bāṛā	sīdhī dauṛ
चाल	घोड़े की मंद चाल	कूद	रस्सी	घोड़ों का बाड़ा	सीधी दौड़
trot	gallop	groom	stable	arena	racecourse
dulkī	sarpaṭ chāl	sāīs	astabal	khel kā maidān	dauṛ kā maidān
दुलकी	सरपट चाल	साईस	अस्तबल	खेल का मैदान	दौड़ का मैदान

fishing • machhlī pakaṛnā • मछली पकड़ना

sinker | bhār | भार

barb
kāṃṭā
कांटा
eye
āṃkh
आंख

fishhook | machhlī huk | मछली हुक

bait | machhlī chārā | मछली–चारा

landing net | machhl
pakaṛne kā jāl | मछली
पकड़ने का जाल

float
floṭ | फ़्लोट

lure
chārā | चारा

fly | kṛtrim makkhī | कृत्रिम मक्खी

tackle box
upkaraṇ baksā
उपकरण बक्सा

keep net | machhlī rakhne kā jāl | मछली रखने का जाल

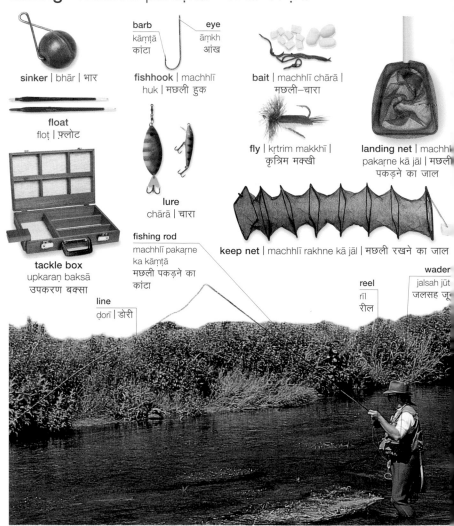

fishing rod
machhlī pakaṛne
ka kāṃṭā
मछली पकड़ने का
कांटा
line
ḍorī | डोरी
reel
rīl
रील
wader
jalsah jūt
जलसह जू

angler | machhlī pakaṛne vālā | मछली पकड़ने वाला

types of fishing • machhlī pakaṛne ke prakār • मछली पकड़ने के प्रकार

freshwater fishing | nadī meṃ machhlī pakaṛnā | नदी में मछली पकड़ना

fly fishing | makkhī se machhlī pakaṛnā | मक्खी से मछली पकड़ना।

surfcasting | samudr kināre machhlī pakaṛnā
समुद्र किनारे मछली पकड़ना

sport fishing
śaukiyā machhlī pakaṛnā
शौक़िया मछली पकड़ना

deep sea fishing
gahre samudr meṃ machhlī pakaṛnā
गहरे समुद्र में मछली पकड़ना

activities • gatividhiyāṃ • गतिविधियां

cast (v)
jāl ḍālnā
जाल डालना

catch (v)
pakaṛnā
पकड़ना

reel in (v)
ḍorī khīṃchnā
डोरी खींचना

net (v)
jāl se pakaṛnā
जाल से पकड़ना

release (v)
pānī meṃ chhoṛnā
पानी में छोड़ना

vocabulary • śabdāvalī • शब्दावली

bait (v) chārā lagānā चारा लगाना	**tackle** upkaraṇ उपकरण	**rain gear** jalvārak जलवारक	**fishing permit** fiśiṅg parmiṭ फ़िशिंग परमिट	**creel** machhlī kī ṭokrī मछली की टोकरी
bite (v) chārā khānā चारा खाना	**spool** charkhī चरखी	**pole** bāṃs बांस	**marine fishing** samudr meṃ machhlī pakaṛnā समुद्र में मछली पकड़ना	**spearfishing** bhāle se machhlī pakaṛnā भाले से मछली पकड़ना

skiing • skīiṅg • स्कीइंग

ski slope
skī slop
स्की स्लोप
chairlif
cheyarlif
चेयरलिफ़्
cable car
kebal kār
केबल कार
ski run
skī mārg
स्की मार्ग
les 3 vallées
glove
dastānā
दस्ताना
ski pole
skī pol
स्की पोल
safety barrier
surakṣā bairiyar
सुरक्षा बैरियर
ski
skī
स्की
tip
nok
नोक
edge
kinārā
किनारा
ski jacket
skī jaikeṭ
स्की जैकेट
ski boot
skī būṭ
स्की बूट
skier
skīyar | स्कीयर

events • pratispardhāeṃ • प्रतिस्पर्धाएं

downhill skiing | ḍāun hil skīiṅg | डाउन हिल स्कीइंग

gate
prārambh sthān
प्रारंभ स्थान

slalom | barfānī dauṛ | बर्फ़ानी दौड़

ski jump
skī kūd | स्की कूद

cross-country skiing
kros-kanṭrī skīiṅg
क्रॉस-कंट्री स्कीइंग

winter sports • śaradiya krīṛāeṃ • शरदीय क्रीड़ाएं

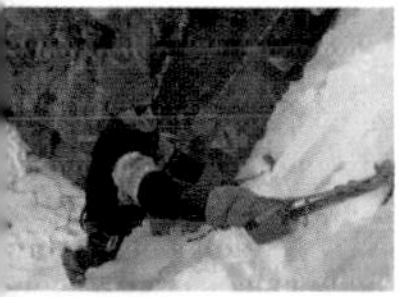

ice climbing
āis klaimbiṅg
आइस क्लाइम्बिंग

ice skating
āis sketiṅg
आइस स्केटिंग

figure skating
figar sketiṅg
फ़िगर स्केटिंग

skate
skeṭ
स्केट

goggles
chaśmā
चश्मा

snowboarding
sno borḍiṅg | स्नो बोर्डिंग

bobsled
slej gāṛī | स्लेज गाड़ी

luge
him vāhan | हिम वाहन

snowmobile
sno mobāil | स्नो मोबाइल

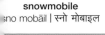

sledding | slej par phisalnā | स्लेज पर फिसलना

vocabulary • śabdāvalī • शब्दावली

alpine skiing
ucch parvatīya skīiṅg
उच्च पर्वतीय स्कीइंग

giant slalom
baṛī barfānī dauṛ
बड़ी बर्फ़ानी दौड़

off-piste
ṭhos baraf par skīiṅg
ठोस बर्फ़ पर स्कीइंग

curling
karliṅg khel
कर्लिंग खेल

dog-sledding
dog slejiṅg
डॉग स्लेजिंग

speed skating
spīḍ sketiṅg
स्पीड स्केटिंग

biathlon
skīiṅg pratiyogitā
स्कीइंग प्रतियोगिता

avalanche
him skhalan
हिम स्खलन

other sports • anya khelkūd • अन्य खेलकूद

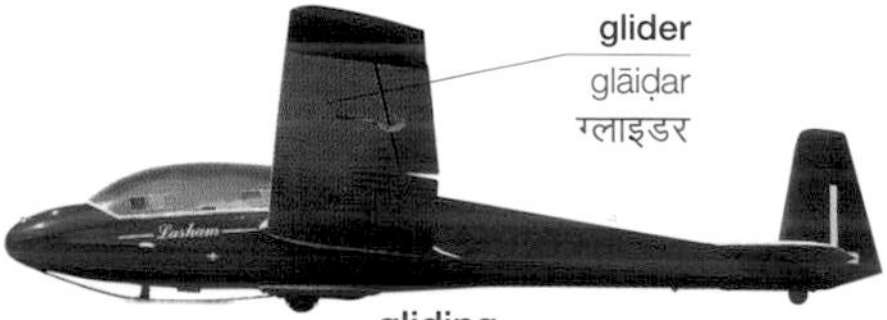

glider
glāiḍar
ग्लाइडर

gliding
glāiḍiṅg
ग्लाइडिंग

hang-glider
haiṅg glāiḍar
हैंग–ग्लाइडर

hang-gliding
haiṅg glāiḍiṅg
हैंग–ग्लाइडिंग

rope
rassī
रस्सी

rock-climbing
parvatārohaṇ | पर्वतारोहण

parachute
pairāśūṭ
पैराशूट

parachuting
pairāśūṭ se utarnā | पैराशूट से उतरना

paragliding
pairāglāiḍiṅg | पैराग्लाइडिंग

skydiving
skāiḍāiving | स्काइडाइविंग

rappelling
parvat avrohaṇ | पर्वत अवरोहण

bungee jumping
bañjī kūd | बंजी कूद

rally driving
railī ḍrāiviṅg
रैली ड्राइविंग

race-car driver
resiṅg ḍrāivar
रेसिंग ड्राइवर

auto racing
moṭar res
मोटर रेस

motocross
moṭar cross
मोटर क्रॉस

motorcycle racing
moṭarbāik res
मोटरबाइक रेस

skateboard
skeṭ borḍ
स्केट बोर्ड

skateboarding
skeṭborḍiṅg
स्केटबोर्डिंग

inline skating
inalāin skeṭiṅg
इनलाइन स्केटिंग

stick
sṭik
स्टिक

lacrosse
cross balle kā khel
क्रॉस बल्ले का खेल

mask
naqāb
नक़ाब

foil
talvār
तलवार

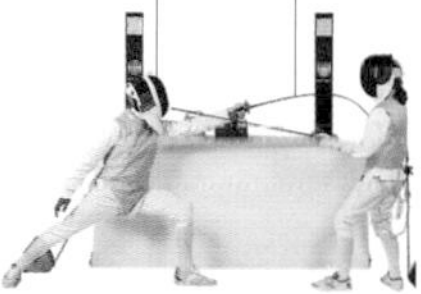

fencing
talvārbāzī
तलवारबाज़ी

pin
pin | पिन

bowling ball
boliṅg ball
बोलिंग बॉल

bowling
boliṅg | बोलिंग

bow
dhanuṣ | धनुष

arrow
tīr
तीर

quiver
tarkaś
तरकश

archery
dhanurvidyā
धनुर्विद्या

target
niśānā | निशाना

target shooting
niśānebāzī
निशानेबाज़ी

pool
pūl biliyarḍ | पूल बिलियर्ड

snooker
snūkar | स्नूकर

fitness • svasthtā • स्वस्थता

exercise bike
vyāyām sāikil
व्यायाम साइकिल

gym machine
jim maśīn
जिम मशीन

bench
bench
बेंच

free weights
vazan
वज़न

bar
chhaṛ
छड़

gym
jim
जिम

rowing machine
roiṅg maśīn
रोइंग मशीन

treadmill
ṭreḍmil
ट्रेडमिल

step machine
sṭep maśīn
स्टेप मशीन

personal trainer
nijī praśikṣak
निजी प्रशिक्षक

cross-trainer
cross ṭrenar
क्रॉस ट्रेनर

swimming pool
taranṭāl
तरणताल

sauna
vāṣp snān
वाष्प स्नान

exercises • vyāyām • व्यायाम

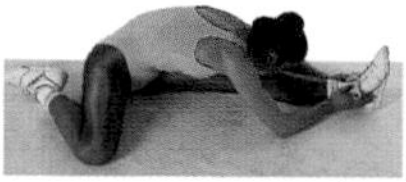

stretch | sṭrech | स्ट्रेच

lunge
āge jhuknā | आगे झुकना

tights
taṅg pajāmī
तंग पजामी

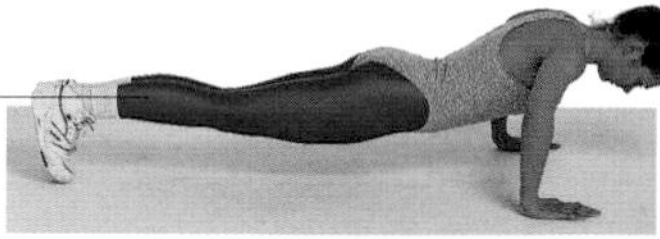

push-up
pres ap | प्रेस अप

squat
squat
स्कवॉट

sit-up
siṭ-ap
सिट—अप

dumb bell
ḍamb bel
डंब बेल

biceps curl
ḍole
डोले

leg press
leg pres
लेग प्रेस

chest press
chesṭ pres
चेस्ट प्रेस

athletic shoes
ṭrenars
ट्रेनर्स

weight bar
vazan chhaṛ
वज़न छड़

weight training
bhārottolan
भारोत्तोलन

jogging
jogging
जॉगिंग

pilates
pilāṭez
पिलाटेज़

vocabulary • śabdāvalī • शब्दावली

train (v)
abhyās karnā
अभ्यास करना

warm up (v)
māṃspeśiyāṃ garmānā
मांसपेशियां गरमाना

circuit training
sarkiṭ ṭreniṅg
सर्किट ट्रेनिंग

flex (v)
jhukānā
झुकाना

extend (v)
baṛhānā
बढ़ाना

pull up (v)
pul-ap karnā
पुल—अप करना

boxercise
boxing vyāyām
बॉक्सिंग व्यायाम

rope-jumping
rassī kūd
रस्सी कूद

jog in place (v)
ek jagah jog karnā
एक जगह जॉग करना

leisure

manorañjan

मनोरंजन

theater • thieṭar • थिएटर

curtain
pardā
पर्दा

wings
pārśv
पार्श्व

set
saiṭ
सैट

audience
darśak
दर्शक

orchestra
orchestra
ऑर्केस्ट्रा

stage | manch | मंच

seat
sīṭ
सीट

upper balcony
ūprī dīrghā
ऊपरी दीर्घा

row
ḳatār
क़तार

box
box
बॉक्स

circle
dīrghā
दीर्घा

balcony
bālkanī
बालकनी

aisle
vīthikā
वीथिका

orchestra
stalls
स्टॉल

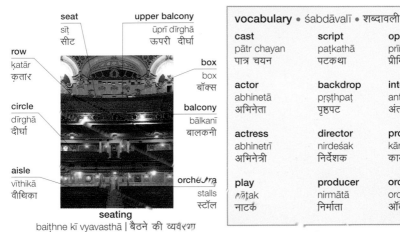

seating
baiṭhne kī vyavasthā | बैठने की व्यवस्था

vocabulary • śabdāvalī • शब्दावली

cast	script	opening night
pātr chayan	paṭkathā	prīmiyar
पात्र चयन	पटकथा	प्रीमियर
actor	backdrop	intermission
abhinetā	pṛṣṭhpaṭ	antarāl
अभिनेता	पृष्ठपट	अंतराल
actress	director	program
abhinetrī	nirdeśak	kāryakram
अभिनेत्री	निर्देशक	कार्यक्रम
play	producer	orchestra pit
nāṭak	nirmātā	orchestra sthal
नाटक	निर्माता	ऑर्केस्ट्रा स्थल

concert
concert | कॉन्सर्ट

musical
myūzikal | म्यूज़िकल

ballet
baile | बैले

opera
opera | ऑपेरा

vocabulary • śabdāvalī • शब्दावली

usher
praveśak
प्रवेशक

classical music
śāstrīya saṅgīt
शास्त्रीय संगीत

musical score
svarlipi
स्वरलिपि

soundtrack
dhvani paṭṭī
ध्वनि पट्टी

applaud (v)
tālī bajānā
ताली बजाना

encore
punaḥ prastuti
पुनः प्रस्तुति

What time does it start?
yah kis samaya śurū hogā?
यह किस समय शुरू होगा?

I'd like two tickets for tonight's performance.
mujhe āj rāt ke kāryakram kī do ṭikṭeṃ chāhie
मुझे आज रात के कार्यक्रम की दो टिकटें चाहिए।

cinema • sinemā • सिनेमा

box office
box office
बॉक्स ऑफ़िस

lobby
lobby
लॉबी

movie theater
sinemā hall | सिनेमा हॉल

screen
pardā | पर्दा

vocabulary • śabdāvalī • शब्दावली

comedy
comedy
कॉमेडी

thriller
thrilar
थ्रिलर

horror movie
ḍarāvanī film
डरावनी फ़िल्म

Western
paśchimī
पश्चिमी

romance
romāns
रोमांस

science fiction movie
vijñān kathā film
विज्ञान कथा फ़िल्म

adventure
romānch kathā
रोमांच कथा

animated film
ainimeṭeḍ film
ऐनिमेटेड फ़िल्म

orchestra • vādyavṛṁd • वाद्यवृंद

strings • tantrī vādya • तंत्री वाद्य

harp hārp हार्प

conductor sanchālak संचालक

double bass ḍabal bās डबल बास

violin vāyalin वायलिन

podium poḍiyam पोडियम

viola vāyolā वायोला

cello chelo चेलो

score svar lipi स्वर लिपि

piano | piyāno | पियानो

treble clef ṭrebal klaif ट्रेबल क्लैफ़

note svar स्वर

staf sṭā स्टाफ़

bass clef bās klaif बास क्लैफ़

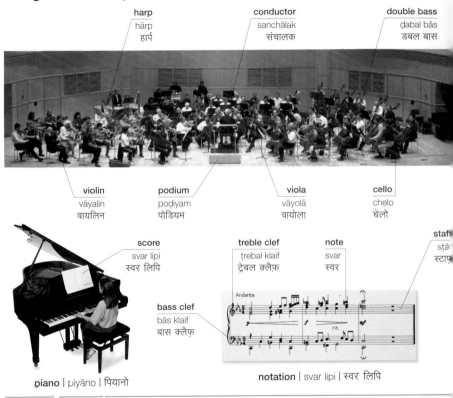

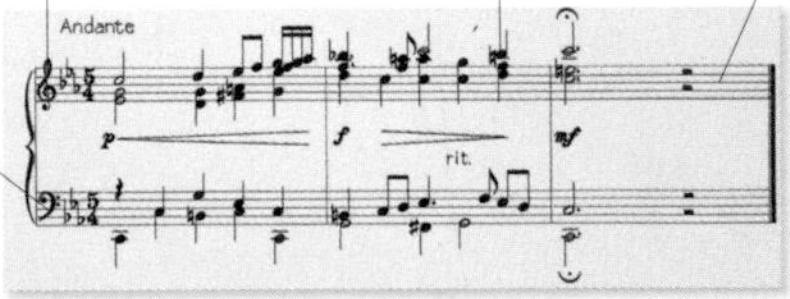

notation | svar lipi | स्वर लिपि

vocabulary • śabdāvalī • शब्दावली

overture pūrvrang पूर्वरंग	**sonata** sonāṭā सोनाटा	**rest** virām विराम	**sharp** ucch svar उच्च स्वर	**natural** piyāno kā śvet pardā पियानो का श्वेत पर्दा	**scale** saptak सप्तक
symphony svar saṅgati स्वर संगति	**instruments** vādya yantr वाद्य यंत्र	**pitch** svarmān स्वरमान	**flat** komal sur कोमल सुर	**bar** tālkhaṇḍ तालखंड	**baton** chhaṛī छड़ी

woodwind • kāṣṭh vādya yantr • काष्ठ वाद्य यंत्र

piccolo
piccolo | पिकॉलो

flute
bāṃsurī | बांसुरी

oboe
obo | ओबो

English horn
aṅgrezī bīn | अंग्रेज़ी बीन

clarinet
klairineṭ
क्लैरिनेट

bass clarinet
mandr klairineṭ
मंद्र क्लैरिनेट

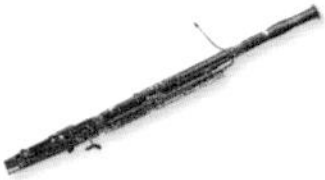

bassoon
basūn
बसून

double bassoon
ḍabal basūn
डबल बसून

saxophone
saiksofon
सैक्सोफ़ोन

percussion • tāl vādya • ताल वाद्य

kettle drum
nagāṛā | नगाड़ा

gong
ghaṇṭā | घंटा

vibraphone
vāibrāfon | वाइब्राफ़ोन

foot pedal
fuṭ paiḍal
फुट पैडल

bongos
bauṃgo
बौंगो

snare drum
chhoṭā ḍram
छोटा ड्रम

cymbals
manjīrā | मंजीरा

tambourine
ḍaphlī | डफली

triangle
ṭrāieṅgal
ट्राइएंगल

maracas
marākas
मराकस

brass • pītal ke vādya • पीतल के वाद्य

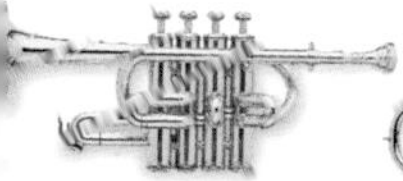

trumpet
ṭrampeṭ | ट्रम्पेट

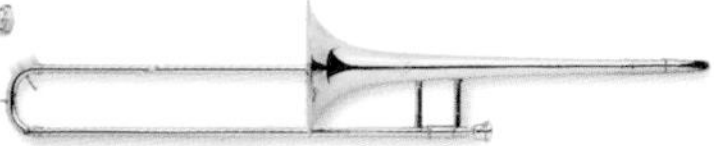

trombone
trombone | ट्रॉमबोन

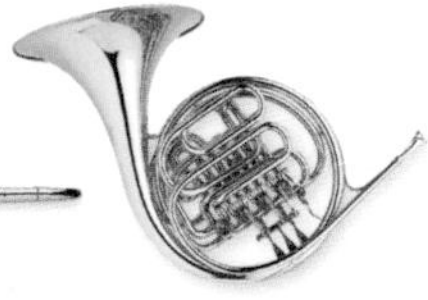

French horn
french horn | फ्रेंच हॉर्न

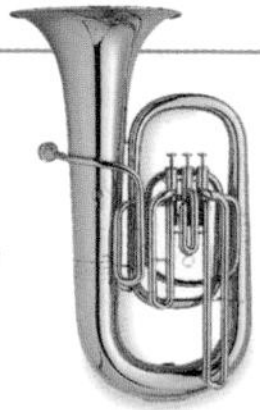

tuba
ṭyūbā | ट्यूबा

concert • concert • कॉन्सर्ट

speaker
spīkar | स्पीकर
fans
praśansak
प्रशंसक
lead singer
pramukh gāyak
प्रमुख गायक
guitarist
gitār vādak
गिटार वादक
microphone
māikrofon
माइक्रोफ़ोन
drummer
ḍramar
ड्रमर

rock concert | rock concert | रॉक कॉन्सर्ट

instruments • vādya yantr • वाद्य यंत्र

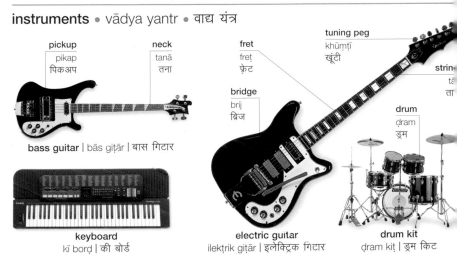

pickup
pikap
पिकअप
neck
tanā
तना

bass guitar | bās giṭār | बास गिटार

keyboard
kī borḍ | की बोर्ड

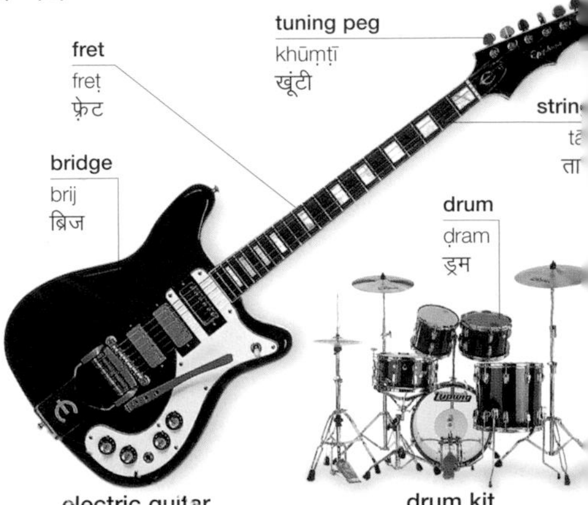
fret
freṭ
फ़्रेट
tuning peg
khūṃṭī
खूंटी
strin
tā
ता
bridge
brij
ब्रिज

electric guitar
ilekṭrik giṭār | इलेक्ट्रिक गिटार

drum
ḍram
ड्रम

drum kit
ḍram kiṭ | ड्रम किट

nusical styles • saṅgīt śailiyāṃ • संगीत शैलियां

jazz | jaiz | जैज़

blues | blūz | ब्लूज़

punk | paṅk | पंक

folk music
lok saṅgīt | लोक संगीत

pop | pop | पॉप

dance | nṛitya | नृत्य

rap
raip | रैप

heavy metal
rock | रॉक

classical music
śāstrīya saṅgīt | शास्त्रीय संगीत

vocabulary • śabdāvalī • शब्दावली

song	**lyrics**	**melody**	**beat**	**reggae**	**country**	**spotlight**
gānā	gīt	madhur saṅgīt	thāp	raige	kanṭrī myūzik	spot lāiṭ
गाना	गीत	मधुर संगीत	थाप	रैगे	कंट्री म्यूज़िक	स्पॉट लाइट

sightseeing • sair-sapāṭā • सैर–सपाटा

tourist
paryaṭak
पर्यटक

tourist attraction
paryaṭan sthal | पर्यटन स्थल

itinerary
mārg nirdeśikā
मार्ग निर्देशिका

open-top
khulī chha
खुली छत

tour bus | paryaṭan bas | पर्यटन बस

tour guide
paryaṭan gāiḍ
पर्यटन–गाइड

figurine
laghu pratimā
लघु प्रतिमा

guided tour
mārgdarśit paryaṭan
मार्गदर्शित पर्यटन

souvenirs
smṛti chihn
स्मृति चिह्न

vocabulary • śabdāvalī • शब्दावली

open khulā खुला	**guidebook** nirdeśikā निर्देशिका	**camcorder** haiṇḍīkaim हैंडीकैम	**left** bāyāṃ बायां
straight ahead sīdh meṃ सीध में	**film closed** band बंद	**camera** kaimrā कैमरा	**right** dāyāṃ दायां
admission charge praveś śulk प्रवेश शुल्क	**batteries** baiṭriyāṃ बैटरियां	**directions** nirdeśan निर्देशन	**film** film फ़िल्म

Where is…?
… kahāṃ hai?
… कहां है?

I'm lost.
maiṃ kho gayā hūṃ
मैं खो गया हूं।

Can you tell me the way to…?
kyā āp mujhe… jāne kā rāstā batā sakte haiṃ?
क्या आप मुझे… जाने का रास्ता बता सकते हैं?

ttractions • ramaṇīya sthal • रमणीय स्थल

painting
penṭiṅg
पेंटिंग

exhibit
pradarśit vastu
प्रदर्शित वस्तु

art gallery
alā dīrghā | कला दीर्घा

monument
smārak | स्मारक

exhibition
pradarśanī | प्रदर्शनी

museum
saṅgrahālya | संग्रहालय

famous ruin
prasiddh khaṅḍahar
प्रसिद्ध खंडहर

historic building
aitihāsik imārat
ऐतिहासिक इमारत

casino
juāghar | जुआघर

gardens
bāg̣ | बाग़

national park
rāṣṭrīya udyān | राष्ट्रीय उद्यान

nformation • jānkarī • जानकारी

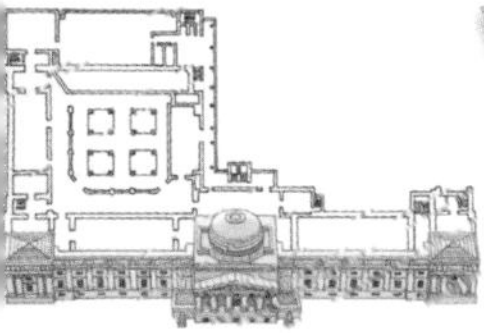

floor plan
bhavan nakśā | भवन नक़्शा

map
nakśā | नक़्शा

times
samaya
समय

schedule
samaya sāriṇī
समय सारिणी

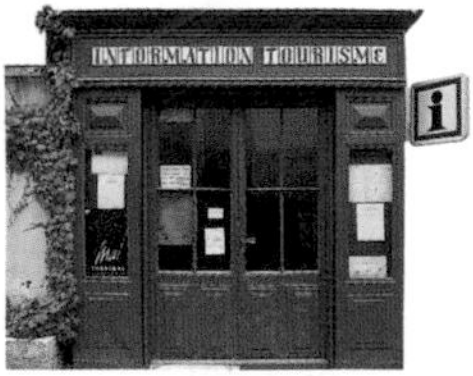

tourist information
paryaṭak sūchnā kendr
पर्यटक सूचना केंद्र

outdoor activities • bāhrī gatividhiyāṃ • बाहरी गतिविधियां

footpath
paidal rāstā
पैदल रास्ता

sundial
dhūp ghaṛī
धूप घड़ी

café
kaife
कैफ़े

park | udyān | उद्यान

grass
ghās
घास

bench
bench
बेंच

formal garden
bagīchā
बग़ीचा

roller coaster
rolar kosṭar
रोलर कोस्टर

fairground
melā sthal | मेला स्थल

theme park
thīm pārk | थीम पार्क

safari park
safārī pārk | सफ़ारी पार्क

zoo
chiṛiyāghar | चिड़ियाघर

ctivities • gatividhiyāṃ • गतिविधियां

cycling | sāikil chalānā
साइकिल चलाना

jogging
jogging | जॉगिंग

skateboarding | sket̤
bording | स्केट बोर्डिंग

rollerblading | rolar
bleding | रोलर ब्लेडिंग

bridle path
aśv mārg
अश्व मार्ग

bird-watching | pakṣī
nihārnā | पक्षी निहारना

horseback riding
ghuṛsavārī | घुड़सवारी

hiking
padyātrā | पदयात्रा

hamper
ṭokrī
टोकरी

picnic
piknik | पिकनिक

playground • khel kā maidān • खेल का मैदान

sandbox
ret kā akhāṛā
रेत का अखाड़ा

wading pool
kṛtrim tālāb
कृत्रिम तालाब

swing
jhūlā | झूला

climbing frame
sīṛhīnumā jhūlā | सीढ़ीनुमा झूला

seesaw | seesaw | सीसॉ

slide | phisal paṭṭī | फिसल पट्टी

beach • taṭ • तट

hotel
hoṭal
होटल

beach umbrella
taṭīya chhātā
तटीय छाता

beach hut
taṭīya jhopṛī
तटीय झोपड़ी

sand
ret
रेत

wave
lahar
लहर

se
samud
समु

beach bag
bīch thailā
बीच थैला

bikini
biknī
बिकनी

sunbathe (v) | sūrya snān karnā | सूर्य स्नान करना

lifeguard
jīvan rakṣak
जीवन रक्षक

lifeguard tower jīvan rakṣak ṭāvar जीवन रक्षक टावर

windbreak | havā rodhak | हवा रोधक

boardwalk | vihār sthal विहार स्थल

deck chair | ḍaik kursī | डैक कुर्सी

sunglasses | dhūp kā chaśmā | धूप का चश्मा

sun hat haiṭ | हैट

suntan lotion | sanṭain lośan | सनटैन लोशन

sunblock | san block | सन ब्लॉक

beach ball bīch ball | बीच बॉल

inflatable ring | rabaṛ kī ṭyūb | रबड़ की ट्यूब

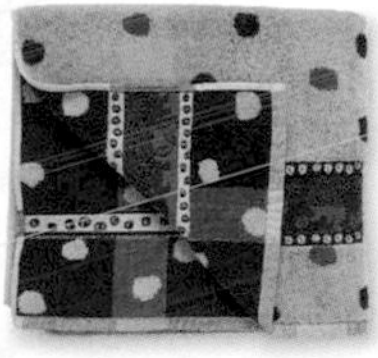

beach towel bīch tauliyā | बीच तौलिया

swimsuit
tairākī sūṭ
तैराकी सूट

shovel
khurpī
खुरपी

pail
ṭokrī
टोकरी

sandcastle
ret kā mahal
रेत का महल

shell
sīp
सीप

camping • śivir lagānā • शिविर लगाना

restrooms
śauchālaya
शौचालय
waste disposal
kūṛedān
कूड़ेदान
shower block
snān sthal
स्नान स्थल
electric hookup
ilekṭrik huk ap
इलेक्ट्रिक हुक–अप
flysheet
dvār pardā
द्वार पर्दा
tent peg
khūṃṭā
खूंटा
guy rope
rassī
रस्सी
camper
gāṛī
गाड़ी

campground
śivir sthal | शिविर स्थल

vocabulary • śabdāvalī • शब्दावली

camp (v)
śivir lagānā
शिविर लगाना

site manager's office
sāiṭ prabandhak kāryālaya
साइट प्रबंधक कार्यालय

sites available
sthān uplabdh
स्थान उपलब्ध

full
pūrā
पूरा

site
sthān
स्थान

pitch a tent (v)
tambū gāṛnā
तंबू गाड़ना

tent pole
tambū kā khambhā
तंबू का खंभा

camp bed
safrī palaṅg
सफ़री पलंग

picnic bench
piknik bench
पिकनिक बेंच

hammock
jhūlā
झूला

camper van
śivir vāhan
शिविर वाहन

trailer
ṭrelar
ट्रेलर

charcoal
kacchā koyalā
कच्चा कोयला

firelighter
āg jalāne kā upkaraṇ
आग जलाने का उपकरण

light a fire (v)
āg jalānā
आग जलाना

campfire
alāv
अलाव

frame
frem
फ़्रेम
backpack
piṭṭhū
पिट्ठू
water bottle
pānī kī botal
पानी की बोतल
groundsheet
darī
दरी
vacuum flask
vaikyūm flāsk
वैक्यूम फ़्लास्क

tent
śivir | शिविर

insect repellent
macchhar avrodhak
मच्छर अवरोधक

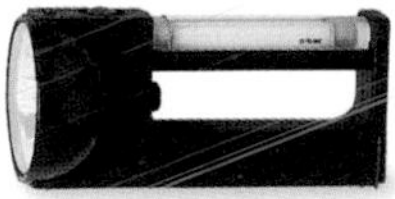

flashlight
torch | टॉर्च

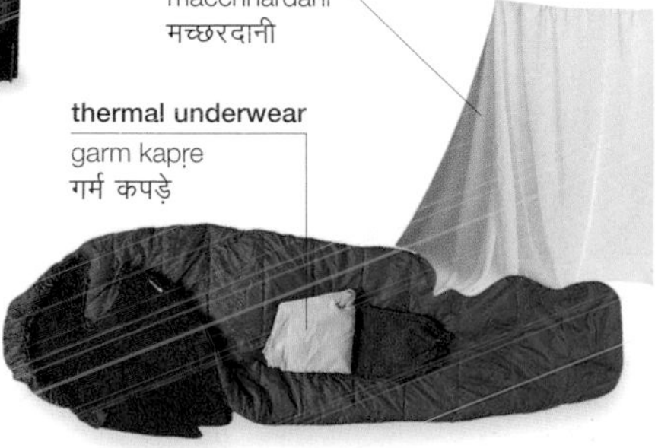
mosquito net
macchhardānī
मच्छरदानी
thermal underwear
garm kapṛe
गर्म कपड़े

sleeping bag
slīpiṅg baig | स्लीपिंग बैग

hiking boots
jūte | जूते

rain gear
waterproofs | वॉटरप्रूफ़

camping stove
safrī sṭov | सफ़री स्टोव

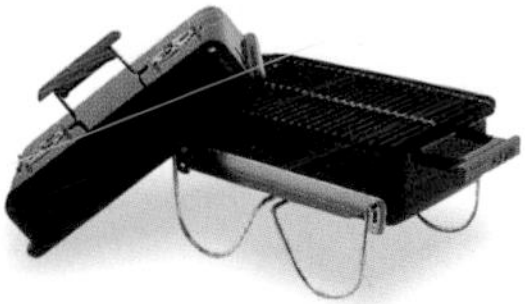

barbecue grill
gril | ग्रिल

sleeping mat
gaddā
गद्दा

air mattress | havā bharā gaddā | हवा भरा गद्दा

home entertainment • gharelū manorañjan • घरेलू मनोरंजन

digital radio
ḍijiṭal reḍiyo
डिजिटल रेडियो

iPod©
āī poḍ | आई पॉड

DVD disk
DVD ḍisk
डीवीडी डिस्क

DVD player
DVD pleyar
डीवीडी प्लेयर

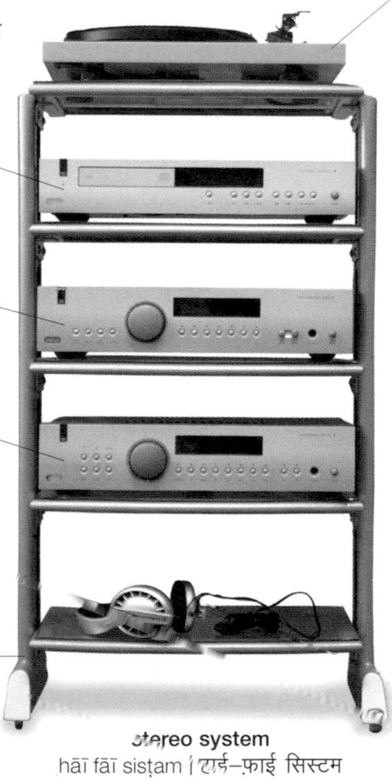

record player
record pleyar
रिकॉर्ड प्लेयर

CD player
CD pleyar
सीडी प्लेयर

radio
reḍiyo
रेडियो

amplifier
emplīfāyar
एंम्लीफ़ायर

headphones
haiḍfon
हैडफ़ोन

stand
sṭaiṇḍ
स्टैंड

stereo system
hāī fāī sisṭam | हाई–फ़ाई सिस्टम

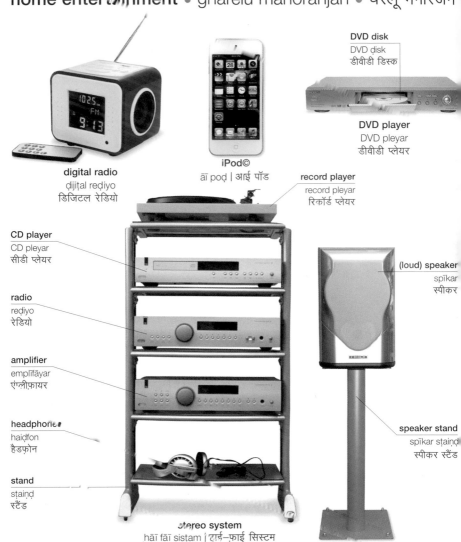

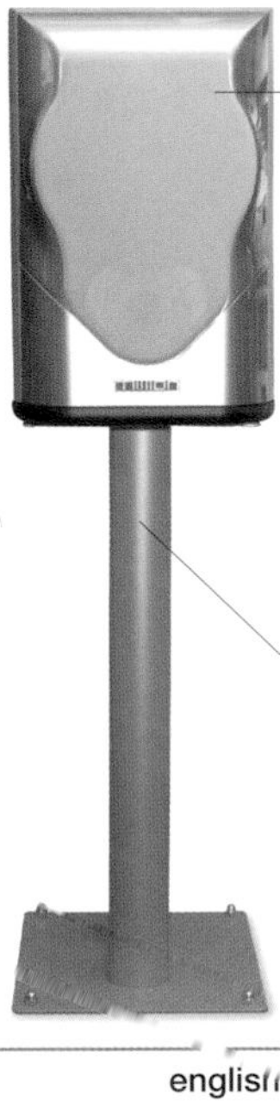

(loud) speaker
spīkar
स्पीकर

speaker stand
spīkar sṭaiṇḍ
स्पीकर स्टैंड

screen
skrīn
स्क्रीन

eyecup
aī kap
आई कप

DTV converter box
ḍijiṭal boks | डिजिटल बॉक्स

camcorder
haiṇḍīkaim | हैंडीकैम

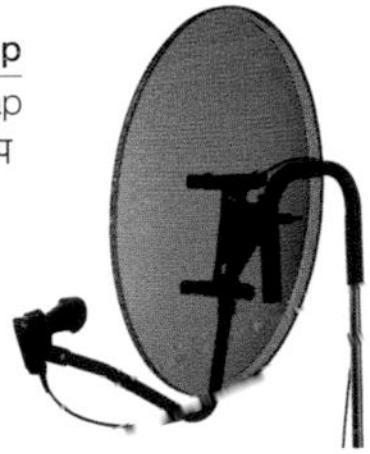

satellite dish
upgrah ḍiś | उपग्रह डिश

flatscreen TV
flaiṭskrīn ṭīvī
फ्लैटस्क्रीन टीवी

console
consolo
कॉन्सोल

controller
kanṭrolar
कंट्रोलर

video game | vīḍiyo gem | वीडियो गेम

fast-forward
fāsṭ forward
फ़ास्ट फ़ॉरवर्ड

pause
pause
पॉज

record
record
रिकॉर्ड

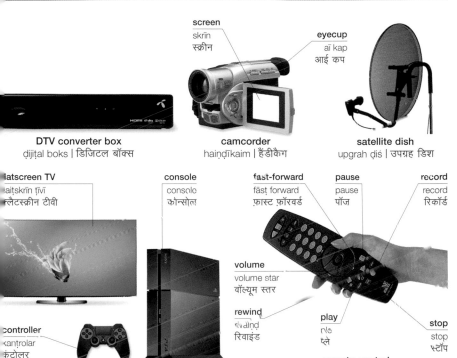

volume
volume star
वॉल्यूम स्तर

rewind
rivāinḍ
रिवाइंड

play
ple
प्ले

stop
stop
स्टॉप

remote control
rimoṭ kanṭrol | रिमोट कंट्रोल

vocabulary • śābdāvalī • शब्दावली

CD
kompaikṭ ḍisk
कॉम्पैक्ट डिस्क

cassette tape
kaiseṭ ṭep
कैसेट टेप

cassette player
kaiseṭ pleyar
कैसेट प्लेयर

streaming
sṭrīmiṅg
स्ट्रीमिंग

feature film
fīchar film
फ़ीचर फ़िल्म

advertisement
vijñāpan
विज्ञापन

digital
ḍijiṭal
डिजिटल

wifi
wāī fāī
वाई फाई

program
kāryakram
कार्यक्रम

stereo
sṭīriyo
स्टीरियो

cable television
kebal ṭelīvizan
केबल टेलीविज़न

high-definition
haī-ḍefiniśan
हाइ–डेफ़िनिशन

freeview box
frīvyū box
फ्रीव्यू बॉक्स

change channels (v)
chainal badalnā
चैनल बदलना

tune the radio (v)
reḍiyo saiṭ karnā
रेडियो सैट करना

watch television (v)
ṭīvī dekhnā
टीवी देखना

turn on the television (v)
ṭelīvizan chalānā
टेलीविज़न चलाना

turn off the television (v)
ṭelīvizan band karnā
टेलीविज़न बंद करना

pay-per-view channel
prati chainal bhugtān
प्रति चैनल भुगतान

photography • foṭogrāfī • फ़ोटोग्राफ़ी

shutter release
śaṭar rilīz
शटर रिलीज़

aperture dial
aparchar niyantrak
अपर्चर नियंत्रक

lens
lens
लेंस

SLR camera | SLR kaimrā | एस एल आर कैमरा

filter
filṭar | फ़िल्टर

lens cap
lens kaip | लेंस कैप

flash gun
flaiś gan | फ़्लैश गन

light meter
lāiṭmīṭar | लाइटमीटर

zoom lens
zūm lens | ज़ूम लेंस

tripod
tipāyā sṭaiṇḍ | तिपाया स्टैंड

types of camera • kaimre ke prakār • कैमरे के प्रकार

Polaroid
Polaroiḍ kaimrā
पोलरॉइड कैमरा

digital camera
ḍijiṭal kaimrā
डिजीटल कैमरा

cameraphone
kaimrāfon
कैमराफ़ोन

disposable camera
ḍispozebal kaimrā
डिस्पोज़ेबल कैमरा

photograph (v) • foṭo khīṃchnā • फ़ोटो खींचना

film roll
film rīl
फ़िल्म रील

film
film | फ़िल्म

focus (v) | kendrit karnā | केंद्रित करना

develop (v)
film dhonā | फ़िल्म धोना

negative
negeṭiv | नेगेटिव

landscape
prākṛtik dṛśya
प्राकृतिक दृश्य

portrait
vyakti chitr
व्यक्ति चित्र

photograph | tasvīr | तस्वीर

photo album
foṭo elbam | फ़ोटो एल्बम

picture frame | foṭo frem | फ़ोटो फ़्रेम

problems • samasyāeṃ • समस्याएं

underexposed
kam udbhāsit
कम उद्भासित

overexposed
atyadhik udbhāsit
अत्यधिक उद्भासित

out of focus | fokas se bāhar | फ़ोकस से बाहर

red eye
reḍ āī | रेड आई

vocabulary • śabdāvalī • शब्दावली

viewfinder
dṛśyadarśī
दृश्यदर्शी

print
foṭo prati
फ़ोटो प्रति

camera case
kaimrā kes
कैमरा केस

matt
khurdarā
खुरदरा

exposure
udbhāsan
उद्भासन

gloss
chiknā
चिकना

darkroom
ḍārk rūm
डार्क रूम

enlargement
foṭo baṛī karānā
फ़ोटो बड़ी कराना

I'd like this film processed
maiṃ yah rīl dhulvānā chāhtā hūṃ
मैं यह रील धुलवाना चाहता हूं।

games • khel • खेल

chessboard
bisāt
बिसात

black
kālā
काला

white
safed
सफ़ेद

queen
vazīr
वज़ीर

king
rājā
राजा

bishop
ūṃṭ
ऊंट

pawn
pyādā
प्यादा

knight
ghoṛā
घोड़ा

rook
hāthī
हाथी

chess
śatranj | शतरंज

square
ḳhānā
ख़ाना

piece
goṭī
गोटी

checkers | draughts | ड्रॉट्स

tile
ṭā
टाइल

Scrabble | skraibal | स्क्रैबल

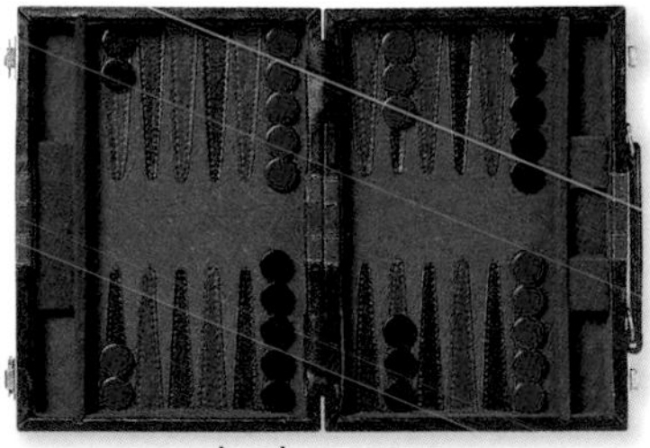

backgammon
baik gaiman | बैक गैमन

dice
pāsā
पासा

counter
mohrā | मोहरा

Monopoly
monopol
मोनोपोली

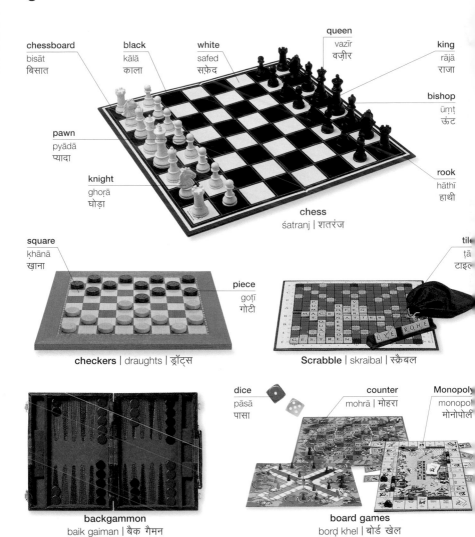

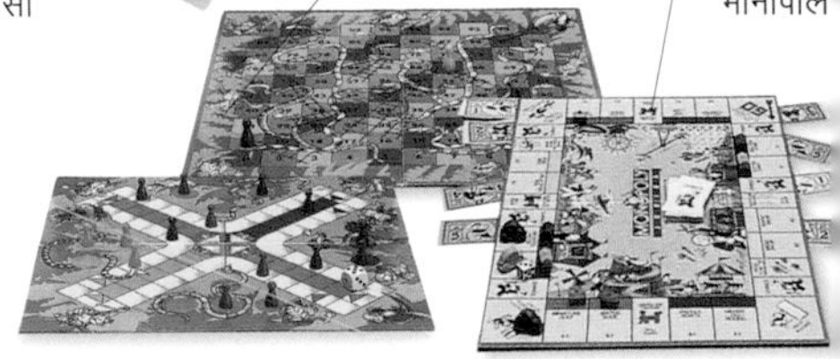

board games
borḍ khel | बोर्ड खेल

stamp collecting
ḍāk ṭikaṭ saṅgrah
डाक टिकट संग्रह

jigsaw puzzle | chitrakhaṇḍ pahelī | चित्रखंड पहेली

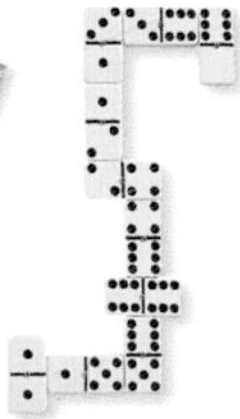

dominoes
ḍominos | डोमिनोस

dartboard
ḍārṭ borḍ
डार्टबोर्ड

bullseye
lakṣya
लक्ष्य

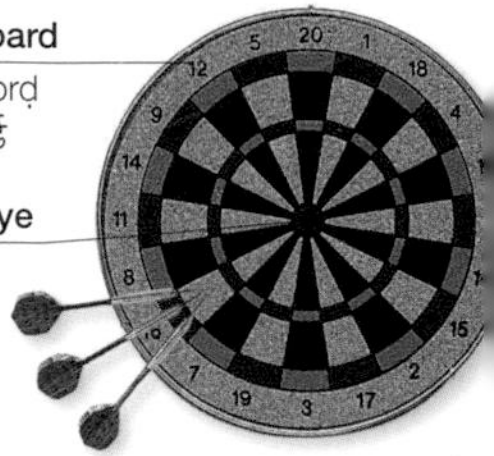

darts
ḍārṭs | डार्ट्स

joker
jokar
जोकर

ack
ulām
लाम

ueen
egam
गम

ing
ādśāh
ादशाह

ace
ikkā
इक्का

diamond
īṇṭ
ईंट

spade
hukum
हुकुम

heart
pān
पान

club
chiṛī
चिड़ी

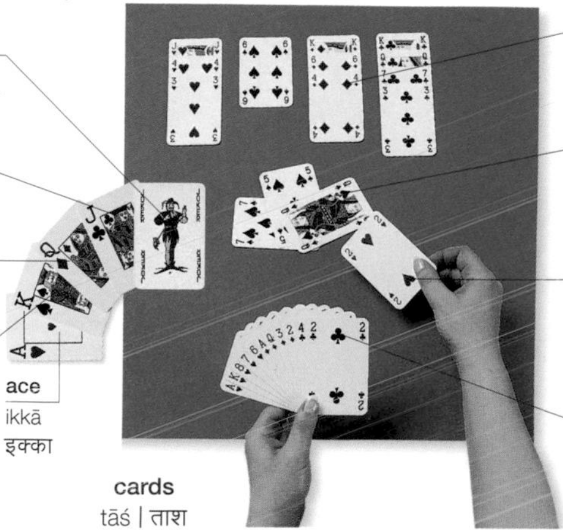

cards
tāś | ताश

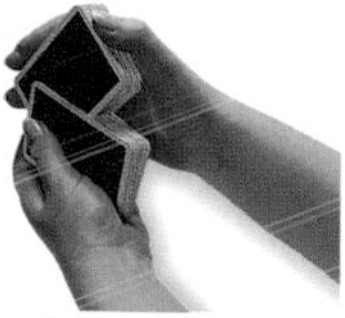

shuffle (v)
tāś pheṃṭnā | ताश फेंटना

deal (v)
patte bāṃṭnā | पत्ते बांटना

vocabulary • śabdāvalī • शब्दावली

move
chāl
चाल

play (v)
khelnā
खेलना

player
khilāṛī
खिलाड़ी

win (v)
jītnā
जीतना

winner
vijetā
विजेता

lose (v)
hārnā
हारना

loser
parājit
पराजित

game
khel
खेल

bet
śart
शर्त

point
nambar
नंबर

score
arjit aṃk
अर्जित अंक

poker
pokar
पोकर

bridge
brij
ब्रिज

deck of cards
tāś kī gaḍḍī
ताश की गड्डी

suit
tāś raṅg
ताश रंग

Roll the dice.
pāsā pheṃko
पासा फेंको

Whose turn is it?
kiskī bārī hai?
किसकी बारी है?

It's your move.
ab tumhārī chāl hai
अब तुम्हारी चाल है।

arts and crafts 1 • kalā aur śilp 1 • कला और शिल्प 1

painting | chitrakārī | चित्रकारी

colours • raṅg • रंग

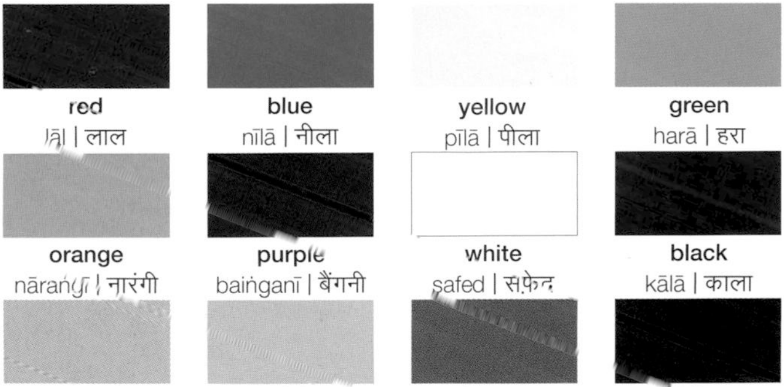

red lāl | लाल

blue nīlā | नीला

yellow pīlā | पीला

green harā | हरा

orange nāraṅgī | नारंगी

purple baiṅganī | बैंगनी

white safed | सफ़ेद

black kālā | काला

gray slēṭī | स्लेटी

pink gulābī | गुलाबी

brown bhūrā | भूरा

indigo nīl | नील

paints • raṅg • रंग

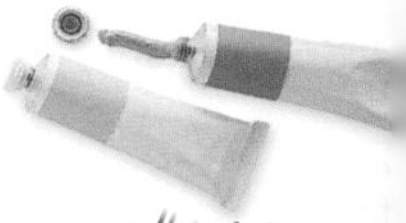

oil paints
tail raṅg | तैल रंग

watercolor paint
pānī ke raṅg | पानी के रं

pastels
raṅgīn khaṛiyā | रंगीन ख

acrylic paint
aikrilīk raṅg | ऐक्रिलीक

poster paint
pōsṭar raṅg | पोस्टर रं

other crafts • anya kalāeṃ • अन्य कलाएं

ketchpad
khāṅkan paṭal
खांकन पटल
sketch
ḳhākā
ख़ाका
encil
ensil
सिल
charcoal
koyalā battī
कोयला बत्ती

drawing | rekhāṅkan | रेखांकन

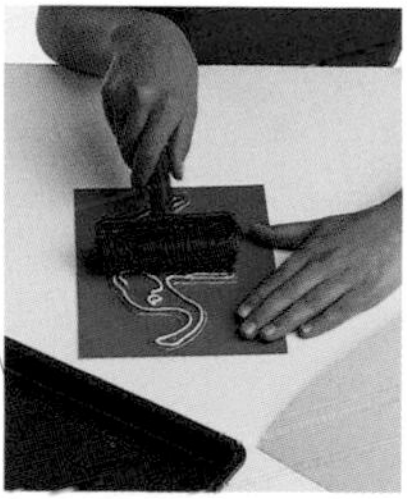
ink
syāhī
स्याही

printing
chhapāī | छपाई

engraving
utkīrṇan | उत्कीर्णन

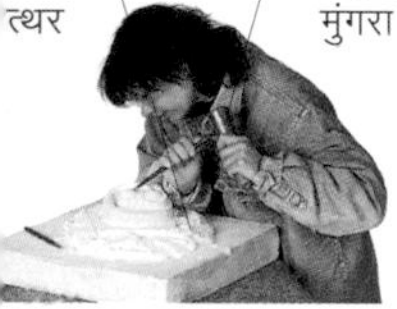
tone
atthar
त्थर
mallet
muṅgrā
मुंगरा

sculpting
mūrti śilp | मूर्ति शिल्प

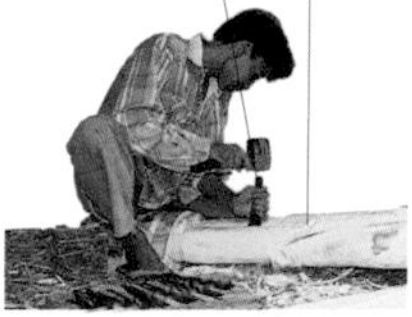
chisel
chhainī
छैनी
wood
lakṛī
लकड़ी

woodworking
kāṣṭh-kalā | काष्ठ–कला

modeling tool
hastkalā upkaraṇ
हस्तकला उपकरण
potter's wheel
chāk
चाक
clay
chiknī miṭṭī
चिकनी
मिट्टी

pottery
kumhār karm | कुम्हार कर्म

lue
ond
ोंद
cardboard
gattā
गत्ता

collage | kolāj | कोलाज

welry-making | ābhūṣaṇ-nirmāṇ | आभूषण निर्माण

papier-mâché | paipya māśe | पैप्य माशे

origami
aurigāmī | औरिगामी

model-making | model banānā | मॉडल बनाना

arts and crafts 2 • kalā aur śilp 2 • कला और शिल्प 2

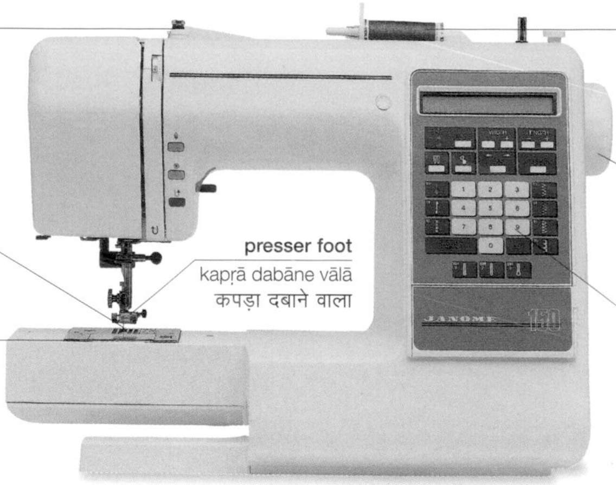
thread guide
dhāgā
धागा
thread ree
dhāge kī r
धागे की रीत
needle
sūī
सूई
balance whee
pahiy
पहिय
presser foot
kapṛā dabāne vālā
कपड़ा दबाने वाला
needle plate
sūī ke nīche
kī pattī
सूई के नीचे
की पत्ती
stitch selecto
silāī chayan baṭa
सिलाई चयन बट

sewing machine
silāī maśīn | सिलाई मशीन

scissors
kaiṃchī
कैंची

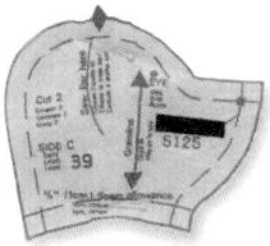

pattern
ḳhākā
ख़ाका

tape measure
inchṭep
इंचटेप

material
kapṛā | कपड़ा

pincushion
pinkuśan
पिनकुशन
pin
pin
पिन

sewing basket
silāī kī ṭokrī | सिलाई की टोकरी

bobbin
phirkī
फिरकी

thread
dhāgā
धागा

eye
āī | आई

hook
huk
हुक

thimble
aṃguśtānā
अंगुश्ताना

tailor's chalk
darzī kā chalk
दर्ज़ी का चॉक

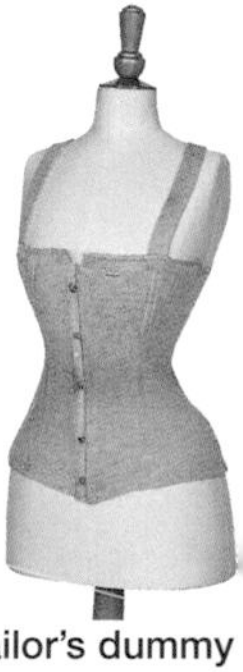

tailor's dummy
darzī kī ḍamī
दर्ज़ी की डमी

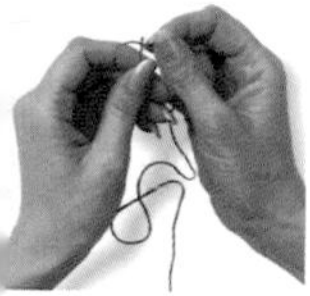

thread (v)
dhāgā ḍālnā
धागा डालना

stitch
bakhiyā
बखिया

sew (v)
silnā
सिलना

darn (v)
rafū karnā
रफ़ू करना

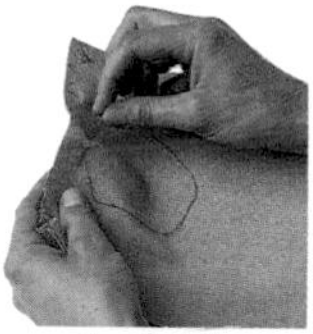

tack (v)
ṭāṃknā
टांकना

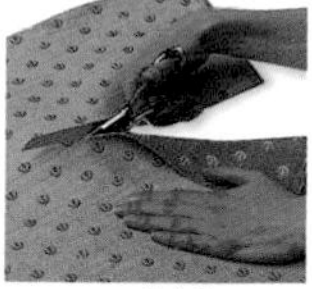

cut (v)
kāṭnā
काटना

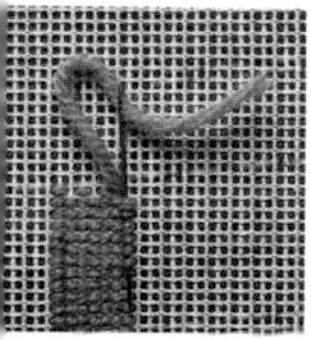

needlepoint
sūī kī nok
सूई की नोक

embroidery
kaṛhāī
कढ़ाई

crochet hook
krośiyā huk
क्रोशिया हुक

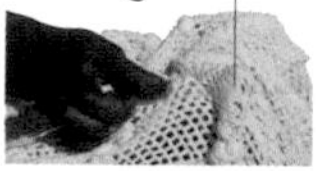

crochet
krośiyā
क्रोशिया

macramé
jhālar
झालर

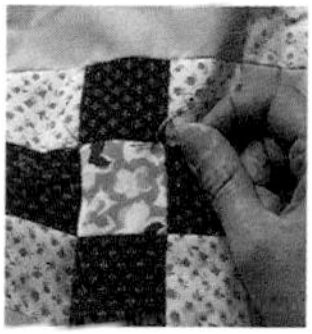

patchwork
paiband
पैबंद

quilting
parat lagānā
परत लगाना

lace bobbin
les bobbin
लेस बॉबिन

lace-making
les banānā
लेस बनाना

loom
karghā
करघा

weaving
bunnā
बुनना

vocabulary • śabdāvalī • शब्दावली

unpick (v)
udheṛnā
उधेड़ना

fabric
kapṛā
कपड़ा

cotton
sūtī kapṛā
सूती कपड़ा

linen
linen
लिनेन

polyester
polyester
पॉलीएस्टर

nylon
nāyalon
नायलोन

silk
reśam
रेशम

designer
ḍizāinar
डिज़ाइनर

fashion
faiśan
फ़ैशन

zipper
zip
ज़िप

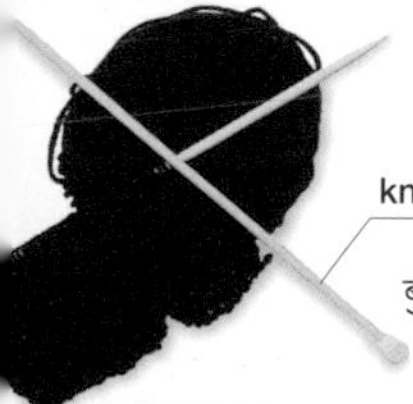

knitting needle
bunne kī slāī
बुनने की सलाई

knitting
bunāī | बुनाई

wool
ūn
ऊन

skein
lacchhī | लच्छी

environment
paryāvaraṇ
पर्यावरण

space • antarikṣ • अंतरिक्ष

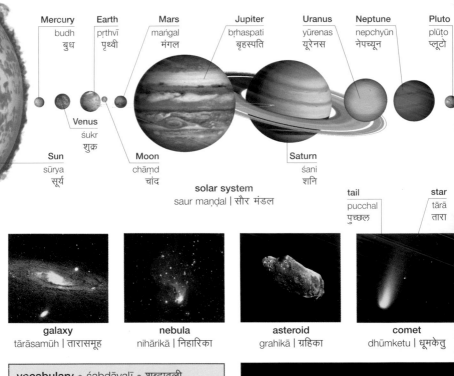

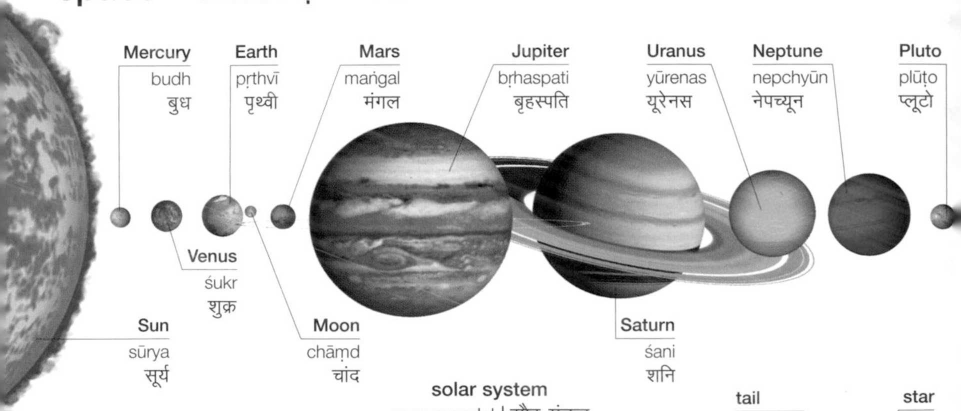
Mercury
budh
बुध
Earth
pṛthvī
पृथ्वी
Mars
maṅgal
मंगल
Jupiter
bṛhaspati
बृहस्पति
Uranus
yūrenas
यूरेनस
Neptune
nepchyūn
नेपच्यून
Pluto
plūṭo
प्लूटो
Venus
śukr
शुक्र
Sun
sūrya
सूर्य
Moon
chāṃd
चांद
Saturn
śani
शनि

solar system
saur maṇḍal | सौर मंडल

galaxy
tārāsamūh | तारासमूह

nebula
nihārikā | निहारिका

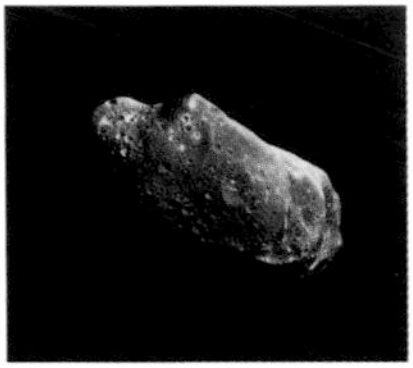

asteroid
grahikā | ग्रहिका

tail
pucchal
पुच्छल
star
tārā
तारा

comet
dhūmketu | धूमकेतु

vocabulary • śabdāvalī • शब्दावली

universe
brahamāṇḍ
ब्रह्मांड

black hole
blaik hol
ब्लैक होल

full moon
pūrā chāṃd
पूरा चांद

orbit
kakṣā
कक्षा

planet
grah
ग्रह

new moon
pratipadā kā chāṃd
प्रतिपदा का चांद

gravity
gurutv
गुरुत्व

meteor
ulkā
उल्का

crescent moon
ardhchandr
अर्धचंद्र

eclipse | grahan | ग्रहण

pace exploration • antarikṣ anveṣaṇ • ंतरिक्ष अन्वेषण

pace shuttle
ntarikṣ yān
ंतरिक्ष यान

ooster
ūsṭar
्स्टर

launch pad
prakṣepaṇ sthal
प्रक्षेपण स्थल

launch
prakṣepaṇ | प्रक्षेपण

space suit
antarikṣ sūṭ
अंतरिक्ष सूट

astronaut | antarikṣ yātrī | अंतरिक्ष यात्री

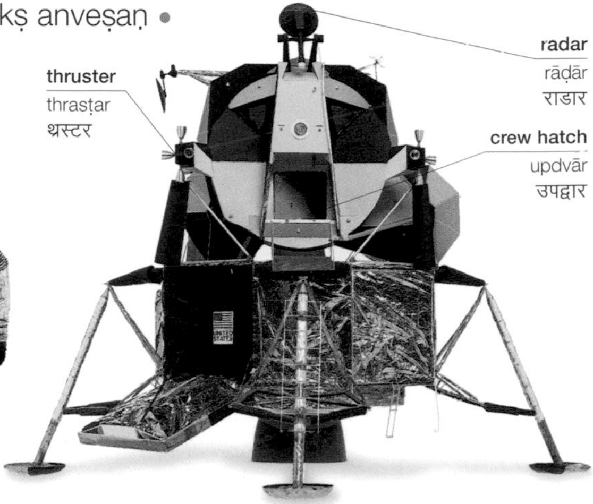

thruster
thrasṭar
थ्रस्टर

radar
rāḍār
राडार

crew hatch
updvār
उपद्वार

lunar module | chandryān | चंद्रयान

satellite
upgrah | उपग्रह

space station | antarikṣ kendr
अंतरिक्ष केंद्र

astronomy • khagol vijñān • खगोल विज्ञान

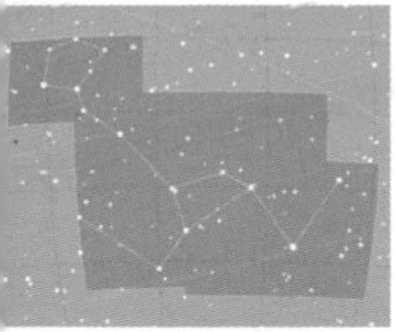

constellation
tārāmaṇḍal | तारामंडल

binoculars
dūrbīn | दूरबीन

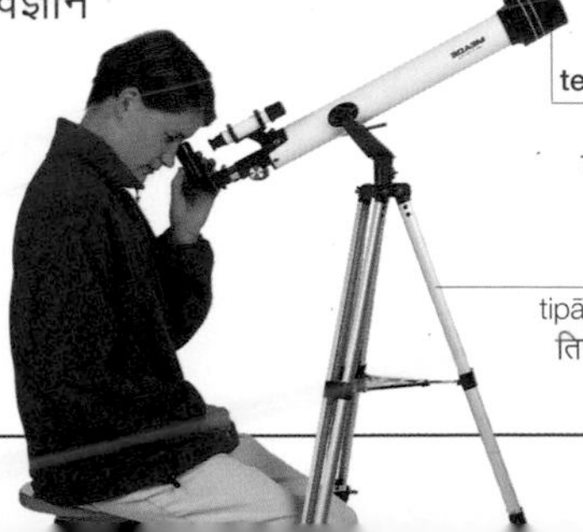

telescope
ṭelīskop
टेलीस्कोप

tripod
tipāyā sṭaiṇḍ
तिपाया स्टैंड

Earth • pṛthvī • पृथ्वी

pole
dhruv
ध्रुव
land
bhūmi
भूमि
ocean
mahāsāgar
महासागर
mountain rang
parvat śre
पर्वत श्रे
sea
sāgar
सागर
peninsul
prāyadvī
प्रायद्वी
continent
mahādvīp
महाद्वीप
island
dvīp
द्वीप

planet | grah | ग्रह

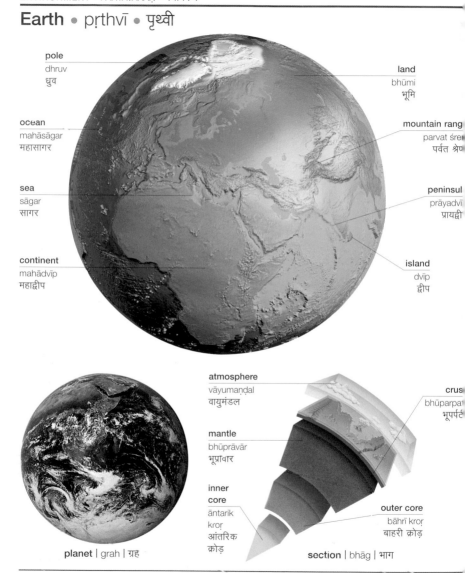

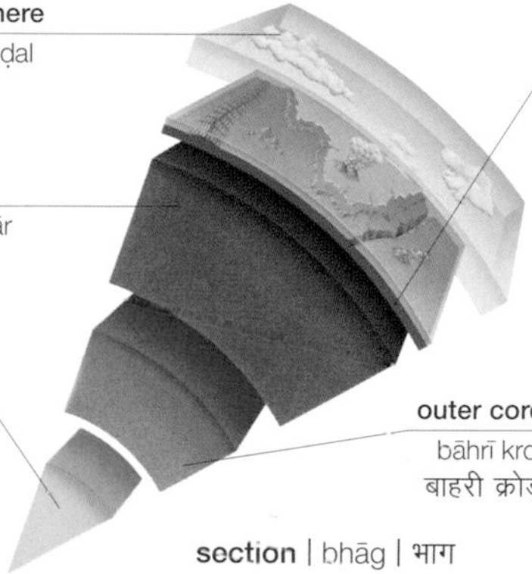
atmosphere
vāyumaṇḍal
वायुमंडल
crus
bhūparpat
भूपर्पट
mantle
bhūprāvār
भूप्रावार
inner core
āntarik kroṛ
आंतरिक क्रोड़
outer core
bāhrī kroṛ
बाहरी क्रोड़

section | bhāg | भाग

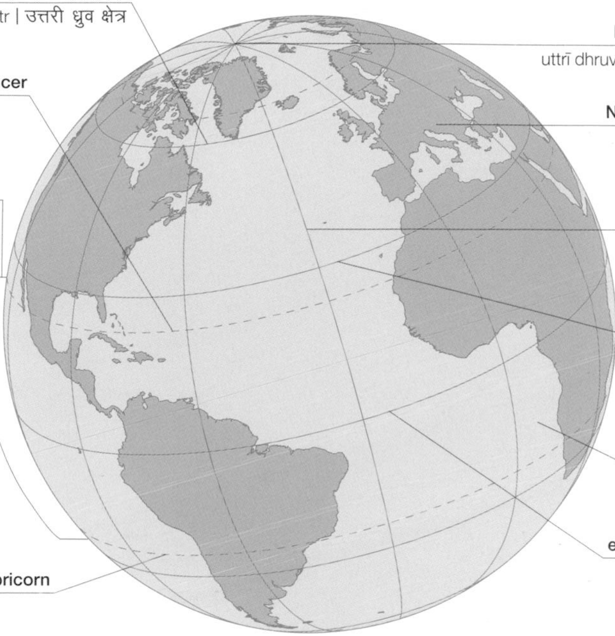
rctic Circle
trī dhruv kṣetr | उत्तरी ध्रुव क्षेत्र
North Pole
uttrī dhruv | उत्तरी ध्रुव
ropic of Cancer
ark rekhā
र्क रेखा
Northern Hemisphere
uttrī golārdh
उत्तरी गोलार्ध
opics
ṣṇ kaṭibandh
ष्ण कटिबंध
longitude
deśāntar rekhāṅś
देशांतर रेखांश
latitude
akṣāṅś
अक्षांश
Southern Hemisphere
dakṣiṇī golārdh
दक्षिणी गोलार्ध
equator
viṣuvat
विषुवत
ropic of Capricorn
nakar rekhā
कर रेखा

zones | kaṭibandh | कटिबंध

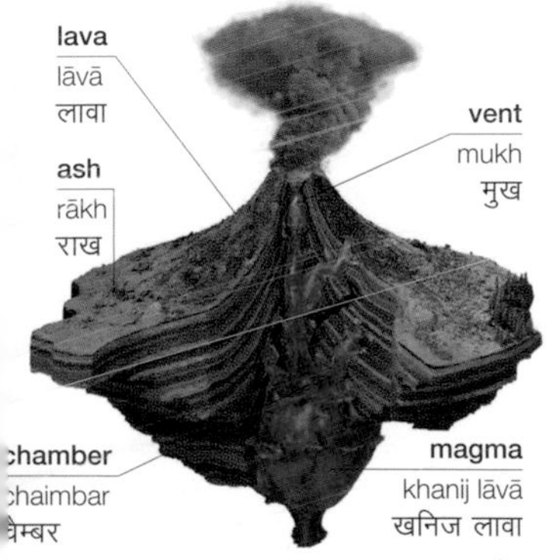
lava
lāvā
लावा
vent
mukh
मुख
ash
rākh
राख
chamber
chaimbar
चेम्बर
magma
khanij lāvā
खनिज लावा

volcano | jvālāmukhī | ज्वालामुखी

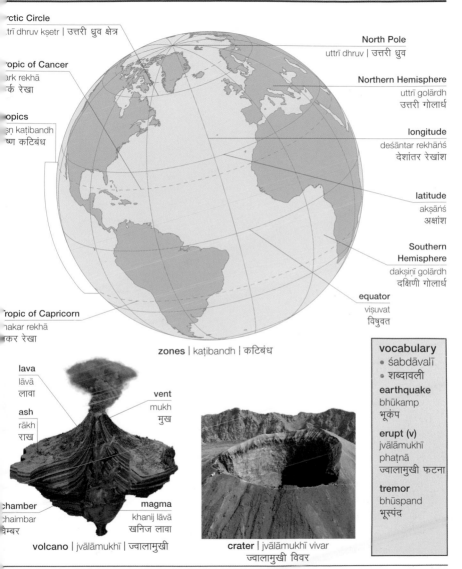

crater | jvālāmukhī vivar
ज्वालामुखी विवर

vocabulary • śabdāvalī • शब्दावली

earthquake
bhūkamp
भूकंप

erupt (v)
jvālāmukhī phaṭnā
ज्वालामुखी फटना

tremor
bhūspand
भूस्पंद

landscape • bhūdṛśaya • भूदृश्य

mountain
parvat | पर्वत
slope
ḍhalān
ढलान
bank
kinārā
किनारा
river
nadī
नदी
rapids
tīvr dhārā
तीव्र धारा
rocks
chaṭṭān
चट्टान

glacier
himnad | हिमनद

valley | ghāṭī | घाटी

hill
pahāṛī | पहाड़ी

plateau
paṭhār | पठार

gorge
darrā | दर्रा

cave
guphā | गुफा

plain | maidān | मैदान

desert | registān
रेगिस्तान

forest | jaṅgal | जंगल

woods | van | वन

rainforest
varṣā van | वर्षा वन

swamp
daldal | दलदल

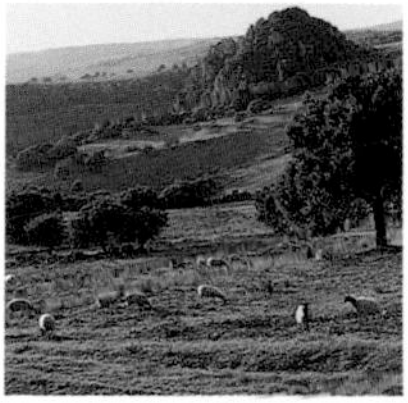

meadow
charāgāh | चरागाह

grassland | ghās kā
maidān | घास का मैदान

waterfall
jalprapāt | जलप्रपात

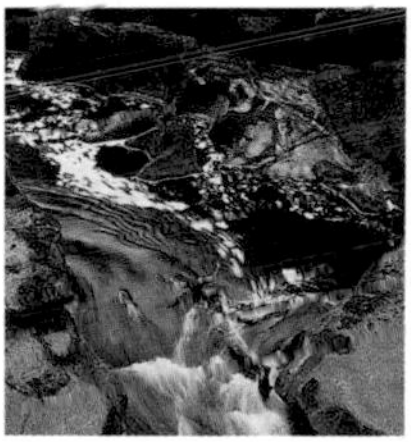

stream
dhārā | धारा

lake
jhīl | झील

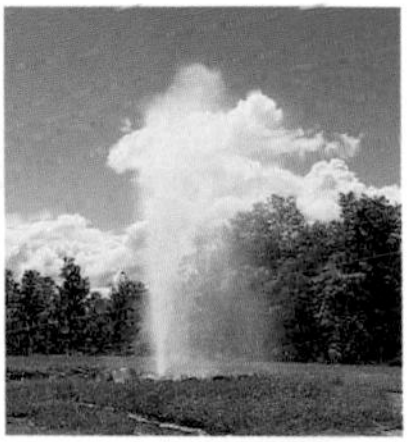

geyser
garm jalsarot | गर्म जलस्रोत

coast
samudr taṭ | समुद्र तट

cliff | kharī chaṭṭān
खड़ी चट्टान

coral reef
pravāl dvīp | प्रवाल द्वीप

estuary | sāgar vilyan
सागर विलयन

weather • mausam • मौसम

exosphere
parāmaṇḍal
परामंडल

aurora
dhruvjyoti
ध्रुवज्योति

thermosphere
tāpmaṇḍal
तापमंडल

sunshine | dhūp | धूप

ionosphere
āyan maṇḍal
आयन मंडल

mesosphere
madhya maṇḍal
मध्य मंडल

ultraviolet rays
parābaiṅganī kirṇem
पराबैंगनी किरणें

stratosphere
samtāp maṇḍal
समताप मंडल

ozone layer
ozon parat
ओज़ोन परत

troposphere
nimntāp maṇḍal
निम्नताप मंडल

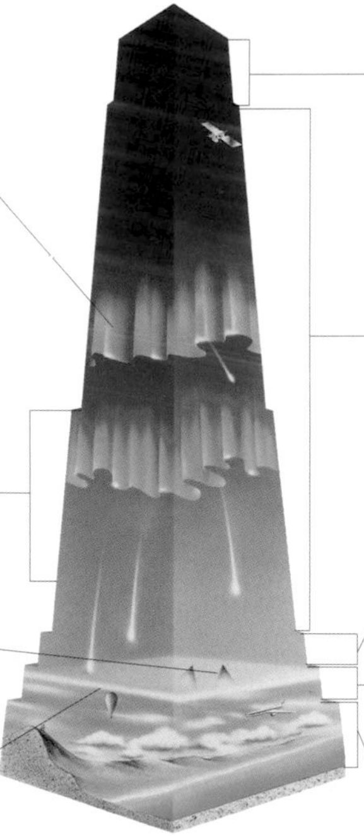

atmosphere | vayumaṇḍal | वायुमंडल

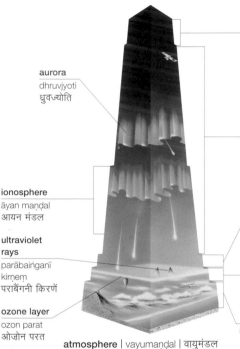

wind | pavan | पवन

---

vocabulary • śabdāvalī • शब्दावली

sleet	**shower**	**hot**	**dry**	**windy**	**I'm hot/cold.**
himvarṣā	bauchhār	garm	sūkhā	tūfānī	mujhe garmī / ṭhaṇḍ lag rahī hai
हिमवर्षा	बौछार	गर्म	सूखा	तूफ़ानी	मुझे गर्मी/ठंड लग रही है।
hail	**sunny**	**cold**	**wet**	**gale**	**It's raining.**
ole	dhūpdār	ṭhaṇḍā	gīlā	āṅdhī	bāriś ho rahī hai
ओले	धूपदार	ठंडा	गीला	आंधी	बारिश हो रही है।
thunder	**cloudy**	**warm**	**humid**	**temperature**	**It's … degrees.**
garaj	meghācchhann	gungunā	nam	tāpmān	tāpmān … ḍigrī hai
गरज	मेघाच्छन्न	गुनगुना	नम	तापमान	तापमान… डिग्री है।

cloud | bādal | बादल

rain | bāriś | बारिश

storm | tūfān | तूफ़ान

mist | kohrā | कोहरा

fog | dhundh | धुंध

rainbow | indrdhanuṣ | इंद्रधनुष

snow | him | हिम

frost | tuṣār | तुषार

ice | baraf | बर्फ़

freeze | ṭhaṇḍ | ठंड

hurricane
chakrvāt | चक्रवात

tornado
bavaṇḍar | बवंडर

monsoon
varṣā | वर्षा

flood
bāṛh | बाढ़

rocks • pāṣāṇ • पाषाण

igneous • jvalāmukhīya śail • ज्वालामुखीय शैल

granite
grenāiṭ
ग्रेनाइट

obsidian
obsiḍiyan
ओबसिडियन

basalt
kālā patthar
काला पत्थर

pumice
jhāmak
झामक

sedimentary • avsādī śail • अवसादी शैल

sandstone
baluā patthar
बलुआ पत्थर

limestone
chūnā patthar
चूना पत्थर

chalk
khaṛiyā
खड़िया

flint
chakmak
चकमक

conglomerate
pāṣāṇit kaṅkaṛ
पाषाणित कंकड़

coal
koyalā
कोयला

metamorphic • rūpāntarit śail • रूपांतरित शैल

slate
sleṭ
स्लेट

schist
starit chaṭṭān
स्तरित चट्टान

gneiss
śail
शैल

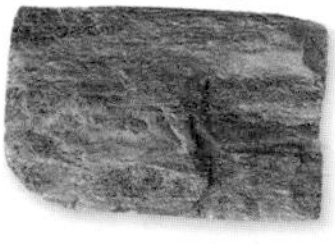

marble
saṅgmarmar
संगमरमर

gems • ratan • रत्न

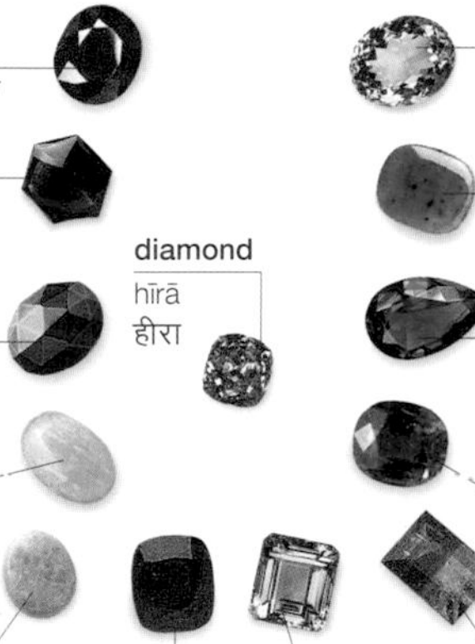

ruby
māṇik | माणिक

amethyst
jambumaṇi
जंबुमणि

diamond
hīrā
हीरा

jet
lāvā maṇi
लावा मणि

opal
upal
उपल

moonstone
chandrakānt maṇi
चंद्रकांत मणि

garnet
raktmaṇi
रक्तमणि

topaz
pukhrāj
पुखराज

aquamarin
haritnī
हरितनील

jad
je
जे

emeral
pann
पन्न

sapphir
nīlan
नीलम

tourmalin
turmal
तुरमली

minerals • khanij • खनिज

quartz
sphaṭik
स्फटिक

mica
abhrak
अभ्रक

sulfur
gandhak
गंधक

hematite
hemeṭāiṭ
हेमेटाइट

calcite
kailsāiṭ
कैल्साइट

malachite
melākāiṭ
मेलाकाइट

turquoise
firojā
फ़ीरोजा

onyx
sarpmaṇi
सर्पमणि

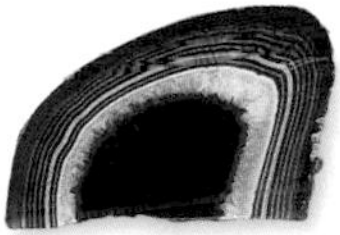

agate
akīk
अकीक

graphite
grefāiṭ
ग्रेफ़ाइट

metals • dhātu • धातु

gold
sonā | सोना

silver
chāndī
चांदी

platinum
pleṭinam
प्लेटिनम

nickel
nikal | निकल

iron
lohā | लोहा

copper
tāmbā | तांबा

tin
ṭin | टिन

aluminum
alyūminiyam
अल्यूमिनियम

mercury
pārā | पारा

zinc
jastā | जस्ता

animals 1 • paśu 1 • पशु

mammals • standhārī jīv • स्तनधारी जीव

rabbit
ḳhargoś
ख़रगोश

whiskers
mūṃchheṃ
मूंछें

hamster
haimsṭar | हैमस्टर

mouse
mūṣak | मूषक

tail
pūṃchh
पूंछ

rat
chūhā | चूहा

hedgehog
sāhī | साही

squirrel
gilahrī
गिलहरी

bat
chamgādaṛ
चमगादड़

raccoon
raikūn
रैकून

fox
lomṛī
लोमड़ी

wolf
bheṛiyā
भेड़िया

puppy
pillā
पिल्ला

dog
kuttā | कुत्ता

kitten
billī kā bacchā
बिल्ली का बच्चा

cat
billī | बिल्ली

otter
ūdbilāv | ऊदबिलाव

pup
śiśu sīl
शिशु सील

seal
sīl | सील

sea lion
samudr siṅh
समुद्र सिंह

flipper
mīn paṅkh
मीन पंख

walrus
hāthī sīl
हाथी सील

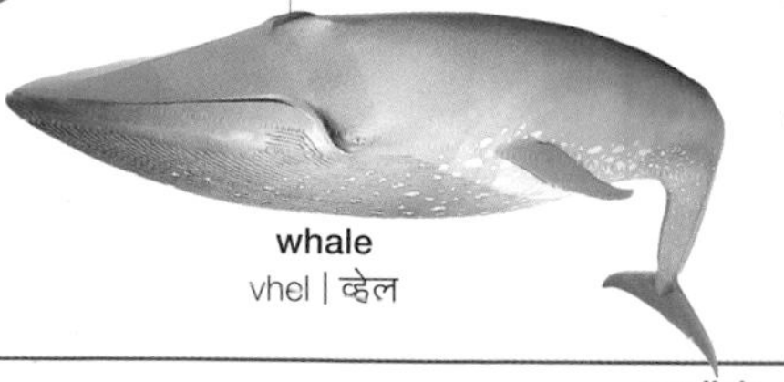

blowhole
śvās chhidr
श्वास छिद्र

whale
vhel | व्हेल

dolphin
dolphin
डॉल्फ़िन

antler
sīng
सींग

deer
hiran | हिरन

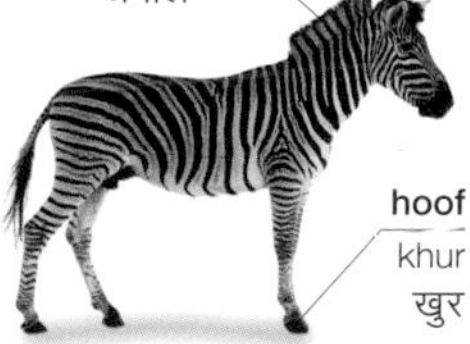
mane
ayāl
अयाल
hoof
khur
खुर

zebra
zebrā | ज़ेबरा

giraffe
jirāf | जिराफ़

hump
kūbaṛ
कूबड़

camel
ūṃṭ | ऊंट

hippopotamus
dariyāī ghoṛā | दरियाई घोड़ा

trunk
sūṃṛ | सूंड़
tusk
hāthī dāṃt
हाथी दांत

elephant
hāthī | हाथी

horn
sīng | सींग

rhinoceros
gaiṇḍā | गैंडा

tiger
bāgh | बाघ

mane
ayāl | अयाल

lion
babbar śer | बब्बर शेर

monkey
bandar | बंदर

gorilla
gorillā | गोरिल्ला

koala
koālā | कोआला

pouch
thailī
थैली

kangaroo
kaṅgārū | कंगारू

claw
panjā
पंजा

bear
bhālū | भालू

polar bear
dhruviya bhālū | ध्रुवीय भालू

panda
pāṃḍā
पांडा

animals 2 • paśu • पशु

birds • pakṣī • पक्षी

canary
chhoṭī pīlī chiṛiyā
छोटी पीली चिड़िया

sparrow
goraiyā | गोरैया

hummingbird | marmar pakṣī | मर्मर पक्षी

swallow
abābīl | अबाबील

crow
kauā | कौआ

pigeon
kabūtar | कबूतर

woodpecker
kaṭhphoṛvā
कठफोड़वा

falcon
bāz | बाज़

owl
ullū | उल्लू

gull
ghomrā | घोमरा

eagle
uḳāb | उक़ाब

pelican
pelikan | पेलिकन

flamingo
rājhaṃs | राजहंस

stork
bag̣ulā | बग़ुला

crane
sāras | सारस

penguin
penguin | पेंगुइन

ostrich
śuturmurg̣ | शुतुर्मुर्ग़

goose
bataḳh | बतख़

swan
haṃs | हंस

peacock
mor | मोर

pheasant
tītar | तीतर

turkey
ṭarkī | टर्की

cockatoo
kākātū totā
काकातू तोता

beak
chomch
चोंच
feather
far
फ़र
wing
paṅkh
पंख
claw
panjā
पंजा

parrot
totā | तोता

reptiles • sarīsṛp • सरीसृप

scales
sūkhī chamṛī
सूखी चमड़ी

alligator
ghaṛiyāl | घड़ियाल

lizard
chhipkalī | छिपकली

iguana
goh | गोह

shell
kavach
कवच

turtle | samudrī
kachhuā | समुद्री कछुआ

tortoise
kachhuā | कछुआ

snake
sāṃp | सांप

snout
thūthnī
थूथनी

crocodile
magarmacchh | मगरमच्छ

animals 3 • paśu 3 • पशु

amphibians • ubhayachar jīv • उभयचर जीव

frog
memḍhak | मेंढक

toad
thal memḍhak | थल मेंढक

tadpole
śiśu memḍhak | शिशु मेंढक

salamander
sarṭak | सरटक

fish • machhlī • मछली

eel
bām machhlī | बाम मछली

shark
śārk | शार्क

seahorse
aśvmīn | अश्वमीन

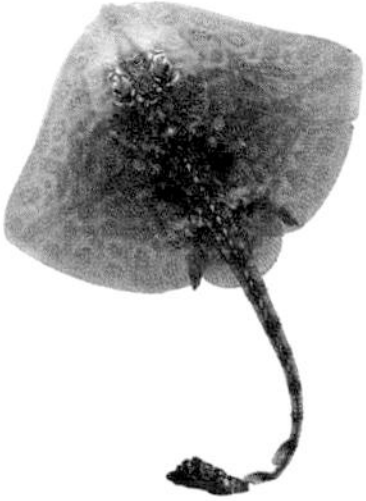

skate
skeṭ machhlī | स्केट मछली

ray
re | रे

goldfish
sonmāchhī | सोनमाछी

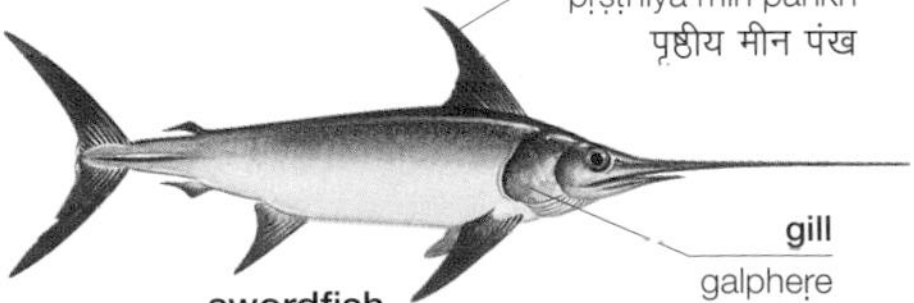
dorsal fin
pṛṣṭhīya mīn paṅkh
पृष्ठीय मीन पंख
gill
galpheṛe
गलफेड़े

swordfish
khaṅgmīn | खंगमीन

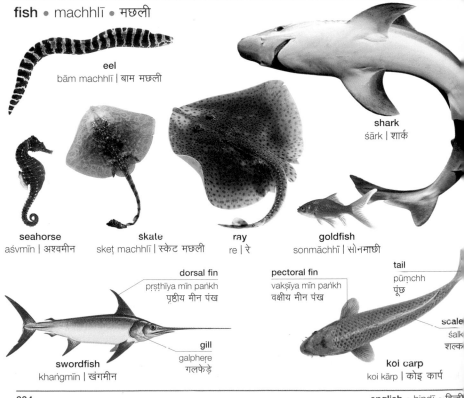

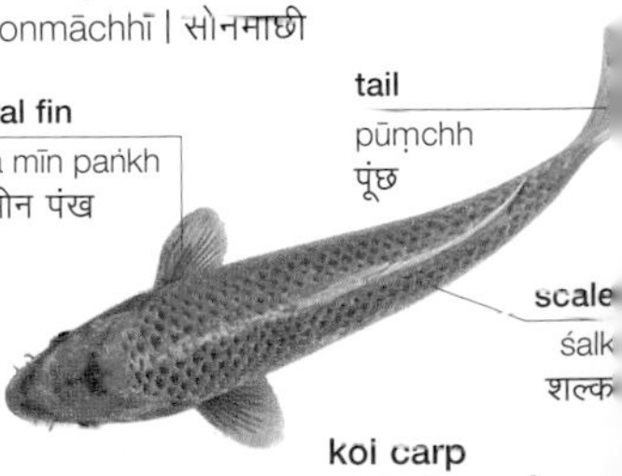
pectoral fin
vakṣīya mīn paṅkh
वक्षीय मीन पंख
tail
pūṃchh
पूंछ
scale
śalk
शल्क

koi carp
koi kārp | कोइ कार्प

invertebrates • akaśerukī jīv • अकशेरुकी जीव

ant
chīṃṭī | चींटी

termite
dīmak | दीमक

bee
madhumakkhī | मधुमक्खी

wasp
barr | बर्र

beetle
phuṅgā | फूंगा

cockroach
tilchaṭṭā | तिलचट्टा

moth
pataṅgā | पतंगा

butterfly
titlī | तितली

cocoon
koyā | कोया

caterpillar
illī | इल्ली

cricket
jhiṅgur | झींगुर

grasshopper
ṭiḍḍā | टिड्डा

praying mantis
mantris
मंत्रिस

scorpion
bicchhū | बिच्छू

centipede
kankhajūrā | कनखजूरा

dragonfly
ḍraigan flāī
ड्रैगन फ़्लाई

fly
makkhī | मक्खी

mosquito
macchhar | मच्छर

ladybug
leḍībarḍ | लेडीबर्ड

spider
makṛī | मकड़ी

slug
kambu | कंबु

snail
ghoṃghā | घोंघा

worm
kṛmi | कृमि

starfish
sṭār fiś | स्टार फ़िश

mussel
śambuk | शंबुक

crab
kekṛā | केकड़ा

lobster
lobster | लॉबस्टर

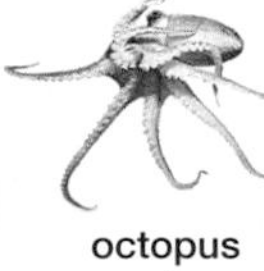

octopus
aṣṭbhuj | अष्टभुज

squid
skviḍ | स्क्विड

jellyfish
jailī fiś | जैली फ़िश

plants • vanaspati • वनस्पति

tree • peṛ • पेड़

branch
śākhā
शाखा
bark
chhāl
छाल
root
jaṛ
जड़
trunk
tanā
तना

oak | bāṃj | बांज

leaf
pattī
पत्ती
twig
ṭahnī
टहनी

willow
śarpat | शरपत

poplar | vilāyatī pīpal | विलायती पीपल

eucalyptus
nīlgiri | नीलगिरि

larch
śrīdāru | श्रीदारु

beech
bīch | बीच

birch
bhojvṛkṣ | भोजवृक्ष

pine
chīṛ | चीड़

cedar
devdār | देवदार

maple
mepal | मेपल

elm
chirābel | चिराबेल

lime | nībū kā vṛkṣ | नीबू का वृक्ष

berry
saras phal
सरस फल

holly
śūlparṇī | शूलपर्णी

palm
tāṛ | ताड़

lowering plant • puṣpī paudhe • पुष्पी पौधे

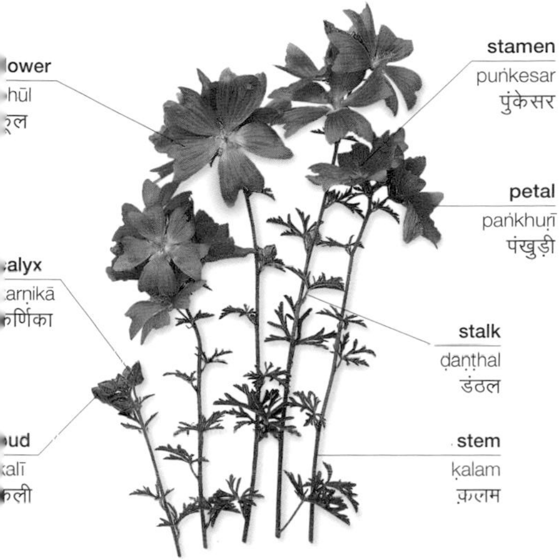
lower
hūl
ूल
stamen
puṅkesar
पुंकेसर
petal
paṅkhuṛī
पंखुड़ी
alyx
arṇikā
र्णिका
stalk
ḍaṇṭhal
डंठल
ud
alī
ली
stem
ḳalam
क़लम

buttercup
baṭarkap | बटरकप

daisy
ḍezī | डेज़ी

thistle
ikṣugandhā
इक्षुगंधा

dandelion
kukrauṃdhā
कुकरौंधा

heather
haidar
हैदर

poppy
ahipuṣp
अहिपुष्प

foxglove
apsaroṅguli
अप्सरोंगुलि

honeysuckle
hanīsakal
हनीसकल

sunflower
sūryamukhī
सूर्यमुखी

clover
tinpatiyā
तिनपतिया

bluebells
jaṅglī gomed
जंगली गोमेद

primrose
primroz
प्रिमरोज़

lupines
lyūpin
ल्यूपिन

nettle
bicchhū-būṭī
बिच्छू–बूटी

town • śahar • शहर

street
saṛak
सड़क

curb
paṭrī
पटरी

street corner
galī kā nukkaṛ
गली का नुक्कड़

stor
dukā
दुका

intersectio
chaurāh
चौराह

one-wa
systen
iktarfā rāst
इकतरफ़ा रास्त

sidewal
fuṭpāt
फ़ुटपा

offic
buildin
karyālay
khan
कार्यालय खं

apartmen
buildin
apārṭmen
khan
अपार्टमेंट खं

alley
galī
गली

parking lot
kār pārk
कार पार्क

street sign
mārg saṅketak
मार्ग संकेतक

barrier
khambhā
खंभा

streetligh
sṭrīṭ lāi
स्ट्रीट लाइ

buildings • imārat • इमारत

town hall
ṭāun hall | टाउन हॉल

library
pustakālaya | पुस्तकालय

movie theater
sinemā | सिनेमा

theater
thieṭar | थिएटर

university
viśvavidyālaya | विश्वविद्यालय

school
vidyālaya | विद्यालय

skyscraper
gaganchumbī imārat
गगनचुंबी इमारत

areas • kṣetr • क्षेत्र

industrial park
audyogik kṣetr
औद्योगिक क्षेत्र

city
śahar | शहर

suburb
upnagar | उपनगर

village
gāṃv | गांव

vocabulary • śabdāvalī • शब्दावली

pedestrian zone
paidal rāstā
पैदल रास्ता

side street
galī
गली

manhole
mainhol
मैनहोल

gutter
nālā
नाला

church
charch
चर्च

avenue
rāstā
रास्ता

square
chauk
चौक

bus stop
bas stop
बस स्टॉप

factory
kārḳhānā
कारख़ाना

drain
nālī
नाली

architecture • vāstuśilp • वास्तुशिल्प

buildings and structures • bhavan evam imārateṃ • भवन एवं इमारतें

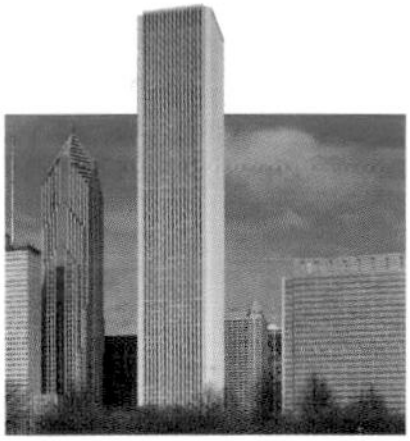

skyscraper | gaganchumbī imārat | गगनचुंबी इमारत

turret
burj
बुर्ज
moat
khāī
खाई

castle
ḳilā | क़िला

church
girjāghar | गिरजाघर

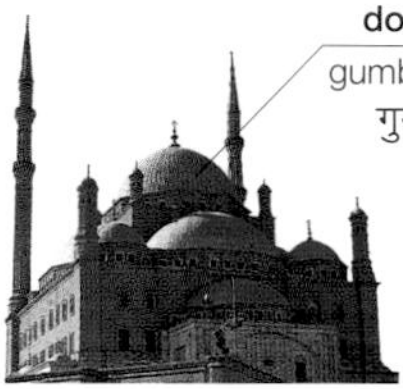
dome
gumbad
गुम्बद

mosque
masjid | मस्जिद

temple
mandir | मंदिर

vault
mehrābdār chhat
मेहराबदार छत

synagogue | yahūdī pūjāsthal
यहूदी पूजास्थल

dam
bāndh | बांध

bridge
pul | पुल

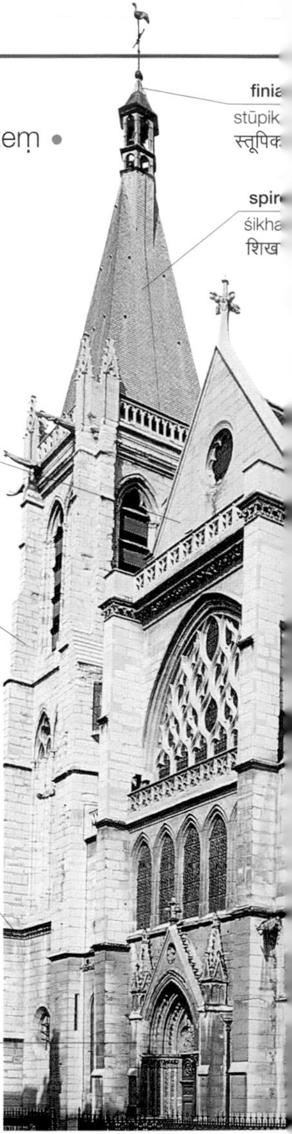
finia
stūpik
स्तूपिक
spir
śikha
शिख
gable
triyankī chhat
त्रियंकी छत
tower
mīnār
मीनार
cornice
cornice
कॉर्निस
pillar
khambhā
खंभा

cathedral
baṛā girjāghar | बड़ा गिरजाघर

styles • śailī • शैली

gothic
gothic | गॉथिक

architrave
prastarpād
प्रस्तरपाद

renaissance
renesāns | रेनेसान्स

baroque
bārok | बारोक

arch
mehrāb
मेहराब

frieze
chitr vallarī
चित्र वल्लरी

buttress
puśtā
पुश्ता

choir
gāyan sthal
गायन स्थल

rococo
rokoko | रोकोको

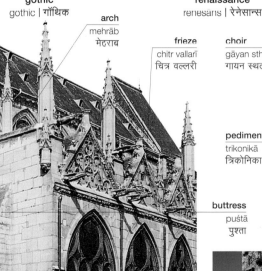

pediment
trikonikā
त्रिकोनिका

neoclassical
navśāstrīya | नवशास्त्रीय

Art Nouveau
ārṭ nūvo | आर्ट नूवो

Art Deco
ārṭ ḍeko | आर्ट डेको

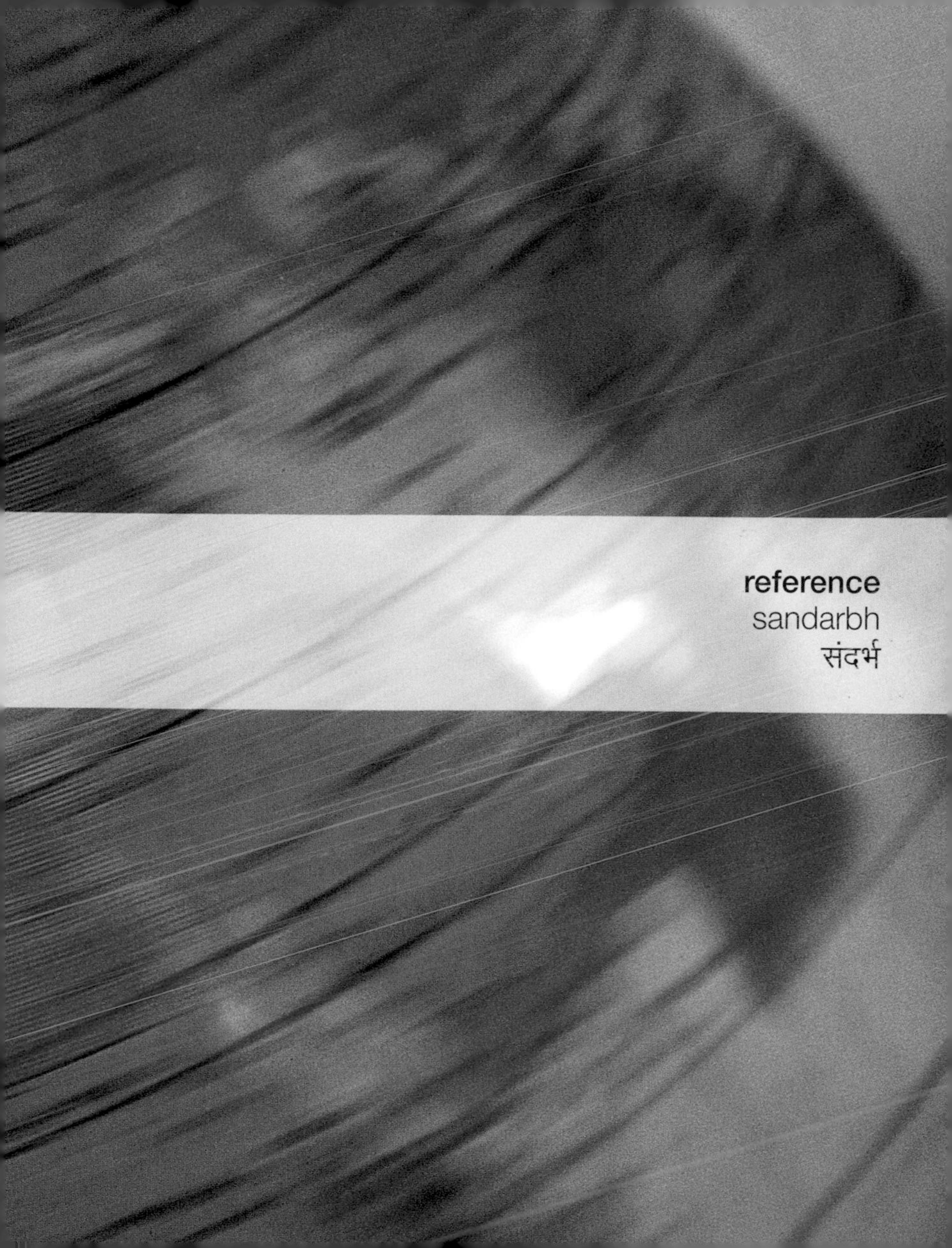

reference
sandarbh
संदर्भ

time • samaya • समय

minute hand
minaṭ kī sūī
मिनट की सूई

hour hand
ghaṇṭe kī sūī
घंटे की सूई

clock | gharī | घड़ी

vocabulary • śabdāvalī • शब्दावली

second saikaṇḍ सैकंड	**now** abhī अभी	**15 minutes** pandrah minaṭ पंद्रह मिनट
minute minaṭ मिनट	**later** bād meṃ बाद में	**twenty minutes** bīs minaṭ बीस मिनट
hour ghaṇṭā घंटा	**half an hour** ādhā ghaṇṭā आधा घंटा	**forty minutes** chālīs minaṭ चालीस मिनट

What time is it?
kyā samaya huā hai ?
क्या समय हुआ है?

It's three o'clock.
tīn baj gae haiṃ
तीन बज गए हैं।

five after one
ek baj kar pāṃch minaṭ
एक बज कर पांच मिनट

ten after one
ek baj kar das minaṭ
एक बज कर दस मिनट

quarter after one
savā ek
सवा एक

twenty after one
ek baj kar bīs minaṭ
एक बज कर बीस मिन

second hand
saikaṇḍ kī sūī
सैकंड की सूई

twenty-five after one
ek baj kar pacchīs minaṭ
एक बज कर पच्चीस मिनट

one-thirty
ḍeṛh
डेढ़

twenty-five to two
do bajne meṃ pacchīs minaṭ
दो बजने में पच्चीस मिनट

twenty to two
do bajne meṃ bīs m
दो बजने में बीस मिन

quarter to two
paune do
पौने दो

ten to two
do bajne meṃ das minaṭ
दो बजने में दस मिनट

five to two
do bajne meṃ pāṃch minaṭ
दो बजने में पांच मिनट

two o'clock
do baje
दो बजे

night and day • rāt aur din • रात और दिन

midnight
ardhrātri | अर्धरात्रि

sunrise
sūryodaya | सूर्योदय

dawn
bhor | भोर

morning
subah | सुबह

sunset
sūryāst | सूर्यास्त

noon
madhyāhn | मध्याह्न

dusk
sāyaṃkāl | सायंकाल

evening
sandhyā | संध्या

afternoon
dopahar | दोपहर

vocabulary • śabdāvalī • शब्दावली

early
jaldī
जल्दी

on time
samaya par
समय पर

late
der
देर

You're early.
āp jaldī ā gae haiṃ
आप जल्दी आ गए हैं।

You're late.
āp der se āe haiṃ
आप देर से आए हैं।

I'll be there soon.
maiṃ jaldī hī pahuṃch jāūṃgā
मैं जल्दी ही पहुंच जाऊंगा।

Please be on time.
kṛpyā samaya par pahuṃcheṃ
कृपया समय पर पहुंचें।

What time does it start?
yah kis samaya śurū hogā?
यह किस समय शुरू होगा?

I'll see you later.
maiṃ āpse bād meṃ milūṅgā
मैं आपसे बाद में मिलूंगा।

It's getting late.
der ho rahī hai
देर हो रही है।

How long will it last?
yah kab tak chalegā?
यह कब तक चलेगा?

What time does it finish?
yah kab samāpt hogā?
यह कब समाप्त होगा?

calendar • kaileṇḍar • कैलेंडर

month
mās
मास

year
varṣ
वर्ष

January
janvarī
जनवरी

2010

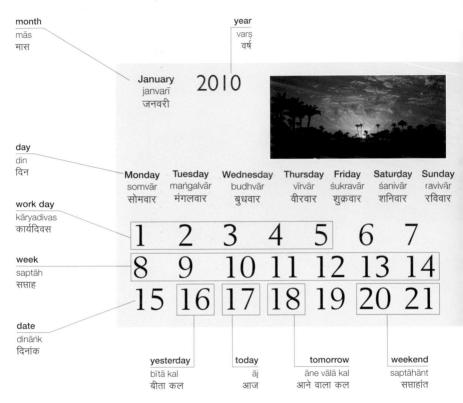

day
din
दिन

Monday somvār सोमवार	**Tuesday** maṅgalvār मंगलवार	**Wednesday** budhvār बुधवार	**Thursday** vīrvār वीरवार	**Friday** śukravār शुक्रवार	**Saturday** śanivār शनिवार	**Sunday** ravivār रविवार
1	2	3	4	5	6	7
8	9	10	11	12	13	14
15	16	17	18	19	20	21

work day
kāryadivas
कार्यदिवस

week
saptāh
सप्ताह

date
dināṅk
दिनांक

yesterday
bītā kal
बीता कल

today
āj
आज

tomorrow
āne vālā kal
आने वाला कल

weekend
saptāhānt
सप्ताहांत

vocabulary • śabdāvalī • शब्दावली

January janvarī जनवरी	**March** mārch मार्च	**May** maī मई	**July** julāī जुलाई	**September** sitambar सितंबर	**November** navambar नवंबर
February farvarī फ़रवरी	**April** aprail अप्रैल	**June** jūn जून	**August** agast अगस्त	**October** akṭūbar अक्टूबर	**December** disambar दिसंबर

years • varṣ • वर्ष

1900 nineteen hundred • unnīs sau • उन्नीस सौ

1901 nineteen hundred and one • unnīs sau ek • उन्नीस सौ एक

1910 nineteen ten • unnīs sau das • उन्नीस सौ दस

2000 two thousand • do hazār • दो हज़ार

2001 two thousand and one • do hazār ek • दो हज़ार एक

seasons • ṛtueṃ • ऋतुएं

spring
basant
बसंत

summer
grīṣm
ग्रीष्म

fall
patjhaṛ
पतझड़

winter
śarad
शरद

vocabulary • śabdāvalī • शब्दावली

century
śatābdī
शताब्दी

decade
daśak
दशक

fortnight
pakhvāṛā
पखवाड़ा

this week
is hafte
इस हफ़्ते

last week
pichhle hafte
पिछले हफ़्ते

the day before yesterday
bītā parsoṃ
बीता परसों

weekly
sāptāhik
साप्ताहिक

monthly
māsik
मासिक

annual
vārṣik
वार्षिक

millennium
sahsrābdī
सहस्राब्दी

next week
agle hafte
अगले हफ़्ते

the day after tomorrow
parsoṃ
परसों

What's the date today?
āj kyā tārīkh hai?
आज क्या तारीख़ है?

It's February seventh, two thousand and two.
āj 7 farvarī 2002 hai
आज 7 फ़रवरी, 2002 है।

numbers • aṃk • अंक

0 zero • śūnya • शून्य

1 one • ek • एक

2 two • do • दो

3 three • tīn • तीन

4 four • chār • चार

5 five • pāṃch • पांच

6 six • chhah • छह

7 seven • sāt • सात

8 eight • āṭh • आठ

9 nine • nau • नौ

10 ten • das • दस

11 eleven • gyārah • ग्यारह

12 twelve • bārah • बारह

13 thirteen • terah • तेरह

14 fourteen • chaudah • चौदह

15 fifteen • pandrah • पंद्रह

16 sixteen • solah • सोलह

17 seventeen • satrah • सत्रह

18 eighteen • aṭhārah • अठारह

19 nineteen • unnīs • उन्नीस

20 twenty • bīs • बीस

21 twenty-one • ikkīs • इक्कीस

22 twenty-two • bāīs • बाईस

30 thirty • tīs • तीस

40 forty • chālīs • चालीस

50 fifty • pachās • पचास

60 sixty • sāṭh • साठ

70 seventy • sattar • सत्तर

80 eighty • assī • अस्सी

90 ninety • nabbe • नब्बे

100 one hundred • sau • सौ

110 one hundred and ten • ek sau das • एक सौ दस

200 two hundred • do sau • दो सौ

300 three hundred • tīn sau • तीन सौ

400 four hundred • chār sau • चार सौ

500 five hundred • pāṃch sau • पांच सौ

600 six hundred • chhah sau • छह सौ

700 seven hundred • sāt sau • सात सौ

800 eight hundred • āṭh sau • आठ सौ

900 nine hundred • nau sau • नौ सौ

1,000	**one thousand** • ek hazār • एक हज़ार
10,000	**ten thousand** • das hazār • दस हज़ार
20,000	**twenty thousand** • bīs hazār • बीस हज़ार
50,000	**fifty thousand** • pachās hazār • पचास हज़ार
55,500	**fifty-five thousand five hundred** • pachpan hazār pāṃch sau • पचपन हज़ार पांच सौ
100,000	**one hundred thousand** • ek lākh • एक लाख
1,000,000	**one million** • das lākh • दस लाख
1,000,000,000	**one billion** • ek arab • एक अरब

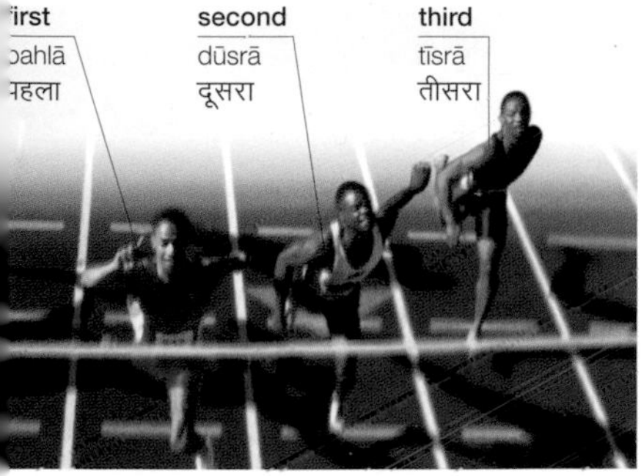
first
pahlā
पहला
second
dūsrā
दूसरा
third
tīsrā
तीसरा

fourth • chauthā • चौथा

fifth • pāṃchvāṃ • पांचवां

sixth • chhaṭhā • छठा

seventh • sātvāṃ • सातवां

eighth • āṭhvāṃ • आठवां

ninth • nauvāṃ • नौवां

tenth • dasvāṃ • दसवां

eleventh • gyārahavāṃ • ग्यारहवां

twelfth • bārhavāṃ • बारहवां

thirteenth • terhavāṃ • तेरहवां

fourteenth • chaudhavāṃ • चौदहवां

fifteenth • pandrahavāṃ • पंद्रहवां

sixteenth • solahavāṃ • सोलहवां

seventeenth • satrahavāṃ • सत्रहवां

eighteenth • aṭhārahavāṃ • अठारहवां

nineteenth • unnīsvāṃ • उन्नीसवां

twentieth • bīsvāṃ • बीसवां

twenty-first • ikkisvāṃ • इक्कीसवां

twenty-second • bāisvāṃ • बाईसवां

twenty-third • teisvāṃ • तेइसवां

thirtieth • tīsvāṃ • तीसवां

fortieth • chālīsvāṃ • चालीसवां

fiftieth • pachāsvāṃ • पचासवां

sixtieth • sāṭhvāṃ • साठवां

seventieth • sattarvāṃ • सत्तरवां

eightieth • assīvāṃ • अस्सीवां

ninetieth • nabbevāṃ • नब्बेवां

one hundredth • sauvāṃ • सौवां

weights and measures • bhār aur māpak • भार और मापक

area • kṣetr • क्षेत्र

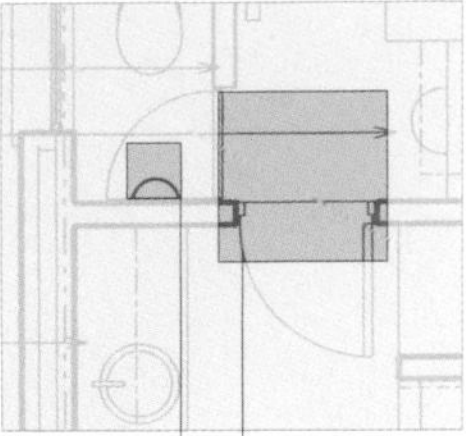

square foot
varg fuṭ
वर्ग फुट

square meter
vargmīṭar
वर्गमीटर

distance • dūrī • दूरी

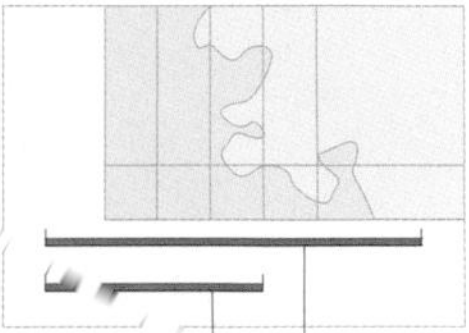

kilometer
kilomīṭar
किलोमीटर

mile
mīl
मील

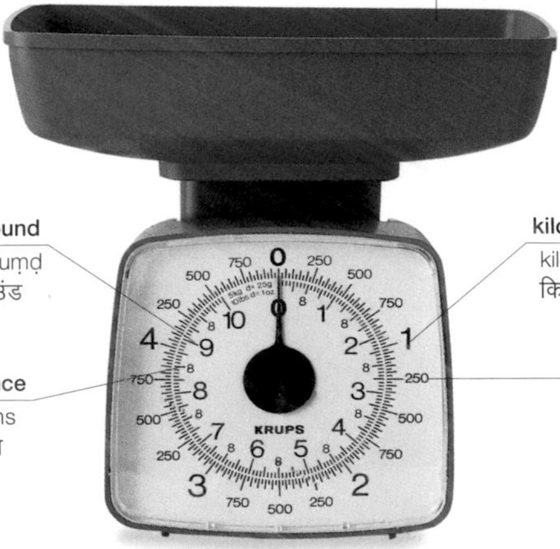

pan
pain
पैन

pound
pāuṃḍ
पाउंड

ounce
auṃs
औंस

kilogram
kilogrām
किलोग्राम

gram
grām
ग्राम

scales | tarāzū | तराजू

vocabulary • śabdāvalī • शब्दावली

yard
gaz
गज़

meter
mīṭar
मीटर

ton
ṭan
टन

milligram
milīgrām
मिलीग्राम

measure (v)
māpnā
मापना

weigh (v)
tolnā
तोलना

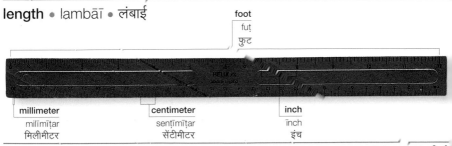

length • lambāī • लंबाई

foot
fuṭ
फुट

millimeter
milīmīṭar
मिलीमीटर

centimeter
senṭīmīṭar
सेंटीमीटर

inch
īnch
इंच

capacity • kṣamtā • क्षमता

half-liter
ādhā līṭar
आधा लीटर

pint
pāinṭ | पाइंट

milliliter
milīlīṭar
मिलीलीटर

measuring cup
māpak jag | मापक जग

volume
āyatan
आयतन

measure
māp | माप

vocabulary • śabdāvalī • शब्दावली

gallon
gailan
गैलन

quart
kvārṭ
क्वार्ट

liter
līṭar
लीटर

container • kanṭenar • कंटेनर

carton
kārṭan | कार्टन

packet
paikeṭ | पैकेट

bottle
botal | बोतल

bag
thailā
थैला

tub | ṭab | टब

jar | jār | जार

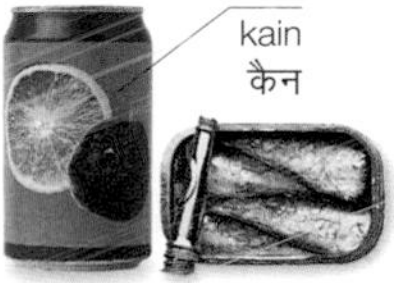

can
kain
कैन

tin | ṭin | टिन

spray bottle
ḍispensar | डिस्पेंसर

bar
ṭikiyā
टिकिया

tube | ṭyūb | ट्यूब

roll | rol | रोल

pack | paik | पैक

spray can
spre kain | स्प्रे कैन

world map • viśv mānchitr • विश्व मानचित्र

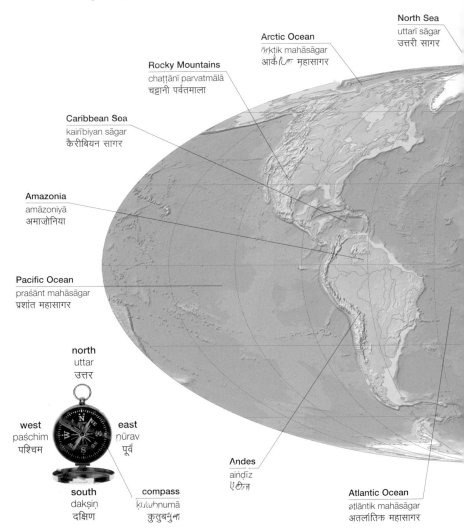

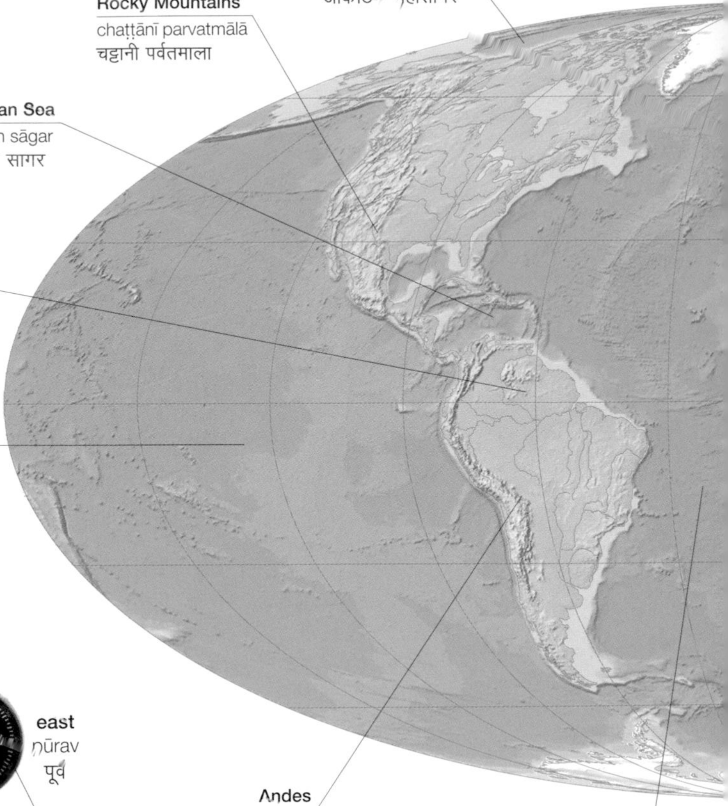
North Sea
uttarī sāgar
उत्तरी सागर
Arctic Ocean
ārktik mahāsāgar
आर्कटिक महासागर
Rocky Mountains
chaṭṭānī parvatmālā
चट्टानी पर्वतमाला
Caribbean Sea
kairībiyan sāgar
कैरीबियन सागर
Amazonia
amāzoniyā
अमाज़ोनिया
Pacific Ocean
praśānt mahāsāgar
प्रशांत महासागर
Andes
aiṇḍīz
एंडीज़
Atlantic Ocean
atlāntik mahāsāgar
अतलांतिक महासागर

north
uttar
उत्तर
west
paśchim
पश्चिम
east
pūrav
पूर्व
south
dakṣiṇ
दक्षिण
compass
kutubnumā
कुतुबनुमा

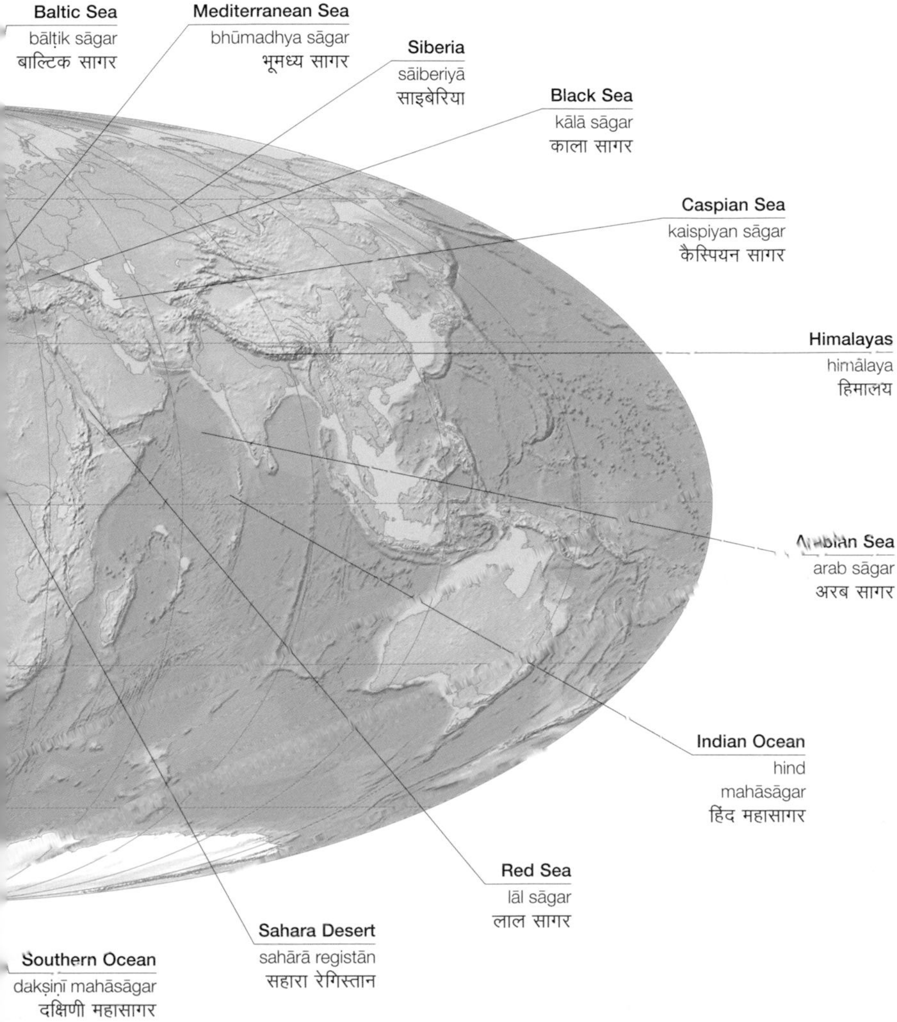
Baltic Sea
bālṭik sāgar
बाल्टिक सागर
Mediterranean Sea
bhūmadhya sāgar
भूमध्य सागर
Siberia
sāiberiyā
साइबेरिया
Black Sea
kālā sāgar
काला सागर
Caspian Sea
kaispiyan sāgar
कैस्पियन सागर
Himalayas
himālaya
हिमालय
Arabian Sea
arab sāgar
अरब सागर
Indian Ocean
hind mahāsāgar
हिंद महासागर
Red Sea
lāl sāgar
लाल सागर
Sahara Desert
sahārā registān
सहारा रेगिस्तान
Southern Ocean
dakṣiṇī mahāsāgar
दक्षिणी महासागर

North and Central America • uttar aur madhya amerikā • उत्तर और मध्य अमेरिका

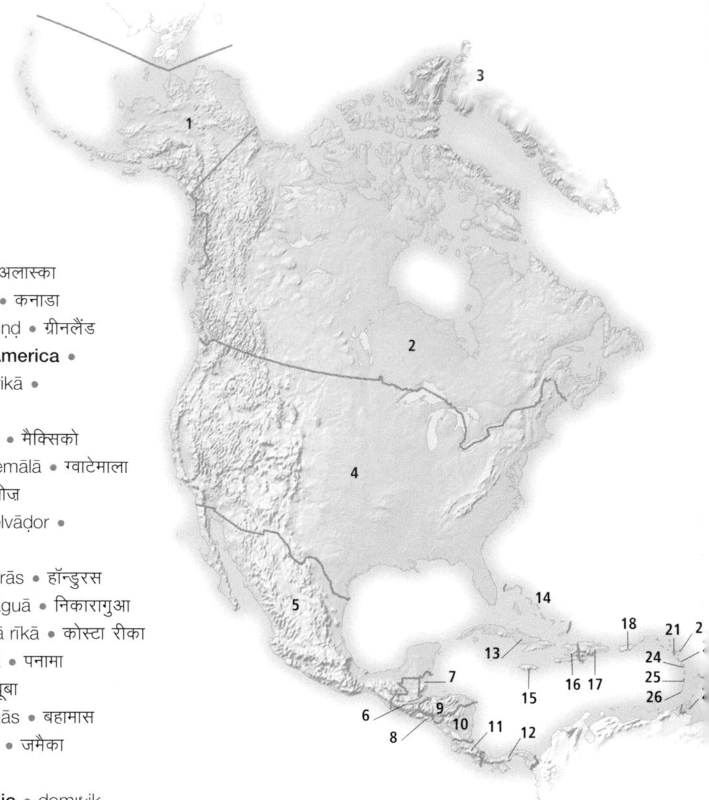

1 **Alaska** • alāskā • अलास्का
2 **Canada** • kanāḍā • कनाडा
3 **Greenland** • grīnlainḍ • ग्रीनलैंड
4 **United States of America** • saṃyūkt rājya amerikā • सयुंक्त राज्य अमेरिका
5 **Mexico** • maiksiko • मैक्सिको
6 **Guatemala** • gvāṭemālā • ग्वाटेमाला
7 **Belize** • belīz • बेलीज़
8 **El Salvador** • el selvāḍor • एल सेल्वाडोर
9 **Honduras** • honḍurās • हॉन्डुरस
10 **Nicaragua** • nikārāguā • निकारागुआ
11 **Costa Rica** • kosṭā rīkā • कोस्टा रीका
12 **Panama** • panāmā • पनामा
13 **Cuba** • kyūbā • क्यूबा
14 **Bahamas** • bahāmās • बहामास
15 **Jamaica** • jamaikā • जमैका
16 **Haiti** • haitī • हैटी
17 **Dominican Republic** • ḍominik ganrājya • डोमिनिक गणराज्य
18 **Puerto Rico** • pyūrto rīko • प्यूर्तो रीको
19 **Barbados** • bārbāḍos • बारबाडोस
20 **Trinidad and Tobago** • trinidād enḍ ṭobāgo • त्रिनिदाद एंड टोबागो
21 **St. Kitts and Nevis** • senṭ kiṭs enḍ nevis • सेंट किट्स एंड नेविस
22 **Antigua and Barbuda** • enṭīguā aur bārbuḍā • एंटीगुआ और बारबुडा
23 **Dominica** • ḍominikā • डोमिनिका
24 **St. Lucia** • senṭ luchiā • सेंट लुचिया
25 **St. Vincent and The Grenadines** • senṭ vinsenṭ enḍ da grenāḍins • सेंट विन्सेंट एंड द ग्रेनाडिन्स
26 **Grenada** • grenāḍā • ग्रेनाडा

South America • dakṣiṇ amerikā • दक्षिण अमेरिका

1 **Venezuela** • venezuelā • वेनेजुएला
2 **Colombia** • kolambiyā • कोलम्बिया
3 **Ecuador** • ikveḍor • एक्वेडोर
4 **Peru** • perū • पेरू
5 **Galapagos Islands** • gālāpāgos dvip samūh • गालापागोस द्वीप समूह
6 **Guyana** • guyānā • गुयाना
7 **Suriname** • sūrīnām • सूरीनाम
8 **French Guiana** • french gayānā • फ़्रेंच गयाना
9 **Brazil** • brāzīl • ब्राज़ील
10 **Bolivia** • bolīviyā • बोलीविया
11 **Chile** • chilī • चिली
12 **Argentina** • arjenṭīnā • अर्जेंटीना
13 **Paraguay** • pairāgue • पैरागुए
14 **Uruguay** • urūgue • उरूगुए
15 **Falkland Islands** • falkland dvip samūh • फ़ॉकलैंड द्वीप समूह

Vocabulary • śabdāvalī • शब्दावली

country deś देश	**province** prānt प्रांत	**zone** anchal अंचल
continent mahādvīp महाद्वीप	**territory** ilāqā इलाक़ा	**district** zilā ज़िला
nation rāṣṭr राष्ट्र	**colony** colony कॉलोनी	**region** kṣetra क्षेत्र
state rājya राज्य	**principality** sāmrājya साम्राज्य	**capital** rājdhānī राजधानी

Europe • yūrop • यूरोप

1 **Ireland** • āyarlaiṇḍ • आयरलैंड
2 **United Kingdom** • yūnāiṭeḍ kiṅgḍam • यूनाइटेड किंग्डम
3 **Portugal** • purtgāl • पुर्तगाल
4 **Spain** • spen • स्पेन
5 **Balearic Islands** • bailirik dvīp samūh • बैलिरिक द्वीप समूह
6 **Andorra** • anḍorā • अन्डोरा
7 **France** • frāṃs • फ़्रांस
8 **Belgium** • beljiyam • बेल्जियम
9 **Netherlands** • nīdarlaiṇḍ • नीदरलैंड
10 **Luxembourg** • lakzambarg • लक्ज़मबर्ग
11 **Germany** • jarmanī • जर्मनी
12 **Denmark** • ḍenmārk • डेनमार्क
13 **Norway** • nārve • नार्वे
14 **Sweden** • svīḍan • स्वीडन
15 **Finland** • finlaiṇḍ • फ़िनलैंड
16 **Estonia** • esṭoniyā • एस्टोनिया
17 **Latvia** • lāṭviyā • लाटविया
18 **Lithuania** • lithuāniyā • लिथुआनिया
19 **Kaliningrad** • kailinin grāḍ • कैलिनिनग्राड
20 **Poland** • polaiṇḍ • पोलैंड
21 **Czech Republic** • chek gaṇrājya • चेक गणराज्य
22 **Austria** • austria • ऑस्ट्रिया
23 **Liechtenstein** • liktensṭāin • लिक्टेन्स्टाइन
24 **Switzerland** • sviṭzarlaiṇḍ • स्विट्जरलैंड
25 **Italy** • iṭlī • इटली
26 **Monaco** • monāko • मोनाको
27 **Corsica** • corsica • कॉरसिका
28 **Sardinia** • sārḍīniyā • सार्डीनिया
29 **San Marino** • sān marīno • सान मरीनो
30 **Vatican City** • veṭikan siṭī • वेटिकन सिटी
31 **Sicily** • sisilī • सिसिली
32 **Malta** • māltā • माल्टा
33 **Slovenia** • sloveniyā • स्लोवेनिया
34 **Croatia** • kroeśiyā • क्रोएशिया
35 **Hungary** • haṅgarī • हंगरी
36 **Slovakia** • slovākiyā • स्लोवाकिया
37 **Ukraine** • yūkren • यूक्रेन
38 **Belarus** • belārūs • बेलारूस
39 **Moldova** • moldova • मॉल्डोवा
40 **Romania** • romāniyā • रोमानिया
41 **Serbia** • sarbiyā • सर्बिया
42 **Bosnia and Herzogovina** • bosniyā eṇḍ harzogovinā • बोस्निया एंड हर्ज़ोगोविना
43 **Albania** • albāniyā • अल्बानिया
44 **Macedonia** • meseḍoniyā • मेसेडोनिया
45 **Bulgaria** • bulgāriyā • बुल्गारिया
46 **Greece** • grīs • ग्रीस
47 **Kosovo** • kōsōvō • कोसोवो
48 **Montenegro** • mōntenegro • मोंटेनेग्रो
49 **Iceland** • āislaiṇḍ • आइसलैंड

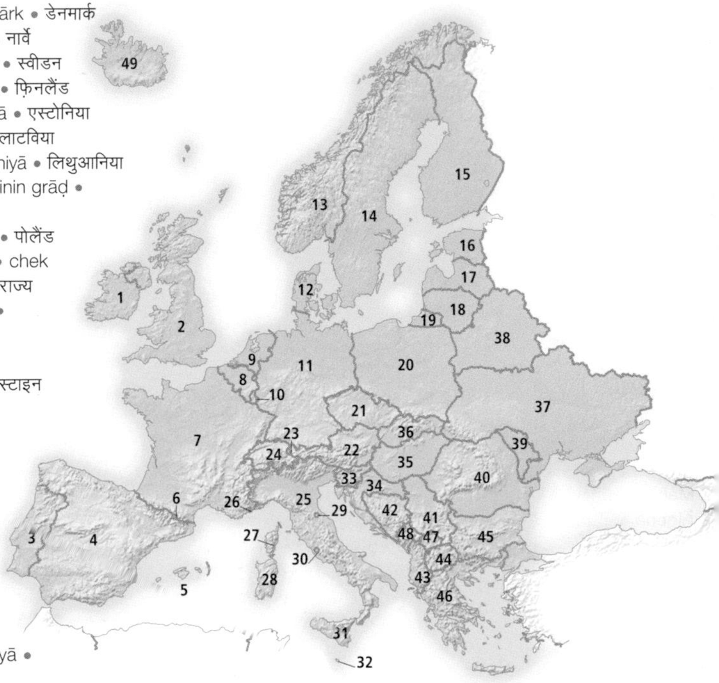

Africa • afrīkā • अफ़्रीका

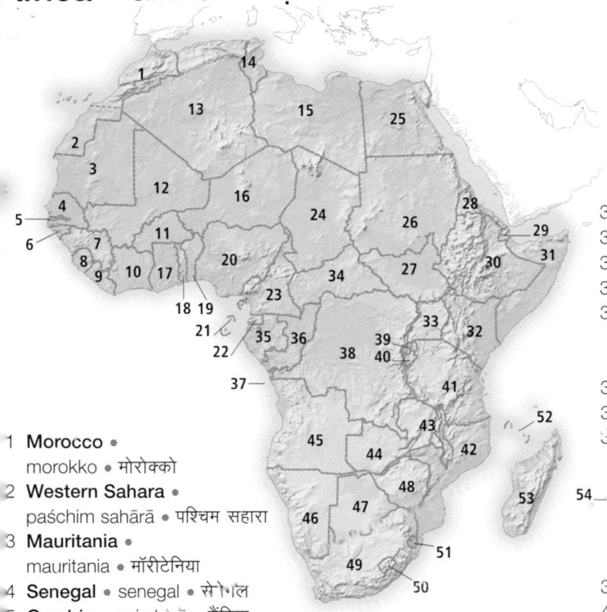

1 **Morocco** • morokko • मोरोक्को
2 **Western Sahara** • paśchim sahārā • पश्चिम सहारा
3 **Mauritania** • mauritania • मॉरीटेनिया
4 **Senegal** • senegal • सेनेगल
5 **Gambia** • gaimbiyā • गैंबिया
6 **Guinea-Bissau** • ginībissāū • गिनीबिस्साऊ
7 **Guinea** • ginī • गिनी
8 **Sierra Leone** • sierā lione • सिएरा लिओने
9 **Liberia** • lāiberiyā • लाइबेरिया
10 **Ivory Coast** • āivarī kosṭ • आइवरी कोस्ट
11 **Burkina Faso** • burkina fāso • बुर्किना फ़ासो
12 **Mali** • mālī • माली
13 **Algeria** • aljīriyā • अल्जीरिया
14 **Tunisia** • ṭyūnīśiyā • ट्यूनीशिया
15 **Libya** • lībiyā • लीबिया
16 **Niger** • nāijar • नाइजर
17 **Ghana** • ghānā • घाना
18 **Togo** • ṭogo • टोगो
19 **Benin** • benin • बेनिन
20 **Nigeria** • nāijīriyā • नाइजीरिया
21 **São Tomé and Principe** • são tome aiṇḍ prinsipe • साओ टोमे एंड प्रिंसिपे
22 **Equatorial Guinea** • ekveṭoriyal ginī • एक्वेटोरियल गिनी
23 **Cameroon** • kaimrūn • कैमरून
24 **Chad** • chāḍ • चाड
25 **Egypt** • misr • मिस्र
26 **Sudan** • sūḍān • सूडान
27 **South Sudan** • dakṣiṇ sūḍān • दक्षिण सूडान
28 **Eritrea** • eriṭriyā • एरिट्रिया
29 **Djibouti** • jibūtī • जिबूती
30 **Ethiopia** • ithiyopiyā • इथियोपिया
31 **Somalia** • somāliyā • सोमालिया
32 **Kenya** • kenyā • केन्या
33 **Uganda** • yugāṇḍā • युगांडा
34 **Central African Republic** • madhya afrīkī gaṇrajya • मध्य अफ़्रीकी गणराज्य
35 **Gabon** • gaibon • गैबोन
36 **Congo** • congo • कॉन्गो
37 **Cabinda (Angola)** • kebindā (aṅgōlā) • केबिंदा (अंगोला)
38 **Democratic Republic of the Congo** • congo loktāntrik gaṇrājya • कॉन्गो लोकतांत्रिक गणराज्य
39 **Rwanda** • ruāṇḍā • रुआंडा
40 **Burundi** • burūṇḍī • बुरूंडी
41 **Tanzania** • tanzāniyā • तंज़ानिया
42 **Mozambique** • mozāmbīk • मोज़ाम्बीक़
43 **Malawi** • malāvī • मलावी
44 **Zambia** • zāmbiyā • ज़ाम्बिया
45 **Angola** • aṅgolā • अंगोला
46 **Namibia** • nāmībiyā • नामीबिया
47 **Botswana** • botsvānā • बोत्सवाना
48 **Zimbabwe** • zimbābve • ज़िम्बाब्वे
49 **South Africa** • dakṣiṇ afrīkā • दक्षिण अफ़्रीका
50 **Lesotho** • lesotho • लेसोथो
51 **Swaziland** • svāzīlaiṇḍ • स्वाज़ीलैंड
52 **Comoros** • komoros • कोमोरॉस
53 **Madagascar** • maiḍāgāskar • मैडागास्कर
54 **Mauritius** • mauritius • मॉरीशस

Asia • eśiyā • एशिया

1 **Turkey** • turkī • तुर्की
2 **Cyprus** • sāipras • साइप्रस
3 **Russian Federation** • rūs • रूस
4 **Georgia** • georgia • जॉर्जिया
5 **Armenia** • ārmeniyā • आर्मेनिया
6 **Azerbaijan** • azarbaijān • अज़रबैजान
7 **Iran** • īrān • ईरान
8 **Iraq** • irāk̤ • इराक़
9 **Syria** • sīriyā • सीरिया
10 **Lebanon** • lebnān • लेबनान
11 **Israel** • izrāil • इज़राइल
12 **Jordan** • jordan • जॉर्डन
13 **Saudi Arabia** • saūdī arab • सऊदी अरब
14 **Kuwait** • k̤uvait • क़ुवैत
15 **Bahrain** • baharīna • बहरीन
16 **Qatar** • k̤atar • क़तर
17 **United Arab Emirates** • sanyukt arab amīrāt • संयुक्त अरब अमीरात
18 **Oman** • omān • ओमान
19 **Yemen** • yaman • यमन
20 **Kazakhstan** • kazākistān • कज़ाकिस्तान
21 **Uzbekistan** • uzbekistān • उज़्बेकिस्तान
22 **Turkmenistan** • turkmenistān • तुर्कमेनिस्तान
23 **Afghanistan** • afgānistān • अफ़ग़ानिस्तान
24 **Tajikistan** • tajākistān • तजाकिस्तान
25 **Kyrgyzstan** • kirgistān • किर्गिस्तान
26 **Pakistan** • pākistān • पाकिस्तान
27 **India** • bhārat • भारत
28 **Maldives** • māldīv • मालदीव
29 **Sri Lanka** • śrīlaṅkā • श्रीलंका
30 **China** • chīn • चीन
31 **Mongolia** • maṅgoliyā • मंगोलिया
32 **North Korea** • uttar koriyā • उत्तर कोरिया
33 **South Korea** • dakṣiṇ koriyā • दक्षिण कोरिया
34 **Japan** • jāpān • जापान
35 **Nepal** • nepāl • नेपाल
36 **Bhutan** • bhūṭān • भूटान
37 **Bangladesh** • bāṅglādeś • बांग्लादेश
38 **Burma (Myanmar)** • barmā (myānmār) • बर्मा (म्यांमार)
39 **Thailand** • thāilaiṇḍ • थाइलैंड
40 **Laos** • lāos • लाओस
41 **Vietnam** • viyatnām • वियतनाम

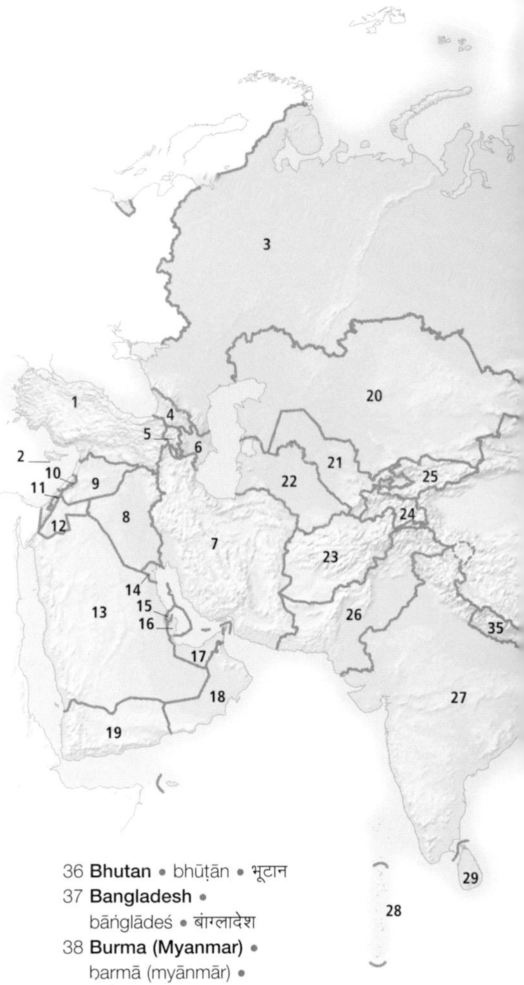

Australasia • australasia • ऑस्ट्रेलेशिया

1 **Australia** • australia • ऑस्ट्रेलिया
2 **Tasmania** • tasmāniyā • तस्मानिया
3 **New Zealand** • nyūzīlaiṇḍ • न्यूज़ीलैंड

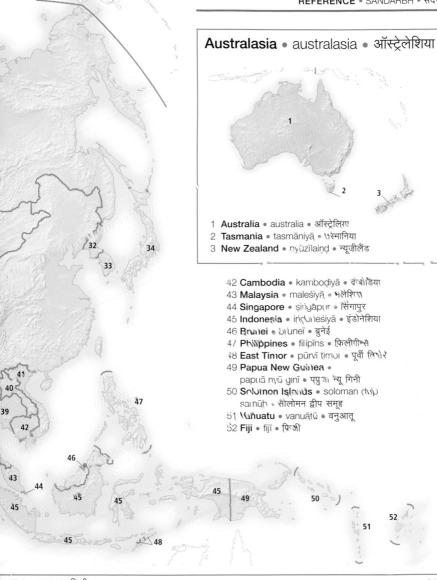

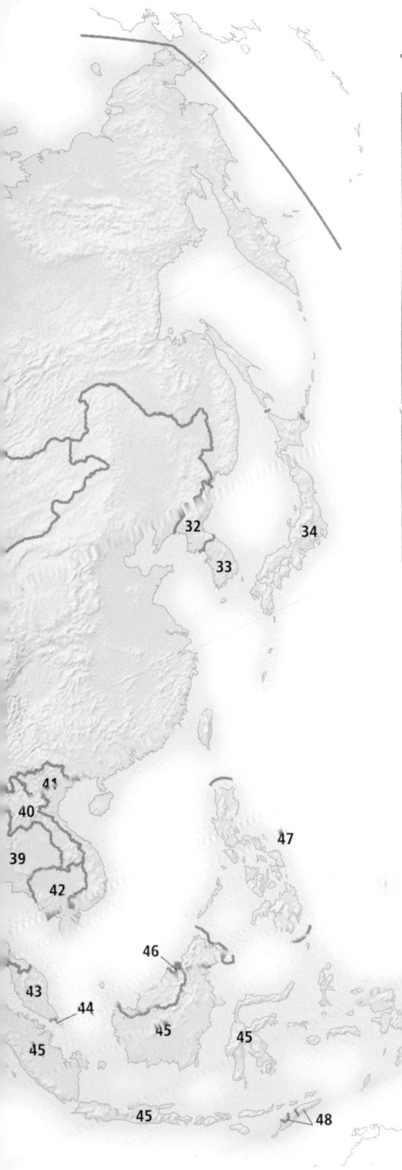

42 **Cambodia** • kamboḍiyā • कंबोडिया
43 **Malaysia** • maleśiyā • मलेशिया
44 **Singapore** • siṅgāpur • सिंगापुर
45 **Indonesia** • iṇḍoneśiyā • इंडोनेशिया
46 **Brunei** • brunei • ब्रुनेई
47 **Philippines** • filīpīns • फ़िलीपीन्स
48 **East Timor** • pūrvī timor • पूर्वी तिमोर
49 **Papua New Guinea** • papuā nyū ginī • पपुआ न्यू गिनी
50 **Solomon Islands** • soloman dvīp samūh • सोलोमन द्वीप समूह
51 **Vanuatu** • vanuātū • वनुआतू
52 **Fiji** • fijī • फ़िजी

particles and antonyms • upsarg, pratyaya aur vilom śabd • उपसर्ग, प्रत्यय और विलोम शब्द

to ko • को	**from** se • से	**for** ke lie • के लिए	**towards** kī taraf • की तरफ़
over ūpar • ऊपर	**under** nīche • नीचे	**with** sāth • साथ	**without** bagair • बग़ैर
in front of sāmne • के सामने	**behind** pīchhe • पीछे	**before** pahle • पहले	**after** bād meṃ • बाद में
onto ke ūpar • के ऊपर	**into** ke andar • के अंदर	**by** tab tak • तब तक	**until** jab tak • जब तक
in andar • अंदर	**out** bāhar • बाहर	**early** jaldī • जल्दी	**late** der • देर
above ūpar • ऊपर	**below** nīche • नीचे	**now** abhī • अभी	**later** bād meṃ • बाद में
inside andar • अंदर	**outside** bāhar • बाहर	**always** hameśā • हमेशा	**never** kabhī nahīṃ • कभी नहीं
up ūpar • ऊपर	**down** nīche • नीचे	**often** aksar • अक्सर	**rarely** kabhī-kabhī • कभी–कभी
at par • पर	**beyond** pare • परे	**yesterday** bītā kal • बीता कल	**tomorrow** āgāmī kal • आगामी कल
on top of ke ūpar • के ऊपर	**beside** ke pās • के पास	**first** pahlā • पहला	**last** āk͟hrī • आख़री
between ke bīch • के बीच	**opposite** viprīt • विपरीत	**every** harek • हरेक	**some** kuchh • कुछ
near nikaṭ • निकट	**far** dūr • दूर	**about** lagbhag • लगभग	**exactly** saṭīk • सटीक
here yahāṃ • यहां	**there** vahāṃ • वहां	**a little** thoṛā sā • थोड़ा सा	**a lot** bahut sā • बहुत सा
through ārampār • आरम्पार	**around** ghūm kar • घूम कर	**along** sāth-sāth • साथ–साथ	**across** ke pār • के पार

arge aṛā • बड़ा	**small** chhoṭā • छोटा	**hot** garm • गर्म	**cold** ṭhanḍā • ठंडा
vide haurā • चौड़ा	**narrow** saṅkrā • संकरा	**open** khulā • खुला	**closed** band • बंद
all ambā • लंबा	**short** chhoṭā • छोटा	**full** bharā • भरा	**empty** ḳhālī • ख़ाली
igh ṃchā • ऊंचा	**low** nīchā • नीचा	**new** nayā • नया	**old** purānā • पुराना
hick oṭā • मोटा	**thin** patlā • पतला	**light** halkā • हल्का	**dark** gahrā • गहरा
ght alkā • हल्का	**heavy** bhārī • भारी	**easy** āsān • आसान	**difficult** kaṭhin • कठिन
ard aṭhor • कठोर	**soft** mulāyam • मुलायम	**free** ḳhālī • ख़ाली	**occupied** vyast • व्यस्त
vet īlā • गीला	**dry** sūkhā • सूखा	**fat** moṭā • मोटा	**thin** patlā • पतला
ood cchhā • अच्छा	**bad** burā • बुरा	**young** javān • जवान	**old** būṛhā • बूढ़ा
ast ez • तेज़	**slow** dhīre • धीरे	**better** behtar • बेहतर	**worse** badtar • बदतर
orrect ahī • सही	**wrong** ġalat • ग़लत	**black** kālā • काला	**white** safed • सफ़ेद
lean āf • साफ़	**dirty** gandā • गंदा	**interesting** rochak • रोचक	**boring** ubāū • उबाऊ
eautiful hūbsūrat • ख़ूबसूरत	**ugly** badsūrat • बदसूरत	**sick** bīmār • बीमार	**well** svasth • स्वस्थ
xpensive ahaṅgā • महंगा	**cheap** sastā • सस्ता	**beginning** ārambh • आरंभ	**end** ant • अंत
uiet ānt • शांत	**noisy** • śor karne vālā शोर करने वाला	**strong** mazbūt • मज़बूत	**weak** kamzor • कमज़ोर

useful phrases • upyogī vākyāṅś • उपयोगी वाक्यांश

essential phrases
āvaśyak vākyāṅś
आवश्यक वाक्यांश

Yes • hāṃ • हां

No • nahīṃ • नहीं

Maybe • ho saktā hai
हो सकता है।

Please • kṛpyā • कृपया

Thank you
dhanyavād • धन्यवाद

You're welcome
āpkā svāgat hai
आपका स्वागत है।

Excuse me • māf kījiegā
माफ़ कीजिएगा

I'm sorry
maiṃ māfī chāhtā hūṃ
मैं माफ़ी चाहता हूं।

Don't
mat karo • मत करो।

OK • acchhā • अच्छा

That's fine
yah ṭhīk hai • यह ठीक है।

That's correct
yah sahī hai • यह सही है।

That's wrong
yah ġalat hai • यह ग़लत है।

greetings
abhivādan
अभिवादन

Hello
namaskār • नमस्कार

Goodbye
namaskār • नमस्कार

Good morning
suprabhāt • सुप्रभात

Good afternoon
namaskār • नमस्कार

Good evening
namaskār • नमस्कार

Good night
śubh rātri • शुभ रात्रि

How are you?
āp kaise haiṃ?
आप कैसे हैं?

My name is...
merā nām ... hai
मेरा नाम ... है।

What is your name?
āpkā kyā nām hai?
आपका क्या नाम है?

What is his/her name?
unkā kyā nām hai?
उनका क्या नाम है?

May I introduce...
maiṃ āpko ... se
milvānā chāhtā hūṃ
मैं आपको ... से मिलवाना
चाहता हूं।

This is...
ye ... haiṃ • ये ... हैं।

Pleased to meet you
āpse milkar ķhuśī huī
आपसे मिलकर ख़ुशी हुई।

See you later
bād meṃ milte haiṃ
बाद में मिलते हैं।

signs • chihn • चिह्न

Tourist information
paryaṭak jānkārī
पर्यटक जानकारी

Entrance
praveś • प्रवेश

Exit • nikās • निकास

Emergency exit
saṅkaṭ dvār
संकट द्वार

Push • dhakeleṃ • धकेलें

Danger • ķhatrā • ख़तरा

No smoking • dhūmrpān
varjit • धूम्रपान वर्जित

Out of order
ķharāb • ख़राब

Opening times
khulne kā samaya
खुलने का समय

Free admission
muft praveś • मुफ़्त प्रवेश

Open all day • pūre
din khulā • पूरे दिन खुला

Reduced price • kam
mūlya par • कम मूल्य पर

Sale • sel • सेल

Knock before entering
praveś karne se pahle
dastak deṃ • प्रवेश करने
से पहले दस्तक दें

Keep off the grass
kṛpyā ghās par na chaleṃ
कृपया घास पर न चलें

help • sahāyatā
सहायता

Can you help me?
kyā āp merī madad kar
sakte haiṃ?
क्या आप मेरी मदद कर
सकते हैं?

I don't understand
maiṃ samjhā nahīṃ
मैं समझा नहीं।

I don't know
mujhe patā nahīṃ hai
मुझे पता नहीं है।

Do you speak English, French...?
kyā āp aṅgrezī, french
... bolte haiṃ?
क्या आप अंग्रेज़ी, फ्रेंच ...
बोलते हैं?

I speak English, Spanish...
maiṃ aṅgrezī, speniś ...
boltā hūṃ
मैं अंग्रेज़ी, स्पेनिश ...
बोलता हूं।

Please speak more slowly
kṛpyā aur dhīre boleṃ
कृपया और धीरे बोलें।

Please write it down for me • kṛpyā ye mere
lie likh deṃ
कृपया ये मेरे लिए लिख दें।

I have lost...
merā ... kho gayā hai
मेरा ... खो गया है।

ɪirections
ɪirdeś • निर्देश

am lost
naim bhaṭak gayā hūṃ.
ं भटक गया हूं।

Vhere is the...? •...
ahāṃ haiṃ? •... कहां हैं?

Vhere is the
earest...?
ɪazdīkī ... kahāṃ hai?
जदीकी ... कहां है?

Vhere are the
estrooms?
auchālaya kahāṃ hai?
ौचालय कहां है?

łow do I get to...?
naiṃ ... kaise pahuṃch
aktā hūṃ?
... कैसे पहुंच सकता हूं?

o the right
āīṃ taraf • दाईं तरफ़

o the left
āīṃ taraf • बाईं तरफ़

traight ahead
ge jākar sīdhā
ागे जाकर सीधा

łow far is...? •
.. kitnī dūr hai?
.. कितनी दूर है?

oad signs • mārg
ɪhihn • मार्ग चिह्न

ll directions • sabhī
iśāeṃ • सभी दिशाएं

aution
āvdhānī • सावधानी

lo entry
raveś varjit • प्रवेश वर्जित

Slow down
raftār dhīmī kareṃ
रफ़्तार धीमी करें

Detour • parivartit mārg
परिवर्तित मार्ग

Keep right
dāīṃ taraf raheṃ
दाईं तरफ़ रहें

No parking
pārkiṅg niṣedh hai
पार्किंग निषेध है

No through road
ām rāstā nahīṃ hai
आम रास्ता नहीं है

One-way street
iktarfā rāstā
इकतरफ़ा रास्ता

Other directions
anya nirdeś • अन्य निर्देश

Residents only
keval nivāsiyoṃ ke lie
केवल निवासियों के लिए

Dangerous bend
khatarnāk moṛ
ख़तरनाक मोड़

accommodation
āvās • आवास

I have a reservation
mere pās ārakṣaṇ hai
मेरे पास आरक्षण है।

My room number is...
merā kamrā nambar ...
hai. • मेरा कमरा नंबर ... है।

What time is breakfast?
nāśte kā kyā samaya
hai?
नाश्ते का क्या समय है?

I'll be back at...
o'clock • maiṃ ... baje
lauṭūṅgā • मैं ... बजे लौटूंगा

I'm leaving tomorrow
maiṃ kal jā rahā hūṃ
मैं कल जा रहा हूं।

eating and drinking
khānā-pīnā
खाना–पीना

It's delicious • yah
svādiṣṭ hai • यह स्वादिष्ट है।

I don't drink/smoke
maiṃ śarāb/sigreṭ
nahīṃ pītā
मैं शराब/सिगरेट नहीं पीता।

I don't eat meat
maiṃ māṃs nahīṃ khātā
मैं मांस नहीं खाता।

No more for me, thank
you • mujhe aur nahīṃ
chāhie, dhanyavād
मुझे और नहीं चाहिए, धन्यवाद।

May I have some
more? • kyā mujhe
thoṛā aur mil saktā hai?
क्या मुझे थोड़ा और मिल
सकता है?

May we have the
check? • kyā hameṃ
bil mil saktā hai? • क्या
हमें बिल मिल सकता है?

Can I have a receipt?
kyā mujhe rasīd mil saktī
hai? • क्या मुझे रसीद मिल
सकती है?

No-smoking area
dhūmrpān varjit kṣetr
धूम्रपान वर्जित क्षेत्र

health • svāsthya
स्वास्थ्य

I don't feel well • merī
tabīyat ṭhīk nahīṃ hai
मेरी तबीयत ठीक नहीं है।

I feel sick
maiṃ bīmār mahsūs kar
rahā hūṃ
मैं बीमार महसूस कर रहा हूं।

What is the telephone
number of the nearest
doctor?
sabse nazdīkī doctor kā
fon nambar kyā hai?
सबसे नज़दीकी डॉक्टर का
फ़ोन नंबर क्या है?

It hurts here
yahāṃ dukhtā hai
यहां दुखता है।

I have a fever
mujhe bukhār hai
मुझे बुख़ार है।

I'm ... months
pregnant
mujhe ... mahīne kā
garbh hai
मुझे ... महीने का गर्भ है।

I need a prescription
for ... • mujhe ... ke lie
docterī nuskhā chāhie
मुझे ... के लिए डॉक्टरी
नुस्ख़ा चाहिए।

I normally take...
sāmānyataḥ maiṃ ...
letā hūṃ
सामान्यत: मैं ... लेता हूं।

I'm allergic to...
mujhe ... se elarjī hai
मुझे ... से एलर्जी है।

hindi pronunciation

the hindi alphabet

The Hindi script, which is called Devnagari, is made up of 12 vowels and 36 consonants. In this book we have adapted the usual romanization of Hindi by dropping the "a" normally used to represent the Hindi vowel "अ" that is attached to all Hindi consonants. Roman consonants, such as "w", only have a sound of their own once they are joined to vowels such as "a" or "e", as in "water" or "wet". In Hindi, however, every consonant incorporates the vowel "अ", so is a complete sound in itself. The sound of the consonant changes when another vowel is added to it. For example, the Hindi consonant "क" is romanized as "ka". When more vowels are added it becomes "की" (kee) or "के" (ke).

In this book we have used Roman consonants to represent each Devnagari consonant, and its accompanying vowel. For example, traditionally "लोग" ("people") would be transcribed as "loga", but we have used "log" to help you pronounce it more accurately. The exception to this is the Hindi consonant "य", represented by the Roman "ya", where we have retained the "a" to keep the pronunciation accurate.

We have kept the Roman spellings for words such as ball, monitor, coffee, and sauce, which are commonly used in everyday Hindi.

hindi vowels

vowel	english equivalent	phonetic symbol	guide to pronunciation
अ	a	a	as "u" in cut
आ	aa	ā	as "a" in class
इ	i	i	as "i" in bit
ई	ee	ī	as "ea" in beat
उ	u	u	as "u" in put
ऊ	oo	ū	as "oo" in hoot
ए	e	e	as "a" in late
ऐ	ai	ai	as "a" in rack
ओ	o	o	as "oa" in goat
औ	au	au	as "o" in floppy
अं	un	ṃ	as "un" in clung
अ:	ah	ḥ	as "ah" in blah

hindi consonants

Instances marked with a bullet (•) have no equivalent in English pronunciation.

consonant	english equivalent	phonetic symbol	guide to pronunciation
क	ka	k	as “cu” in cut
ख	kh	kh	as “kh” in Khaki
ग	ga	g	as “g” in girl
घ	gha	gh	as “gh” in Ghana
ङ	angah	ṅ	as “ung” in clung
च	cha	ch	as “chu” in church
छ	chha	chh	•
ज	ja	j	as “ju” in jug
झ	jha	jh	•
ञ	yan	ñ	•
ट	ta	ṭ	as “tu” in turtle
ठ	tha	ṭh	as “th” in lothar
ड	da	ḍ	as “du” in dump
ड़	ra	ṛ	•
ढ	dha	ḍh	as “dh” in Dhaka
ढ़	rha	ṛh	•
ण	na	ṇ	•
त	ta	t	as “t” in Tashkent
थ	tha	th	as “th” in Pythagoras
द	da	d	as “the” in the (pronounced softly)
ध	dha	dh	•
न	na	n	as “nu” in nursing
प	pa	p	as “pu” in puckered
फ	pha	ph	as “fu” in fur
ब	ba	b	as “bu” in bubble
भ	bha	bh	as “bha” in bharat
म	ma	m	as “mu” in mutter
य	ya	ya	as “yu” in yuppie
र	ra	r	as “ru” in rub

... continued on next page

continued from previous page

consonant	english equivalent	phonetic symbol	guide to pronunciation
ल	la	l	as "lo" in love
व	wa	v	as "wo" in word
श	sha	ś	as "shu" in shut
ष	sa	ṣ	•
स	sa	s	as "si" in sin
ह	ha	h	as "hu" in hurt
क्ष	ksha	kṣ	as "ksha" in rickshaw
त्र	tra	tr	as "tr" in trinidad
ज्ञ	jna	jñ	•

combining consonants and vowels

To show how vowel sounds change, we have taken the consonant "क" (ka) and shown how the vowel sound changes when each of the 12 vowels is joined with it.

k क	+	**a** अ	=	**ka** क	**ka** as "cu" in cut
k क	+	**ā** आ	=	**kā** का	**kā** as "ka" in kamikaze
k क	+	**i** इ	=	**ki** कि	**ki** as "ki" in kiss
k क	+	**ī** ई	=	**kī** की	**kī** as "kee" in keen
k क	+	**u** उ	=	**ku** कु	**ku** as "cu" in cushion
k क	+	**ū** ऊ	=	**kū** कू	**kū** as "coo" in cool
k क	+	**e** ए	=	**ke** के	**ke** as "ka" in kate
k क	+	**ai** ऐ	=	**kai** कै	**kai** as "ca" in California
k क	+	**o** ओ	=	**ko** को	**ko** as "coa" in coarse
k क	+	**au** औ	=	**kau** कौ	**kau** as "co" in copy
k क	+	**ṃ** अं	=	**kang** कं	**kang** as "kan" in kangaroo
n न	+	**ḥ** अः	=	**nah** नः	•

You can repeat this exercise with other consonants as the vowel sounds will change in the same way.

key to romanization

अ	आ	इ	ई	उ	ऊ	ऋ	
a	ā	i	ī	u	ū	ṛ	
			ए	ऐ	ओ	औ	
			e	ai	o	au	
क	क़	ख	ख़	ग	ग़	घ	ङ
k	ḳ	kh	ḳh	g	g̣	gh	ṅ
च	छ	ज	ज़	झ	ञ		
ch	chh	j	z	jh	ñ		
ट	ठ	ड	ड़	ढ	ढ़	ण	
	ṭh	ḍ	ṛ	ḍh	ṛh	ṇ	
त	थ	द	ध	न			
	th	d	dh	n			
प	फ	फ़	ब	भ	म		
p	ph	f	b	bh	m		
य	र	ल	व	श			
ya	r	l	v	ś			
ष	स	ह	:				
ṣ	s	h	ḥ				
क्ष	त्र	ज्ञ					
kṣ	tr	jña					

A "~" over a vowel shows it is pronounced nasally.

A consonant with a dot below it, for example "ṃ", is an anuswar, or a half consonant, which means it is a consonant without an accompanying vowel sound.

Certain letters in Hindi, though pronounced differently, have been romanized with the same consonants, as there aren't enough characters in the Roman alphabet to represent similar sounds. For example:

hindi consonant	**roman transliteration**
द	d
ढ	ḍh
ढ़	ṛh
ध	dh
ड़ & ऋ	ṛ
ड	ḍ

We have used the *nukta* (a dot) below certain consonants to denote Urdu pronunciation. Consonants with *nuktas*, for example, have been romanized as follows:

क़	ख़	ग़	ज़	फ़
ḳ	ḳh	g̣	z	f

Some of these consonants without a *nukta* have been romanized as follows:

क	ख	ग	ज	फ
k	kh	g	j	ph

index • tālikā • तालिका

C

E

F

G

H

Q

R

T

U

acknowledgments • ābhār • आभार

DORLING KINDERSLEY would like to thank Tracey Miles and Christine Lacey for design assistance, Georgina Garner for editorial and administrative help, Sonia Gavira, Polly Boyd, and Cathy Meeus for editorial help, and Claire Bowers for compiling the DK picture credits.

The publisher would like to thank the following for their kind permission to reproduce their photographs:
Abbreviations key. a above; b-below/bottom; c-centre; f-far; l-left; r-right; t-top)

123RF.com: Andriy Popov 34tl; Daniel Ernst 179tc; Hongqi Zhang 24cla. 175cr; Ingvar Bjork 60c; Kobby Dagan 259c; leonardo255 269c; Liubov Vadimovna (Luba) Nel 39cla; Ljupco Smokovski 75crb; Oleksandr Marynchenko 60bl; Olga Popova 33c; oneblink 49bc; Racorn 162tl; Robert Churchill 94c; Roman Gorielov 33bc; Ruslan Kudrin 35bc, 35br; Subbotina 39cra; Sutichak Yachaingkham 39tc; Tarzhanova 37tc; Vitaly Valua 39tl; Wavebreak Media Ltd 188bl; Wilawan Khasawong 75cb; **Action Plus:** 224bc; **Alamy Images:** 154t; A.T. Willett 287bcl; Alex Segre 105ca, 105cb, 195cl; Ambrophoto 24cra; Blend Images 168cr; Cultura RM 33r; Doug Houghton 107fbr; Ekkapon Sriharun 172bl; Hugh Threlfall 35tl; 176tr; Ian Allenden 48br; Ian Dagnall (iPod is a trademark of Apple Inc., registered in the U.S. and other countries) 268tc, 270t; Ievgen Chepil 250bc; imagebroker 199tl, 249c; keith morris 178c; Martyn Evans 210b; MBI 175tl; Michael Burrell 213cra; Michael Foyle 184bl; Oleksiy Maksymenko 105tc; Paul Weston 168br; Prisma Bildagentur AG 246b; Radharc Images 197tr; RBtravel 112tl; Ruslan Kudrin 176tl; Sasa Huzjak 258t; Sergey Kravchenko 37ca; Sergio Azenha 270bc; Stanca Sanda (iPad is a trademark of Apple Inc., registered in the U.S. and other countries) 176bc; Stock Connection 287bcr; tarczas 35cr; vitaly suprun 176cl; Wavebreak Media ltd 39cl, 174b, 175tr; **Allsport/Getty Images:** 238cl; **Alvey and Towers:** 209 acr, 215bcl, 215bcr, 241cr; **Peter Anderson:** 188bbr, 271br. **Anthony Blake Photo Library:** Charlie Stebbings 114cl; John Sims 114tcl; **Andyalte:** 98tl; **apple mac computers:** 268tcr; **Arcaid:** John Edward Linden 301bl; Martine Hamilton Knight, Architects: Chapman Taylor Partners, 213cl; Richard Bryant 301br; **Argos:** 41tcl, 66cbl, 66cl, 66br, 66bcl, 69cl, 70bcl, 71t, 77tl, 269tc, 270tl; **Axiom:** Eitan Simanor 105bcr; Ian Cumming 104; Vicki Couchman 148cr; **Beken Of Cowes Ltd:** 215cbc; **Bosch:** 76tcr, 76tc, 76tcl; **Camera Press:** 38tr, 256t, 257cr; Barry J. Holmes 148tr; Jane Hanger 159cr; Mary Germanou 259bc; **Corbis:** 78b; Anna Clopet 247tr; Ariel Skelley / Blend Images 52l; Bettmann 181tl, 181tr; Blue Jean Images 48bl; Bo Zauders 156t; Bob Rowan 152bl; Bob Winsett 247cbl; Brian Bailey 247br; Carl and Ann Purcell 162l; Chris Rainer 247ctl; Craig Aurness 215bl; David H.Wells 249cbr; Dennis Marsico 274bl; Dimitri Lundt 236bc; Duomo 211tl; Gail Mooney 277ctcr; George Lepp 248c; Gerald Nowak 239b; Gunter Marx 248cr; Jack Hollingsworth 231bl; Jacqui Hurst 277cbr; James L. Amos 247bl, 191ctr, 220bcr; Jan Butchofsky 277cbc; Johnathan Blair 243cr; Jose F. Poblete 191br; Jose Luis Pelaez.Inc 153tc; Karl Weatherly 220bl, 247tcr; Kelly Mooney Photography 259tl; Kevin Fleming 249bc; Kevin R. Morris 105tr, 243tl, 243tc; Kim Sayer 249tcr; Lynn Goldsmith 258t; Macduff Everton 231bcl; Mark Gibson 249bl; Mark L. Stephenson 249tcl; Michael Pole 115tr, Michael S. Yamashita 247ctcl; Mike King 247cbl; Neil Rabinowitz 214br; Pablo Corral 115bc; Paul A. Sounders 169br, 249ctcl; Paul J. Sutton 224c, 224br; Phil Schermeister 227b, 248tr; R. W Jones 309; Richard Morrell 189bc; Rick Doyle 241ctr; Robert Holmes 97br, 277ctc; Roger Ressmeyer 169tr; Russ Schleipman 229; The Purcell Team 211ctr; Vince Streano 194t; Wally McNamee 220br, 220bcl, 224bl; Wavebreak Media LTD 191bc; Yann Arhus-Bertrand 249tl; **Demetrio Carrasco / Dorling Kindersley (c) Herge / Les Editions Casterman:** 112ccl; **Dorling Kindersley:** Banbury Museum 35c; Five Napkin Burger 152t; **Dixons:** 270cl, 270cr, 270bl, 270bcl, 270bcr, 270ccr; **Dreamstime.com:** Alexander Podshivalov 179tr, 191cr; Alexxl66 268tl; Andersastphoto 176tc; Andrey Popov 191bl; Arne9001 190tl; Chaoss 26c; Designsstock 269cl; Monkey Business Images 26clb; Paul Michael Hughes 162tr; Serghei Starus 190bc; **Education Photos:** John Walmsley 26tl; **Empics Ltd:** Adam Day 236br; Andy Heading 243c; Steve White 249cbc; **Getty Images:** 48bcl, 100t, 114bcr, 154bl, 287tr; 94tr; Don Farrall / Digital Vision 176c; Ethan Miller 270bl; Inti St Clair 179bl; Liam Norris 188br; Sean Justice / Digital Vision 24br; **Dennis Gilbert:** 106tc; **Hulsta:** 70t; **Ideal Standard Ltd:** 72r; **The Image Bank/Getty Images:** 58; **Impact Photos:** Eliza Armstrong 115cr; Philip Achache 246t; **The Interior Archive:** Henry Wilson, Alfie's Market 114bl; Luke White, Architect: David Mikhail, 59tl; Simon Upton, Architect: Phillippe Starck, St Martins Lane Hotel 100bcr, 100br; **iStockphoto.com:** asterix0597 163tl; EdStock 190br, RichLegg 26bc; SorinVidis 27cr; **Jason Hawkes Aerial Photography:** 216t; **Dan Johnson:** 35r; **Kos Pictures Source:** 215cbl, 240tc, 240tr; David Williams 216b; **Lebrecht Collection:** Kate Mount 169bc; **MP Visual.com:** Mark Swallow 202t; **NASA:** 280cr, 280ccl, 281tl; **P&O Princess Cruises:** 214bl; **P A Photos:** 181br; **The Photographers' Library:** 186bl, 186bc, 186t; **Plain and Simple Kitchens:** 66t, **Powerstock Photolibrary:** 169tl, 256t, 287tc; **PunchStock:** Image Source 195tr; **Rail Images:** 208c, 208 cbl, 209br; **Red Consultancy:** Odeon cinemas 257br; **Redferns:** 259br; Nigel Crane 259c; **Rex Features:** 106br, 259tc, 259tr, 259bl, 280b; Charles Ommaney 114tcr; J.F.F Whitehead 243cl; Patrick Barth 101tl; Patrick Frilet 189cbl; Scott Wiseman 287bl; **Royalty Free Images:** Getty Images/Eyewire 154bl; **Science & Society Picture Library:** Science Museum 202b; **Science Photo Library:** IBM Research 190cla; NASA 281cr; **SuperStock:** Ingram Publishing 62; Juanma Aparicio / age fotostock 172t; Nordic Photos 269tl; **Skyscan:** 168t, 182c, 298; Quick UK Ltd 212; **Sony:** 268bc; **Robert Streeter:** 154br; **Neil Sutherland:** 82tr, 83tl, 90t, 118, 188ctr, 196tl, 196tr, 299cl, 299bl; **The Travel Library:** Stuart Black 264t; **Travelex:** 97cl; **Vauxhall:** Technik 198t, 199tl, 199tr, 199cl, 199cr, 199ctcl, 199ctcr, 199tcl, 199tcr, 200; **View Pictures:** Dennis Gilbert, Architects: ACDP Consulting, 106t; Dennis Gilbert, Chris Wilkinson Architects, 209tr; Peter Cook, Architects: Nicholas Crimshaw and partners, 208t; **Betty Walton:** 185br; **Colin Walton:** 2, 4, 7, 9, 10, 28, 42, 56, 92, 95c, 99tl, 99tcl, 102, 116, 120t, 138t, 146, 150t, 160, 170, 191ctcl, 192, 218, 252, 260br, 260l, 261tr, 261c, 261cr, 271cbl, 271cbr, 271ct, 278, 287br, 302, 401.

DK PICTURE LIBRARY:
Akhil Bahkshi; Patrick Baldwin; Geoff Brightling; British Museum; John Bulmer; Andrew Butler; Joe Cornish; Brian Cosgrove; Andy Crawford and Kit Hougton; Philip Dowell; Alistair Duncan; Gables; Bob Gathany; Norman Hollands; Kew Gardens; Peter James Kindersley; Vladimir Kozlik; Sam Lloyd; London Northern Bus Company Ltd; Tracy Morgan; David Murray and Jules Selmes; Musée Vivant du Cheval, France; Museum of Broadcast Communications; Museum of Natural History; NASA; National History Museum; Norfolk Rural Life Museum; Stephen Oliver; RNLI; Royal Ballet School; Guy Ryecart; Science Museum; Neil Setchfield; Ross Simms and the Winchcombe Folk Police Museum; Singapore Symphony Orchestra; Smart Museum of Art; Tony Souter; Erik Svensson and Jeppe Wikstrom; Sam Tree of Keygrove Marketing Ltd; Barrie Watts; Alan Williams; Jerry Young.

Additional Photography by Colin Walton.

Colin Walton would like to thank:
A&A News, Uckfield; Abbey Music, Tunbridge Wells; Arena Mens Clothing, Tunbridge Wells; Burrells of Tunbridge Wells; Gary at Di Marco's; Jeremy's Home Store, Tunbridge Wells; Noakes of Tunbridge Wells; Ottakar's, Tunbridge Wells; Selby's of Uckfield; Sevenoaks Sound and Vision; Westfield, Royal Victoria Place, Tunbridge Wells.